6th Workshop on Asian Translation (WAT 2019)

Hong Kong, China
4 November 2019

ISBN: 978-1-7138-0087-3

WAT 2019

The 6th Workshop on Asian Translation

Proceedings of the 6th Workshop on Asian Translation

November 4, 2019
Hong Kong, China

Preface

Many Asian countries are rapidly growing these days and the importance of communicating and exchanging the information with these countries has intensified. To satisfy the demand for communication among these countries, machine translation technology is essential.

Machine translation technology has rapidly evolved recently and it is seeing practical use especially between European languages. However, the translation quality of Asian languages is not that high compared to that of European languages, and machine translation technology for these languages has not reached a stage of proliferation yet. This is not only due to the lack of the language resources for Asian languages but also due to the lack of techniques to correctly transfer the meaning of sentences from/to Asian languages. Consequently, a place for gathering and sharing the resources and knowledge about Asian language translation is necessary to enhance machine translation research for Asian languages.

The Workshop on Machine Translation (WMT), the world's largest machine translation workshop, mainly targets on European languages and does not include Asian languages. The International Workshop on Spoken Language Translation (IWSLT) has spoken language translation tasks for some Asian languages using TED talk data, but these is no task for written language.

The Workshop on Asian Translation (WAT) is an open machine translation evaluation campaign focusing on Asian languages. WAT gathers and shares the resources and knowledge of Asian language translation to understand the problems to be solved for the practical use of machine translation technologies among all Asian countries. WAT is unique in that it is an "open innovation platform": the test data is fixed and open, so participants can repeat evaluations on the same data and confirm changes in translation accuracy over time. WAT has no deadline for the automatic translation quality evaluation (continuous evaluation), so participants can submit translation results at any time.

Following the success of the previous WAT workshops (WAT2014 – WAT2018), WAT2019 will bring together machine translation researchers and users to try, evaluate, share and discuss brand-new ideas about machine translation. For the 6th WAT, we included 5 new translation subtasks. We had 25 teams who submitted their translation results, and about 400 submissions in total.

In addition to the shared tasks, WAT2019 also feature scientific papers on topics related to the machine translation, especially for Asian languages. The program committee accepted 6 papers, which focus on on neural machine translation, and construction and evaluation of language resources.

We are grateful to "SunFlare Co., Ltd.", "Japan Exchange Group, Inc. (JPX)", "Asia-Pacific Association for Machine Translation (AAMT)" and "Kawamura International" for partially sponsoring the workshop. We would like to thank all the authors who submitted papers. We express our deepest gratitude to the committee members for their timely reviews. We also thank the EMNLP-IJCNLP 2019 organizers for their help with administrative matters.

WAT 2019 Organizers

Organizers:

Toshiaki Nakazawa, The University of Tokyo, Japan

Chenchen Ding, National Institute of Information and Communications Technology (NICT), Japan

Raj Dabre, National Institute of Information and Communications Technology (NICT), Japan

Anoop Kunchukuttan, Microsoft AI and Research, India

Win Pa Pa, University of Computer Studies, Yangon (UCSY), Myanmar

Nobushige Doi, Japan Exchange Group (JPX), Japan

Yusuke Oda, Google, Japan

Ondřej Bojar, Charles University, Prague, Czech Republic

Shantipriya Parida, Idiap Research Institute, Martigny, Switzerland

Isao Goto, Japan Broadcasting Corporation (NHK), Japan

Hideya Mino, Japan Broadcasting Corporation (NHK), Japan

Hiroshi Manabe, National Institute of Information and Communications Technology (NICT), Japan

Katsuhito Sudoh, Nara Institute of Science and Technology (NAIST), Japan

Sadao Kurohashi, Kyoto University, Japan

Pushpak Bhattacharyya, Indian Institute of Technology Bombay (IIT), India

Program Committee:

Hailong Cao, Harbin Institute of Technology, China

Michael Carl, Kent State University, USA

Chenhui Chu, Osaka University, Japan

Fabien Cromières, Kyoto University, Japan

Kenji Imamura, NICT, Japan

Hideto Kazawa, Google, Japan

Anoop Kunchookuttan, Microsoft, India

Yang Liu, Tsinghua University, China

Takashi Ninomiya, Ehime University, Japan

Liling Tan, Rakuten Institute of Technology, Singapore

Masao Utiyama, NICT, Japan

Jiajun Zhang, Chinese Academy of Sciences, China

Dongdong Zhang, Microsoft Research Asia, China

Technical Collaborators:

Luis Fernando D'Haro, Universidad Politécnica de Madrid, Spain
Rafael E. Banchs, Nanyang Technological University, Singapore
Haizhou Li, National University of Singapore, Singapore

Invited talk: Multitask Learning from Multilingual Mutimodal Data

Desmond Elliott

The University of Copenhagen

Abstract

I will talk about two perspectives on learning from multilingual multimodal data: as a language generation problem and as cross-modal retrieval problem. In the language generation problem of multimodal machine translation, I will discuss whether we should learn grounded representations by using the additional visual context as a conditioning input or as a variable that the model learns to predict, and highlight some recent arguments about whether models are actually sensitive to the visual context. As a multilingual image–sentence retrieval problem, I will discuss experiments that highlight situations in which it is useful to train with multilingual annotations, as opposed to monolingual annotations, and the challenges in learning from disjoint cross-lingual datasets.

Biography

Desmond is an Assistant Professor at the University of Copenhagen. He received his PhD from the University of Edinburgh, and was a postdoctoral researcher at CWI Amsterdam, the University of Amsterdam, and the University of Edinburgh, funded by an Alain Bensoussan Career Development Fellowship and an Amazon Research Award. His research interests include multimodal and multlingual machine learning, which has appeared in papers ACL, CoNLL, EMNLP and NAACL. He was involved in the creation the Multi30K and How2 multilingual multimodal datasets and has developed a variety of models that learn from these types of data. He co-organised the How 2 Challenge Workshop at ICML 2019, the Multimodal Machine Translation Shared Task from 2016–2018, and the 2018 Frederick Jelinek Memorial Workshop on Grounded Sequence-to-Sequence Learning.

Table of Contents

Workshop Program

Monday, November 4, 2019

09:00–09:30   **Welcome and Overview**

Overview of the 6th Workshop on Asian Translation
Toshiaki Nakazawa, Nobushige Doi, Shohei Higashiyama, Chenchen Ding, Raj Dabre, Hideya Mino, Isao Goto, Win Pa Pa, Anoop Kunchukuttan, Shantipriya Parida, Ondřej Bojar and Sadao Kurohashi

09:30–10:30   **Research Paper I**

Compact and Robust Models for Japanese-English Character-level Machine Translation
Jinan Dai and Kazunori Yamaguchi

Controlling Japanese Honorifics in English-to-Japanese Neural Machine Translation
Weston Feely, Eva Hasler and Adrià de Gispert

Designing the Business Conversation Corpus
Matīss Rikters, Ryokan Ri, Tong Li and Toshiaki Nakazawa

10:30–10:50   **Poster Booster I**

10:50–12:30   **System Description Paper (Poster) I**

English to Hindi Multi-modal Neural Machine Translation and Hindi Image Captioning
Sahinur Rahman Laskar, Rohit Pratap Singh, Partha Pakray and Sivaji Bandyopadhyay

Supervised and Unsupervised Machine Translation for Myanmar-English and Khmer-English
Benjamin Marie, Hour Kaing, Aye Myat Mon, Chenchen Ding, Atsushi Fujita, Masao Utiyama and Eiichiro Sumita

NICT's participation to WAT 2019: Multilingualism and Multi-step Fine-Tuning for Low Resource NMT
Raj Dabre and Eiichiro Sumita

KNU-HYUNDAI's NMT system for Scientific Paper and Patent Tasks onWAT 2019
Cheoneum Park, Young-Jun Jung, Kihoon Kim, Geonyeong Kim, Jae-Won Jeon, Seongmin Lee, Junseok Kim and Changki Lee

Monday, November 4, 2019 (continued)

12:30–14:00   **Lunch Break**

14:00–14:45   **Invited Talk by Dr. Desmond Elliott**

14:45–15:05   **Poster Booster II**

15:05–15:10   **Commemorative Photo**

15:10–16:30   **System Description Paper (Poster) II**

SYSTRAN @ WAT 2019: Russian-Japanese News Commentary task
Jitao Xu, TuAnh Nguyen, MinhQuang PHAM, Josep Crego and Jean Senellart

UCSYNLP-Lab Machine Translation Systems for WAT 2019
Yimon ShweSin, Win Pa Pa and KhinMar Soe

16:30–17:30   Research Paper II

Sentiment Aware Neural Machine Translation
Chenglei Si, Kui Wu, Ai Ti Aw and Min-Yen Kan

Overcoming the Rare Word Problem for low-resource language pairs in Neural Machine Translation
Thi-Vinh Ngo, Thanh-Le Ha, Phuong-Thai Nguyen and Le-Minh Nguyen

Neural Arabic Text Diacritization: State of the Art Results and a Novel Approach for Machine Translation
Ali Fadel, Ibraheem Tuffaha, Bara' Al-Jawarneh and Mahmoud Al-Ayyoub

17:30–17:35   Closing

Overview of the 6th Workshop on Asian Translation

Toshiaki Nakazawa
The University of Tokyo
nakazawa@logos.t.u-tokyo.ac.jp

Nobushige Doi
Japan Exchange Group
n-doi@jpx.co.jp

Shohei Higashiyama and Chenchen Ding and Raj Dabre
National Institute of
Information and Communications Technology
{shohei.higashiyama, chenchen.ding, raj.dabre}@nict.go.jp

Hideya Mino and Isao Goto
NHK
{mino.h-gq, goto.i-es}@nhk.or.jp

Win Pa Pa
University of Conputer Study, Yangon
winpapa@ucsy.edu.mm

Anoop Kunchukuttan
Microsoft AI and Research
anoop.kunchukuttan@microsoft.com

Shantipriya Parida
Idiap Research Institute
shantipriya.parida@idiap.ch

Ondřej Bojar
Charles University, MFF, ÚFAL
bojar@ufal.mff.cuni.cz

Sadao Kurohashi
Kyoto University
kuro@i.kyoto-u.ac.jp

Abstract

This paper presents the results of the shared tasks from the 6th workshop on Asian translation (WAT2019) including Ja↔En, Ja↔Zh scientific paper translation subtasks, Ja↔En, Ja↔Ko, Ja↔En patent translation subtasks, Hi↔En, My↔En, Km↔En, Ta↔En mixed domain subtasks, Ru↔Ja news commentary translation task, and En→Hi multi-modal translation task. For the WAT2019, 25 teams participated in the shared tasks. We also received 10 research paper submissions out of which 7[1] were accepted. About 400 translation results were submitted to the automatic evaluation server, and selected submissions were manually evaluated.

1 Introduction

The Workshop on Asian Translation (WAT) is an open evaluation campaign focusing on Asian languages. Following the success of the previous workshops WAT2014-WAT2018 (Nakazawa et al., 2014, 2015, 2016, 2017, 2018), WAT2019 brings together machine translation researchers and users to try, evaluate, share and discuss brand-new ideas for machine translation. We have been working toward practical use of machine translation among all Asian countries.

For the 6th WAT, we adopted new translation subtasks with Khmer↔English and Tamil↔English mixed domain corpora,[2] Russian↔Japanese news commentary corpus and English→Hindi multi-modal corpus[3] in addition to most of the subtasks of WAT2018.

WAT is a unique workshop on Asian language translation with the following characteristics:

- Open innovation platform
  Due to the fixed and open test data, we can repeatedly evaluate translation systems on the same dataset over years. WAT receives submissions at any time; i.e., there is no submission deadline of translation results w.r.t automatic evaluation of translation quality.

---

[1] One paper was withdrawn post acceptance and hence only 6 papers will be in the proceedings.

[2] http://lotus.kuee.kyoto-u.ac.jp/WAT/my-en-data/

[3] https://ufal.mff.cuni.cz/hindi-visual-genome/wat-2019-multimodal-task

Proceedings of the 6th Workshop on Asian Translation, pages 1–35
Hong Kong, China, November 4, 2019. ©2019 Association for Computational Linguistics

Lang	Train	Dev	DevTest	Test
JE	3,008,500	1,790	1,784	1,812
JC	672,315	2,090	2,148	2,107

Table 1: Statistics for ASPEC

Lang	Train	Dev	DevTest	Test-N
zh-ja	1,000,000	2,000	2,000	5,204
ko-ja	1,000,000	2,000	2,000	5,230
en-ja	1,000,000	2,000	2,000	5,668

Lang	Test-N1	Test-N2	Test-N3	Test-EP
zh-ja	2,000	3,000	204	1,151
ko-ja	2,000	3,000	230	–
en-ja	2,000	3,000	668	–

Table 2: Statistics for JPC

- Domain and language pairs
  WAT is the world's first workshop that targets scientific paper domain, and Chinese↔Japanese and Korean↔Japanese language pairs. In the future, we will add more Asian languages such as Vietnamese, Thai and so on.

- Evaluation method
  Evaluation is done both automatically and manually. Firstly, all submitted translation results are automatically evaluated using three metrics: BLEU, RIBES and AMFM. Among them, selected translation results are assessed by two kinds of human evaluation: pairwise evaluation and JPO adequacy evaluation.

2 Datasets

2.1 ASPEC

ASPEC was constructed by the Japan Science and Technology Agency (JST) in collaboration with the National Institute of Information and Communications Technology (NICT). The corpus consists of a Japanese-English scientific paper abstract corpus (ASPEC-JE), which is used for ja↔en subtasks, and a Japanese-Chinese scientific paper excerpt corpus (ASPEC-JC), which is used for ja↔zh subtasks. The statistics for each corpus are shown in Table 1.

2.1.1 ASPEC-JE

The training data for ASPEC-JE was constructed by NICT from approximately two million Japanese-English scientific paper abstracts owned by JST. The data is a comparable corpus and sentence correspondences are found automatically using the method from Utiyama and Isahara (2007). Each sentence pair is accompanied by a similarity score calculated by the method and a field ID that indicates a scientific field. The correspondence between field IDs and field names, along with the frequency and occurrence ratios for the training data, are described in the README file of ASPEC-JE.

The development, development-test and test data were extracted from parallel sentences from the Japanese-English paper abstracts that exclude the sentences in the training data. Each dataset consists of 400 documents and contains sentences in each field at the same rate. The document alignment was conducted automatically and only documents with a 1-to-1 alignment are included. It is therefore possible to restore the original documents. The format is the same as the training data except that there is no similarity score.

2.1.2 ASPEC-JC

ASPEC-JC is a parallel corpus consisting of Japanese scientific papers, which come from the literature database and electronic journal site J-STAGE by JST, and their translation to Chinese with permission from the necessary academic associations. Abstracts and paragraph units are selected from the body text so as to contain the highest overall vocabulary coverage.

The development, development-test and test data are extracted at random from documents containing single paragraphs across the entire corpus. Each set contains 400 paragraphs (documents). There are no documents sharing the same data across the training, development, development-test and test sets.

2.2 JPC

JPO Patent Corpus (JPC) for the patent tasks was constructed by the Japan Patent Office (JPO) in collaboration with NICT. The corpus consists of Chinese-Japanese, Korean-Japanese and English-Japanese patent descriptions whose International Patent Classi-

Disclosure Period	Train	Dev		DevTest		Test	
		Texts	Items	Texts	Items	Texts	Items
2016-01-01 to 2017-12-31	1,089,346 (614,817)	- -	- -	- -	- -	- -	- -
2018-01-01 to 2018-06-30	314,649 (218,495)	1,153 (1,148)	2,845 (2,650)	1.114 (1,111)	2,900 (2,671)	1,153 (1,135)	2,129 (1,763)

Table 3: Statistics for TDDC (The number of unique sentences)

fication (IPC) sections are chemistry, electricity, mechanical engineering, and physics.

At WAT2019, the patent tasks has two subtasks: normal subtask and expression pattern subtask. Both subtasks use common training, development and development-test data for each language pair. The normal subtask for three language pairs uses four test data with different characteristics:

- test-N: union of the following three sets;

- test-N1: patent documents from patent families published between 2011 and 2013;

- test-N2: patent documents from patent families published between 2016 and 2017; and

- test-N3: patent documents published between 2016 and 2017 where target sentences are manually created by translating source sentences.

The expression pattern subtask for zh→ja pair uses test-EP data. The test-EP data consists of sentences annotated with expression pattern categories: title of invention (TIT), abstract (ABS), scope of claim (CLM) or description (DES). The corpus statistics are shown in Table 2. Note that training, development, development-test and test-N1 data are the same as those used in WAT2017.

2.3 TDDC

Timely Disclosure Documents Corpus (TDDC) was constructed by Japan Exchange Group (JPX). The corpus was made by aligning the sentences manually from past Japanese and English timely disclosure documents in PDF format published by companies listed on Tokyo Stock Exchange (TSE). Timely Disclosure tasks focus on Japanese to English translation of sentences extracted from timely disclosure documents in order to avoid mistranslations that would confuse investors.

TSE is one of the largest capital markets in the world that has over 3,600 companies listed as of the end of 2018. Companies are required to disclose material information including financial statements, corporate actions, and corporate governance policies to the public in a timely manner. These timely disclosure documents form an important basis for investment decisions, containing important figures (e.g., sales, profits, significant dates) and proper nouns (e.g., names of persons, places, companies, business and product). Since such information is critical for investors, mistranslations should be avoided and translations should be of a high quality.

The corpus consists of Japanese-English sentence pairs, document hashes, and sentence hashes. A document hash is a hash of the Document ID, which is a unique identifier of the source document. A sentence hash is a hash of the Document ID and the Sentence ID, which is a unique identifier of the sentence in each source document.

The corpus is partitioned into training, development, development-test, and test data. The training data is split into two (2) sets of data from different periods. The first data set was created based on documents disclosed from January 1, 2016 to December 31, 2017, and the second data set was based on documents from January 1, 2018 to June 30, 2018. The development, development-test, and test data set were extracted from timely disclosure documents disclosed from January 1, 2018 to June 30, 2018, excluding documents that were used to create the training data. The documents for the period were randomly selected, and the sentences were extracted from each randomly selected, discrete document set so that the sources extracted are not biased. Therefore, the set of source documents for training, development, development-test and

Lang	Train	Dev	DevTest	Test
en-ja	200,000	2,000	2,000	2,000

Table 4: Statistics for JIJI Corpus

Lang	Train	Dev	Test	Mono
hi-en	1,492,827	520	2,507	–
hi-ja	152,692	1,566	2,000	–
hi	–	–	–	45,075,279

Table 5: Statistics for IITB Corpus. "Mono" indicates monolingual Hindi corpus.

Corpus	Train	Dev	Test
ALT	18,088	1,000	1,018
UCSY	204,539	–	–
All	222,627	1,000	1,018

Table 6: Statistics for the data used in Myanmar-English translation tasks

test data are independent of each other. Furthermore, each data set of the development, development-test, and test is further split into two (2) sets of data: sentences that end with a Japanese period ($_\circ$: U+3002) are classified as 'Texts', which has various sentences, and others are classified as 'Items', which has many duplicates and similar expressions. The statistics for each corpus are shown in Table 3.

2.4 JIJI Corpus

JIJI Corpus was constructed by Jiji Press Ltd. in collaboration with NICT. The corpus consists of news text that comes from Jiji Press news of various categories including politics, economy, nation, business, markets, sports and so on. The corpus is partitioned into training, development, development-test and test data, which consists of Japanese-English sentence pairs. The statistics for each corpus are shown in Table 4.

The sentence pairs in each data are identified in the same manner as that for ASPEC using the method from (Utiyama and Isahara, 2007).

2.5 IITB Corpus

IIT Bombay English-Hindi Corpus contains English-Hindi parallel corpus as well as monolingual Hindi corpus collected from a variety of sources and corpora. This corpus had been developed at the Center for Indian Language Technology, IIT Bombay over the years. The corpus is used for mixed domain tasks hi↔en. The statistics for the corpus are shown in Table 5.

2.6 ALT and UCSY Corpus

The parallel data for Myanmar-English translation tasks at WAT2019 consists of two corpora, the ALT corpus and UCSY corpus.

- The ALT corpus is one part from the Asian Language Treebank (ALT) project (Riza et al., 2016), consisting of twenty thousand Myanmar-English parallel sentences from news articles.

- The UCSY corpus (Yi Mon Shwe Sin and Khin Mar Soe, 2018) is constructed by the NLP Lab, University of Computer Studies, Yangon (UCSY), Myanmar. The corpus consists of 200 thousand Myanmar-English parallel sentences collected from different domains, including news articles and textbooks.

The ALT corpus has been manually segmented into words (Ding et al., 2018, 2019), and the UCSY corpus is unsegmented. A script to tokenize the Myanmar data into writing units is released with the data. The automatic evaluation of Myanmar translation results is based on the tokenized writing units, regardless to the segmented words in the ALT data. However, participants can make a use of the segmentation in ALT data in their own manner.

The detailed composition of training, development, and test data of the Myanmar-English translation tasks are listed in Table 6. Notice that both of the corpora have been modified from the data used in WAT2018.

2.7 ALT and ECCC Corpus

The parallel data for Khmer-English translation tasks at WAT2019 consists of two corpora, the ALT corpus and ECCC corpus.

- The ALT corpus is one part from the Asian Language Treebank (ALT) project (Riza et al., 2016), consisting of twenty thousand Khmer-English parallel sentences from news articles.

Corpus	Train	Dev	Test
ALT	18,088	1,000	1,018
ECCC	104,660	–	–
All	122,748	1,000	1,018

Table 7: Statistics for the data used in Khmer-English translation tasks

Dataset	Items	Tokens	
		English	Hindi
Training Set	28,932	143,178	136,722
D-Test	998	4,922	4,695
E-Test (EV)	1,595	7,852	7,535
C-Test (CH)	1,400	8,185	8,665

Table 8: Data for the English→Hindi multi-modal translation task. One item consists of source English sentence, target Hindi sentence, and a rectangular region within an image. The total number of English and Hindi tokens in the dataset also listed. The abbreviations EV and CH are used in the official task names in WAT scoring tables.

- The ECCC corpus consists of 100 thousand Khmer-English parallel sentences extracted from document pairs of Khmer-English bi-lingual records in Extraordinary Chambers in the Court of Cambodia, collected by National Institute of Posts, Telecoms & ICT, Cambodia.

The ALT corpus has been manually segmented into words (Ding et al., 2018), and the ECCC corpus is unsegmented. A script to tokenize the Khmer data into writing units is released with with the data. The automatic evaluation of Khmer translation results is based on the tokenized writing units, regardless to the segmented words in the ALT data. However, participants can make a use of the segmentation in ALT data in their own manner.

The detailed composition of training, development, and test data of the Khmer-English translation tasks are listed in Table 7.

2.8 Multi-Modal Task Corpus

For English→Hindi multi-modal translation task we asked the participants to use the Hindi Visual Genome corpus (HVG, Parida et al., 2019a,b). The statistics of the corpus are given in Table 8. One "item" in the original HVG consists of an image with a rectangular region highlighting a part of the image, the original English caption of this region and the Hindi reference translation. Depending on the track (see 2.8.1 below), some of these item components are available as the source and some serve as the reference or play the role of a competing candidate solution.

HVG Training, D-Test and E-Test sections were accessible to the participants in advance. The participants were explicitly instructed not to consult E-Test in any way but strictly speaking, they could have used the reference translation (which would mean cheating from the evaluation point of view). C-Test was provided only for the task itself: the source side was distributed to task participants and the target side was published only after output submission deadline.

Note that the original Visual Genome suffers from a considerable level of noise. Some observed English grammar errors are illustrated in Figure 1. We also took the chance and used our manual evaluation for validating the quality of the captions given the picture, see 8.4.1 below.

The multi-modal task includes three tracks as illustrated in Figure 1:

2.8.1 Multi-Modal Task Tracks

1. Text-Only Translation (labeled "TEXT" in WAT official tables): The participants are asked to translate short English captions (text) into Hindi. No visual information can be used. On the other hand, additional text resources are permitted (but they need to be specified in the corresponding system description paper).

2. Hindi Captioning (labeled "HI"): The participants are asked to generate captions in Hindi for the given rectangular region in an input image.

3. Multi-Modal Translation (labeled "MM"): Given an image, a rectangular region in it and an English caption for the rectangular region, the participants are asked to translate the English text into Hindi. Both textual and visual information can be used.

	Text-Only MT	Hindi Captioning	Multi-Modal MT
Image	–		
Source Text	the bird is stand on a tree branch	–	man stand on skateboard
System Output Gloss	चिड़िया एक पेड़ शाखा पर है Bird on a branch of tree	लाल और सफेद चिह्न Red and white sign	स्केटबोर्ड पर मनुष्य स्टेपिंग Man stepping on skateboard
Reference Solution Gloss	पक्षी एक पेड़ की शाखा पर खड़ा है A bird standing on the branch of a tree	सन्केत अंग्रेजी और विदेशी भाषा में लिखे गये हैं A sign is written in English and a foreign language	आदमी स्केटबोर्ड पर खड़ा है A man is standing on a skateboard

Figure 1: An illustration of the three tracks of WAT 2019 Multi-Modal Task. Note the grammatical errors in the English source. The correct sentences would be "The bird is standing on a tree branch." and "A man is standing on a skateboard."

Dataset	Sentences	English tokens	Tamil tokens
train	166,871	3,913,541	2,727,174
test	2,000	47,144	32,847
development	1,000	23,353	16,376
total	169,871	3,984,038	2,776,397
Domain	Sentences	English tokens	Tamil tokens
bible	26,792 (15.77%)	703,838	373,082
cinema	30,242 (17.80%)	445,230	298,419
news	112,837 (66.43%)	2,834,970	2,104,896
total	169,871	3,984,038	2,776,397

Table 9: Data for the Tamil↔English task.

Lang.pair	Partition	#sent.	#tokens	#types
Ja↔Ru	train	12,356	341k / 229k	22k / 42k
	development	486	16k / 11k	2.9k / 4.3k
	test	600	22k / 15k	3.5k / 5.6k
Ja↔En	train	47,082	1.27M / 1.01M	48k / 55k
	development	589	21k / 16k	3.5k / 3.8k
	test	600	22k / 17k	3.5k / 3.8k
Ru↔En	train	82,072	1.61M / 1.83M	144k / 74k
	development	313	7.8k / 8.4k	3.2k / 2.3k
	test	600	15k / 17k	5.6k / 3.8k

Table 10: In-Domain data for the Russian–Japanese task.

2.9 EnTam Corpus

For Tamil↔English translation task we asked the participants to use the publicly available EnTam mixed domain corpus[4] (Ramasamy et al., 2012). This corpus contains training, development and test sentences mostly from the news-domain. The other domains are Bible and Cinema. The statistics of the corpus are given in Table 9.

2.10 JaRuNC Corpus

For the Russian↔Japanese task we asked participants to use the JaRuNC corpus[5] (Imankulova et al., 2019) which belongs to the news commentary domain. This dataset was manually aligned and cleaned and is trilingual. It can be used to evaluate Russian↔English

translation quality as well but this is beyond the scope of this years sub-task. Refer to Table 10 for the statistics of the in-domain parallel corpora. In addition we encouraged the participants to use out-of-domain parallel corpora from various sources such as KFTT,[6] JESC,[7] TED,[8] ASPEC,[9] UN,[10] Yandex[11] and Russian↔English news-commentary corpus.[12]

3 Baseline Systems

Human evaluations of most of WAT tasks were conducted as pairwise comparisons between the translation results for a specific baseline system and translation results for each partic-

[4] http://ufal.mff.cuni.cz/~ramasamy/parallel/html/
[5] https://github.com/aizhanti/JaRuNC

[6] http://www.phontron.com/kftt/
[7] https://datarepository.wolframcloud.com/resources/Japanese-English-Subtitle-Corpus
[8] https://wit3.fbk.eu/
[9] http://lotus.kuee.kyoto-u.ac.jp/ASPEC/
[10] https://cms.unov.org/UNCorpus/
[11] https://translate.yandex.ru/corpus?lang=en
[12] http://lotus.kuee.kyoto-u.ac.jp/WAT/News-Commentary/news-commentary-v14.en-ru.filtered.tar.gz

ipant's system. That is, the specific baseline system was the standard for human evaluation. At WAT 2019, we adopted a neural machine translation (NMT) with attention mechanism as a baseline system.

The NMT baseline systems consisted of publicly available software, and the procedures for building the systems and for translating using the systems were published on the WAT web page.[13] We also have SMT baseline systems for the tasks that started at WAT 2017 or before 2017. The baseline systems are shown in Tables 11, 12, and 13. SMT baseline systems are described in the WAT 2017 overview paper (Nakazawa et al., 2017). The commercial RBMT systems and the online translation systems were operated by the organizers. We note that these RBMT companies and online translation companies did not submit themselves. Because our objective is not to compare commercial RBMT systems or online translation systems from companies that did not themselves participate, the system IDs of these systems are anonymous in this paper.

3.1 Training Data

We used the following data for training the NMT baseline systems.

- All of the training data for each task were used for training except for the ASPEC Japanese–English task. For the ASPEC Japanese–English task, we only used train-1.txt, which consists of one million parallel sentence pairs with high similarity scores.
- All of the development data for each task was used for validation.

3.2 Tokenization

We used the following tools for tokenization.

3.2.1 For ASPEC, JPC, TDDC, JIJI, ALT, UCSY, ECCC, and IITB

- Juman version 7.0[14] for Japanese segmentation.
- Stanford Word Segmenter version 2014-01-04[15] (Chinese Penn Treebank (CTB)

[13]http://lotus.kuee.kyoto-u.ac.jp/WAT/WAT2019/baseline/baselineSystems.html

[14]http://nlp.ist.i.kyoto-u.ac.jp/EN/index.php?JUMAN

[15]http://nlp.stanford.edu/software/segmenter.shtml

System ID	System	Type	ASPEC				JPC					
			ja-en	en-ja	ja-zh	zh-ja	ja-en	en-ja	ja-zh	zh-ja	ja-ko	ko-ja
NMT	OpenNMT's NMT with attention	NMT	✓	✓	✓	✓	✓	✓	✓	✓	✓	✓
SMT Phrase	Moses' Phrase-based SMT	SMT	✓	✓	✓	✓	✓	✓	✓	✓	✓	✓
SMT Hiero	Moses' Hierarchical Phrase-based SMT	SMT	✓	✓	✓	✓	✓	✓	✓	✓	✓	✓
SMT S2T	Moses' String-to-Tree Syntax-based SMT and Berkeley parser	SMT	✓		✓		✓		✓			
SMT T2S	Moses' Tree-to-String Syntax-based SMT and Berkeley parser	SMT		✓		✓		✓		✓		
RBMT X	The Honyaku V15 (Commercial system)	RBMT	✓	✓			✓	✓				
RBMT X	ATLAS V14 (Commercial system)	RBMT	✓	✓			✓	✓				
RBMT X	PAT-Transer 2009 (Commercial system)	RBMT	✓	✓			✓	✓				
RBMT X	PC-Transer V13 (Commercial system)	RBMT										
RBMT X	J-Beijing 7 (Commercial system)	RBMT			✓	✓			✓	✓		
RBMT X	Hohrai 2011 (Commercial system)	RBMT			✓	✓				✓		
RBMT X	J Soul 9 (Commercial system)	RBMT									✓	✓
RBMT X	Korai 2011 (Commercial system)	RBMT									✓	✓
Online X	Google translate	Other	✓	✓	✓	✓	✓	✓	✓	✓	✓	✓
Online X	Bing translator	Other	✓	✓	✓	✓	✓	✓	✓	✓	✓	✓
AIAYN	Google's implementation of "Attention Is All You Need"	NMT	✓	✓								

Table 11: Baseline Systems I

System ID	System	Type	JIJI		IITB				ALT			
			ja-en	en-ja	hi-en	en-hi	hi-ja	ja-hi	my-en	en-my	km-en	en-km
NMT	OpenNMT's NMT with attention	NMT	✓	✓	✓	✓	✓	✓	✓	✓	✓	✓
SMT Phrase	Moses' Phrase-based SMT	SMT	✓	✓	✓	✓	✓	✓				
SMT Hiero	Moses' Hierarchical Phrase-based SMT	SMT	✓	✓								
SMT S2T	Moses' String-to-Tree Syntax-based SMT and Berkeley parser	SMT	✓									
SMT T2S	Moses' Tree-to-String Syntax-based SMT and Berkeley parser	SMT		✓								
RBMT X	The Honyaku V15 (Commercial system)	RBMT	✓	✓								
RBMT X	PC-Transer V13 (Commercial system)	RBMT	✓	✓								
Online X	Google translate	Other	✓	✓	✓	✓	✓	✓	✓	✓	✓	✓
Online X	Bing translator	Other	✓	✓	✓	✓	✓	✓				

Table 12: Baseline Systems II

System ID	System	Type	NewsCommentary		TDDC	EnTam		Multimodal
			ru-ja	ja-ru	ja-en	ta-en	en-ta	en-hi
NMT	OpenNMT's NMT with attention	NMT			✓			
NMT T2T	Tensor2Tensor's Transformer	NMT	✓	✓		✓	✓	
NMT OT	OpenNMT-py's Transformer	NMT						✓
Online X	Azure Custom Translator	Other			✓			

Table 13: Baseline Systems III

model) for Chinese segmentation.

- The Moses toolkit for English and Indonesian tokenization.
- Mecab-ko[16] for Korean segmentation.
- Indic NLP Library[17] for Indic language segmentation.
- The tools included in the ALT corpus for Myanmar and Khmer segmentation.
- subword-nmt[18] for all languages.

When we built BPE-codes, we merged source and target sentences and we used 100,000 for -s option. We used 10 for vocabulary-threshold when subword-nmt applied BPE.

3.2.2 For EnTam, News Commentary

- The Moses toolkit for English and Russian only for the News Commentary data.

- Mecab[19] for Japanese segmentation.

- The EnTam corpus is not tokenized by any external toolkits.

- Both corpora are further processed by tensor2tensor's internal pre/post-processing which includes sub-word segmentation.

3.2.3 For Multi-Modal Task

- Hindi Visual Genome comes untokenized and we did not use or recommend any specific external tokenizer.

- The standard OpenNMT-py sub-word segmentation was used for pre/post-processing for the baseline system and each participant used what they wanted.

3.3 Baseline NMT Methods

We used the following NMT with attention for most of the tasks. We used Transformer (Vaswani et al., 2017) (Tensor2Tensor)) for the News Commentary and English↔Tamil tasks and Transformer (OpenNMT-py) for the Multimodal task.

3.3.1 NMT with Attention

We used OpenNMT (Klein et al., 2017) as the implementation of the baseline NMT systems of NMT with attention (System ID: NMT). We used the following OpenNMT configuration.

- encoder_type = brnn
- brnn_merge = concat
- src_seq_length = 150
- tgt_seq_length = 150
- src_vocab_size = 100000
- tgt_vocab_size = 100000
- src_words_min_frequency = 1
- tgt_words_min_frequency = 1

The default values were used for the other system parameters.

3.3.2 Transformer (Tensor2Tensor)

For the News Commentary and English↔Tamil tasks, we used tensor2tensor's[20] implementation of the Transformer (Vaswani et al., 2017) and use default hyperparameter settings corresponding to the "base" model for all baseline models. The baseline for the News Commentary task is a multilingual model as described in Imankulova et al. (2019) which is trained using only the in-domain parallel corpora. We use the token trick proposed by (Johnson et al., 2017) to train the multilingual model. As for the English↔Tamil task, we train separate baseline models for each translation direction with 32,000 separate sub-word vocabularies.

3.3.3 Transformer (OpenNMT-py)

For the Multimodal task, we used the Transformer model (Vaswani et al., 2018) as implemented in OpenNMT-py (Klein et al., 2017) and used the "base" model with default parameters for the multi-modal task baseline. We have generated the vocabulary of 32k subword types jointly for both the source and target languages. The vocabulary is shared between the encoder and decoder.

4 Automatic Evaluation

4.1 Procedure for Calculating Automatic Evaluation Score

We evaluated translation results by three metrics: BLEU (Papineni et al., 2002), RIBES

---

[16]https://bitbucket.org/eunjeon/mecab-ko/
[17]https://bitbucket.org/anoopk/indic_nlp_library
[18]https://github.com/rsennrich/subword-nmt
[19]https://taku910.github.io/mecab/
[20]https://github.com/tensorflow/tensor2tensor

(Isozaki et al., 2010) and AMFM (Banchs et al., 2015). BLEU scores were calculated using multi-bleu.perl in the Moses toolkit (Koehn et al., 2007). RIBES scores were calculated using RIBES.py version 1.02.4.[21] AMFM scores were calculated using scripts created by the technical collaborators listed in the WAT2019 web page.[22] All scores for each task were calculated using the corresponding reference translations.

Before the calculation of the automatic evaluation scores, the translation results were tokenized or segmented with tokenization/segmentation tools for each language. For Japanese segmentation, we used three different tools: Juman version 7.0 (Kurohashi et al., 1994), KyTea 0.4.6 (Neubig et al., 2011) with full SVM model[23] and MeCab 0.996 (Kudo, 2005) with IPA dictionary 2.7.0.[24] For Chinese segmentation, we used two different tools: KyTea 0.4.6 with full SVM Model in MSR model and Stanford Word Segmenter (Tseng, 2005) version 2014-06-16 with Chinese Penn Treebank (CTB) and Peking University (PKU) model.[25] For Korean segmentation, we used mecab-ko.[26] For Myanmar and Khmer segmentations, we used myseg.py[27] and kmseg.py[28]. For English and Russian tokenizations, we used tokenizer.perl[29] in the Moses toolkit. For Hindi and Tamil tokenizations, we used Indic NLP Library.[30] The detailed procedures for the automatic evaluation are shown on the WAT2019 evaluation web page.[31]

4.2 Automatic Evaluation System

The automatic evaluation system receives translation results by participants and automatically gives evaluation scores to the uploaded results. As shown in Figure 2, the system requires participants to provide the following information for each submission:

- Human Evaluation: whether or not they submit the results for human evaluation;

- Publish the results of the evaluation: whether or not they permit to publish automatic evaluation scores on the WAT2019 web page.

- Task: the task you submit the results for;

- Used Other Resources: whether or not they used additional resources; and

- Method: the type of the method including SMT, RBMT, SMT and RBMT, EBMT, NMT and Other.

Evaluation scores of translation results that participants permit to be published are disclosed via the WAT2019 evaluation web page. Participants can also submit the results for human evaluation using the same web interface.

This automatic evaluation system will remain available even after WAT2019. Anybody can register an account for the system by the procedures described in the registration web page.[32]

4.3 Additional Automatic Scores in Multi-Modal Task

For the multi-modal task, several additional automatic metrics were run aside from the WAT evaluation server, namely: BLEU (now calculated by Moses scorer[33]), characTER (Wang et al., 2016), chrF3 (Popović, 2015), TER (Snover et al., 2006), WER, PER and CDER (Leusch et al., 2006). Except for chrF3 and characTER, we ran Moses tokenizer[34] on the candidate and reference before scoring. For all error metrics, i.e. metrics where better

[21] http://www.kecl.ntt.co.jp/icl/lirg/ribes/index.html

[22] lotus.kuee.kyoto-u.ac.jp/WAT/WAT2019/

[23] http://www.phontron.com/kytea/model.html

[24] http://code.google.com/p/mecab/downloads/detail?name=mecab-ipadic-2.7.0-20070801.tar.gz

[25] http://nlp.stanford.edu/software/segmenter.shtml

[26] https://bitbucket.org/eunjeon/mecab-ko/

[27] http://lotus.kuee.kyoto-u.ac.jp/WAT/my-en-data/wat2019.my-en.zip

[28] http://lotus.kuee.kyoto-u.ac.jp/WAT/km-en-data/km-en.zip

[29] https://github.com/moses-smt/mosesdecoder/tree/RELEASE-2.1.1/scripts/tokenizer/tokenizer.perl

[30] https://bitbucket.org/anoopk/indic_nlp_library

[31] http://lotus.kuee.kyoto-u.ac.jp/WAT/evaluation/index.html

[32] http://lotus.kuee.kyoto-u.ac.jp/WAT/WAT2019/registration/index.html

[33] https://github.com/moses-smt/mosesdecoder/blob/master/mert/evaluator.cpp

[34] https://github.com/moses-smt/mosesdecoder/blob/master/scripts/tokenizer/tokenizer.perl

Figure 2: The interface for translation results submission

scores are lower, we reverse the score by taking $1 - x$ and indicate this by prepending "n" to the metric name. With this modification, higher scores always indicate a better translation result. Also, we multiply all metric scores by 100 for better readability.

5 Human Evaluation

In WAT2019, we conducted three kinds of human evaluations: pairwise evaluation (Section 5.1) and JPO adequacy evaluation (Section 5.2) for text-only language pairs and a pairwise variation of direct assessment (Section 5.3) for the multi-modal task.

5.1 Pairwise Evaluation

We conducted pairwise evaluation for participants' systems submitted for human evaluation. The submitted translations were evaluated by a professional translation company and Pairwise scores were given to the submissions by comparing with baseline translations (described in Section 3).

5.1.1 Sentence Selection and Evaluation

For the pairwise evaluation, we randomly selected 400 sentences from the test set of each task. We used the same sentences as the last year for the continuous subtasks. Baseline and submitted translations were shown to annotators in random order with the input source sentence. The annotators were asked to judge which of the translations is better, or whether they are on par.

5.1.2 Voting

To guarantee the quality of the evaluations, each sentence is evaluated by 5 different annotators and the final decision is made depending on the 5 judgements. We define each judgement $j_i(i = 1, \cdots, 5)$ as:

$$j_i = \begin{cases} 1 & \text{if better than the baseline} \\ -1 & \text{if worse than the baseline} \\ 0 & \text{if the quality is the same} \end{cases}$$

The final decision D is defined as follows using $S = \sum j_i$:

$$D = \begin{cases} win & (S \geq 2) \\ loss & (S \leq -2) \\ tie & (otherwise) \end{cases}$$

5.1.3 Pairwise Score Calculation

Suppose that W is the number of wins compared to the baseline, L is the number of losses and T is the number of ties. The Pairwise score can be calculated by the following formula:

$$Pairwise = 100 \times \frac{W - L}{W + L + T}$$

From the definition, the Pairwise score ranges between -100 and 100.

5.1.4 Confidence Interval Estimation

There are several ways to estimate a confidence interval. We chose to use bootstrap resampling (Koehn, 2004) to estimate the 95%

5	All important information is transmitted correctly. (100%)
4	Almost all important information is transmitted correctly. (80%–)
3	More than half of important information is transmitted correctly. (50%–)
2	Some of important information is transmitted correctly. (20%–)
1	Almost all important information is NOT transmitted correctly. (–20%)

Table 14: The JPO adequacy criterion

confidence interval. The procedure is as follows:

1. randomly select 300 sentences from the 400 human evaluation sentences, and calculate the Pairwise score of the selected sentences

2. iterate the previous step 1000 times and get 1000 Pairwise scores

3. sort the 1000 scores and estimate the 95% confidence interval by discarding the top 25 scores and the bottom 25 scores

5.2 JPO Adequacy Evaluation

We conducted JPO adequacy evaluation for the top two or three participants' systems of pairwise evalution for each subtask.[35] The evaluation was carried out by translation experts based on the JPO adequacy evaluation criterion, which is originally defined by JPO to assess the quality of translated patent documents.

5.2.1 Sentence Selection and Evaluation

For the JPO adequacy evaluation, the 200 test sentences were randomly selected from the 400 test sentences used for the pairwise evaluation. For each test sentence, input source sentence, translation by participants' system, and reference translation were shown to the annotators. To guarantee the quality of the evaluation, each sentence was evaluated by two annotators. Note that the selected sentences are the same as those used in the previous workshops except for the new subtasks at WAT2019.

5.2.2 Evaluation Criterion

Table 14 shows the JPO adequacy criterion from 5 to 1. The evaluation is performed

---

[35]The number of systems varies depending on the subtasks.

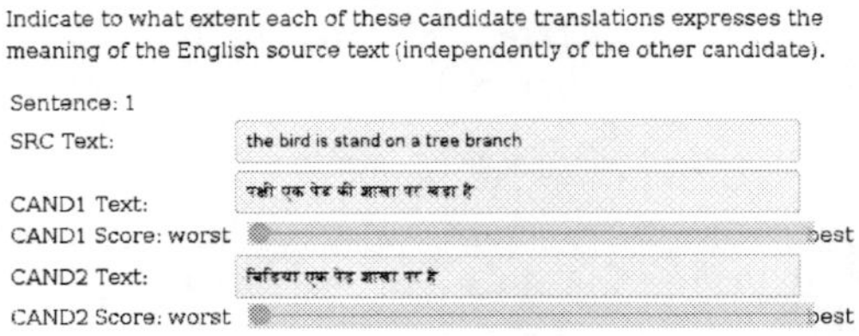

Figure 3: Manual evaluation of text-only translation in the multi-modal task.

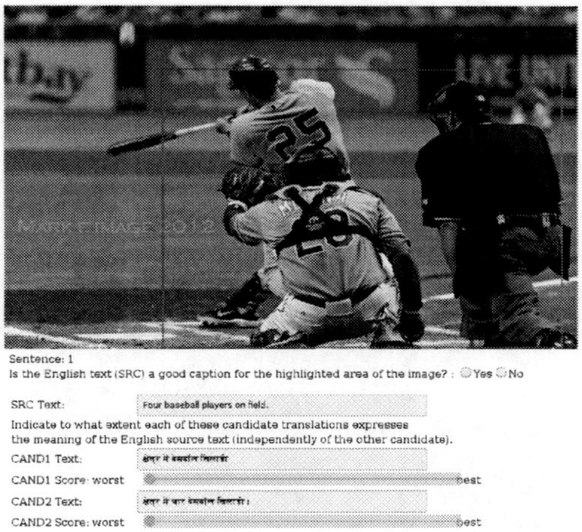

subjectively. "Important information" represents the technical factors and their relationships. The degree of importance of each element is also considered to evaluate. The percentages in each grade are rough indications for the transmission degree of the source sentence meanings. The detailed criterion is described in the JPO document (in Japanese).[36]

5.3 Manual Evaluation for the Multi-Modal Task

The evaluations of the three tracks of the multi-modal task follow the Direct Assessment (DA, Graham et al., 2016) technique by asking annotators to assign a score from 0 to 100 to each candidate. The score is assigned using a slider with no numeric feedback, the scale is therefore effectively continuous. After a certain number of scored items, each of the annotators stabilizes in their predictions.

The collected DA scores can be either directly averaged for each system and track (denoted "Ave"), or first standardized per annotator and then averaged ("Ave Z"). The standardization removes the effect of individual differences in the range of scores assigned: the scores are scaled so that the average score of each annotator is 0 and the standard deviation is 1.

Our evaluation differs from the basic DA in the following respects: (1) we run the evaluation bilingually, i.e. we require the annotators to understand the source English sufficiently to be able to assess the adequacy of the Hindi translation, (2) we ask the annotators to score two distinct segments at once, while the original DA displays only one candidate at a time.

The main benefit of bilingual evaluation is that the reference is not needed for the evalu-

<hr>

[36]http://www.jpo.go.jp/shiryou/toushin/chousa/ tokkyohonyaku_hyouka.htm

Figure 4: Manual evaluation of multi-modal translation.

ation. Instead, the reference can be included among other candidates and the manual evaluation allows us to directly compare the performance of MT to human translators.

The dual judgment (scoring two candidates at once) was added experimentally. The advantage is saving some of the annotators' time (they do not need to read the source or examine the picture again) and the chance to evaluate candidates also in terms of direct pairwise comparisons. In the history of WMT (Bojar et al., 2016), 5-way relative ranking was used for many years. With 5 candidates, the individual pairs may not be compared very precisely. With the single-candidate DA, pairwise comparisons cannot be used as the basis for system ranking. We believe that two candidates on one screen could be a good balance.

For the full statistical soundness, the judgments should be independent of each other. This is not the case in our dual scoring, even if we explicitly ask people to score the candidates independent of each other. The full independence is however not assured even in the original approach because annotators will remember their past judgments. This year, WMT even ran DA with document context available to the annotators by scoring all segments from a given document one after another in their natural order. We thus dare to pretend independence of judgments when interpreting DA scores.

Figure 5: Manual evaluation of Hindi captioning.

The user interface for our annotation for each of the tracks is illustrated in Figure 3, Figure 4, and Figure 5.

In the "text-only" evaluation, one English text (source) and two Hindi translations (candidate 1 and 2) are shown to the annotators. In the "multi-modal" evaluation, the annotators are shown both the image and the source English text. The first question is to validate if the source English text is a good caption for the indicated area. For two translation candidates, the annotators are asked to independently indicate to what extent the meaning is preserved. The "Hindi captioning" evaluation shows only the image and two Hindi candidates. The annotators are reminded that the two captions should be treated independently and that each of them can consider a very different aspect of the region.

6 Participants

Table 15 shows the participants in WAT2019. The table lists 25 organizations from various countries, including Japan, India, Myanmar, USA, Korea, China, France, and Switzerland.

About 400 translation results by 25 teams were submitted for automatic evaluation and about 30 translation results by 8 teams were submitted for pairwise evaluation. We selected about 50 translation results for JPO adequacy evaluation. Table 16 shows tasks for which each team submitted results by the deadline.

7 Evaluation Results

In this section, the evaluation results for WAT2019 are reported from several perspectives. Some of the results for both automatic and human evaluations are also accessible at the WAT2019 website.[37]

7.1 Official Evaluation Results

Figures 6, 7, 8 and 9 show the official evaluation results of ASPEC subtasks, Figures 10, 11, 12, 13, 14 and 15 show those of JPC subtasks, Figures 16 and 17 show those of JIJI subtasks, Figures 18 and 19 show those of NCPD subtasks, Figures 20 and 21 show those of IITB subtasks, Figures 22, 23, 24 and 25 show those of ALT subtasks, Figures 26 and 27 show those of TDDC subtasks and Figures 28 and 29 show those of UFAL subtasks. Each figure contains the JPO adequacy evaluation result and evaluation summary of top systems.

The detailed automatic evaluation results are shown in Appendix A. The detailed JPO adequacy evaluation results for the selected submissions are shown in Tables 17 and 18. The weights for the weighted κ (Cohen, 1968) is defined as $|Evaluation1 - Evaluation2|/4$.

The automatic scores for the multi-modal task along with the WAT evaluation server BLEU scores are provided in Table 20. For each of the test sets (E-Test and C-Test), the scores are comparable across all the tracks (text-only, captioning or multi-modal translation) because of the underlying set of reference translations is the same. The scores for the captioning task will be however very low because captions generated independently of the English source caption are very likely to differ from the reference translation.

For multi-modal task, Table 19 shows the manual evaluation scores for all valid system submissions. As mentioned above, we used the reference translation as if it was one of the competing systems, see the rows "Reference" in the table. The annotation was fully anonymized, so the annotators had no chance of knowing if they are scoring human translation or MT output.

---

[37]http://lotus.kuee.kyoto-u.ac.jp/WAT/evaluation/

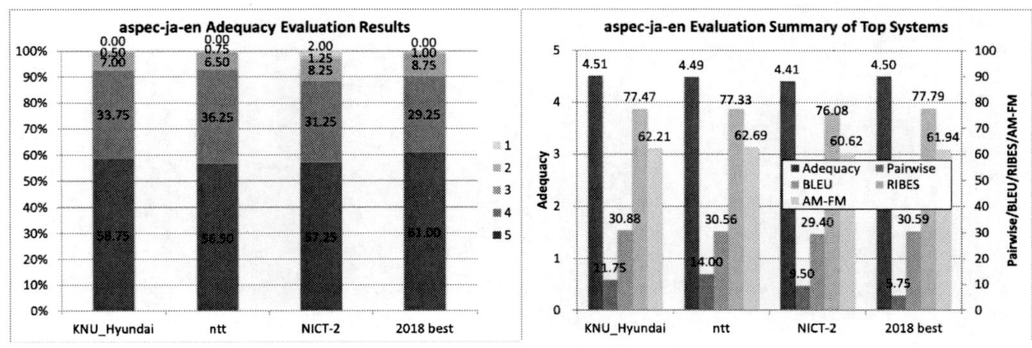

Figure 6: Official evaluation results of aspec-ja-en.

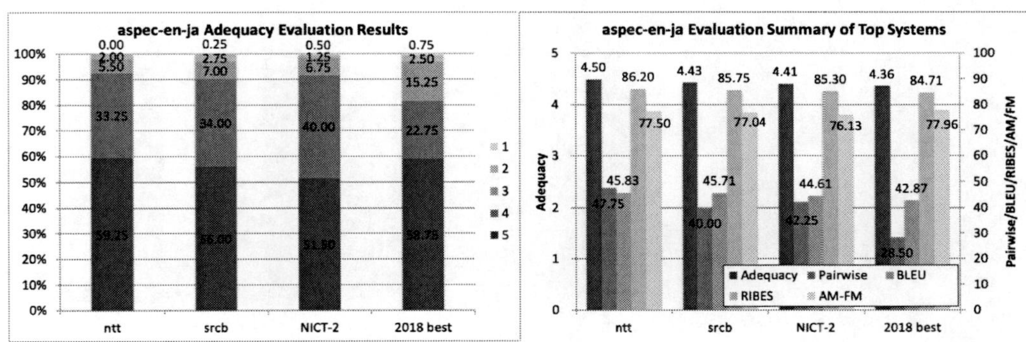

Figure 7: Official evaluation results of aspec-en-ja.

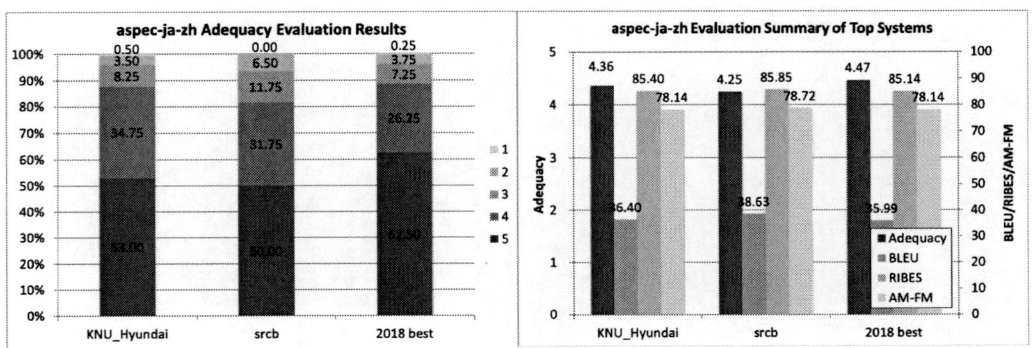

Figure 8: Official evaluation results of aspec-ja-zh.

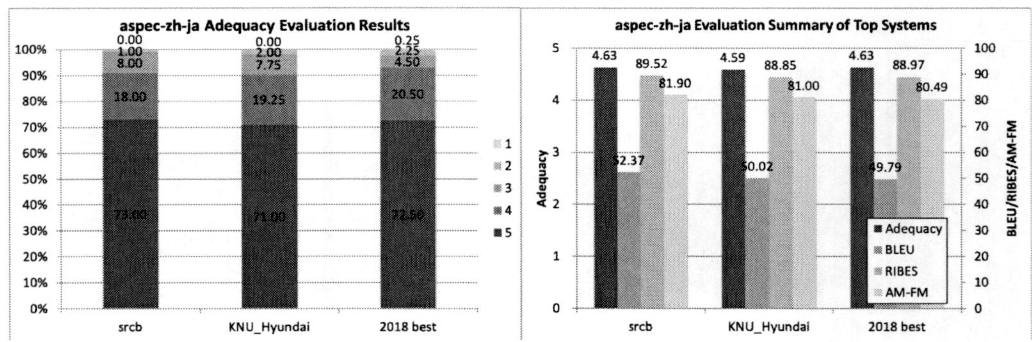

Figure 9: Official evaluation results of aspec-zh-ja.

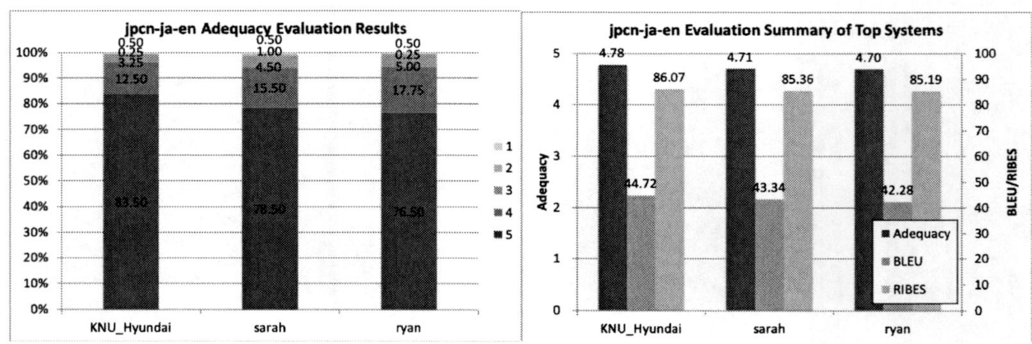

Figure 10: Official evaluation results of jpcn-ja-en.

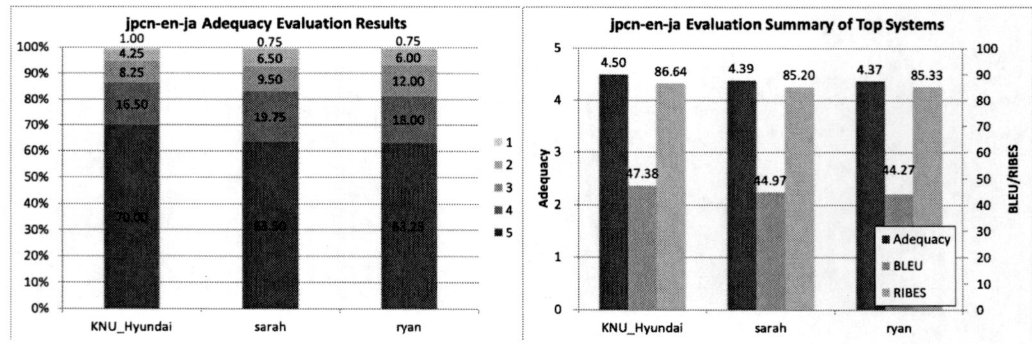

Figure 11: Official evaluation results of jpcn-en-ja.

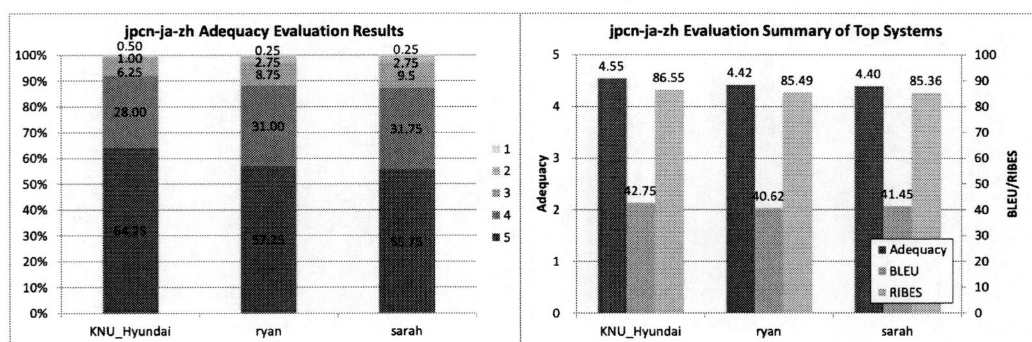

Figure 12: Official evaluation results of jpcn-ja-zh.

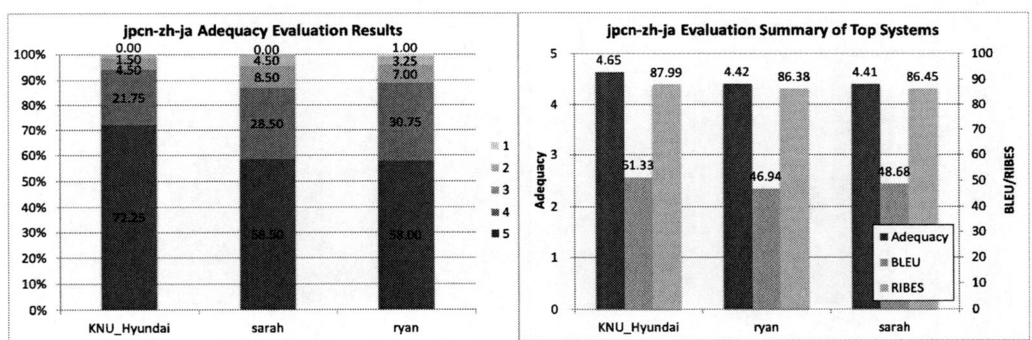

Figure 13: Official evaluation results of jpcn-zh-ja.

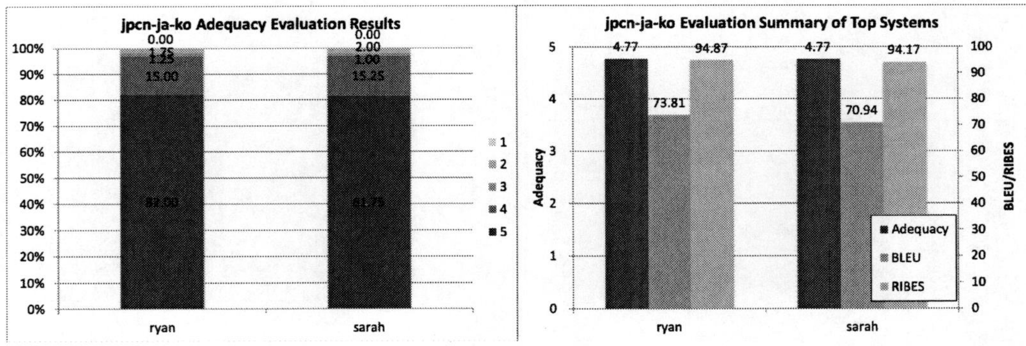

Figure 14: Official evaluation results of jpcn-ja-ko.

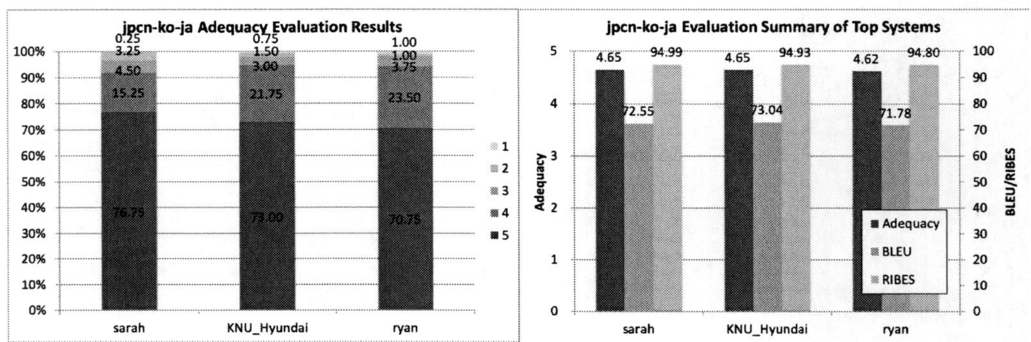

Figure 15: Official evaluation results of jpcn-ko-ja.

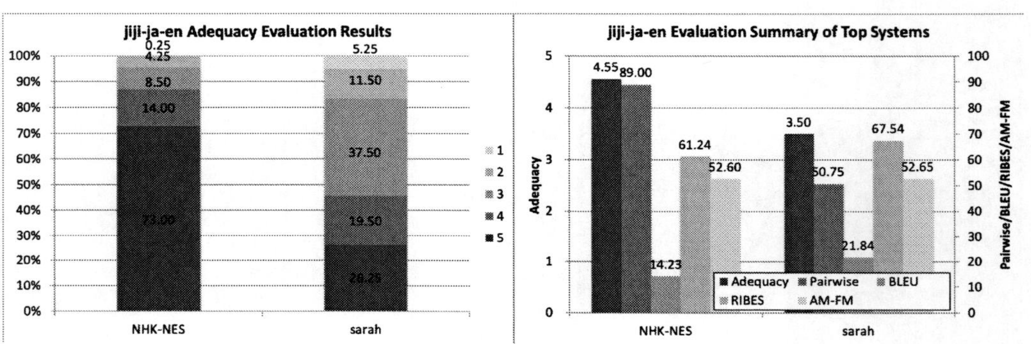

Figure 16: Official evaluation results of jiji-ja-en.

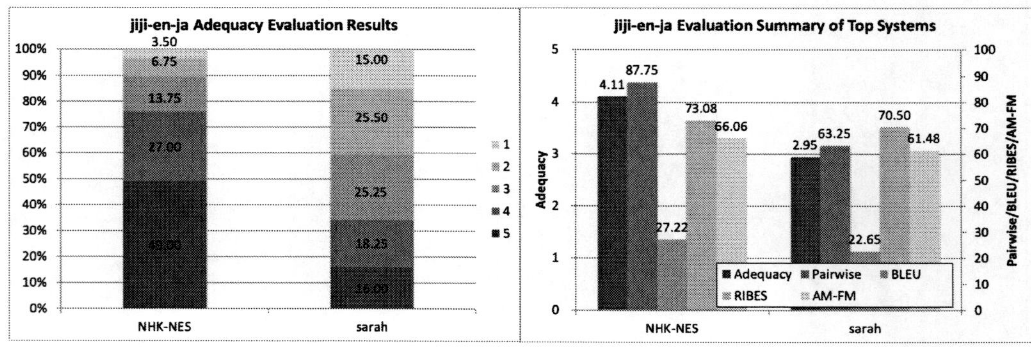

Figure 17: Official evaluation results of jiji-en-ja.

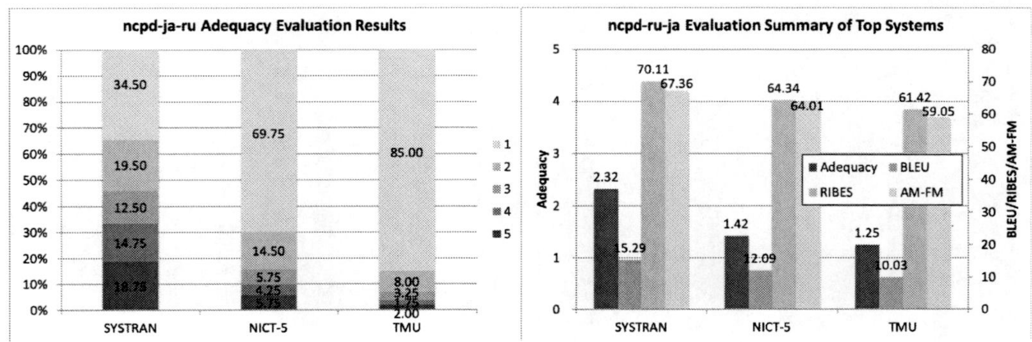

Figure 18: Official evaluation results of ncpd-ja-ru.

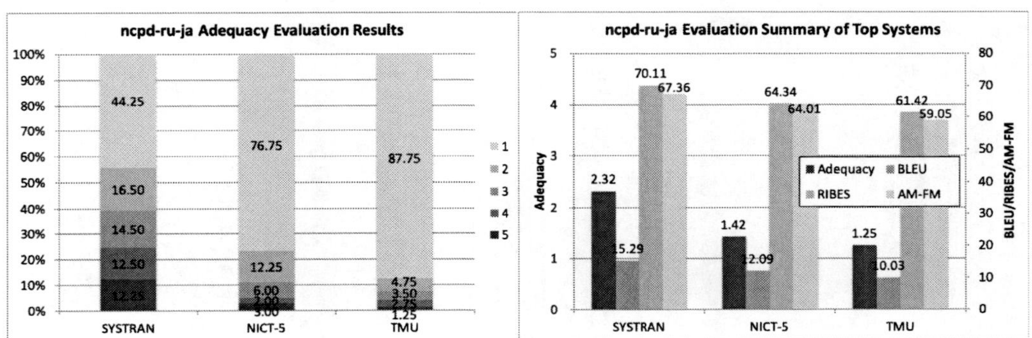

Figure 19: Official evaluation results of ncpd-ru-ja.

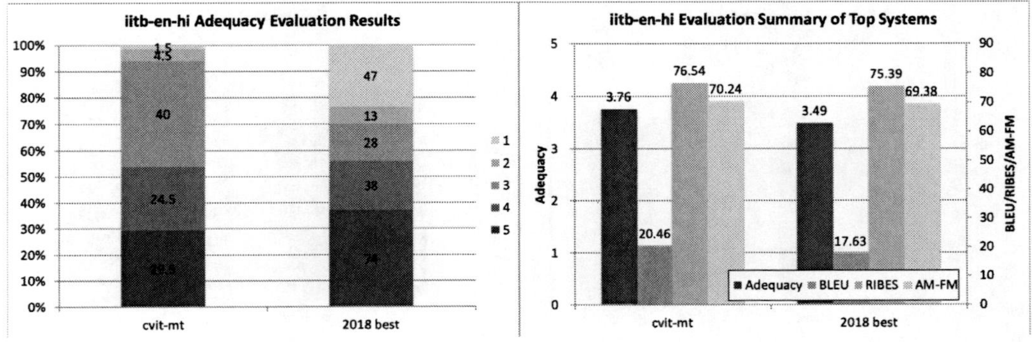

Figure 20: Official evaluation results of iitb-en-hi.

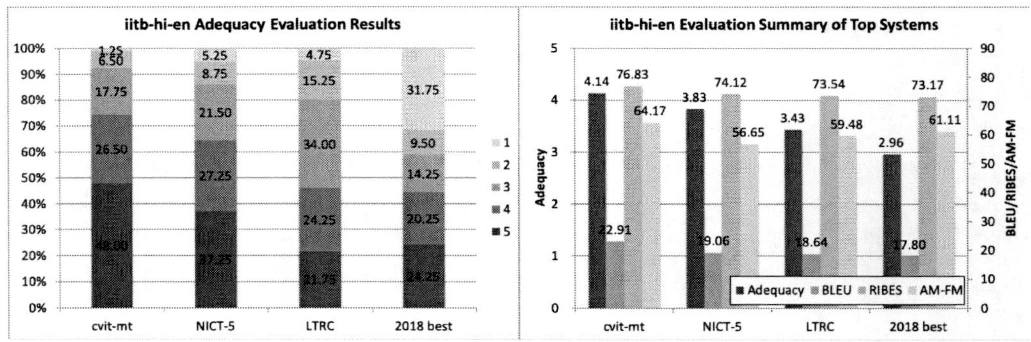

Figure 21: Official evaluation results of iitb-hi-en.

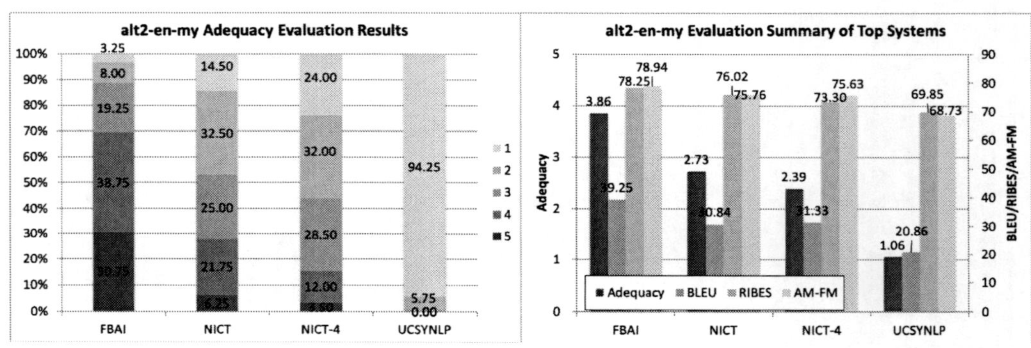

Figure 22: Official evaluation results of alt2-en-my.

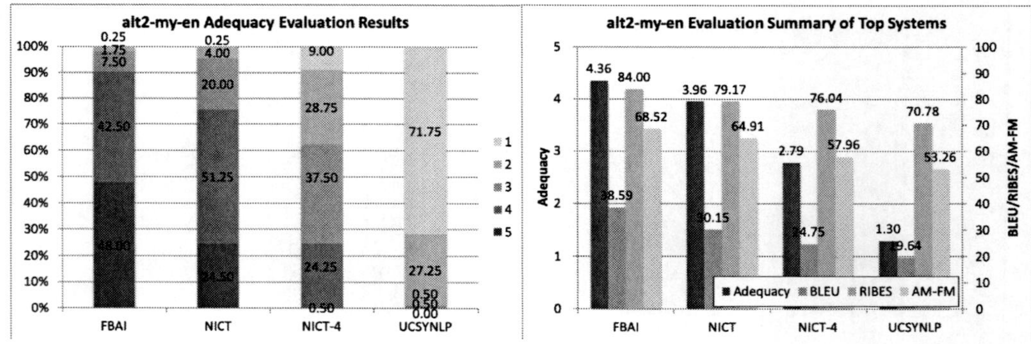

Figure 23: Official evaluation results of alt2-my-en.

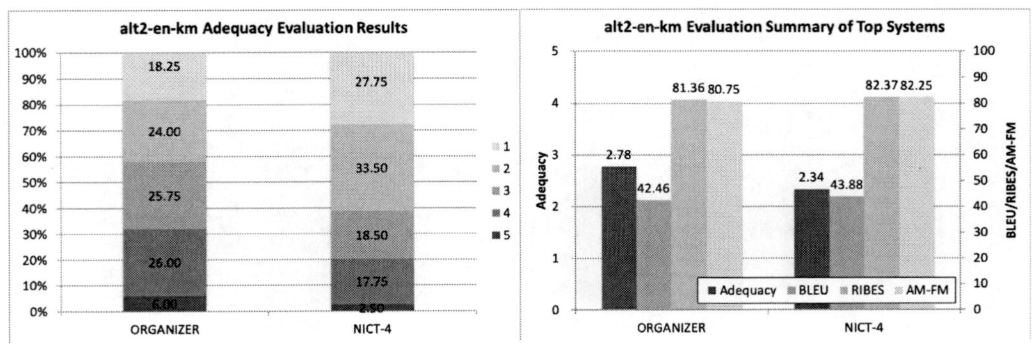

Figure 24: Official evaluation results of alt2-en-km.

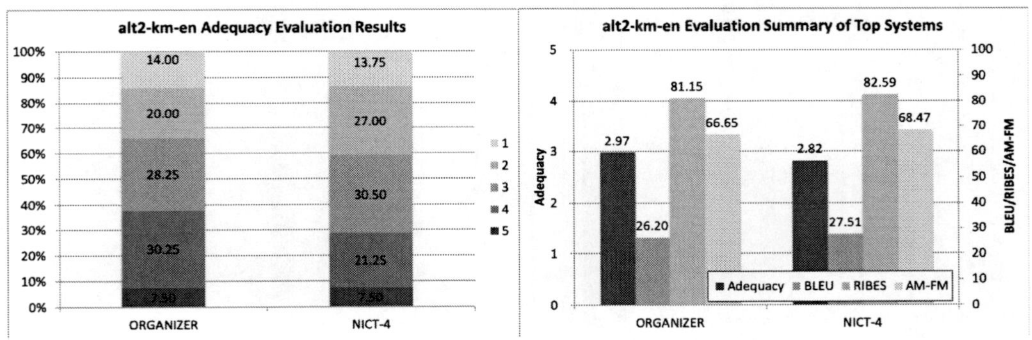

Figure 25: Official evaluation results of alt2-km-en.

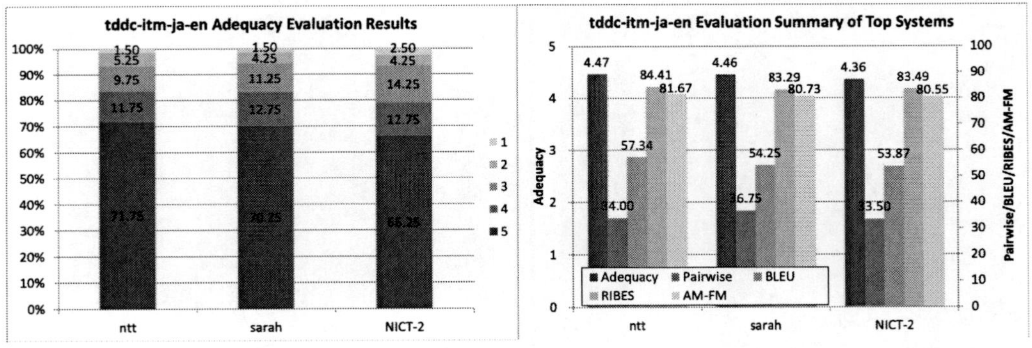

Figure 26: Official evaluation results of tddc-itm-ja-en.

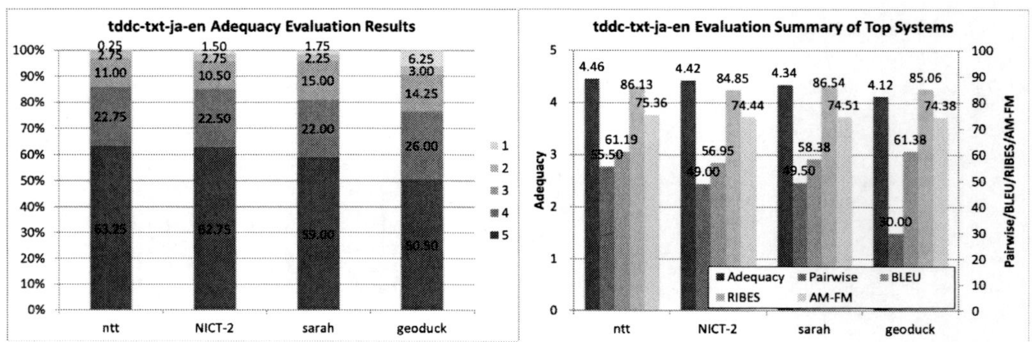

Figure 27: Official evaluation results of tddc-txt-ja-en.

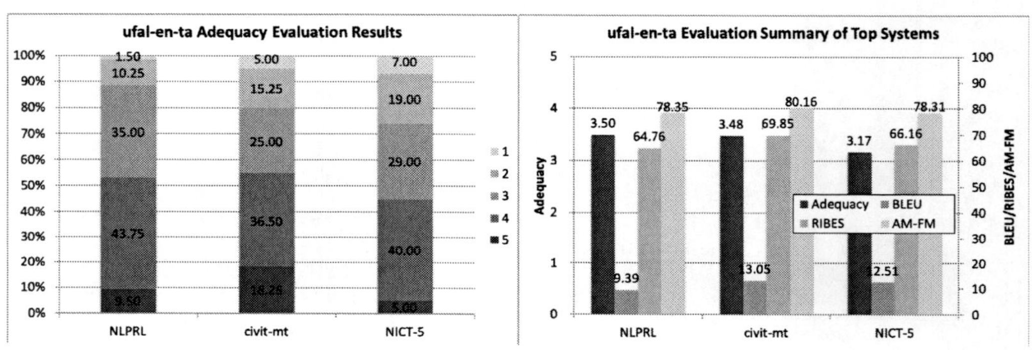

Figure 28: Official evaluation results of ufal-en-ta.

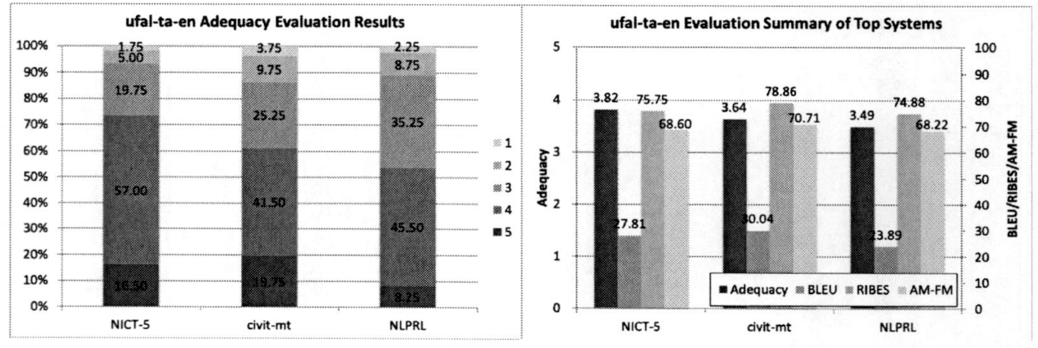

Figure 29: Official evaluation results of ufal-ta-en.

Team ID	Organization	Country
TMU	Tokyo Metropolitan University	Japan
NICT	NICT	Japan
NTT	NTT Corporation	Japan
NICT-2	NICT	Japan
NICT-4	NICT	Japan
NICT-5	NICT	Japan
UCSYNLP	University of Computer Studies, Yangon	Myanmar
UCSMNLP	University of Computer Studies, Mandalay	Myanmar
cvit	IIIT Hyderabad	India
srcb	RICOH Software Research Center Beijing Co.,Ltd	China
sarah	Rakuten Institute of Technology	Japan
683	National Institute of Technology Silchar	India
KNU_Hyundai	Kangwon National University	Korea
NITSNLP	National Institute of Technology Silchar	India
ryan	Kakao Brain	Korea
PUP-IND	Punjabi University Patiala	India
FBAI	Facebook AI Research	USA
AISTAI	National Institute of Advanced Industrial Science and Technology	Japan
SYSTRAN	SYSTRAN	France
NHK-NES	NHK & NHK Engineering System	Japan
geoduck	Microsoft Research	USA
LTRC-MT	IIIT Hyderabad	India
ykkd	The University of Tokyo	Japan
IDIAP	Idiap Research Institute	Switzerland
NLPRL	Indian Institute of Technology (BHU) Varanasi	India

Table 15: List of participants in WAT2019

Team ID	ASPEC				JPC						TDDC	JIJI		NCPD	
	EJ	JE	CJ	JC	EJ	JE	CJ	JC	Ko-J	J-Ko	JE	EJ	JE	RJ	JR
TMU														✓	✓
NTT	✓	✓									✓				
NICT-2	✓	✓									✓				
NICT-5		✓												✓	✓
srcb	✓	✓	✓	✓											
sarah					✓	✓	✓	✓	✓	✓	✓	✓	✓		
KNU_Hyundai	✓	✓	✓	✓	✓	✓	✓	✓	✓						
ryan					✓	✓	✓	✓	✓	✓					
AISTAI	✓														
SYSTRAN														✓	✓
NHK-NES												✓	✓		
geoduck											✓				
ykkd		✓													

Team ID	Mixed-domain tasks								Mutimodal task
	ALT				IITB		UFAL (EnTam)		EV/CH
	EM	ME	E-Kh	Kh-E	EH	HE	ET	TE	EH
NICT	✓	✓							
NICT-4	✓	✓	✓	✓					
NICT-5						✓	✓	✓	
UCSYNLP	✓	✓							
UCSMNLP	✓	✓							
cvit					✓	✓	✓	✓	
sarah	✓								
683									✓
NITSNLP									✓
PUP-IND									✓
FBAI	✓	✓							
LTRC-MT						✓			
IDIAP									✓
NLPRL							✓	✓	

Table 16: Submissions for each task by each team. E, J, C, Ko, R, M, Kh, H, and T denote English, Japanese, Chinese, Korean, Russian, Myanmar, Khmer, Hindi, and Tamil language, respectively.

Subtask	SYSTEM ID	DATA ID	Annotator A		Annotator B		all	weighted	
			average	variance	average	variance	average	κ	κ
aspec-ja-en	KNU_Hyundai	3173	4.63	0.40	4.38	0.41	4.51	0.23	0.31
	ntt	3225	4.62	0.39	4.34	0.42	4.49	0.26	0.32
	NICT-2	3086	4.51	0.74	4.30	0.68	4.41	0.22	0.39
	2018 best	2474	4.37	0.49	4.63	0.44	4.50	0.15	0.25
aspec-en-ja	ntt	3236	4.60	0.51	4.39	0.43	4.50	0.07	0.15
	srcb	3212	4.54	0.62	4.32	0.52	4.43	0.17	0.31
	NICT-2	3182	4.54	0.53	4.28	0.46	4.41	0.22	0.31
	2018 best	2219	4.16	0.90	4.57	0.57	4.36	0.17	0.30
aspec-ja-zh	KNU_Hyundai	3170	4.44	0.47	4.29	0.85	4.36	0.15	0.15
	srcb	3208	4.14	0.74	4.37	0.86	4.25	0.16	0.26
	2018 best	2266	4.67	0.32	4.27	0.90	4.47	0.28	0.36
aspec-zh-ja	srcb	3210	4.80	0.24	4.46	0.61	4.63	0.27	0.31
	KNU_Hyundai	3179	4.76	0.26	4.42	0.71	4.59	0.14	0.16
	2018 best	2267	4.78	0.26	4.48	0.67	4.63	0.31	0.33
jpcn-ja-en	KNU_Hyundai	3188	4.73	0.40	4.83	0.22	4.78	0.36	0.46
	sarah	2927	4.63	0.53	4.78	0.29	4.71	0.44	0.55
	ryan	2962	4.62	0.50	4.77	0.27	4.70	0.33	0.38
jpcn-en-ja	KNU_Hyundai	3192	4.43	0.81	4.57	0.77	4.50	0.36	0.49
	sarah	2926	4.38	0.83	4.40	0.98	4.39	0.35	0.51
	ryan	2961	4.30	0.90	4.44	0.94	4.37	0.36	0.53
jpcn-ja-zh	KNU_Hyundai	3157	4.53	0.45	4.56	0.54	4.54	0.29	0.35
	ryan	2948	4.43	0.49	4.41	0.74	4.42	0.29	0.39
	sarah	2921	4.39	0.50	4.41	0.75	4.40	0.39	0.48
jpcn-zh-ja	KNU_Hyundai	3152	4.72	0.26	4.57	0.55	4.65	0.26	0.35
	ryan	2949	4.42	0.58	4.42	0.81	4.42	0.35	0.48
	sarah	2920	4.45	0.56	4.37	0.80	4.41	0.36	0.51
jpcn-ja-ko	ryan	2850	4.82	0.27	4.73	0.34	4.77	0.56	0.65
	sarah	2925	4.83	0.27	4.71	0.36	4.77	0.31	0.46
jpcn-ko-ja	sarah	2924	4.72	0.39	4.58	0.68	4.65	0.59	0.69
	KNU_Hyundai	2998	4.70	0.35	4.59	0.58	4.65	0.68	0.76
	ryan	2890	4.68	0.35	4.55	0.63	4.62	0.71	0.74
jiji-ja-en	NHK-NES	2884	4.50	0.68	4.61	0.72	4.55	0.26	0.38
	sarah	2793	3.27	1.13	3.73	1.39	3.50	0.23	0.39
jiji-en-ja	NHK-NES	2886	4.04	1.02	4.18	1.37	4.11	0.21	0.42
	sarah	2814	3.00	1.35	2.89	1.99	2.95	0.19	0.42

Table 17: JPO adequacy evaluation results in detail (1).

Subtask	SYSTEM ID	DATA ID	Annotator A		Annotator B		all	weighted	
			average	variance	average	variance	average	κ	κ
ncpd-ja-ru	SYSTRAN	3076	2.65	2.56	2.62	2.12	2.64	0.26	0.47
	NICT-5	3026	1.70	1.39	1.54	1.19	1.62	0.29	0.52
	TMU	3095	1.32	0.65	1.23	0.57	1.28	0.30	0.43
ncpd-ru-ja	SYSTRAN	2912	2.23	2.16	2.42	1.99	2.32	0.24	0.48
	NICT-5	3027	1.41	0.95	1.44	0.74	1.42	0.34	0.57
	TMU	3097	1.21	0.50	1.29	0.65	1.25	0.36	0.56
iitb-en-hi	cvit-mt	2680	3.94	1.02	3.58	0.82	3.76	0.53	0.58
	2018 best	2362	3.58	2.71	3.40	2.52	3.49	0.52	0.74
iitb-hi-en	cvit-mt	2681	4.53	0.53	3.74	1.18	4.13	0.05	0.13
	NICT-5	2865	4.26	0.90	3.39	1.48	3.83	0.10	0.22
	LTRC	3119	3.92	0.91	2.94	1.15	3.43	0.05	0.16
	2018 best	2381	2.96	2.55	2.96	2.52	2.96	0.48	0.76
alt2-en-my	fbai	3203	4.36	0.67	3.36	1.02	3.86	0.02	0.19
	NICT	2818	2.74	1.34	2.71	1.25	2.73	0.97	0.98
	NICT-4	2979	2.40	1.21	2.38	1.13	2.39	0.97	0.98
	UCSYNLP	2858	1.05	0.05	1.06	0.06	1.06	0.59	0.59
alt2-my-en	fbai	3201	4.49	0.53	4.24	0.47	4.36	0.13	0.18
	NICT	2816	3.88	0.78	4.03	0.46	3.96	0.07	0.18
	NICT-4	2977	2.56	0.78	3.01	0.85	2.79	0.26	0.42
	UCSYNLP	3252	1.25	0.27	1.34	0.22	1.30	0.62	0.60
alt2-en-km	organizer	2898	2.54	1.54	3.00	1.19	2.77	0.24	0.49
	NICT-4	2929	2.43	1.35	2.25	1.20	2.34	0.67	0.80
alt2-km-en	organizer	2897	2.60	1.52	3.35	0.92	2.97	0.08	0.31
	NICT-4	2915	2.91	1.33	2.73	1.25	2.82	0.61	0.76
tddc-itm-ja-en	ntt	3002	4.48	0.83	4.46	1.05	4.47	0.17	0.30
	sarah	2807	4.52	0.77	4.40	1.04	4.46	0.29	0.47
	NICT-2	3081	4.42	0.94	4.30	1.19	4.36	0.40	0.52
tddc-txt-ja-en	ntt	3005	4.34	0.65	4.58	0.65	4.46	0.16	0.27
	NICT-2	3084	4.26	0.82	4.58	0.72	4.42	0.22	0.33
	sarah	2808	4.20	0.83	4.49	0.87	4.34	0.26	0.39
	geoduck	3200	4.07	0.99	4.17	1.64	4.12	0.30	0.48
ufal-en-ta	NLPRL018	3015	3.71	0.56	3.29	0.82	3.50	0.17	0.34
	cvit-mt	2830	3.46	1.10	3.50	1.34	3.48	0.84	0.90
	NICT-5	3046	3.15	0.92	3.19	1.16	3.17	0.62	0.74
ufal-ta-en	NICT-5	3054	3.88	0.46	3.75	0.90	3.81	0.39	0.48
	cvit-mt	2833	3.58	0.89	3.70	1.19	3.64	0.75	0.83
	NLPRL018	3014	3.67	0.47	3.31	0.91	3.49	0.10	0.22

Table 18: JPO adequacy evaluation results in detail (2).

	Team ID	Data ID	Ave	Ave Z
EV TEXT	IDIAP	2956	72.85	0.70
	Reference		71.34	0.66
	683	3285	68.89	0.57
	683	3286	61.64	0.36
	NITSNLP	3299	52.53	0.00
CH TEXT	Reference		79.23	0.94
	IDIAP	3277	60.81	0.25
	IDIAP	3267	60.17	0.25
	683	3284	45.69	-0.28
	683	3287	45.52	-0.24
	NITSNLP	3300	28.48	-0.81
EV MM	Reference		70.04	0.60
	683	3271	69.17	0.61
	PUP-IND	3296	62.42	0.35
	PUP-IND	3295	60.22	0.28
	NITSNLP	3288	58.98	0.25
CH MM	Reference		75.96	0.76
	683	3270	54.51	0.08
	NITSNLP	3298	48.45	-0.20
	PUP-IND	3281	48.06	-0.13
	PUP-IND	3280	47.06	-0.17
EV HI	Reference		68.80	0.52
	NITSNLP	3289	51.78	-0.05
CH HI	Reference		72.60	0.61
	NITSNLP	3297	44.46	-0.35
	683	3304	26.54	-0.94

Table 19: Manual evaluation result for WAT Multi-Modal Tasks.

	System	Run	BLEU	chrF3	nCDER	nCharacTER	nPER	nTER	nWER	BLEU$_w$
EV TEXT	IDIAP	2956	52.18	58.81	62.18	57.95	69.32	56.87	55.07	41.32
	683	3285	48.29	54.66	58.18	54.12	65.34	52.52	51.00	38.19
	683	3286	33.47	40.37	45.36	00.11	50.54	43.11	42.13	25.34
	NITSNLP	3299	30.05	34.49	41.36	≀ 10.92	48.23	36.42	35.10	20.13
CH TEXT	IDIAP	3277	40.40	50.18	52.58	44.32	60.19	49.11	46.02	30.94
	IDIAP	3267	39.08	49.30	51.78	41.72	59.49	48.42	45.51	30.34
	683	3284	21.56	30.90	33.92	13.69	41.14	30.53	28.40	14.69
	683	3287	21.50	30.27	≀ 34.66	-65.00	38.98	≀ 32.91	≀ 31.47	≀ 15.85
	NITSNLP	3300	10.50	17.91	23.04	≀ -60.87	28.05	20.87	19.90	5.56
EV MM	683	3271	51.46	57.63	61.51	52.61	68.52	55.99	54.28	40.55
	PUP-IND	3296	39.67	47.76	51.98	46.84	59.50	43.47	41.92	28.27
	NITSNLP	3288	39.13	45.50	49.45	27.92	57.43	≀ 43.91	≀ 42.17	≀ 28.45
	PUP-IND	3295	38.50	45.35	≀ 50.33	≀ 41.40	≀ 58.82	41.84	40.65	27.39
CH MM	683	3270	28.62	37.86	41.60	20.10	48.64	38.38	36.44	20.37
	NITSNLP	3298	19.68	27.99	31.84	-24.40	38.61	29.38	27.16	12.58
	PUP-IND	3281	18.32	27.79	30.08	≀ 19.63	≀ 40.51	23.51	21.12	11.77
	PUP-IND	3280	16.15	25.78	28.57	06.31	37.34	23.38	≀ 21.28	10.19
EV HI	NITSNLP	3289	8.68	14.45	14.27	-15.81	22.51	06.85	06.19	2.59
CH HI	NITSNLP	3297	2.28	8.88	8.00	-50.33	12.97	06.05	05.62	0.00
	683	3304	1.07	8.63	6.65	-19.81	-32.82	-52.44	-52.59	0.00

Table 20: Multi-Modal Task automatic evaluation results. For each test set (EV and CH) and each track (TEXT, MM and HI), we sort the entries by our BLEU scores. The symbol "≀" in subsequent columns indicates fields where the other metric ranks candidates in a different order. BLEU$_w$ denotes the WAT official BLEU scores.

7.2 Statistical Significance Testing of Pairwise Evaluation between Submissions

Table 21 shows the results of statistical significance testing of aspec-ja-en subtasks, Table 22 shows that of JIJI subtasks, Table 23 shows that of TDDC subtasks. $\ggg$, $\gg$ and $>$ mean that the system in the row is better than the system in the column at a significance level of $p < 0.01$, 0.05 and 0.1 respectively. Testing is also done by the bootstrap resampling as follows:

1. randomly select 300 sentences from the 400 pairwise evaluation sentences, and calculate the Pairwise scores on the selected sentences for both systems

2. iterate the previous step 1000 times and count the number of wins (W), losses (L) and ties (T)

3. calculate $p = \frac{L}{W+L}$

Inter-annotator Agreement

To assess the reliability of agreement between the workers, we calculated the Fleiss' κ (Fleiss et al., 1971) values. The results are shown in Table 24. We can see that the κ values are larger for X→J translations than for J→X translations. This may be because the majority of the workers for these language pairs are Japanese, and the evaluation of one's mother tongue is much easier than for other languages in general. The κ values for Hindi languages are relatively higt. This might be because the overall translation quality of the Hindi languages are low, and the evaluators can easily distinguish better translations from worse ones.

8 Findings

In this section, we will show findings of some of the translation tasks.

8.1 TDDC

In the results of both the automatic evaluation and the human evaluation, every system translated most sentences correctly. According to the human evaluation of the subtasks of 'Items' and 'Texts', all evaluators rated more than 70% of all the pairs at 4 or 5. Most of these high-rated pairs consist of typical terms and sentences from timely disclosure documents. This tasks focus on the accurate translation of figures, so the evaluation criteria confirmed there are no mistranslation in the typical sentences containing figures, such as unit of money and dates.

However, uncommon sentences used in timely disclosure documents tend to be mistranslated. For example, uncommon proper nouns tended to be omitted or mistranslated to other meaning words, besides sentences which has complex and uncommon structures, generally long sentences, caused errors at dependency of subordinate clauses.

In addition, some systems translated sentences without subjects into sentences with incorrect subjects. Japanese sentences often omit subjects and objects, which would normally be included in English. For example, a Japanese sentence, "当社普通株式 27,000 株を上限とする。" (Common shares of the Company, limited to a maximum of 27,000 shares), was translated to "(Unrelated company name) common stocks up to 27,000 shares".

Moreover, there are some incorrect modifiers or determiners. In Japanese timely disclosure documents, there are many variable prefix for dates, such as "本"(this), "当"(this), "次" (next), and "前" (last). Some systems translated sentences containing these words with incorrect year. For example, a Japanese sentence contains "当第 3 四半期連結会計期間末"(the end of third quarter of this fiscal year) was translated to "the end of the third quarter of FY 2016".

In summary, the causes of these mistranslations are considered as follows:

- It is difficult for the systems to translate long sentence and proper nouns which TDDC does not contain.

- Some source sentences are unclear due to lack of subjects and/or objects, so these are not suitable for English translation.

- TDDC contains not semantically balanced pairs and the systems might be affected strongly by either of source pair sentences.

On the other hand, some translations seem to be fitted to sentences of TDDC which are

	KNU_Hyundai (3173)	NICT-2 (3086)	srcb (3205)
NTT (3225)	-	≫	⋙
KNU_Hyundai (3173)		-	⋙
NICT-2 (3086)			>

	NICT-2 (3182)	srcb (3212)	AISTAI (3251)	KNU_Hyundai (3172)
NTT (3236)	⋙	⋙	⋙	⋙
NICT-2 (3182)		-	≫	≫
srcb (3212)			>	≫
AISTAI (3251)				-

Table 21: Statistical significance testing of the aspec-ja-en (left) and aspec-en-ja (right) Pairwise scores.

	NHK-NES (2883)	sarah (2793)	sarah (2813)
NHK-NES (2884)	⋙	⋙	⋙
NHK-NES (2883)		⋙	⋙
sarah (2793)			⋙

	NHK-NES (2885)	sarah (2814)	sarah (2815)
NHK-NES (2886)	⋙	⋙	⋙
NHK-NES (2885)		⋙	⋙
sarah (2814)			⋙

Table 22: Statistical significance testing of the jiji-ja-en (left) and jiji-en-ja (right) Pairwise scores.

	sarah (2807)	NTT (3002)	NICT-2 (3081)	sarah (2811)	geoduck (3197)	geoduck (3216)
ORGANIZER (3264)	⋙	⋙	⋙	⋙	⋙	⋙
sarah (2807)		≫	⋙	⋙	⋙	⋙
NTT (3002)			-	⋙	⋙	⋙
NICT-2 (3081)				⋙	⋙	⋙
sarah (2811)					-	≫
geoduck (3197)						⋙

	NTT (3005)	sarah (2808)	NICT-2 (3084)	sarah (2812)	geoduck (3200)	geoduck (3217)
ORGANIZER (3265)	-	⋙	⋙	⋙	⋙	⋙
NTT (3005)		⋙	⋙	⋙	⋙	⋙
sarah (2808)			-	⋙	⋙	⋙
NICT-2 (3084)				⋙	⋙	⋙
sarah (2812)					⋙	⋙
geoduck (3200)						⋙

Table 23: Statistical significance testing of the tddc-itm-ja-en (left) and tddc-txt-ja-en (right) Pairwise scores.

freely and omitted redundant expressions, but evaluators mark them as low scores, probably because they are not literal translations. This result implies that it is necessary to create another evaluation criterion, which evaluates the correctness of transmitting information to investors correctly.

8.2 English↔Tamil Task

We observed that most participants used transfer learning techniques such as fine-tuning and mixed fine-tuning for Tamil→English translation leading to reasonably high quality translations. However, English→Tamil translation is still poor and the main reason is the lack of helping parallel corpora. We expect that utilization of large in-domain monolingual corpora for back-translation should help alleviate this problem. We will provide such corpora for next year's task.

8.3 News Commentary Task

We only received 3 submissions for Russian↔Japanese translation and all submissions leveraged multilingualism and multi-step fine-tuning proposed by Imankulova et al. (2019) and showed that carefully choosing corpora and robust training can dramatically enhance the quality of NMT for language pairs

aspec-ja-en		
SYSTEM	DATA	κ
NTT	3225	0.157
NICT-2	3086	0.187
srcb	3205	0.220
KNU_Hyundai	3173	0.156
ave.		0.180

aspec-en-ja		
SYSTEM	DATA	κ
NTT	3236	0.298
NICT-2	3182	0.319
srcb	3212	0.305
KNU_Hyundai	3172	0.302
AISTAI	3251	0.303
ave.		0.305

jiji-ja-en		
SYSTEM	DATA	κ
sarah	2793	0.146
sarah	2813	0.158
NHK-NES	2883	0.273
NHK-NES	2884	0.159
ave.		0.184

jiji-en-ja		
SYSTEM	DATA	κ
sarah	2814	0.357
sarah	2815	0.299
NHK-NES	2885	0.354
NHK-NES	2886	0.390
ave.		0.350

tddc-itm-ja-en		
SYSTEM	DATA	κ
ORGANIZER	3264	0.382
NTT	3002	0.403
NICT-2	3081	0.423
sarah	2807	0.408
sarah	2811	0.391
geoduck	3197	0.404
geoduck	3216	0.493
ave.		0.415

tddc-txt-ja-en		
SYSTEM	DATA	κ
ORGANIZER	3265	0.135
NTT	3005	0.163
NICT-2	3084	0.175
sarah	2808	0.163
sarah	2812	0.167
geoduck	3200	0.172
geoduck	3217	0.321
ave.		0.185

Table 24: The Fleiss' kappa values for the pairwise evaluation results.

Source Good?	C-Test	E-Test
Yes	1586 (78.7 %)	1348 (66.9 %)
No	20 (1.0 %)	46 (2.3 %)
No Answer	410 (20.3 %)	622 (30.9 %)
Total	2016 (100.0 %)	2016 (100.0 %)

Table 25: Appropriateness of source English captions in the 4032 assessments collected for the multi-modal track.

that have very small in-domain parallel corpora. For next year's task we expect more submissions where participants will leverage additional larger helping monolingual as well as bilingual corpora.

8.4 Multi-Modal Task

8.4.1 Validation of Source English Captions

In the manual evaluation of multimodal track, our annotators saw both the picture and the source text (and the two scored candidates). We took this opportunity to double check the quality of the original HVG data. Prior to scoring the candidates, we asked our annotators to confirm that the source English text is a good caption for the indicated region of the image.

The results in Table 25 indicate that for a surprisingly high number of items we did not receive any answer. This confirms that even non-anonymous annotators can easily provide sloppy evaluations. It is possible that part of these omissions can be attributed to our annotation interface which was showing all items on one page and relying on scrolling. Next time, we will show only one annotation item on each page and also consider highlighting unanswered questions. Strictly requiring an answer would not be always appropriate but we need to ensure that annotators are aware that they are skipping a question.

Luckily, the bad source captions are not a frequent case, amounting to 1 or 2% of assessed examples.

8.4.2 Relation to Human Translation

The bilingual style of evaluation of the multi-modal task allowed us to evaluate the reference translations as if they were yet another competing MT system. Table 19 thus lists also the "Reference".

Across the tracks and test sets (EV vs. CH), humans surpass MT candidates. One single exception is IDIAP run 2956 winning in text-only translation of the E-Test, but this is not confirmed on the C-Test (CH). The score of the anonymized system 683 on E-Test in multi-modal track (MM) has also almost reached human performance. These are not the first cases of MT performing on par with humans and we are happy to see this when targetting an Indian language.

8.4.3 Evaluating Captioning

While the automatic scores are comparable across tasks, the Hindi-only captioning ("HI") must be considered separately. Without a source sentence, both humans and machines are very likely to come up with highly varying textual captions. The same image can be described in many different aspects. All our automatic metrics compare the candidate caption with the reference one generally on the basis of the presence of the same character sequences, words or n-grams. Candidates diverging from the reference will get a low score regardless of their actual quality.

The automatic evaluation score for the "Hindi caption" is very very low as compared to other sub-tasks ("text-only" and "multimodal" translations) as can be seen in the Table 20. Even the human annotators couldn't give any score for most of the segments submitted from the "Hindi caption" entries due to the wrong caption generation.

9 Conclusion and Future Perspective

This paper summarizes the shared tasks of WAT2019. We had 25 participants worldwide, and collected a large number of useful submissions for improving the current machine translation systems by analyzing the submissions and identifying the issues.

For the next WAT workshop, we plan to conduct document-level evaluation using the new dataset with context for some translation subtasks and we would like to consider how to realize context-aware machine translation in WAT. Also, we are planning to do extrinsic evaluation of the translations.

Acknowledgement

The multi-modal shared task was supported by the following grants at Idiap Research Institute and Charles University.

- At Idiap Research Institute, the work was supported by an innovation project (under an InnoSuisse grant) oriented to improve the automatic speech recognition and natural language understanding technologies for German (Title: "SM2: Extracting Semantic Meaning from Spoken Material" funding application no. 29814.1 IP-ICT). The work was also supported by the EU H2020 project "Real-time network, text, and speaker analytics for combating organized crime" (ROXANNE), grant agreement: 833635.

- At Charles University, the work was supported by the grants 19-26934X (NEUREM3) of the Czech Science Foundation and "Progress" Q18+Q48 of Charles University, and using language resources distributed by the LINDAT/CLARIN project of the Ministry of Education, Youth and Sports of the Czech Republic (projects LM2015071 and OP VVV VI CZ.02.1.01/0.0/0.0/16013/0001781).

Some of the human evaluations for the other tasks were supported by "Research and Development of Deep Learning Technology for Advanced Multilingual Speech Translation", the Commissioned Research of National Institute of Information and Communications Technology (NICT), JAPAN.

References

Rafael E. Banchs, Luis F. D'Haro, and Haizhou Li. 2015. Adequacy-fluency metrics: Evaluating mt in the continuous space model framework. IEEE/ACM Trans. Audio, Speech and Lang. Proc., 23(3):472–482.

Ondřej Bojar, Rajen Chatterjee, Christian Federmann, Yvette Graham, Barry Haddow, Matthias Huck, Antonio Yepes, Philipp Koehn, Varvara Logacheva, Christof Monz, Matteo Negri, Aurelie Névéol, Mariana Neves, Martin Popel, Matt Post, Raphael Rubino, Carolina Scarton, Lucia Specia, Marco Turchi, Karin Verspoor, and Marcos Zampieri. 2016. Findings of the 2016 Conference on Machine Translation (WMT16). In Proceedings of the First Conference on Machine Translation (WMT). Volume 2: Shared Task Papers, volume 2, pages 131–198, Stroudsburg, PA, USA. Association for Computational Linguistics, Association for Computational Linguistics.

Jacob Cohen. 1968. Weighted kappa: Nominal scale agreement with provision for scaled disagreement or partial credit. Psychological Bulletin, 70(4):213 – 220.

Chenchen Ding, Hnin Thu Zar Aye, Win Pa Pa, Khin Thandar Nwet, Khin Mar Soe, Masao Utiyama, and Eiichiro Sumita. 2019. Towards Burmese (Myanmar) morphological analysis: Syllable-based tokenization and part-of-speech tagging. ACM Transactions on Asian and Low-Resource Language Information Processing (TALLIP), 19(1):5.

Chenchen Ding, Masao Utiyama, and Eiichiro Sumita. 2018. NOVA: A feasible and flexible annotation system for joint tokenization and part-of-speech tagging. ACM Transactions on Asian and Low-Resource Language Information Processing (TALLIP), 18(2):17.

J.L. Fleiss et al. 1971. Measuring nominal scale agreement among many raters. Psychological Bulletin, 76(5):378–382.

Yvette Graham, Timothy Baldwin, Alistair Moffat, and Justin Zobel. 2016. Can machine translation systems be evaluated by the crowd alone. Natural Language Engineering, FirstView:1–28.

Aizhan Imankulova, Raj Dabre, Atsushi Fujita, and Kenji Imamura. 2019. Exploiting out-of-domain parallel data through multilingual transfer learning for low-resource neural machine translation. In Proceedings of Machine Translation Summit XVII Volume 1: Research Track, pages 128–139, Dublin, Ireland.

Hideki Isozaki, Tsutomu Hirao, Kevin Duh, Katsuhito Sudoh, and Hajime Tsukada. 2010. Automatic evaluation of translation quality for distant language pairs. In Proceedings of the 2010 Conference on Empirical Methods in Natural Language Processing, EMNLP '10, pages 944–952, Stroudsburg, PA, USA. Association for Computational Linguistics.

Melvin Johnson, Mike Schuster, Quoc V. Le, Maxim Krikun, Yonghui Wu, Zhifeng Chen, Nikhil Thorat, Fernanda Viégas, Martin Wattenberg, Greg Corrado, Macduff Hughes, and Jeffrey Dean. 2017. Google's multilingual neural machine translation system: Enabling zero-shot translation. Transactions of the Association for Computational Linguistics, 5:339–351.

Guillaume Klein, Yoon Kim, Yuntian Deng, Jean Senellart, and Alexander Rush. 2017. Opennmt: Open-source toolkit for neural machine translation. In Proceedings of ACL 2017, System Demonstrations, pages 67–72. Association for Computational Linguistics.

Philipp Koehn. 2004. Statistical significance tests for machine translation evaluation. In Proceedings of EMNLP 2004, pages 388–395, Barcelona, Spain. Association for Computational Linguistics.

Philipp Koehn, Hieu Hoang, Alexandra Birch, Chris Callison-Burch, Marcello Federico, Nicola Bertoldi, Brooke Cowan, Wade Shen, Christine Moran, Richard Zens, Chris Dyer, Ondrej Bojar, Alexandra Constantin, and Evan Herbst. 2007. Moses: Open source toolkit for statistical machine translation. In Annual Meeting of the Association for Computational Linguistics (ACL), demonstration session.

T. Kudo. 2005. Mecab : Yet another part-of-speech and morphological analyzer. http://mecab.sourceforge.net/.

Sadao Kurohashi, Toshihisa Nakamura, Yuji Matsumoto, and Makoto Nagao. 1994. Improvements of Japanese morphological analyzer JUMAN. In Proceedings of The International Workshop on Sharable Natural Language, pages 22–28.

Gregor Leusch, Nicola Ueffing, and Hermann Ney. 2006. CDER: Efficient MT Evaluation Using Block Movements. In In Proceedings of EACL, pages 241–248.

Toshiaki Nakazawa, Chenchen Ding, Hideya MINO, Isao Goto, Graham Neubig, and Sadao Kurohashi. 2016. Overview of the 3rd workshop on asian translation. In Proceedings of the 3rd Workshop on Asian Translation (WAT2016), pages 1–46, Osaka, Japan. The COLING 2016 Organizing Committee.

Toshiaki Nakazawa, Shohei Higashiyama, Chenchen Ding, Hideya Mino, Isao Goto, Hideto Kazawa, Yusuke Oda, Graham Neubig, and Sadao Kurohashi. 2017. Overview of the 4th workshop on asian translation. In Proceedings of the 4th Workshop on Asian Translation (WAT2017), pages 1–54. Asian Federation of Natural Language Processing.

Toshiaki Nakazawa, Hideya Mino, Isao Goto, Sadao Kurohashi, and Eiichiro Sumita. 2014. Overview of the 1st Workshop on Asian Translation. In Proceedings of the 1st Workshop on Asian Translation (WAT2014), pages 1–19, Tokyo, Japan.

Toshiaki Nakazawa, Hideya Mino, Isao Goto, Graham Neubig, Sadao Kurohashi, and Eiichiro Sumita. 2015. Overview of the 2nd Workshop on Asian Translation. In Proceedings of the 2nd Workshop on Asian Translation (WAT2015), pages 1–28, Kyoto, Japan.

Toshiaki Nakazawa, Katsuhito Sudoh, Shohei Higashiyama, Chenchen Ding, Raj Dabre, Hideya Mino, Isao Goto, Win Pa Pa, Anoop Kunchukuttan, and Sadao Kurohashi. 2018. Overview of the 5th workshop on Asian translation. In Proceedings of the 32nd Pacific Asia Conference on Language, Information and Computation: 5th Workshop on Asian Translation: 5th Workshop on Asian Translation, Hong

Kong. Association for Computational Linguistics.

Graham Neubig, Yosuke Nakata, and Shinsuke Mori. 2011. Pointwise prediction for robust, adaptable japanese morphological analysis. In Proceedings of the 49th Annual Meeting of the Association for Computational Linguistics: Human Language Technologies: Short Papers - Volume 2, HLT '11, pages 529–533, Stroudsburg, PA, USA. Association for Computational Linguistics.

Kishore Papineni, Salim Roukos, Todd Ward, and Wei-Jing Zhu. 2002. Bleu: a method for automatic evaluation of machine translation. In ACL, pages 311–318.

Shantipriya Parida, Ondřej Bojar, and Satya Ranjan Dash. 2019a. Hindi visual genome: A dataset for multimodal english-to-hindi machine translation. arXiv preprint arXiv:1907.08948.

Shantipriya Parida, Ondřej Bojar, and Satya Ranjan Dash. 2019b. Hindi Visual Genome: A Dataset for Multimodal English-to-Hindi Machine Translation. Computación y Sistemas. In print. Presented at CICLing 2019, La Rochelle, France.

Maja Popović. 2015. chrF: character n-gram F-score for automatic MT evaluation. In Proceedings of the Tenth Workshop on Statistical Machine Translation, Lisboa, Portugal. Association for Computational Linguistics.

Loganathan Ramasamy, Ondřej Bojar, and Zdeněk Žabokrtský. 2012. Morphological processing for english-tamil statistical machine translation. In Proceedings of the Workshop on Machine Translation and Parsing in Indian Languages (MT-PIL-2012), pages 113–122.

Hammam Riza, Michael Purwoadi, Teduh Uliniansyah, Aw Ai Ti, Sharifah Mahani Aljunied, Luong Chi Mai, Vu Tat Thang, Nguyen Phuong Thai, Vichet Chea, Sethserey Sam, Sopheap Seng, Khin Mar Soe, Khin Thandar Nwet, Masao Utiyama, and Chenchen Ding. 2016. Introduction of the asian language treebank. In In Proc. of O-COCOSDA, pages 1–6.

Matthew Snover, Bonnie Dorr, Richard Schwartz, Linnea Micciulla, and John Makhoul. 2006. A study of translation edit rate with targeted human annotation. In In Proceedings of Association for Machine Translation in the Americas, pages 223–231.

Huihsin Tseng. 2005. A conditional random field word segmenter. In In Fourth SIGHAN Workshop on Chinese Language Processing.

Masao Utiyama and Hitoshi Isahara. 2007. A japanese-english patent parallel corpus. In MT summit XI, pages 475–482.

Ashish Vaswani, Samy Bengio, Eugene Brevdo, Francois Chollet, Aidan Gomez, Stephan Gouws, Llion Jones, Łukasz Kaiser, Nal Kalchbrenner, Niki Parmar, Ryan Sepassi, Noam Shazeer, and Jakob Uszkoreit. 2018. Tensor2tensor for neural machine translation. In Proceedings of the 13th Conference of the Association for Machine Translation in the Americas (Volume 1: Research Papers), pages 193–199. Association for Machine Translation in the Americas.

Ashish Vaswani, Noam Shazeer, Niki Parmar, Jakob Uszkoreit, Llion Jones, Aidan N. Gomez, Lukasz Kaiser, and Illia Polosukhin. 2017. Attention is all you need. CoRR, abs/1706.03762.

Weiyue Wang, Jan-Thorsten Peter, Hendrik Rosendahl, and Hermann Ney. 2016. Character: Translation edit rate on character level. In ACL 2016 First Conference on Machine Translation, pages 505–510, Berlin, Germany.

Yi Mon Shwe Sin and Khin Mar Soe. 2018. Syllable-based myanmar-english neural machine translation. In In Proc. of ICCA, pages 228–233.

Appendix A   Submissions

Tables 26 to 31 summarize translation results submitted for WAT2019 pairwise evaluation. Type, RSRC, and Pair columns indicate type of method, use of other resources, and pairwise evaluation score, respectively. The tables also include results by the organizers' baselines, which are listed in Table 13.

System	ID	Type	RSRC	BLEU			RIBES			AMFM			Pair
				juman	kytea	mecab	juman	kytea	mecab	juman	kytea	mecab	
NMT	1900	NMT	NO	36.37	38.48	37.15	0.824985	0.831183	0.833207	0.759910	0.759910	0.759910	–
NTT	3236	NMT	NO	45.83	47.63	46.57	0.861994	0.865640	0.868175	0.774950	0.774950	0.774950	47.75
NICT-2	3182	NMT	NO	44.61	46.59	45.66	0.852970	0.856755	0.859059	0.761340	0.761340	0.761340	42.25
srcb	3212	NMT	NO	45.71	47.55	46.29	0.857506	0.860642	0.862819	0.770440	0.770440	0.770440	40.00
AISTAI	3251	NMT	NO	42.64	44.17	43.34	0.849129	0.851400	0.856177	0.757590	0.757590	0.757590	36.75
KNU_Hyundai	3172	NMT	NO	44.08	45.88	44.78	0.857060	0.859885	0.863400	0.760050	0.760050	0.760050	36.00

Table 26: ASPEC en-ja submissions

System	ID	Type	RSRC	BLEU	RIBES	AMFM	Pair
NMT	1901	NMT	NO	26.91	0.764968	0.595370	–
NTT	3225	SMT	NO	30.56	0.773281	0.626880	14.000
KNU_Hyundai	3173	NMT	NO	30.88	0.774653	0.622070	11.750
srcb	3205	NMT	NO	30.92	0.778832	0.630150	6.500

Table 27: ASPEC ja-en submissions

System	ID	Type	RSRC	BLEU	RIBES	AMFM	Pair
NMT	3262	NMT	NO	38.55	0.758265	0.712040	–
sarah	2807	NMT	NO	54.25	0.832909	0.807250	36.750
NTT	3002	SMT	NO	57.34	0.844086	0.816660	34.000
NICT-2	3081	NMT	NO	53.87	0.834898	0.805460	33.500
sarah	2811	NMT	NO	52.77	0.823336	0.794050	29.250
geoduck	3197	Other	YES	54.27	0.828493	0.800360	27.250
geoduck	3216	Other	YES	46.21	0.703675	0.710630	-32.500

Table 28: TDDC ITM ja-en submissions

System	ID	Type	RSRC	BLEU	RIBES	AMFM	Pair
NMT	3263	NMT	NO	24.11	0.701005	0.583850	–
NTT	3005	NMT	NO	61.19	0.861346	0.753630	55.500
sarah	2808	NMT	NO	58.38	0.865364	0.745110	49.500
NICT-2	3084	NMT	NO	56.95	0.848530	0.744390	49.000
sarah	2812	NMT	NO	54.84	0.845921	0.732790	37.750
geoduck	3200	Other	YES	61.38	0.850551	0.743820	30.000
geoduck	3217	Other	YES	51.08	0.659190	0.623770	-28.250

Table 29: TDDC TXT ja-en submissions

System	ID	Type	RSRC	BLEU			RIBES			AMFM			Pair
				juman	kytea	mecab	juman	kytea	mecab	juman	kytea	mecab	
NMT	1904	NMT	NO	16.63	17.01	16.36	0.653766	0.657279	0.658830	0.514530	0.514530	0.514530	–
NHK-NES	2886	NMT	YES	27.22	28.75	27.63	0.730816	0.731653	0.734618	0.660570	0.660570	0.660570	87.750
NHK-NES	2885	NMT	YES	28.25	29.76	28.63	0.739036	0.741164	0.743977	0.654260	0.654260	0.654260	81.250
sarah	2814	NMT	NO	22.65	23.48	22.76	0.705044	0.707209	0.710111	0.614840	0.614840	0.614840	63.250
sarah	2815	NMT	NO	21.80	22.67	21.91	0.698609	0.699981	0.701739	0.613770	0.613770	0.613770	55.250

Table 30: JIJI en-ja submissions

System	ID	Type	RSRC	BLEU	RIBES	AMFM	Pair
NMT	1905	NMT	NO	16.48	0.640558	0.459080	–
NHK-NES	2884	NMT	YES	14.23	0.612351	0.526010	89.000
NHK-NES	2883	NMT	YES	26.38	0.703808	0.554110	72.000
sarah	2793	NMT	NO	21.84	0.675386	0.526530	50.750
sarah	2813	NMT	NO	21.34	0.676723	0.524530	44.750

Table 31: JIJI ja-en submissions

Compact and Robust Models for Japanese-English Character-level Machine Translation

Jinan Dai
The University of Tokyo
Meguro-ku 153-8902, Tokyo, Japan
`daijinan@graco.c.u-tokyo.ac.jp`

Kazunori Yamaguchi
The University of Tokyo
Meguro-ku 153-8902, Tokyo, Japan
`yamaguch@graco.c.u-tokyo.ac.jp`

Abstract

Character-level translation has been proved to be able to achieve preferable translation quality without explicit segmentation, but training a character-level model needs a lot of hardware resources. In this paper, we introduced two character-level translation models which are mid-gated model and multi-attention model for Japanese-English translation. We showed that the mid-gated model achieved the better performance with respect to BLEU scores. We also showed that a relatively narrow beam of width 4 or 5 was sufficient for the mid-gated model. As for unknown words, we showed that the mid-gated model could somehow translate the one containing Katakana by coining out a close word. We also showed that the model managed to produce tolerable results for heavily noised sentences, even though the model was trained with the dataset without noise.

1 Introduction

In recent years, neural machine translation (NMT) has made a great progress, and its translation quality has far surpassed the conventional statistical machine translation (SMT). At first, NMT had almost relied on word-level modelling with explicit segmentation ,which brought a lot of problems such as big vocabulary (Chung et al., 2016) and frequently appeared unknown tokens. Senrich et al. (2016) provided a subword segmentation method based on byte-pair encoding (BPE) as a solution. Character-level translation is another approach to deal with the big vocabulary and unknown words. Chung et al. (2016), Lee at al. (2017) and Cherry et al. (2018) have proved that character-level can achieve preferable translation quality without any explicit word segmentation. Though for alphabetical languages, a sentence is much longer when represented in character-level

(Lee et al., 2017), Japanese can suffer less from this problem because of the existence of Kanji. However, the sequence is still relatively long, so training in character-level can still take a lot of time. The objective of this paper is to shorten the training time and reduce the storage requirement in Japanese-English translation.

In this paper, in order to increase the convergence speed, we propose two different character-level models which are a mid-gated model and a model with multi-attention, and we will examine their performances in Japanese-English translation.

Our contributions include:

- We show that mid-gated is more efficient than multi-attention in this problem.

- We show that while memory overhead is greater than subword-level translation with respect of sentence pairs used for training, the training speed can be fast in character-level Japanese-English translation.

- We show that a close transliteration can be found for unknown words in Katakana.

- We show that character-level translation can handle heavy noises with moderate performance degradation.

2 Related Work

Cherry el al. (2018) compared character-level translation methods for alphabetical languages. They studied the effect of the model capacity, the corpus size, and the compression by BPE and Multiscale architecture (Chung et al., 2017).

Following this research we tried Hierarchical Multi-scale Long Short-Term Memory (HML-STM) (Chung et al., 2017) for character-level

Proceedings of the 6th Workshop on Asian Translation, pages 36–44
Hong Kong, China, November 4, 2019. ©2019 Association for Computational Linguistics

Japanese-English translation, but in our experiment environment[1], we did not get a preferable result. So, we omit it in our experiment for our objective is to get a compact model.

We found that HMLSTM includes relu $\left(\mathbf{W} \left[\mathbf{h}_t^1; \mathbf{h}_t^2, \cdots, \mathbf{h}_t^l \right] \right)$, which is a "shortcut connection" in (He et al., 2016). Even though HMLSTM is too large for a compact model, the shortcut connection may be incorporated. So, we tested a model with the shortcut connection. The model with the shortcut connection is called a mid-gated model following the terminology of (Chung et al., 2017) in this paper.

As to BPE and its variantes, the following researches are relevent.

Chung et al. (2016) proposed a character-level decoder called Bi-Scale decoder while in their research, the encoder side uses BPE. They proved that neural machine translation can be done directly on a sequence of characters without any explicit word segmentation.

Zhang and Komachi (2018) proposed a sub-character level translation for Japanese and Chinese in which Kanji in Japanese and characters in Chinese are decomposed into ideographs or strokes. However, this approach will increase sequence length a lot and need an extra dictionary to decompose Kanji and Chinese characters into strokes or ideographs,

Costa-jussà and Fonollosa (2016) used convolution layers followed by multiple high-way layers to generate character-based word embedding. Other than embedding layer of the encoder side, both the encoder and the decoder are in the word level.

We think that the methods of these researches may complicate the model and are not suitable to our objective.

In Cherry el al. (2018), the multi-headed attention was not used. But because a simple multi-headed attention may cause a mild overhead, we tried a model with multi-attention in our experiment.

3   Proposed Model

We propose two different models for the character-level translation. These model use six bidirectional LSTMs for encoder and six LSTMs for decoder. We use the multiplicative attention mechanism proposed by Luong et al. (2015) instead of additive attention proposed by Bahdanau et al. (2015) because we found out that it will greatly reduce memory consumption during training.

3.1   Basic Model

The basic model is a simple multi-layer attentional encoder-decoder (Cho et al., 2014; Bahdanau et al., 2015) model. Figure 1 shows the structure of the model. For decoder, only the first-layer LSTM takes context vectors as one of its input. The context vector and the hidden state of the last layer in the decoder are used to predict the next character.

3.2   Mid-Gated Model

We adopt a shortcut in the recurrent network by Chung et al. (2017) and Ákos Kádár (2018) which is originally for three HMLSTM layers. We call the model with the shortcut a mid-gated model.

The mid-gated model is similar to the basic model except that the input of 4th layer $\mathbf{m}_t$ of both encoder and decoder is calculated by

$$\mathbf{m}_t = \text{relu} \left(\mathbf{W}_m \left[\mathbf{h}_t^1; \mathbf{h}_t^2; \mathbf{h}_t^3 \right] \right) \tag{1}$$

where $\mathbf{W}_m \in \mathbb{R}^{\dim(\mathbf{m}_t) \times \sum_{l=1}^{3} \dim(\mathbf{h}_t^l)}$ is a matrix to map the concatenation of three vectors into one vector, and for encoder $\mathbf{h}_t^l$ is the concatenated output of both direction of lth layer, i.e. $\mathbf{h}_t^l = [\overleftarrow{\mathbf{h}_t^l}; \overrightarrow{\mathbf{h}_t^l}]$, and for decoder, the output of lth layer. Equation 1 can be considered as a shortcut from the first three layers to the 4th layer.

We tried changing the size and location of the shortcut, and we also tried adding another shortcut on the last layer, but we did not get further improvement in these attempts.

3.3   Multi-Attention Model

Usually, word-level and subword-level translation use only one attention layer. But for character-level translation, because of the fine temporal granularity, multi-attention may work well. Thus we tried a multi-attention model as shown in Figure 2.

The encoder side of multi-attention model is the same as the basic model. The decoder side contains six recurrent layers. We use four attention layers for the trade-off between performance and overheads. We put attention layers on the 1st and 6th recurrent layers to ensure the first recurrent

---

[1] 2 NVIDIA 2080s. Cherry el al. (2018) used 16 NVIDIA P100s.

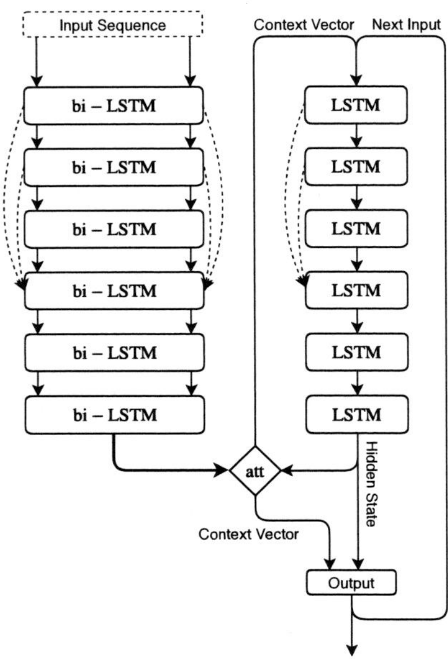

Figure 1: The basic model (without dashed connections) and mid-gated model (with the dashed connections).

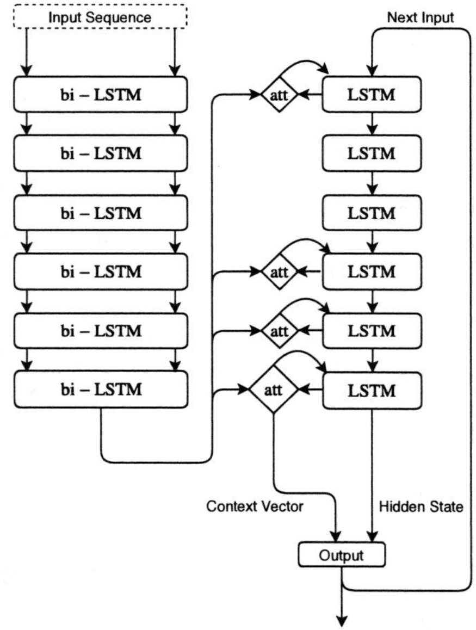

Figure 2: The multi-attention model

	ASPEC-JE	NTCIR-JE
Pairs (train)	1,000,000	1,387,713
Pairs (dev)	1790	2000
Pairs (devtest)	1784	-
Pairs (test)	1812	2300
Vocab (ja)	3084	2966
Vocab (en)	291	98

Table 1: Numbers of sentence pairs and vocabulary of ASPEC-JE and NTCIR-JE.

of the multi-attention model and mid-gated model, but we did not find any improvement in the combination.

4   Experiments Design

4.1   Datasets and Preprocessing

We used ASPEC (Nakazawa et al., 2016) and NTCIR (Goto et al., 2013) as out datasets. The ASPEC dataset contains three training sets `train-1.txt`, `train-2.txt` and `train-3.txt`. We only used the first training set because of our limited hardware resources.

Table 1 shows the sizes of the training set of both datasets. Note that the vocabulary in this paper refers to the number of different characters in the training sets.

For ASPEC dataset, we appended a space at both the beginning and end of each sentence of both languages. Note that this will not influence the final result. We did not perform any other preprocessing. We did not eliminate long sentences. We kept all numbers, characters, punctuations in Japanese side of the datasets as is. We used OpenNMT-tf's built-in character tokenizer for tokenization.

4.2   Training

The model were trained using sentence-level cross entropy loss. Batch sizes were capped at 12,800 tokens, and each batch was divided between two GPUs running synchronously. The dimension of character embedding of Japanese was 512 and for English, 128. All other vector dimensions were 512. The basic and mid-gated models were trained using two NVIDIA's GeForce 1080Ti's, while the multi-attention model was trained using two NVIDIA's RTX 2080Ti's.

We initialized parameters randomly with a uniform (-0.1,0.1) distribution. We used Adam's Optimizer with $\beta_1 = 0.9$, $\beta_2 = 0.999$ and $\epsilon =$

layer taking context as input and the sixth recurrent layer outputting context, and we found out that it is optimal to put other two attention layers on the 4th and 5th recurrent layers in our preliminary experiments. We tried the combination

Models	ASPEC-JE	NTCIR-JE
Basic	26.89 (22.47)	40.82 (36.76)
Mid-Gated	**27.63 (22.98)**	**41.32 (37.34)**
Multi-Attention	27.06 (22.35)	41.11 (37.08)
Yamagishi et al. (2017)	(18.78)	(29.80)
Morishita et al. (2017)	27.62	-
NMT with Attention (Cho et al., 2014; Bahdanau et al., 2015)	26.91	-
Transformer (Vaswani et al., 2017)	28.06	-

Table 2: BLEU scores for various models. Scores calculated by Travatar are shown in parentheses. Scores with references are from the literatures.

	Time	GPU1	GPU2
Basic	43h	4GB	4GB
Mid-Gated	40h	8GB	4GB
Multi-Attention	37h	8GB	4GB

Table 3: The actual training time and GPU overhead of each model. Note that Tensorflow tend to occupy more memory than needed.

10^{-8} (Kingma and Ba, 2015). Gradient norm was clipped to 5.0 (Pascanu et al., 2012). The dropout rate was set to 0.2 for all models. Dropouts were taken place in all bidirectional LSTMs and LSTMs. The initial learning rate was 0.0002, and it decayed with rate 0.9 for every 10k batches after 20k batches. Training stopped when dev set perplexity had not decreased for 6k batches. We implemented the mid-gated and multi-attention models on OpenNMT-tf (1.20.0) for training. The inference was done on version 1.24.0.

Except where mentioned below, the inference used beam search with 4 hypotheses, and the strictness of length normalization was set to 0.2 (Wu et al., 2016).

5 Results

5.1 BLEU Scores

We report our BLEU scores for the three models in Table 2. For ASPEC, we preprocessed the inference result by removing spaces at the beginning and end of translated sentences. For NTCIR, we kept the inference result as is. We used Moses-tokenized case-sensitive BLEU[2] score as our evaluation metric. We report the test-set scores on the

checkpoints having lowest perplexity on the dev set. As we can be seen in the table, the mid-gated model produces the best result among the three models. The parenthesized scores are calculated by bootstrap resampling implemented in Travatar[3].

The organizer's results of WAT 2018 [4] in vanilla encoder-decoder with attention model (Cho et al., 2014; Bahdanau et al., 2015) and Transformer (Vaswani et al., 2017) are also shown.

We also include the best scores in a single model reported by Yamagishi el al. (2017) and Morishita et al. (2017).

The BLEU scores of our models are similar to the subword-level model of Morishita et al. (2017). However our training is much simpler. It takes 10.1 million sentence pairs to train the basic model, and 8.0 million pairs for mid-gated model, and 6.8 million pairs for multi attention model, while Morishita et al. (2017) used 60 million pairs for training in the experiment with the best result in a single model. The actual memory overheads and training time are shown in Table 3. Morishita et al. (2017) used batch of 128 sentence pairs. But in our experiments, setting batch size of each GPU to more than 40 sentence pairs without limiting the sentence length during training caused out-of-memory error. Thus we consider character-level translations uses more memory than subword-level translation while the training speed can be fast with respect to sentence pairs. The BLEU scores of our model are slightly inferior to that of Transformer, but our model has less parameters and is trained easily.

5.2 Translation Examples

We choose two examples from the test set to show the difference of the three models in translation. As shown in Table 4, the translation is the same

[2] http://lotus.kuee.kyoto-u.ac.jp/ WAT/evaluation2/automatic_evaluation_ systems/automaticEvaluationEN.html

[3] http://www.phontron.com/travatar/ evaluation.html

[4] http://lotus.kuee.kyoto-u.ac.jp/WAT/ evaluation/list.php?t=2&o=4

for the simple first sentence, but in the second example, the mid-gated model is superior on fluency and accuracy. As for the word "演えきシステム", which means "deduction system", none of the models translates exactly the same as the reference, while the results by the basic and mid-gated model are only different in articles and suffices.

We also want to check how multi-attention works. As shown in Figure 3, the first two attention layers barely catch the right alignment. The third attention layer got some alignments in the middle of the sentence. In the forth attention layer, when the length of English word is longer than the corresponding Japanese word, the model tend to align the first N characters to the corresponding Japanese characters, where N is the length of the Japanese word, and the remaining characters to the beginning of the sentence.

5.3   Noise

Algorithm 1 $\text{AddNoise}_{dropRate, insertRate}$

for $sentence$ in $testset$ **do**
  for $char$ in $sentence$ **do**
    $drop \leftarrow$ **true** for probability of $dropRate$
    $insert \leftarrow$ **true** for probability of $insertRate$
    if $drop =$ **true** and $insert =$ **true then**
      Replace $char$ with a random character
    else if $drop =$ **true** and $insert =$ **false then**
      Drop $char$ in $sentence$
    else if $drop =$ **false** and $insert =$ **true then**
      Add a randomly chosen character before $char$
    end if
  end for
end for

We tested whether the models can handle noise. We added noise to the ASPEC's test set by randomly dropping and inserting characters to the Japanese side. The inserted characters are chosen randomly from the vocabulary. The insert and drop rate ranges over $5\%, 4\%, 3\%, 2\%, 1\%, 0.1\%, 0.01\%, 0.001\%$, and 0%. Algorithm 1 shows this noising procedure. For each insert and drop rate pair, we built three test set for each drop-insert rate pair and averaged the BLEU scores.

The result is shown in Figure 4. We notice that even with a heavy noise with drop rate of 5% and insert rate of 5%, the three models still managed to yield a tolerable result. Also, we can conclude that dropping characters can cause more decrease in BLEU scores compared to inserting. We speculate that although both inserting and dropping will interfere the inference, the information loss caused by dropping has more impact. Table 5 shows a noise-added example and its translations.

5.4   Beam Width and Length Normalization

As suggested by Morishita et al. (2017) and Wu et al. (2016), we use length normalization with strictness of 0.2. Figure 5 shows how BLEU score changes when increasing beam width.

We can find out that the BLEU scores decrease drastically as beam width increases after 4 or 5 if length normalization is not adopted. While with length normalization, the BLEU scores only decrease by less than 0.7, this is different from BPE translation shown by Morishita et al. (2017) where the scores stay increasing even after beam width of 25.

In character-level translation, we observed that all three models tended to produce a few empty sentences, but with layer normalization with strictness of 0.2, this tendency is suppressed.

Note that the largest beam width is 221 because we employ the character-level translation. We do not try stricter length normalization since in our preliminary experiments, more strictness would decrease the performance with a large beam width.

5.5   Unknown Words

Like BPE, character-level translation is also hoped for predicting candidates for unknown words. In this paper, we define unknown words as follow:

Definition A string is an unknown word if and only if

1. it is a token of a tokenized sentence outside the training dataset, and,
2. it is not substring of any sentence in the training dataset.

For example, the Japanese word "データベース" which means "database" in English, is a token of the second sentence in Table 4 after tokenization. In the training set, the sentence is not included, but there exists some other sentence, one of whose substring is the token, thus this is not unknown

Src	リサイクルに関する話題を紹介した
Ref	Recent topics on recycling are introduced.
Basic	Recent topics on recycling are introduced.
Mid-Gated	Recent topics on recycling are introduced.
Multi-Attention	Recent topics on recycling are introduced.
Src	超伝導材料開発のためのデータベースを構築し,材料設計用演えきシステムの開発を行った。
Ref	A database for development of superconducting material was constructed, and deduction system for material design was developed.
Basic	The database for the development of superconducting material was constructed, and deductive system for material design was developed.
Mid-Gated	A database for the development of superconducting materials was constructed and deduced system for material design was developed.
Multi-Attention	The database for the superconducting material development was constructed, and the development system for material design was developed.

Table 4: Translation example by three models.

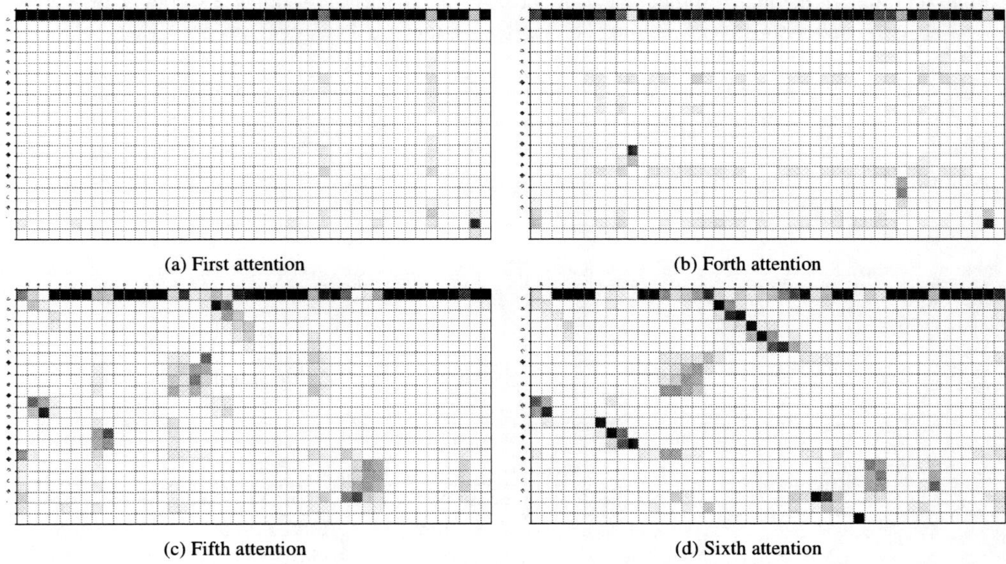

(a) First attention   (b) Forth attention

(c) Fifth attention   (d) Sixth attention

Figure 3: Attentions of the multi-attention model for the first sample in Table 4.

word. Further, the string "超電導材料開発のためのデータベースを構築し" is not a substring of any sentence in the training set, but it is not a token of the tokenized sentence, so this is not unknown word either.

Further, we categorize unknown words into three types:

1. Words only containing Katakana, which is usually transliteration of other language.

2. Words only containing Hiragana and Kanji that is in the character vocabulary.

3. Words containing unseen Kanji.

In order to find sentences with unknown words, we first tokenized the Japanese source sentences in dev, devtest, an test sets using MeCab and constructed vocabulary. For each word in vocabulary, we check if it is a substring of any sentence in the train set. Finally, we eliminated all words with

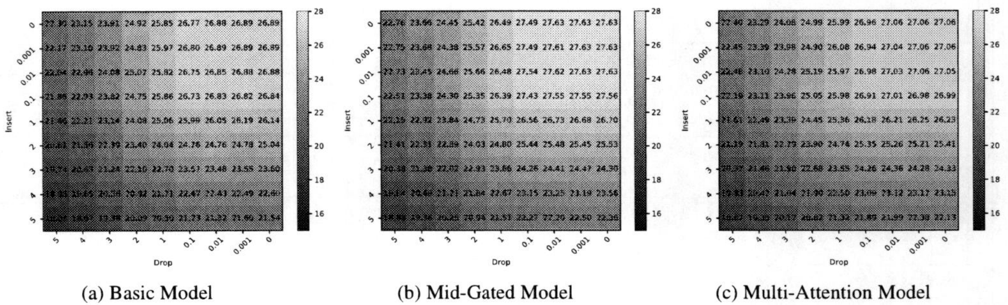

(a) Basic Model   (b) Mid-Gated Model   (c) Multi-Attention Model

Figure 4: The translation scores for different drop-insert probability pairs.

Src	材料製造プロセスでは,物質の融解・凝固・急冷などの熱的現象を,精密に制御すること が 必要である。
Ref	For material production, it is necessary to precisely control thermal phenomena such as fusion, solidification, and rapid cooling of a substance.
Noised	材料製造プロセスで 談 は,物質の融解・凝 べ 固・急 ρ 冷 卒 な 坂 どの熱的現象を,精密に制御すること 必要である。
Basic	In the material manufacturing process, it is necessary to precisely control the thermal phenomenon of melting, <u>compatible solution</u>, and <u>proper</u> ρ <u>compound sake</u> of materials.
Mid-Gated	It is necessary to precisely control the thermal phenomenon of melting, solidification, and rapid ρ <u>collapse</u> of materials in the material manufacturing process.
Multi-Attention	In the material manufacturing process, it is necessary to precisely control the thermal phenomenon of melting and <u>flocculation</u> of the material, and <u>thermal phenomenon of</u> rapid ρ <u>cooling sake</u>.

Table 5: A translation result of the noised sentence. The boxed characters in the Src sentence is the one dropped out, and the boxed characters in the Modified sentence is the one inserted. The words translated wrongly are underlined.

Type	Src	Ref	Basic	Mid-Gated	Multi-Attention
1	アンタゴニスティック	antagonistic	antagonistic	antagonistic	antagonistic
	エコマティAX	Ecomatie AX	ecomater AX	Ecomatey AX	ecomate AX
2	福島大学	Fukushima University	Fukushima University	Fukushima University	Fukushima University
	長谷山俊郎	Toshio Hasegawa	Nagayama Yamato	**IGNORED**	Nakayama
	友ケ島	Tomoga Island	Fiken Island	**IGNORED**	**IGNORED**
3	<u>嘔</u>気・<u>嘔</u>吐	nausea and vomiting	air and vomiting	air and vomiting	air and vomiting
	捏造	fabrication	structure	**IGNORED**	construction

Table 6: Examples of translations of unknown words. The cases of each words are kept as is. Unknown Kanji, i.e., Kanji that do not exist in the vocabulary, are underlined. The translations of words "嘔気" and "嘔吐" were not contained in the reference, so we show the dictionary meaning of these words in Ref.

only alphabets and numbers since it is trivial to translate these "words".

For the first type of unknown words, all models can easily predict the translation and the mid-gated

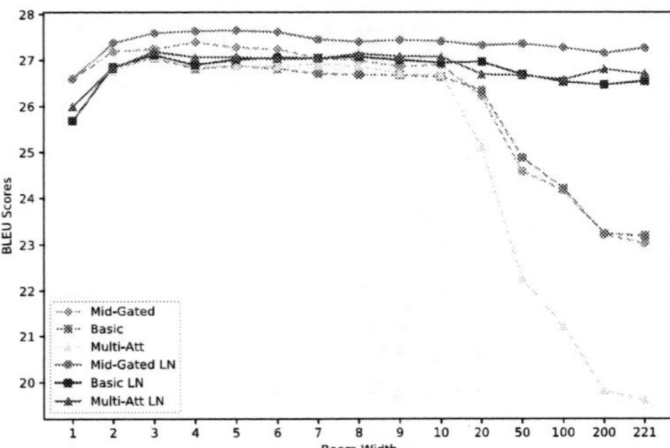

Figure 5: BLEU scores for different beam widths. Here "LN" stands for length normalization.

model can predict translation better for it can also identify proper nouns such that the first character is in the upper case.

For the second type, all models can somehow predict the translation, while as for people's name and hard-to-read name of places, the mid-gated model tends to ignore them while the other two models are trying to translate in their own way.

For the third type of unknown words, the models tend to predict the translation using only known characters. Table 6 gives some examples. Due to limited space, we only give the unknown words and their translations in the reference set and translation results.

The fact that the mid-gated model tends to ignore the second and third types of unknown words does not contradict to the result in Table 2, since even though other models translate the second and third type in their own way, the result is not exactly the correct answer and it is ignored in the BLEU scores. The number of the first type of unknown words in dev, devtest and test sets are twice as many as the sum of numbers of other two types of unknown words, and for the first type of unknown words, mid-gated model tends to predict them better, as shown in Table 6.

6 Conclusion

The objective of this paper is to get a computationally and spatially cheaper character-level translation model while keeping performance in BLEU scores. We proposed three models and showed that one of the models, the mid-gated model, was much better in speed and space consumption than the previous models with similar BLEU scores. We also showed that a relatively narrow beam of width 4 or 5 was sufficient for the mid-gated model.

In character-level translation, no word is made unknown because the vocabulary, which is a set of characters in character-level translation, is small and there is no need to limit vocabulary. Still occurring unknown word in character-level translation is unseen transliteration, an unseen word containing Hiragana and Kanji, or a word with unseen Kanji. Such an unknown word is difficult to translate, but we showed that, as to an unseen transliteration, the mid-gated model could somehow translate it by coining out a close word.

We also showed that the model managed to produce tolerable results for heavily noised sentences. Remarkable here is that the model was trained with the dataset without noise.

For future work, we want to explore a way to correctly translate an unknown word containing Hiragana and Kanji and a word with unseen Kanji. We want to handle typos including conversion error and swapping as well as comparing their performance against word-level and subword-level translations. We also want to investigate the mid-gated model's ability in translating alphabetical languages.

7 Acknowledgment

We also appreciate the reviewers for their insightful comments. This work was supported by JSPS KAKENHI Grant Number 17H01837.

References

Dzmitry Bahdanau, Kyunghyun Cho, and Yoshua Bengio. 2015. Neural machine translation by jointly learning to align and translate. In (Bengio and LeCun, 2015).

Yoshua Bengio and Yann LeCun, editors. 2015. *3rd International Conference on Learning Representations, ICLR 2015, San Diego, CA, USA, May 7-9, 2015, Conference Track Proceedings*.

Colin Cherry, George Foster, Ankur Bapna, Orhan Firat, and Wolfgang Macherey. 2018. Revisiting character-based neural machine translation with capacity and compression. In *Proceedings of the 2018 Conference on Empirical Methods in Natural Language Processing (EMNLP)*, pages 4295–4305, Brussels, Belgium. Association for Computational Linguistics.

Kyunghyun Cho, Bart van Merriënboer, Caglar Gulcehre, Dzmitry Bahdanau, Fethi Bougares, Holger Schwenk, and Yoshua Bengio. 2014. Learning phrase representations using RNN encoder–decoder for statistical machine translation. In *Proceedings of the 2014 Conference on Empirical Methods in Natural Language Processing (EMNLP)*, pages 1724–1734, Doha, Qatar. Association for Computational Linguistics.

Junyoung Chung, Sungjin Ahn, and Yoshua Bengio. 2017. Hierarchical multiscale recurrent neural networks. In *5th International Conference on Learning Representations, ICLR 2017, Toulon, France, April 24-26, 2017, Conference Track Proceedings*. OpenReview.net.

Junyoung Chung, Kyunghyun Cho, and Yoshua Bengio. 2016. A character-level decoder without explicit segmentation for neural machine translation. In *Proceedings of the 54th Annual Meeting of the Association for Computational Linguistics (Volume 1: Long Papers)*, pages 1693–1703, Berlin, Germany. Association for Computational Linguistics.

Marta R. Costa-jussà and José A. R. Fonollosa. 2016. Character-based neural machine translation. In *Proceedings of the 54th Annual Meeting of the Association for Computational Linguistics (Volume 2: Short Papers)*, pages 357–361, Berlin, Germany. Association for Computational Linguistics.

Isao Goto, Ka Po Chow, Bin Lu, Eiichiro Sumita, and Benjamin Tsou. 2013. Overview of the patent machine translation task at the ntcir-10 workshop.

Kaiming He, Xiangyu Zhang, Shaoqing Ren, and Jian Sun. 2016. Deep residual learning for image recognition. In *2016 IEEE Conference on Computer Vision and Pattern Recognition, CVPR 2016, Las Vegas, NV, USA, June 27-30, 2016*, pages 770–778. IEEE Computer Society.

Ákos Kádár, Marc-Alexandre Côté, Grzegorz Chrupala, and Afra Alishahi. 2018. Revisiting the hierarchical multiscale LSTM. *CoRR*, abs/1807.03595.

Diederik P. Kingma and Jimmy Ba. 2015. Adam: A method for stochastic optimization. In (Bengio and LeCun, 2015).

Jason Lee, Kyunghyun Cho, and Thomas Hofmann. 2017. Fully character-level neural machine translation without explicit segmentation. *Transactions of the Association for Computational Linguistics*, 5:365–378.

Thang Luong, Hieu Pham, and Christopher D. Manning. 2015. Effective approaches to attention-based neural machine translation. In *Proceedings of the 2015 Conference on Empirical Methods in Natural Language Processing*, pages 1412–1421, Lisbon, Portugal. Association for Computational Linguistics.

Makoto Morishita, Jun Suzuki, and Masaaki Nagata. 2017. NTT neural machine translation systems at WAT 2017. In *Proceedings of the 4th Workshop on Asian Translation (WAT2017)*, pages 89–94, Taipei, Taiwan. Asian Federation of Natural Language Processing.

Toshiaki Nakazawa, Manabu Yaguchi, Kiyotaka Uchimoto, Masao Utiyama, Eiichiro Sumita, Sadao Kurohashi, and Hitoshi Isahara. 2016. Aspec: Asian scientific paper excerpt corpus. In *Proceedings of the Ninth International Conference on Language Resources and Evaluation (LREC 2016)*, pages 2204–2208, Portorož, Slovenia. European Language Resources Association (ELRA).

Razvan Pascanu, Tomas Mikolov, and Yoshua Bengio. 2012. On the difficulty of training recurrent neural networks. In *ICML*.

Rico Sennrich, Barry Haddow, and Alexandra Birch. 2016. Neural machine translation of rare words with subword units. In *Proceedings of the 54th Annual Meeting of the Association for Computational Linguistics (Volume 1: Long Papers)*, pages 1715–1725, Berlin, Germany. Association for Computational Linguistics.

Ashish Vaswani, Noam Shazeer, Niki Parmar, Jakob Uszkoreit, Llion Jones, Aidan N. Gomez, Lukasz Kaiser, and Illia Polosukhin. 2017. Attention is all you need. In *NIPS*.

Yonghui Wu, Mike Schuster, Zhifeng Chen, Quoc V. Le, Mohammad Norouzi, Wolfgang Macherey, Maxim Krikun, Yuan Cao, Qin Gao, Klaus Macherey, Jeff Klingner, Apurva Shah, Melvin Johnson, Xiaobing Liu, Lukasz Kaiser, Stephan Gouws, Yoshikiyo Kato, Taku Kudo, Hideto Kazawa, Keith Stevens, George Kurian, Nishant Patil, Wei Wang, Cliff Young, Jason Smith, Jason Riesa, Alex Rudnick, Oriol Vinyals, Gregory S. Corrado, Macduff Hughes, and Jeffrey Dean. 2016. Google's neural machine translation system: Bridging the gap between human and machine translation. *ArXiv*, abs/1609.08144.

Hayahide Yamagishi, Shin Kanouchi, Takayuki Sato, and Mamoru Komachi. 2017. Improving Japanese-to-English neural machine translation by voice prediction. In *Proceedings of the Eighth International Joint Conference on Natural Language Processing (Volume 2: Short Papers)*, pages 277–282, Taipei, Taiwan. Asian Federation of Natural Language Processing.

Longtu Zhang and Mamoru Komachi. 2018. Neural machine translation of logographic language using sub-character level information. In *Proceedings of the Third Conference on Machine Translation: Research Papers*, pages 17–25, Belgium, Brussels. Association for Computational Linguistics.

Controlling Japanese Honorifics in English-to-Japanese Neural Machine Translation

Weston Feely* Eva Hasler† Adrià de Gispert†
SDL Research
*Los Angeles, CA, †Cambridge, UK
`{wfeely,ehasler,agispert}@sdl.com`

Abstract

In the Japanese language different levels of honorific speech are used to convey respect, deference, humility, formality and social distance. In this paper, we present a method for controlling the level of formality of Japanese output in English-to-Japanese neural machine translation (NMT). By using heuristics to identify honorific verb forms, we classify Japanese sentences as being one of three levels of informal, polite, or formal speech in parallel text. The English source side is marked with a feature that identifies the level of honorific speech present in the Japanese target side. We use this parallel text to train an English-Japanese NMT model capable of producing Japanese translations in different honorific speech styles for the same English input sentence.

1 Introduction

Languages differ in the way they express the same ideas depending on social context. In English different words or phrases are used in a more casual or familiar context compared to a more formal context. In languages such as Japanese or Korean formality distinctions are grammatically encoded using a system of honorifics. These honorifics are part of Japanese verbal morphology, which allows the same concept to be expressed in multiple levels of formality by altering the inflection of the main verb of the sentence. The examples in Table 1 show one sentence in three different levels of formality. In all three examples the meaning is the same, but the inflection of the main verb is different.

It is important to note that these formality distinctions in Japanese are not optional. All sentences must use one verb inflection or another, so speakers are always making a choice of what level of formality to use depending on social context.

Formality	Japanese sentence and transcription
Informal	駅の 近くに たくさんの お店が ある。 eki-no chikaku-ni takusan-no omise-ga aru
Polite	駅の 近くに たくさんの お店が あります。 eki-no chikaku-ni takusan-no omise-ga arimasu
Formal	駅の 近くに たくさんの お店が ございます。 eki-no chikaku-ni takusan-no omise-ga gozaimasu

Table 1: Three sentences meaning "There are many shops near the train station", in different levels of formality

For example, when speaking with family, close friends, or others of equal social status, the informal ある (aru "there are") is used. When speaking to superiors, strangers, or older individuals the polite expression あります (arimasu "there are") is used. When expressing deference or humility, the formal expression ございます (gozaimasu "there are") is used. In this paper we use the terms informal, polite, and formal to refer to these three levels of formality as shown in Table 1. Traditional Japanese grammars may make finer-grained, more nuanced distinctions than this.

While there is this nuance to Japanese grammar, in English there is no such distinction, so when translating from English into Japanese, a translator must choose one level of formality or another. This poses a challenge for English-Japanese NMT, since for a translation to be adequate it needs to both capture the meaning of the source sentence and use the appropriate level of formality.

We propose a method to allow English-Japanese NMT to produce translations in a particular level of formality, using an additional feature on the source side marking the desired level of formality to be used in the translation. With this feature provided at both training and test time, a single NMT system can learn to distinguish these levels of formality and produce multiple translations for the same input sentence. We evaluate our ap-

Proceedings of the 6th Workshop on Asian Translation, pages 45–53
Hong Kong, China, November 4, 2019. ©2019 Association for Computational Linguistics

English Source	The number at the bottom of the list drops off.
Modified English Source	<polite> The number at the bottom of the list drops off.
Japanese Target	リストの一番下にある番号がリストから削除されます。 risuto-no ichiban shita-ni aru bangō-ga risuto kara sakujo saremasu

Table 2: Attaching a single token to the beginning of an English training data source sentence, based on the predicted formality of the Japanese target side

proach on multiple data sets and show that it successfully produces sentences in the requested level of formality. Apart from yielding more consistent outputs, it improves general translation quality as measured by BLEU on all data sets. We see particularly strong gains on the polite and formal portions of the test sets. We also release the following resources that were developed as part of our work towards formality-aware NMT

- A set of manual formality labels for a portion of the Tanaka corpus

- Code for a rule-based formality converter which can be applied as a translation post-processing step

We hope that these resources will spur further research on translation into Japanese.

2   Formality-Aware NMT

This section describes our approach for creating a formality-aware English-Japanese NMT system.

2.1   Choosing Formality in Translation

Our proposed method starts with identifying the formality of every Japanese target sentence in our parallel training corpus. We can determine that the Japanese sentence is informal, polite, or formal based on the verb inflection of the main verb of the sentence, which is often the last word in the sentence.

For example, in Table 2 the suffix ます (masu) at the end of the Japanese target sentence is a common politeness marker that identifies this as a polite sentence. This is particular to Japanese grammar, and from the English source sentence alone you cannot determine what level of formality the Japanese translation should have. So to inform our English-Japanese NMT system what formality level we are translating into, we attach the token *<polite>* to the beginning of the English source sentence. For every sentence pair in our training

corpus, we must attach such a token to the beginning of the English source side, depending on the formality of the Japanese target side.

At test time the resulting English-Japanese NMT model will need to be provided the same kind of informal, polite, or formal tokens at the beginning of every English input sentence to be translated. This allows the user of the NMT system to choose which level of formality they would like their Japanese translation to use. There are applications where these labels could be determined automatically from the context; we leave this for future work as our current data sets do not have context beyond the sentence level.

2.2   Automatic Identification of Honorifics

In order to label our training and test data with these formality tokens, we need to be able to identify the formality of a Japanese sentence automatically. To do this we look for the presence or absence of certain Japanese honorific verb forms as a heuristic. We created a set of common verbs and verbal inflections that correspond to each formality level, such as the informal expression じゃなかった (janakatta "was not"), the suffixes です (desu) and ます (masu), which attach to verb stems to express politeness, as well as several honorific and humble verbs such as なさいます (nasaimasu "to do" *honorific*) and 致します (itashimasu "to do" *humble*), which are used in formal social contexts to either show respect to the listener or show humility from the speaker, respectively. The full set of verb forms can be found in Table 3.

We apply our heuristics to a 21 million sentence Japanese monolingual corpus, composed of web-crawled text from multiple domains. We categorize sentences into three classes which we label informal, polite, or formal by looking for the verb forms in Table 3. We start with the formal verb forms. If any of these verbs are present we consider the sentence to be formal, if not then we proceed to looking for the polite verb forms, then the

Formality	Verb forms
Informal	だ, だった, じゃない, じゃなかった, だろう, da, datta, janai, janakatta, darou, だから, だけど, だって, だっけ, そうだ, ようだ dakara, dakedo, datte, dakke, souda, youda
Polite	です, でした, ない, なかった, ます, ました, ません, desu, deshita, nai, nakatta, masu, mashita, masen, ましょう, でしょう, ください, なさい, である, ではない mashou, deshou, kudasai, nasai, dearu, dewanai
Formal	ございます, いらっしゃいます, おります, なさいます, 致します, gozaimasu, irrashaimasu, orimasu, nasaimasu, itashimasu, ご覧になります, 拝見します, お目に掛かります, goranninarimasu, haikenshimasu, omenikakarimasu, おいでになります, 伺います, 参ります, 存知します, 存じ上げます, oideninarimasu, ukagaimasu, mairimasu, zonjishimasu, zonjiagemasu, 召し上がります, 頂く, 頂きます, 頂いて, 差しあげます, meshiagemasu, itadaku, itadakimasu, itadaite, sashiagemasu, 下さいます, おっしゃいます, 申し上げます kudasaimasu, osshaimasu, moushiagemasu

Table 3: Common verbs and suffixes for each level of formality, used as identifying heuristics.

informal verb forms. If none of the verb forms in Table 3 are present in the sentence it is ignored. From the original 21 million sentences, 1 million were unable to be categorized by our heuristics.

We hypothesize that a text classifier trained on the resulting 20 million sentences selected by our heuristics will learn more nuanced distinctions in word choice and style than using the heuristics alone, which only identify a small set of verb forms. We tokenize this data set with the KyTea morphological analyzer (Neubig, 2011b) and train a model on the tokenized monolingual data and labels with the text classification tools provided by the FastText (Joulin et al., 2017) toolkit, using word trigram features.

To evaluate our classifier's performance, we enlisted the help of a Japanese linguist to make formality judgments on a small test set of 150 Japanese sentences drawn from the publicly-available Tanaka corpus (Tanaka, 2001). Out of these 150 total sentences, 68 were labeled *informal*, 45 were labeled *polite* and 37 were labeled *formal* by the annotator. These sentences and annotations will be made publicly available alongside the publication of this paper.

Table 4 contains a precision-recall evaluation of our formality classifier, showing strong F1 scores for all three classes. The formality classifier output matches the exact classifications made by our

	Informal	Polite	Formal
Precision	1.00	0.82	0.72
Recall	0.74	0.91	0.97
F1	0.85	0.86	0.83

Table 4: Evaluation scores of labels produced by the formality classifier compared to gold test set labels for each formality category (n=150).

heuristic rules on this test set, but we hypothesize that it generalizes better to unseen text and therefore use it in our translation experiments. The results show that our classifier has higher precision on the informal category, but lower recall, and higher recall on the polite and formal categories, but lower precision.

2.3 Rule-Based Formality Conversion

We also compare our method of formality-aware NMT with a simple rule-based tool which converts a Japanese sentence from one level of formality to another. This is done by identifying the main verb in a Japanese sentence and either replacing the verb itself or just the verbal inflection with the inflection for the desired level of formality. The code will be made available open-source alongside this publication.

Rule-based formality conversion is non-trivial since there are many conjugations to consider for a single verb, which differ based on the class the verb belongs to. For example, to convert the verb 歩きました (arukimashita "walked" *polite*)" to an informal inflection, the polite suffix ました (mashita) is removed from the stem of the verb and a new suffix is appended to create 歩いた (aruita). The き (ki) at the end of the verb stem marks this as a verb in a particular verb class. All verbs with *ki* at the end of their stem belong to the same class and have the same conjugation pattern.

In order to use this rule-based method to compare to our English-Japanese formality-aware NMT, we can simply take our baseline NMT system, trained without the formality tokens described above in section 2.1, and apply the rules to convert the NMT output into the desired level of formality. However, this rule-based method is imperfect and relies on tokenization and part-of-speech information from the KyTea morphological analyzer. Incorrect part of speech tags or tokenization that doesn't match our rule-based tool's dictionary will lead to errors in changing verbal inflection. In our evaluation, we show how using this rule-based method compares to our formality-aware NMT.

3 Evaluation

In this section, we evaluate the translation quality of our formality-aware NMT models as well as their ability to produce the desired formality level in the output.

3.1 Datasets

We use three publicly-available parallel data sets for our NMT experiments. The Asian Scientific Paper Excerpt Corpus (ASPEC) (Nakazawa et al., 2016), a corpus of scientific paper abstracts, the Japanese-English Subtitle Corpus (JESC) (Pryzant et al., 2018), a corpus of sentence-aligned movie and television subtitles, and the Kyoto Free Translation Task (KFTT) (Neubig et al., 2011a), a corpus of Wikipedia data about the city of Kyoto. In our experiments we use the standard training and test sets for each parallel corpus. We also use a proprietary parallel training data set which contains web-crawled data from a mix of domains and a corresponding test set. Training and test set sizes are reported in Table 5.

Dataset	Train	Test
Proprietary	23,781,990	300
ASPEC	1,000,000	1,812
JESC	3,237,376	2,001
KFTT	329,882	1,160

Table 5: Parallel training and test data set sizes in number of sentences

3.2 Experimental Setup

The English source of each bitext was tokenized with the Moses (Koehn et al., 2007) tokenizer.perl script and the Japanese target was tokenized with KyTea. We limit sentence length to 80 tokens on either side of the bitext and train a Moses truecaser for the English source side, except for the JESC data set because the English side of the JESC corpus is already entirely lowercased. We use 32k subword unit vocabularies (Sennrich et al., 2016b) separate for source and target. We use the resulting tokenized, truecased, subworded training data to train our NMT models.

Our experiments use the Transformer (Vaswani et al., 2018) to train NMT models. We use 512 hidden units, 6 hidden layers, 8 heads, and a batch size of 4096. We train for 200k training steps using the Adam optimizer (Kingma and Ba, 2015).

For each parallel corpus, we train a formality-aware NMT model by classifying the formality of the Japanese target side and attaching a corresponding feature to the beginning of each English source segment, identifying the target as being informal, polite, or formal. For comparison, we also train a baseline NMT model without these formality annotations.

3.3 Experimental Results

To evaluate our formality-aware NMT models, we first need to choose the right level of formality for each sentence in the test sets. We do this by applying the formality classifier to the test reference and prepending the predicted labels to the source side of each test sentence. We then provide this input to our formality-aware NMT models and compare the output to test set translations from our baseline NMT using BLEU (Papineni et al., 2002). We tokenize the Japanese MT output and reference using KyTea before computing BLEU. We evaluate on the overall test set, as well as each separate portion of the test set where the test reference was classified as informal, polite or formal. Table 6 shows our results on the test set using BLEU.

3.3.1 Performance of Rule-Based Conversion

We first evaluate the performance of the rule-based conversion method described in Section 2.3. The rule-based tool currently has the capability to convert to informal or polite verbal inflections, lacking rules for formal verb inflections. Thus, we only report results on the informal and polite sections of our test sets.

As shown in Table 6, the rule-based method yields improvements on the informal test portion for all models except ASPEC where performance remains the same. On the polite portion, we only see gains for the JESC model but a notable decrease in performance on ASPEC and no changes for the proprietary and KFTT test sets. This shows that while it is possible to adjust the formality level through post-processing, it is a non-trivial task and will require more work to improve the coverage of the tool. However, the rule-based tool could also be used for other tasks such as creating additional synthetic training data.

3.3.2 Performance of formality-aware NMT

The BLEU scores in Table 6 show that on the overall test set, our formality-aware NMT models show an improvement over the baseline NMT models. This holds true for both the model trained on the proprietary training data set, and the models trained on the publicly-available training data sets. Out of the models trained on publicly-available data, the ASPEC model shows the smallest improvement (+0.3 BLEU), the KFTT model improves more (+0.9 BLEU), and the JESC model shows the highest improvement (+1.5 BLEU).

When looking at the individual portions of the test set, as identified by our classifier, we see a larger quality improvement for the model trained on proprietary data on the informal and formal sections of its test set, and a smaller improvement on the polite section. The ASPEC formality-aware NMT is not better on the informal section of its test set, but there are larger gains in quality on the polite and formal test sections. The JESC and KFTT models improve on all three sections, with the largest gains seen in the formal section. Finally, formality-aware NMT improves over the rule-based method for all models and test sections, indicating that the NMT model is more effective at producing the desired formality level in context.

3.3.3 Evaluating formality levels

Since choosing the appropriate formality level in Japanese is very important to conform with social norms, we want to show that our formality-aware NMT models can provide translations in the desired level of formality. As our test sets do not have gold labels from a human annotator for each reference, we use our formality classifier to predict the level of formality for both the MT output and the test reference and compute F1 scores using the predicted reference labels.

Our F1 comparison in Table 7 shows to what extent the formality-aware NMT output matches the predicted formality level of the reference translation when the system is provided with the correct input label. We can see that the F1 scores for the formality-aware NMT are high for all three levels of formality, above 0.9 in all cases. We also see a big improvement over the baseline NMT models for each test set, especially in the polite and formal categories. From this we conclude that our formality-aware NMT models can produce a translation in the desired level of formality.

An imbalance of the training data may partly explain the difference in quality improvement across the three formality sections of the test sets. Table 8 shows how much of the training data for each data set was classified as being informal, polite, or formal. The proprietary data set contains mostly polite and informal data. In contrast, the majority of the three publicly available data sets is informal data, with a much smaller portion of polite data. For all data sets there is very little formal data, leading to the weak baseline performance on that category. By modelling formality levels more explicitly, our models are better able to compensate the inherent bias towards informal style.

4 Analysis and Examples

To show some concrete examples of our formality-aware translations, Table 9 contains an example of the MT output from the JESC formality-aware NMT model and the corresponding JESC NMT baseline trained without formality annotations. For this single English source sentence, there are multiple different MT outputs depending on which formality label is attached to the source before passing it to the NMT model for translation. The informal expression ない (nai "there is not") is used in the MT output by both the baseline model and the formality-aware NMT model when

		test BLEU			
Dataset	Model	Overall	Informal	Polite	Formal
Proprietary	Baseline NMT	24.6	17.8	28.0	17.4
	Rule-Based Conversion	-	18.3	28.0	-
	Formality-Aware NMT	25.5	18.7	28.4	22.3
ASPEC	Baseline NMT	43.0	42.8	45.7	33.0
	Rule-Based Conversion	-	42.8	44.5	-
	Formality-Aware NMT	43.3	42.8	47.1	43.9
JESC	Baseline NMT	18.8	18.0	19.4	22.1
	Rule-Based Conversion	-	18.7	20.6	-
	Formality-Aware NMT	20.3	19.4	21.9	29.3
KFTT	Baseline NMT	24.6	26.0	18.1	11.4
	Rule-Based Conversion	-	26.4	18.1	-
	Formality-Aware NMT	25.5	26.5	20.7	19.3

Table 6: KyTea-tokenized BLEU, comparing baseline NMT, rule-based conversion and formality-aware NMT models on heldout test

		F1		
Dataset	Model	Informal	Polite	Formal
Internal	Baseline NMT	0.59	0.82	0.29
	Formality-Aware NMT	0.97	0.99	0.91
ASPEC	Baseline NMT	0.95	0.67	0.19
	Formality-Aware NMT	1.00	1.00	0.96
JESC	Baseline NMT	0.85	0.50	0.28
	Formality-Aware NMT	1.00	0.99	0.96
KFTT	Baseline NMT	0.93	0.41	0.00
	Formality-Aware NMT	1.00	0.96	0.74

Table 7: F1 scores for each formality category when comparing predicted labels for MT output and reference translation.

Train	Informal	Polite	Formal
Internal	41.5%	56.9%	1.6%
ASPEC	87.6%	11.2%	1.2%
JESC	80.7%	18.3%	0.9%
KFTT	90.9%	8.4%	0.7%

Table 8: Percentage of each training data set classified as informal, polite, or formal

'informal' is attached to the source segment. The polite expression ありません (arimasen "there is not") is used by the formality-aware NMT model when 'polite' is attached, and the formal expression ございません (gozaimasen "there is not") is used by the formality-aware NMT model when 'formal' is attached. All of these expressions have the same meaning, but correspond correctly to the desired level of formality.

Table 10 shows another example of the MT output from the internal formality-aware NMT model and the corresponding internal NMT baseline trained without formality annotations. Again there are multiple different MT outputs depending on which formality label is attached to the source. The informal expression 戦う (tatakau "to fight") is used in the MT output by the formality-aware NMT model when 'informal' is attached to the source segment. The polite expression 戦います (tatakaimasu "to fight") is used by the baseline NMT model and the formality-aware NMT model when 'polite' is attached, and the formal expression 戦いをいたします (tatakai-wo itashimasu "to do battle" *humble*) is used by the formality-aware NMT model when 'formal' is attached. All of these expressions have the same meaning, but correspond correctly to the desired level of formality. Here the formality-aware NMT model is closest to the reference when 'informal' is attached, but all three formality-aware NMT translations are

Source	There's nothing to apologize for.
Reference	謝ることなんかなにもないさ ayamaru koto nanka nanimo nai sa
NMT Model	MT Output and Transcription
Baseline	謝ることなんて何もない ayamaru koto nante nanimo nai
Formality-Aware - Informal	別に謝ることはない betsu ni ayamaru koto wa nai
Formality-Aware - Polite	謝ることはありません ayamaru koto wa arimasen
Formality-Aware - Formal	お詫びのことは何もございません owabi no koto wa nanimo gozaimasen

Table 9: Example output from JESC NMT baseline model and formality-aware NMT model, when each formality level is attached to the source segment.

equally adequate.

5 Related Work

Sennrich et al. (2016a) showed that side constraints can be added to the source side of a parallel text to provide control over the politeness of translation output in an English-German translation task. Following this paper's suggestion, we take a similar approach towards Japanese honorifics.

Niu et al. (2017) also use a similar approach, termed "Formality-Sensitive Machine Translation", in a French-English translation task. In (Niu et al., 2018) French-English parallel text with formality features is combined with English-English parallel text, where the source and target are of similar meaning but different formality, to create a multi-task model that performs both formality-sensitive MT and monolingual formality transfer.

In related work on Japanese-English NMT, Yamagishi et al. (2016) use a side-constraint approach to control the voice (active or passive) of an English translation. Takeno (2017) apply side constraints more broadly to control translation length, bidirectional decoding, domain adaptation, and unaligned target word generation.

Our paper follows the modeling approach introduced by Johnson et al. (2017), who showed that by adding a token to the source side of parallel text allows for training a single NMT model on data for multiple language pairs. Their token specifies the desired target language, allowing the user control over the language of machine translation output, even for source-target language pairs that were not seen during training, which they call "zero-shot"

translation. The same approach has been successfully used in other applications, such as in distinguishing standard versus back-translated translation parallel corpora (Caswell et al., 2019).

6 Conclusion

We have shown how the distinctions between levels of formality in the Japanese language can be learned by an NMT model, by identifying Japanese honorifics in parallel training data and labeling the source side with an additional feature. We find that this technique provides control over the honorifics present in the MT output and provides an improvement in translation quality, particularly in polite and formal sentences in each test set. This improvement holds for models trained on proprietary data as well as models trained on three widely-used publicly available Japanese data sets. In future work, we would like to explore augmenting the training data for each of the comparisons we showed. We would like to explore creating artificial English-Japanese data by doing a rule-based transformation of the Japanese side of the bitext into different formality levels. We would also like to do further human evaluation of our Japanese formality classifier and the NMT models we trained, and we may explore applying this technique to English-Korean NMT because Korean also has a similar system of honorifics.

References

Isaac Caswell, Ciprian Chelba, and David Grangier. 2019. Tagged back-translation. In *Proceedings of the Fourth Conference on Machine Translation*,

Source	King Arthur's knights do battle with a killer rabbit.
Reference	円卓の騎士たちはキラーラビットと戦う。 entaku-no kishitachi-wa kirā rabitto-to tatakau
NMT Model	MT Output and Transcription
Baseline	アーサー王の騎士はキラーウサギと戦います。 āsā ō-no kishitachi-wa kirā usagi-to tatakaimasu
Formality-Aware - Informal	キング アーサーの騎士たちはキラーウサギと戦う。 kingu āsā-no kishitachi-wa kirā usagi-to tatakau
Formality-Aware - Polite	キング アーサーの騎士たちはキラーウサギと戦います。 kingu āsā-no kishitachi-wa kirā usagi-to tatakaimasu
Formality-Aware - Formal	キング アーサーの騎士たちはキラーウサギと戦いをいたします。 kingu āsā-no kishitachi-wa kirā usagi-to tatakai-wo itashimasu

Table 10: Example output from internal NMT baseline model and formality-aware NMT model, when each formality level is attached to the source segment.

pages 53–63, Florence, Italy. Association for Computational Linguistics.

Melvin Johnson, Mike Schuster, Quoc V Le, Maxim Krikun, Yonghui Wu, Zhifeng Chen, Nikhil Thorat, Fernanda Viégas, Martin Wattenberg, Greg Corrado, et al. 2017. Google's multilingual neural machine translation system: Enabling zero-shot translation. *Transactions of the Association for Computational Linguistics*, 5:339–351.

Armand Joulin, Edouard Grave, Piotr Bojanowski, and Tomáš Mikolov. 2017. Bag of tricks for efficient text classification. In *Proceedings of the 15th Conference of the European Chapter of the Association for Computational Linguistics: Volume 2, Short Papers*, pages 427–431. Association for Computational Linguistics.

Diederik P Kingma and Jimmy Lei Ba. 2015. Adam: A method for stochastic optimization. In *3rd International Conference on Learning Representations*. arXiv.org.

Philipp Koehn, Hieu Hoang, Alexandra Birch, Chris Callison-Burch, Marcello Federico, Nicola Bertoldi, Brooke Cowan, Wade Shen, Christine Moran, Richard Zens, Chris Dyer, Ondrej Bojar, Alexandra Constantin, and Evan Herbst. 2007. Moses: Open source toolkit for statistical machine translation. In *Proceedings of the 45th Annual Meeting of the Association for Computational Linguistics Companion Volume Proceedings of the Demo and Poster Sessions*, pages 177–180. Association for Computational Linguistics.

Toshiaki Nakazawa, Manabu Yaguchi, Kiyotaka Uchimoto, Masao Utiyama, Eiichiro Sumita, Sadao Kurohashi, and Hitoshi Isahara. 2016. ASPEC: Asian scientific paper excerpt corpus. In *Proceedings of the Tenth International Conference on Language Resources and Evaluation (LREC 2016)*, pages 2204–2208. European Language Resources Association (ELRA).

Graham Neubig. 2011b. The Kyoto free translation task.

Graham Neubig, Yosuke Nakata, and Shinsuke Mori. 2011a. Pointwise prediction for robust, adaptable Japanese morphological analysis. In *Proceedings of the 49th Annual Meeting of the Association for Computational Linguistics: Human Language Technologies*, pages 529–533. Association for Computational Linguistics.

Xing Niu, Marianna Martindale, and Marine Carpuat. 2017. A study of style in machine translation: Controlling the formality of machine translation output. In *Proceedings of the 2017 Conference on Empirical Methods in Natural Language Processing*, pages 2814–2819.

Xing Niu, Sudha Rao, and Marine Carpuat. 2018. Multi-task neural models for translating between styles within and across languages. In *Proceedings of the 27th International Conference on Computational Linguistics*, pages 1008—-1021.

Kishore Papineni, Salim Roukos, Todd Ward, and Wei-Jing Zhu. 2002. BLEU: a method for automatic evaluation of machine translation. In *Proceedings of the 40th Annual Meeting of the Association for Computational Linguistics*, pages 311–318. Association for Computational Linguistics.

Reid Pryzant, Youngjoo Chung, Dan Jurafsky, and Denny Britz. 2018. JESC: Japanese-English subtitle corpus. In *Proceedings of the 11th Language Resources and Evaluation Conference*. European Language Resource Association.

Rico Sennrich, Barry Haddow, and Alexandra Birch. 2016a. Controlling politeness in neural machine translation via side constraints. In *Proceedings of NAACL-HLT 2016*, pages 35–40. Association for Computational Linguistics.

Rico Sennrich, Barry Haddow, and Alexandra Birch. 2016b. Neural machine translation of rare words with subword units. In *Proceedings of the 54th Annual Meeting of the Association for Computational Linguistics (Volume 1: Long Papers)*, pages 1715–1725. Association for Computational Linguistics.

Nagata Masaaki Yamamoto Kazuhide Takeno, Shunsuke. 2017. Controlling target features in neural machine translation via prefix constraints. In *Proceedings of the 4th Workshop on Asian Translation*, pages 55–63.

Yasuhito Tanaka. 2001. Compilation of a multilingual parallel corpus. In *Proceedings of PACLING 2001*, pages 265–268.

Ashish Vaswani, Samy Bengio, Eugene Brevdo, François Chollet, Aidan Gomez, Stephan Gouws, Llion Jones, Łukasz Kaiser, Nal Kalchbrenner, Niki Parmar, Ryan Sepassi, Noam Shazeer, and Jakob Uszkoreit. 2018. Tensor2Tensor for neural machine translation. In *Proceedings of the 13th Conference of the Association for Machine Translation in the Americas (Volume 1: Research Papers)*, pages 193–199. Association for Machine Translation in the Americas.

Hayahide Yamagishi, Shin Kanouchi, Takayuki Sato, and Mamoru Komachi. 2016. Controlling the voice of a sentence in Japanese-to-English neural machine translation. In *Proceedings of the 3rd Workshop on Asian Translation*, pages 203–210.

Designing the Business Conversation Corpus

Matīss Rikters[*] and **Ryokan Ri**[*] and **Tong Li**[*] and **Toshiaki Nakazawa**

The University of Tokyo

7-3-1 Hongo, Bunkyo-ku, Tokyo, Japan

{matiss, li0123, litong, nakazawa}@logos.t.u-tokyo.ac.jp

Abstract

While the progress of machine translation of written text has come far in the past several years thanks to the increasing availability of parallel corpora and corpora-based training technologies, automatic translation of spoken text and dialogues remains challenging even for modern systems. In this paper, we aim to boost the machine translation quality of conversational texts by introducing a newly constructed Japanese-English business conversation parallel corpus. A detailed analysis of the corpus is provided along with challenging examples for automatic translation. We also experiment with adding the corpus in a machine translation training scenario and show how the resulting system benefits from its use.

1 Introduction

There are a lot of ready-to-use parallel corpora for training machine translation systems, however, most of them are in written languages such as web crawl, news-commentary[1], patents (Goto et al., 2011), scientific papers (Nakazawa et al., 2016) and so on. Even though some of the parallel corpora are in spoken language, they are mostly spoken by only one person (in other words, they are monologues) (Cettolo et al., 2012; Di Gangi et al., 2019) or contain a lot of noise (Tiedemann, 2016; Pryzant et al., 2018). Most of the machine translation evaluation campaigns such as WMT[2], IWSLT[3] and WAT[4] adopt the written language, monologue or noisy dialogue parallel corpora for their translation tasks. Among them, there is only one clean, dialogue parallel corpus (Salesky et al., 2018) adopted by IWSLT in the conversational

speech translation task, nevertheless, the availability of such kind of corpus is still limited.

The quality of machine translation for written text and monologue has vastly improved due to the increase in the amount of the available parallel corpora and the recent neural network technologies. However, there is much room for improvement in the context of dialogue or conversation translation. One typical case is the translation from pro-drop language to the non-pro-drop language where correct pronouns must be supplemented according to the context. The omission of the pronouns occurs more frequently in spoken language than written language. Recently, context-aware translation models attract attention from many researchers (Tiedemann and Scherrer, 2017; Voita et al., 2018, 2019) to solve this kind of problem, however, there are almost no conversational parallel corpora with context information except noisy OpenSubtitles corpus.

Taking into consideration the factors mentioned above, a document and sentence-aligned conversational parallel corpus should be advantageous to push machine translation research in this field to the next stage. In this paper, we introduce a newly constructed Japanese-English business conversation parallel corpus. This corpus contains 955 scenarios, 30,000 parallel sentences. Table 1 shows an example of the corpus.

We choose the business conversation as the domain of the corpus because 1) the business domain is neither too specific nor too general, and 2) we think that a clean conversational parallel corpus is useful to open new machine translation research directions. We hope that this corpus becomes one of the standard benchmark data sets for machine translation.

What is unique for this corpus is that each scenario is annotated with scene information, as shown in the top of Table 1. In conversations,

---

[*]equal contribution

[1]http://www.statmt.org/wmt19/translation-task.html

[2]http://www.statmt.org/wmt19/

[3]http://workshop2019.iwslt.org

[4]http://lotus.kuee.kyoto-u.ac.jp/WAT/

Proceedings of the 6th Workshop on Asian Translation, pages 54–61

Hong Kong, China, November 4, 2019. ©2019 Association for Computational Linguistics

Scene: telephone consultation about intrafirm export

Japanese		English	
Speaker	Content	Speaker	Content
山本	もしもし、山本と申します。	Yamamoto	Hello, this is Yamamoto.
田中	販売部門の田中と申します。	Tanaka	This is Tanaka from the Department of Sales.
田中	輸出に関してご助言いただきたくお電話しました。	Tanaka	I called you to get some advice from you concerning export.
山本	はい、どのようなご用件でしょう？	Yamamoto	Okay, what's the matter?
田中	イランの会社から遠視カメラの引き合いを受けているのですが、イランに対しては輸出制限があると新聞で読んだことがある気がして。	Tanaka	We got an inquiry from an Iranian company about our far-sight cameras, but I think I read in the newspaper that there are export restrictions against Iran.
田中	うちで売っているようなカメラなら、特に問題にならないのでしょうか？	Tanaka	Is there no problem with cameras like the ones we sell?
山本	恐れ入りますが、イランへの輸出は、かなり制限されているのが事実です。	Yamamoto	I'm afraid that the fact is, exports to Iran are highly restricted.
...	...	...	...

Table 1: An example of the Japanese-English business conversation parallel corpus.

the utterances are often very short and vague, therefore it is possible that they should be translated differently depending on the situations where the conversations are taking place. For example, Japanese expression 「すみません」 can be translated into several English expressions such as "Excuse me." (when you call a store attendant), "Thank you." (when you are given some gifts) or "I'm sorry." (when you need to apologise). By using the scene information, it is possible to discriminate the translations, which is hard to do with only the contextual sentences. Furthermore, it might be possible to connect the scene information to the multi-modal translation, which is also hardly studied recently, such as estimating the scenes by the visual information.

The structure of this paper is as follows: we explain how the corpus is constructed in Section 2, show the fundamental analysis of the corpus in Section 3, report results of machine translation experiments in Section 4, and give a conclusion in Section 5.

2 Description and Statistics of the Corpus

The Japanese-English business conversation corpus, namely Business Scene Dialogue (BSD) corpus, is constructed in 3 steps: 1) selecting business scenes, 2) writing monolingual conversation scenarios according to the selected scenes, and 3) translating the scenarios into the other language. The whole construction process was supervised by a person who satisfies the following conditions to guarantee the conversations to be natural:

- has the experience of being engaged in lan-

Scene	Scenarios	Sentences
JA → EN		
face-to-face	165	5,068
phone call	77	2,329
general chatting	101	3,321
meeting	106	3,561
training	16	608
presentation	4	113
sum	469	15,000
EN → JA		
face-to-face	158	4,876
phone call	99	2,949
general chatting	102	2,988
meeting	103	3,315
training	9	326
presentation	15	546
sum	486	15,000

Table 2: Statistics for the corpus, where JA → EN represents scenarios which are written in Japanese then translated into English and EN → JA represents scenarios constructed in the reverse way.

guage learning programs, especially for business conversations

- is able to smoothly communicate with others in various business scenes both in Japanese and English

- has the experience of being involved in business

2.1 Business Scene Selection

The business scenes were carefully selected to cover a variety of business situations, including meetings and negotiations, as well as so-called water-cooler chats. Details are shown in Table 2. We also paid attention not to select specialised scenes which are suitable only for a limited number of industries. We made sure that all of the selected scenes are generic to a broad range of industries.

2.2 Monolingual Dialogue Scenario Writing

Dialogue scenarios were monolingually written for each of the selected business scenes. Half of the monolingual scenarios were written in Japanese and the other half were written in English (15,000 sentences for each language). This is because we want to cover a wide range of lexicons and expressions for both languages in the corpus. Writing the scenarios only in one language might fail to cover useful, important expressions in the other language when they are translated in the following step.

2.3 Scenario Translation

The monolingual scenarios were translated into the other language by human translators. They were asked to make the translations not only accurate, but also as fluent and natural as a real dialogue at the same time. This principle is adopted to eliminate several common tendencies of human translators when performing Japanese-English translation on a written text. For example, Japanese pronouns are usually omitted in a dialogue, however, when the English sentences are literally translated into Japanese, the translators tend to include unnecessary pronouns. It is acceptable as a written text, but would be rather unusual as a spoken text.

3   Analysis of the Corpus

To understand the difficulty of translating conversations, we conduct an analysis regarding the newly constructed corpus. We choose to use Google Translate [5], one of the most powerful neural machine translation (NMT) systems which are publicly available, to produce the translations.

Our primary focus is to understand how many sentences require context to be properly translated. We randomly sample 10 scenarios (322 sentences) from the corpus, and check the translations for fatal translation errors, ignoring fluency or minor grammatical mistakes. As a result, 12 sentences have errors due to phrase ambiguity that needs understanding the context, or the real-world situation, and 18 errors of pronouns due to zero anaphora, which is described in the following sec-

____

[5]https://translate.google.com/ (May 2019)

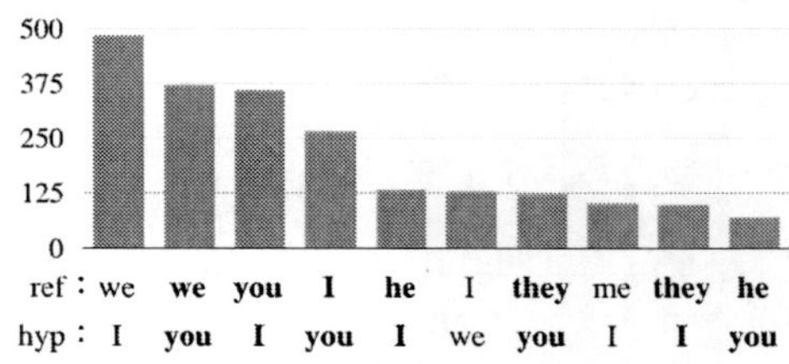

Figure 1: The top 10 frequent errors of pronoun translation (fatal errors denoted in boldface)

tion, in the source language (Japanese). Now we focus on the latter errors.

3.1 Zero Anaphora

As an important preliminary, we briefly introduce a grammatical phenomenon called *zero anaphora*. In Japanese, some arguments of verbs are often omitted from the phrases when they are obvious from the context. When translating them into English, one often has to identify the referent of the omitted argument and recover it in English, as English does not allow omitting the core arguments (i.e., subject, object). In the following Japanese example, the subject of the verb 買った is omitted, but in the English translation a pronoun, for example *he*, has to be recovered. Note that the subject could be anyone, not necessarily *he*, depending on the context. The task of identifying the referent of zero anaphora is called *zero anaphora resolution*, which is one of the most difficult tasks of NLP.

太郎は　　　買った　　　牛乳を　　　飲んだ
Taro-SBJ   buy-PST   milk-OBJ   drink-PST
"Taro drank the milk **he** bought."

3.2 Quantitative Analysis

To estimate how many sentences need zero anaphora resolution in the business conversation corpus, we counted the number of sentences with the personal pronouns (*e.g.*, 彼, 彼女, 私, あなた in Japanese, *I*, *you*, *he*, *she* in English) in both Japanese and English. As a result, 62% of English sentences contain personal pronouns, while only 11% of Japanese sentences do. This means about 50% of the sentences in the corpus potentially need zero reference resolution when we translate them from Japanese into English.

To reveal what kinds of zero pronouns are hard to translate, we again heuristically count the number of the translation errors of the pronouns for

Previous Source:	支店長はポールをクビにするみたいだよ。
Previous Reference:	It seems like the branch manager will be firing **Paul**.
Source:	仕事もあまりしない上に、休み、早退ばかりを希望するから。
Reference:	**He** doesn't work much , and **he** takes days off and asks to leave early often.
Google Translate:	**I** do not have much work , and **I** would like to leave early and leave early.

Figure 2: An example of Japanese to English Google Translate output. The words in boldface are supposed to denote the same referent(Paul).

Previous Source:	**[Speaker1]** 彼の代わりに、優秀な人が入ってくれれば、僕の仕事量が減るはずなんだ。
Previous Reference:	I think I can work less if there's someone excellent coming in as a replacement for him.
Source:	**[Speaker2]** もう少しの辛抱だよ。
Reference:	**You** just need a bit more patience.
Google Translate:	**I** have a little more patience.

Figure 3: An example of Japanese to English Google Translate output. Correct translation needs the speaker information.

the entire corpus. We counted the number of the translated sentences that have pronouns different from their reference sentences. By this heuristic, we detected 3,653 errors (12% of the whole corpus). The top 10 frequent errors are shown in Figure 1.

Some errors such as *we* → *I, I* → *me*, might be not fatal, and not be regarded as translation errors. However, there are still many fatal errors among first, second and third-person pronouns (denoted in boldface in the graph).

Looking at the pronouns that the NMT system produced, we can see the tendency of the system to generate frequent pronouns such as *you, I*. This suggests that the current system tries to compensate source (Japanese) zero pronouns simply by generating frequent target (English) pronouns. When the referent is denoted in relatively infrequent pronouns in the target language, it is hard to be correctly translated. To deal with this problem, We need to develop more sophisticated systems that take context into account.

3.3 Qualitative Analysis

This section exemplifies some zero-anaphora translation errors and discusses what kind of information is needed to perform correct translation.

A translation that needs world knowledge and inference

In Figure 2, the subjects of the verbs are omitted in the source sentence 「（彼は: he）仕事もあまりしない上に、（彼は: he）休み、早退ばかりを希望するから」. This causes the NMT system to incorrectly translate the zero pronouns into *I*, although they actually refer to *Paul* in the previous sentence and thus have to be translated into *he*.

Resolving these zero pronouns, however, is not straightforward, even if one has access to the information of the previous sentence. For example, to identify the subject of 「仕事もあまりしない」 (doesn't work much), one has to know "laziness can lead to being fired" and thereby infer that Paul, who is about to be fired, is the subject. Existing contextual NMT systems (Voita et al., 2018; Bawden et al., 2018; Maruf et al., 2019) still do not seem to be able to handle this complexity.

A translation that needs to know who is talking

In Figure 3, again, the subject is omitted in the source sentence 「（君は: you）もう少しの辛抱だよ。」. The NMT system incorrectly translates the zero pronouns into *I*.

It is worth noting that the type of the zero pronoun differs from the one in Figure 2 in that the referent in Figure 3 does not linguistically appear within the text (called *exophora*), while the other does (*endophora*) (Brown and Yule, 1983). The referent of the zero pronoun in Figure 3 is the listener of the utterance (*you*), and it usually does not have another linguistic item (such as the name of the person) that can be referred to. Although some modality expressions and verb types can give constraints to the possible referents (Nakaiwa and Shirai, 1996), essentially, the resolution of exophora needs the reference to situation.

In this case, the correct translation depends on who is speaking. In the original conversation, the utterance is from Speaker 2 to Speaker 1, and

Data Set	Devel	Eval	Train
BSD	1000	1000	28,000
AMI	1000	1000	108,499
ON	1000	1000	26,439
Total			162,938

Table 3: Training, development and evaluation data statistics.

given the context, one can infer that Speaker 2 is speaking to give a consolation to Speaker 1 and thus the subject should be *you* (Speaker 1). However, if the utterance was from Speaker 1, he would then just be complaining about his situation saying *"I just need a bit more patience"*. This example emphasises that the speaker information is essential to translate some utterances in conversation correctly.

4 Machine Translation Experiments

The BSD corpus was created with the intended use of training NMT systems. Thus, we trained NMT models using the corpus in both translation directions. As the BSD corpus is rather small for training reasonable MT systems, we also experimented with combining it with two larger conversational domain corpora. We employed translators to translate the AMI Meeting Corpus (McCowan et al., 2005) (AMI) and the English part of Onto Notes 5.0 (Weischedel et al., 2013) (ON) into Japanese with the same instructions as for translating the BSD corpus. Afterwards, we used them as additional parallel corpora in our experiments.

4.1 Data Preparation

Before training, we split each of the corpora into 3 parts - training, development and evaluation data sets. The sizes of each corpus are shown in Table 3. We used Sentencepiece (Kudo and Richardson, 2018) to create a shared vocabulary of 4000 tokens. We did not perform other tokenisation or truecasing for the training data. We used Mecab (Kudo, 2006) to tokenise the Japanese side of the evaluation data, which we used only for scoring. The English side remained as-is.

4.2 Experiment Setup

We used Sockeye (Hieber et al., 2017) to train transformer architecture models with 6 encoder and decoder layers, 8 transformer attention heads per layer, word embeddings and hidden layers of size 512, dropout of 0.2, maximum sentence length of 128 symbols, and a batch size of 1024

		JA-EN	EN-JA
BSD	SMT	1.90	5.16
	NMT	8.32	8.34
AMI, BSD, ON	SMT	7.27	5.76
	NMT	12.88	13.53
AMI, ON	SMT	2.18	5.74
	NMT	7.08	10.00

Table 4: NMT and SMT experiments using the conversational corpora. Evaluated on the Business Conversation evaluation set.

words, checkpoint frequency of 4000 updates. All models were trained until they reached convergence (no improvement for 10 checkpoints) on development data.

For contrast we also trained statistical MT (SMT) systems using using the Moses (Koehn et al., 2007) toolkit and the following parameters: Word alignment using fast-align (Dyer et al., 2013); 7-gram translation models and the 'wbe-msd-bidirectional-fe-allff' reordering models; Language model trained with KenLM (Heafield, 2011); Tuned using the improved MERT (Bertoldi et al., 2009).

4.3 Results

Since there are almost no spaces in the Japanese raw texts, we used Mecab to tokenise the Japanese translations and references for scoring. The results in BLEU scores (Papineni et al., 2001) are shown in Table 4 along with several ablation experiments on training NMT and SMT systems using only the BSD data, all 3 conversational corpora, and excluding the BSD corpus from the training data. The results show that adding the BSD to the two larger corpora significantly improves both SMT and NMT performance. For Japanese → English using only BSD as training data achieves a higher BLEU score than using only AMI and ON, while for English → Japanese the opposite is true. Nevertheless, in both translation directions using all 3 corpora outperforms the other results.

We also evaluate the highest-scoring NMT system (trained on all corpora) on all 3 evaluation sets and report BLEU scores and ChrF2 scores (Popović, 2015) in Table 5. We do this to verify that the models are not overfitting on the BSD data, i.e. BLEU and ChrF2 scores are not significantly higher for the BSD evaluation sets when compared to the ON and AMI sets. Results on the ON evaluation set are fairly similar to the BSD results, while results on the AMI evaluation set are

Source:	では、終了する前に、この健康とストレスに関するセルフチェックシートに記入をして頂きたいと思います。
Our Best NMT:	So before we finish, I'd like to fill in the health check-streams with this health and staff check-book.
Google Translate:	I would like you to fill out this health and stress self-check sheet before you finish.
Reference:	Before we finish off, we would like you to fill out this self-check sheet about health and stress.

Figure 4: An example of Japanese to English NMT output comparing our best NMT to Google Translate.

Previous Source:	あぁ、マネージャーはよく休みを取ってるみたいですよ。
Previous Reference:	Well, seems like our manager is taking quite a bit of time off.
Source:	自分が取らないと、他の人が取らないだろと思ってるんでしょうね。
Our Best NMT:	You think other people won't take it if they don't.
Google Translate:	If you don't take it, you might think that other people won't take it.
Reference:	Maybe he thinks if he doesn't take any, then nobody else will.

Figure 5: An example of Japanese to English NMT output, where a context-aware system could be more useful.

	BLEU	ChrF2
ON		
JA → EN	9.08	34.38
EN → JA	14.52	19.73
AMI		
JA → EN	20.88	46.93
EN → JA	23.35	30.25
BSD		
JA → EN	12.88	35.37
EN → JA	13.53	21.97

Table 5: BLEU and ChrF2 scores for all three evaluation data sets using the NMT system trained on all data.

noticeably higher. This can be explained by the fact that the AMI training data set is approximately four times larger than the BSD training data set, and the ON training data set is about the same size as the BSD set.

4.4 Machine Translation Examples

In Figure 4 we can see one of the difficult situations mentioned in Section 3.3, where MT systems find it challenging to generate the correct pronouns in the translation. Of the three pronouns that are in the reference (we, we, you), each system translates one correctly and fails to translate the rest - both systems generate *I* where it should have been *we*, but our system completely omits *you* while Google Translate generates *you* where it should have been *we*.

Figure 5 shows an example where both - our translation and the one from Google Translate are acceptable at the sentence-level, but when looking at the previous source and reference it becomes clear that different personal pronouns should have been used. Our system did generate "they" in the second part of the sentence, which could be a more casual alternative to "he", but both systems still failed to find the correct pronoun for the first part by producing "you" instead of "he". This is an issue that can not be fully resolved by using sentence-level MT and requires a document-level or context-aware solutions.

5 Conclusion

In this paper, we presented a parallel corpus of English-Japanese business conversations. The intended use-cases for the corpus are machine translation system training and evaluation. We describe the corpus in detail and indicate which linguistic phenomena are challenging to translate even for modern MT systems. We also show how adding the BSD corpus to machine translation system training helps to improve translation output of conversational texts.

We point out several examples, where sentence-level MT is unable to produce the correct translation due to lack of context from previous sentences. As the corpus is both - sentence-aligned and document-aligned, we hope that it gets used and inspires new future work such directions as document-level and context-aware neural machine translation, as well as analysing other linguistic phenomena that are relevant to translating conversational texts.

In the near future, we plan to release the full set of business conversational corpora. The set will contain all 3 corpora described in section 4 - an extended version of the Business Scene Dialogue corpus as well as parallel versions of the

AMI Meeting Corpus and Onto Notes 5.0.

Acknowledgements

This work was supported by "Research and Development of Deep Learning Technology for Advanced Multilingual Speech Translation", the Commissioned Research of National Institute of Information and Communications Technology (NICT), JAPAN.

References

Rachel Bawden, Rico Sennrich, Alexandra Birch, and Barry Haddow. 2018. Evaluating Discourse Phenomena in Neural Machine Translation. In *Proceedings of the Conference of the North American Chapter of the Association for Computational Linguistics: Human Language Technologies*.

Nicola Bertoldi, Barry Haddow, and Jean-Baptiste Fouet. 2009. Improved Minimum Error Rate Training in Moses. *The Prague Bulletin of Mathematical Linguistics*, 91(1):7—-16.

Gillian Brown and George Yule. 1983. *Discourse Analysis*. Cambridge University Press, Cambridge.

Mauro Cettolo, Christian Girardi, and Marcello Federico. 2012. Wit^3: Web inventory of transcribed and translated talks. In *Proceedings of the 16th Conference of the European Association for Machine Translation (EAMT)*, pages 261–268, Trento, Italy.

Mattia Antonino Di Gangi, Roldano Cattoni, Luisa Bentivogli, Matteo Negri, and Marco Turchi. 2019. MuST-C: a Multilingual Speech Translation Corpus. In *Proceedings of the 2019 Conference of the North American Chapter of the Association for Computational Linguistics: Human Language Technologies, Volume 2 (Short Papers)*, Minneapolis, MN, USA.

Chris Dyer, Victor Chahuneau, and Noah A Smith. 2013. A simple, fast, and effective reparameterization of ibm model 2. In *Proceedings of NAACL-HLT 2013*. Association for Computational Linguistics.

Isao Goto, Bin Lu, Ka Po Chow, Eiichiro Sumita, and Benjamin Tsou. 2011. Overview of the patent machine translation task at the ntcir-9 workshop. In *Proc. of NTCIR-9 Workshop Meeting*, pages 559–578.

Kenneth Heafield. 2011. Kenlm: Faster and smaller language model queries. In *Proceedings of the Sixth Workshop on Statistical Machine Translation*, pages 187–197. Association for Computational Linguistics.

Felix Hieber, Tobias Domhan, Michael Denkowski, David Vilar, Artem Sokolov, Ann Clifton, and Matt Post. 2017. Sockeye: A toolkit for neural machine translation. *ArXiv e-prints*.

Philipp Koehn, Hieu Hoang, Alexandra Birch, Chris Callison-Burch, Marcello Federico, Nicola Bertoldi, Brooke Cowan, Wade Shen, Christine Moran, Richard Zens, Chris Dyer, Ondřej Bojar, Alexandra Constantin, and Evan Herbst. 2007. Moses: open source toolkit for statistical machine translation.

Taku Kudo. 2006. Mecab: Yet another part-of-speech and morphological analyzer. *http://mecab. source-forge. jp*.

Taku Kudo and John Richardson. 2018. Sentencepiece: A simple and language independent subword tokenizer and detokenizer for neural text processing. In *Proceedings of the 2018 Conference on Empirical Methods in Natural Language Processing: System Demonstrations*, pages 66–71.

Sameen Maruf, André FT Martins, and Gholamreza Haffari. 2019. Selective attention for context-aware neural machine translation. In *Proceedings of the 2019 Conference of the North American Chapter of the Association for Computational Linguistics: Human Language Technologies, Volume 1 (Long and Short Papers)*, pages 3092–3102.

Iain McCowan, Jean Carletta, Wessel Kraaij, Simone Ashby, S Bourban, M Flynn, M Guillemot, Thomas Hain, J Kadlec, Vasilis Karaiskos, et al. 2005. The ami meeting corpus. In *Proceedings of the 5th International Conference on Methods and Techniques in Behavioral Research*, volume 88, page 100.

Hiromi Nakaiwa and Satoshi Shirai. 1996. Anaphora Resolution of Japanese Zero Pronouns with Deictic Reference. In *Proceedings of International Conference on Computational Linguistics*.

Toshiaki Nakazawa, Manabu Yaguchi, Kiyotaka Uchimoto, Masao Utiyama, Eiichiro Sumita, Sadao Kurohashi, and Hitoshi Isahara. 2016. Aspec: Asian scientific paper excerpt corpus. In *Proceedings of the Ninth International Conference on Language Resources and Evaluation (LREC 2016)*, pages 2204–2208, Portorož, Slovenia. European Language Resources Association (ELRA).

Kishore Papineni, Salim Roukos, Todd Ward, and Wei-Jing Zhu. 2001. BLEU. In *Proceedings of the 40th Annual Meeting on Association for Computational Linguistics - ACL '02*, page 311, Morristown, NJ, USA. Association for Computational Linguistics.

Maja Popović. 2015. chrf: character n-gram f-score for automatic mt evaluation. In *Proceedings of the Tenth Workshop on Statistical Machine Translation*, pages 392–395.

R. Pryzant, Y. Chung, D. Jurafsky, and D. Britz. 2018. JESC: Japanese-English Subtitle Corpus. *Language Resources and Evaluation Conference (LREC)*.

Elizabeth Salesky, Susanne Burger, Jan Niehues, and Alex Waibel. 2018. Towards fluent translations from disfluent speech. In *Proceedings of the IEEE Workshop on Spoken Language Technology (SLT)*, Athens, Greece.

Jörg Tiedemann. 2016. Finding alternative translations in a large corpus of movie subtitle. In *Proceedings of the Tenth International Conference on Language Resources and Evaluation (LREC 2016)*, pages 3518–3522, Portorož, Slovenia. European Language Resources Association (ELRA).

Jörg Tiedemann and Yves Scherrer. 2017. Neural machine translation with extended context. In *Proceedings of the Third Workshop on Discourse in Machine Translation*, pages 82–92, Copenhagen, Denmark. Association for Computational Linguistics.

Elena Voita, Rico Sennrich, and Ivan Titov. 2019. When a good translation is wrong in context: Context-aware machine translation improves on deixis, ellipsis, and lexical cohesion. In *Proceedings of the 57th Annual Meeting of the Association for Computational Linguistics*, pages 1198–1212, Florence, Italy. Association for Computational Linguistics.

Elena Voita, Pavel Serdyukov, Rico Sennrich, and Ivan Titov. 2018. Context-aware neural machine translation learns anaphora resolution. In *Proceedings of the 56th Annual Meeting of the Association for Computational Linguistics (Volume 1: Long Papers)*, pages 1264–1274, Melbourne, Australia. Association for Computational Linguistics.

Ralph Weischedel, Martha Palmer, Mitchell Marcus, Eduard Hovy, Sameer Pradhan, Lance Ramshaw, Nianwen Xue, Ann Taylor, Jeff Kaufman, Michelle Franchini, et al. 2013. Ontonotes release 5.0 ldc2013t19. *Linguistic Data Consortium, Philadelphia, PA*, 23.

English to Hindi Multi-modal Neural Machine Translation and Hindi Image Captioning

Sahinur Rahman Laskar, Rohit Pratap Singh, Partha Pakray and **Sivaji Bandyopadhyay**
Department of Computer Science and Engineering
National Institute of Technology Silchar
Assam, India
{sahinurlaskar.nits,rohitkako,parthapakray,sivaji.cse.ju}@gmail.com

Abstract

With the widespread use of Machine Translation (MT) techniques, attempt to minimize communication gap among people from diverse linguistic backgrounds. We have participated in Workshop on Asian Translation 2019 (WAT2019) multi-modal translation task. There are three types of submission track namely, multi-modal translation, Hindi-only image captioning and text-only translation for English to Hindi translation. The main challenge is to provide a precise MT output. The multi-modal concept incorporates textual and visual features in the translation task. In this work, multi-modal translation track relies on pre-trained convolutional neural networks (CNN) with Visual Geometry Group having 19 layered (VGG19) to extract image features and attention-based Neural Machine Translation (NMT) system for translation. The merge-model of recurrent neural network (RNN) and CNN is used for the Hindi-only image captioning. The text-only translation track is based on the transformer model of the NMT system. The official results evaluated at WAT2019 translation task, which shows that our multi-modal NMT system achieved Bilingual Evaluation Understudy (BLEU) score 20.37, Rank-based Intuitive Bilingual Evaluation Score (RIBES) 0.642838, Adequacy-Fluency Metrics (AMFM) score 0.668260 for challenge test data and BLEU score 40.55, RIBES 0.760080, AMFM score 0.770860 for evaluation test data in English to Hindi multi-modal translation respectively.

1 Introduction

The multi-modal translation is an emerging task of the MT community, where visual features of image combine with textual features of parallel source-target text to translate sentences (Shah et al., 2016). Interestingly, multi-modal concept improved the translation quality of generating the captions of the images (Dash et al., 2019) as well as significant improvement over text-only NMT system (Huang et al., 2016). In text-only NMT system, the encoder-decoder framework of NMT is a widely accepted technique used in the task of MT. Because it handles sequence to sequence learning problem for variable length source and target sentences and also, handles long term dependency problem using long short term memory (LSTM) (Sutskever et al., 2014). The demerits of basic encoder-decoder model is that it fails to encode all necessary information into the context vector when the sentence is too long. Hence, to handle such problem attention-based encoder-decoder model is introduced, which allows the decoder to focus on different parts of the source sequence at different decoding steps (Bahdanau et al., 2015). (Luong et al., 2015) enhanced the attention model that merges global, accompanying to all source words and local, only pay attention to a part of source words. The attention-based NMT system shows a promising outcome in various languages (Pathak and Pakray, 2018; Pathak et al., 2018; Laskar et al., 2019). Current work has been investigated for English to Hindi translation. There are three different tracks, namely, multi-modal translation, Hindi-only image captioning and text-only translation using NMT system and participated in WAT2019 multi-modal translation task.

2 Related Works

Literature survey mainly focused on multimodal based NMT works, where multimodal informa-

Proceedings of the 6th Workshop on Asian Translation, pages 62–67
Hong Kong, China, November 4, 2019. ©2019 Association for Computational Linguistics

tion (text and image) integrating into the attention-based encoder-decoder architecture. (Huang et al., 2016), proposed a model using attention based NMT, where regional and global visual features are attached in parallel with multiple encoding threads and each thread is followed by the text sequence. They obtained BLEU score 36.5, which outperformed the text-only baseline model BLEU score 34.5. (Calixto and Liu, 2017) used bi-directional recurrent neural network (RNN) with gated recurrent unit (GRU) in the encoding phase instead of single-layer unidirectional LSTM in (Huang et al., 2016) and also, used image features separately either as a word in the source sentence or directly for encoder or decoder initialization unlike word only in (Huang et al., 2016), achieved BLEU score 38.5, 43.9 in English to German and German to English translation respectively. (Calixto et al., 2017), introduced two independent attention mechanisms over source language words and visual features in a single decoder RNN, which significantly improve over the models used in (Huang et al., 2016), obtained BLEU score 39.0, 43.2 in English to German and German to English translation respectively. (Dutta Chowdhury et al., 2018), investigated multimodel NMT following settings of (Calixto and Liu, 2017) for Hindi to English translation and acquired BLEU score 24.2.

3 System Description

The primary steps of the system operations are data preprocessing, system training and system testing and the same have been illustrated in following subsections. The multimodal NMT toolkit (Calixto and Liu, 2017; Calixto et al., 2017) is employed to build the multimodal NMT system for multimodal translation task, which are based on the pytorch port of OpenNMT (Klein et al., 2017). For text-only translation task, OpenNMT is deployed to build the NMT system and in the case of Hindi-only image captioning track, publicly available VGG16 and LSTM in Keras library, are used to build the system (Simonyan and Zisserman, 2015; Tanti et al., 2018). We have used Hindi visual genome dataset in each track of WAT2019 multi-modal translation task provided by the organizer (Nakazawa et al., 2019). We have not used image coordinates (Width, Height) provided in the dataset to indicate the rectangular region in the image described by the caption. Because, we

have used global features of the images.

3.1 Data Preprocessing

The data preprocessing steps of each track are carried out separately. In the multi-modal translation track, firstly, image features for training, validation and test data are extracted from the image data set as mentioned in Table 1. We have used publicly available pre-trained CNN with VGG19 via batch normalization for extraction of both global and local visual features from the image dataset as shown in Table 1. Secondly, primary functions of preprocessing step, tokenization, lowercasing and applying byte pair encoding (BPE) model of source and target sentences. For this purpose, OpenNMT toolkit is used to make a dictionary of vocabulary size of dimension 8300, 7984 for English-Hindi parallel sentence pairs, which indexes the words during the training process. In the text-only translation track, we have considered only source-target corresponding sentences as shown in Table 1 to build the dictionary, vocabulary size of dimension 8300, 7984 using the OpenNMT toolkit. In the Hindi-only image captioning track, image features are extracted via pre-trained CNN with VGG16 from the image data set as shown in Table 1. The image extracted features are 1-dimensional 4,096 element vector. The text input sequences, maximum description length of 22 words, are cleaned to get the vocabulary size of 5605.

3.2 System Training

After preprocessing of data, the system training process is performed in each track separately in Multiple Graphics Processing Units (GPU) environment to boost the performance of training. In the multi-modal translation track, the source (English) and target (Hindi) sentences are fed into encoder-decoder RNN. The multi-modal NMT system is trained using doubly-attentive decoder following settings of (Calixto et al., 2017), where the multi-modal NMT incorporates two different attention mechanism across the source-language words and visual features in a single decoder RNN. Both encoder and decoder consists of a two-layer network of LSTM nodes, which contains 500 units in each layer. The multi-modal NMT system is trained up to 100 epoch. The default settings drop out of 0.3, batch size 40 and layer normalization are used for a stable training run. In the

Nature of corpus	Name of Corpus	Number of instances/items
Training	Englsih-Hindi (Text data)	28,929
	Image data	28,929
Test (Evaluation Set)	English to Hindi (Text data)	1595
	Image data	1595
Test (Challenge Set)	English to Hindi (Text data)	1400
	Image data	1400
Validation	English-Hindi (Text data)	998
	Image data	998

Table 1: Corpus Statistics (Nakazawa et al., 2019).

training process of text-only translation track, the NMT system is trained up to 25,000 epoch to build the train models by transformer model of NMT system. For a small dataset in text-only translation, it is not required up to 25,000 epoch. But in this dataset, we need to trained up to 25,000 because of learning curve grows up to 24,000 then falls. Hence, we have chosen predicted translation at an optimum point on 24,000 epoch. In the training process of Hindi-only image captioning track, we have used merge-model following settings of (Tanti et al., 2018). The preprocessed image feature vector of 4096 elements are processed by a dense layer to provide 256 elements for representation of the image. Afterward, the input text sequence of 22 words length are fed into a word embedding layer to convert it into vector form which is followed by LSTM based RNN layer contains 256 nodes. Both the fixed-length vectors (Image and text) generated are merged together and processed by a dense layer to build the train models up to 20 epoch.

3.3 System Testing

System training is followed by the system testing process in each track separately. This process is required for predicting translations of test instances/items as shown in Table 1.

4 Result and Analysis

The official evaluation results of the competition for English to Hindi multi-modal translation task are reported by the organizer [1]. Automatic evaluation metrics namely, BLEU (Papineni et al.,

2002), RIBES (Isozaki et al., 2010) and AMFM (Banchs et al., 2015) are used to measure performance of predicted translations. We have participated in all the track of the multi-modal translation task and our team name is 683. In multi-modal translation track, a total of three teams, including our team participated for both challenge and evaluation test data in English to Hindi translation. We have acquired BLEU, RIBES, AMFM score 20.37, 0.642838, 0.668260 for challenge test set and BLEU, RIBES, AMFM score 40.55, 0.760080, 0.770860 for evaluation test set respectively, higher than other teams as shown in Table 2. However, we have attained lower BLEU, RIBES and AMFM scores than other teams in text-only and Hindi-only image captioning translation track as shown in Table 3 and 4 respectively. Moreover, from Table 2, 3 and 4, it is observed that when translating English to Hindi our multi-modal translation outperforms our text only translation as well as our Hindi-only image captioning. To further analyze the best and worst performance of multi-modal translation in comparison to text-only and Hindi-only image captioning, sample predicted sentences on challenge test data, reference target sentences and Google translation on same test data are considered in Table 5, 6. In Table 5, our multi-modal NMT system provides perfect prediction like reference target sentence, Google translation and close to text-only translation but wrong translation in Hindi-only image captioning. However, in Table 6, prediction of source word "court" is inappropriate like Google translation, text-only translation and wrong translation in Hindi-only image captioning.

---

[1] http://lotus.kuee.kyoto-u.ac.jp/WAT/evaluation/index.html

System	BLEU	
	Challenge Test Set	Evaluation Test Set
System-1 (Our system)	**20.37**	**40.55**
System-2	12.58	28.45
System-3	11.77	28.27
System-4	10.19	27.39
	RIBES	
	Challenge Test Set	Evaluation Test Set
System-1 (Our system)	**0.642838**	**0.760080**
System-2	0.507192	0.692880
System-3	0.487897	0.676444
System-4	0.482373	0.634567
	AMFM	
	Challenge Test Set	Evaluation Test Set
System-1 (Our system)	**0.668260**	**0.770860**
System-2	0.659840	0.722110
System-3	0.632060	0.707520
System-4	0.559990	0.682060

Table 2: BLEU, RIBES and AMFM scores result of participated teams for multi-modal translation track.

System	BLEU	
	Challenge Test Set	Evaluation Test Set
System-1	30.94	41.32
System-2	30.34	-
System-3	-	38.95
System-4 (Our system)	**15.85**	**38.19**
System-5 (Our system)	**14.69**	**25.34**
System-6	5.56	20.13
	RIBES	
	Challenge Test Set	Evaluation Test Set
System-1	0.734435	0.770754
System-2	0.726998	-
System-3	-	0.749535
System-4 (Our system)	**0.550964**	**0.744158**
System-5 (Our system)	**0.550568**	**0.636152**
System-6	0.373560	0.574366
	AMFM	
	Challenge Test Set	Evaluation Test Set
System-1	0.775890	0.784950
System-2	0.773260	-
System-3 (Our system)	**0.632910**	**0.763940**
System-4	-	0.762180
System-5 (Our system)	**0.578930**	**0.656370**
System-6	0.461110	0.615290

Table 3: BLEU, RIBES and AMFM scores result of participated teams for text-only translation track.

System	Challenge Test Set	
	RIBES	AMFM
System-1	0.080028	0.385960
System-2 (Our system)	**0.034482**	**0.335390**

Table 4: RIBES, AMFM scores result of participated teams for Hindi-only image captioning track.

5 Conclusion and Future Work

Current work participates in three different translation tracks at WAT2019 namely, multi-modal, text-only and Hindi-only image captioning for

English to Hindi translation. In the current competition, our multi-modal NMT system obtained higher BLEU scores than other participants in case of challenge as well as evaluation test data. The multi-modal NMT system is based on a doubly-attentive decoder to predict sentences, which shows better performance than text-only as well as Hindi-only image captioning. The combination of textual as well as visual features reasons about multi-modal translation outperforms text-only translation as well as Hindi-only image captioning tasks. However, close analysis of predicted sentences on the given test data remarks that more experiment and analysis are needed in future work to enhance the performance of multi-modal NMT system.

Image id: 2407547	
Multi-modal translation track Source Language: English Target Language: Hindi	
Source Test Sentence	there are two players in the court
Predicted Target Sentence	अदालत में दो खिलाड़ी हैं
Reference Target Sentence	कोर्ट में दो खिलाड़ी हैं
Google Translation	अदालत में दो खिलाड़ी हैं
Text-only translation track Predicted Target Sentence: अदालत में दो खिलाड़ी हैं	
Hindi-only image captioning track Predicted Caption: एक व्यक्ति के हाथ में एक सफेद और सफेद टेनिस खिलाड़ी	

Table 6: Worst performance example in English to Hindi multi-modal translation.

Acknowledgement

Authors would like to thank WAT2019 Translation task organizers for organizing this competition and also, thank Centre for Natural Language Processing (CNLP) and Department of Computer Science and Engineering at National Institute of Technology, Silchar for providing the requisite support and infrastructure to execute this work.

Image id: 2417491	
Multi-modal translation track Source Language: English Target Language: Hindi	
Source Test Sentence	wooden sign with white letters on second bus
Predicted Target Sentence	दूसरी बस पर सफेद अक्षरों के साथ लकड़ी के चिन्ह
Reference Target Sentence	दूसरी बस में सफेद अक्षरों के साथ लकड़ी का चिन्ह
Google Translation	दूसरी बस में सफेद अक्षरों के साथ लकड़ी का चिन्ह
Text-only translation track Predicted Target Sentence: दूसरे बस बस पर सफेद अक्षर के साथ लकड़ी संकेत	
Hindi-only image captioning track Predicted Caption: एक सड़क पर एक बस	

Table 5: Best performance examples in English to Hindi multi-modal translation.

References

Dzmitry Bahdanau, Kyunghyun Cho, and Yoshua Bengio. 2015. Neural machine translation by jointly learning to align and translate. In *3rd International Conference on Learning Representations, ICLR 2015, San Diego, CA, USA, May 7-9, 2015, Conference Track Proceedings*.

Rafael E. Banchs, Luis F. D'Haro, and Haizhou Li. 2015. Adequacy-fluency metrics: Evaluating mt in the continuous space model framework. *IEEE/ACM*

Trans. Audio, Speech and Lang. Proc., 23(3):472–482.

Iacer Calixto and Qun Liu. 2017. Incorporating global visual features into attention-based neural machine translation. In *Proceedings of the 2017 Conference on Empirical Methods in Natural Language Processing*, pages 992–1003, Copenhagen, Denmark. Association for Computational Linguistics.

Iacer Calixto, Qun Liu, and Nick Campbell. 2017. Doubly-attentive decoder for multi-modal neural machine translation. In *Proceedings of the 55th Annual Meeting of the Association for Computational Linguistics, ACL 2017, Vancouver, Canada, July 30 - August 4, Volume 1: Long Papers*, pages 1913–1924.

Sandeep Kumar Dash, Saurav Saha, Partha Pakray, and Alexander Gelbukh. 2019. Generating image captions through multimodal embedding. *Journal of Intelligent and Fuzzy Systems*, 36(5):4787–4796.

Koel Dutta Chowdhury, Mohammed Hasanuzzaman, and Qun Liu. 2018. Multimodal neural machine translation for low-resource language pairs using synthetic data. pages 33–42.

Po-Yao Huang, Frederick Liu, Sz-Rung Shiang, Jean Oh, and Chris Dyer. 2016. Attention-based multimodal neural machine translation. In *Proceedings of the First Conference on Machine Translation: Volume 2, Shared Task Papers*, pages 639–645, Berlin, Germany. Association for Computational Linguistics.

Hideki Isozaki, Tsutomu Hirao, Kevin Duh, Katsuhito Sudoh, and Hajime Tsukada. 2010. Automatic evaluation of translation quality for distant language pairs. In *Proceedings of the 2010 Conference on Empirical Methods in Natural Language Processing*, pages 944–952, Cambridge, MA. Association for Computational Linguistics.

Guillaume Klein, Yoon Kim, Yuntian Deng, Jean Senellart, and Alexander Rush. 2017. Opennmt: Open-source toolkit for neural machine translation. In *Proceedings of ACL 2017, System Demonstrations*, pages 67–72, Vancouver, Canada. Association for Computational Linguistics.

Sahinur Rahman Laskar, Partha Pakray, and Sivaji Bandyopadhyay. 2019. Neural machine translation: Hindi-Nepali. In *Proceedings of the Fourth Conference on Machine Translation (Volume 3: Shared Task Papers, Day 2)*, pages 202–207, Florence, Italy. Association for Computational Linguistics.

Thang Luong, Hieu Pham, and Christopher D. Manning. 2015. Effective approaches to attention-based neural machine translation. In *Proceedings of the 2015 Conference on Empirical Methods in Natural Language Processing*, pages 1412–1421, Lisbon, Portugal. Association for Computational Linguistics.

Toshiaki Nakazawa, Chenchen Ding, Raj Dabre, Hideya Mino, Isao Goto, Win Pa Pa, Nobushige Doi, Yusuke Oda, Anoop Kunchukuttan, Shantipriya Parida, Ondej Bojar, and Sadao Kurohashi. 2019. Overview of the 6th workshop on Asian translation. In *Proceedings of the 6th Workshop on Asian Translation*, Hong Kong. Association for Computational Linguistics.

Kishore Papineni, Salim Roukos, Todd Ward, and Wei-Jing Zhu. 2002. Bleu: A method for automatic evaluation of machine translation. In *Proceedings of the 40th Annual Meeting on Association for Computational Linguistics*, ACL '02, pages 311–318, Stroudsburg, PA, USA. Association for Computational Linguistics.

Amarnath Pathak and Partha Pakray. 2018. Neural machine translation for indian languages. *Journal of Intelligent Systems*, pages 1–13.

Amarnath Pathak, Partha Pakray, and Jereemi Bentham. 2018. English–mizo machine translation using neural and statistical approaches. *Neural Computing and Applications*, 30:1–17.

Kashif Shah, Josiah Wang, and Lucia Specia. 2016. SHEF-multimodal: Grounding machine translation on images. In *Proceedings of the First Conference on Machine Translation: Volume 2, Shared Task Papers*, pages 660–665, Berlin, Germany. Association for Computational Linguistics.

Karen Simonyan and Andrew Zisserman. 2015. Very deep convolutional networks for large-scale image recognition. In *3rd International Conference on Learning Representations, ICLR 2015, San Diego, CA, USA, May 7-9, 2015, Conference Track Proceedings*.

Ilya Sutskever, Oriol Vinyals, and Quoc V. Le. 2014. Sequence to sequence learning with neural networks. In *Proceedings of the 27th International Conference on Neural Information Processing Systems - Volume 2*, NIPS'14, pages 3104–3112, Cambridge, MA, USA. MIT Press.

Marc Tanti, Albert Gatt, and Kenneth P. Camilleri. 2018. Where to put the image in an image caption generator. *Natural Language Engineering*, 24(3):467–489.

Supervised and Unsupervised Machine Translation
for Myanmar-English and Khmer-English

Benjamin Marie   **Hour Kaing**   **Aye Myat Mon**   **Chenchen Ding**
Atsushi Fujita   **Masao Utiyama**   **Eiichiro Sumita**
National Institute of Information and Communications Technology
3-5 Hikaridai, Seika-cho, Soraku-gun, Kyoto, 619-0289, Japan
{bmarie,hour_kaing,ayemyatmon,chenchen.ding}@nict.go.jp
{atsushi.fujita,mutiyama,eiichiro.sumita}@nict.go.jp

Abstract

This paper presents the NICT's supervised and unsupervised machine translation systems for the WAT2019 Myanmar-English and Khmer-English translation tasks. For all the translation directions, we built state-of-the-art supervised neural (NMT) and statistical (SMT) machine translation systems, using monolingual data cleaned and normalized. Our combination of NMT and SMT performed among the best systems for the four translation directions. We also investigated the feasibility of unsupervised machine translation for low-resource and distant language pairs and confirmed observations of previous work showing that unsupervised MT is still largely unable to deal with them.

1 Introduction

This paper describes neural (NMT) and statistical machine translation systems (SMT) built for the participation of the National Institute of Information and Communications Technology (NICT) in the WAT2019 (Nakazawa et al., 2019) Myanmar-English (my-en) and Khmer-English (km-en) translation tasks.[1] We present supervised systems built using the parallel data provided by the organizers and external additional monolingual data. For all the translation directions, we trained supervised NMT and SMT systems, and combined them through n-best list reranking using several informative features (Marie and Fujita, 2018a), as in our previous participation to WAT2018 (Marie et al., 2018). This simple combination method achieved the best results among the submitted MT systems for these tasks according to BLEU (Papineni et al.,

2002). We also show that the use of monolingual data can dramatically improve translation quality and that an advanced cleaning and normalization of the data further boosts the translation quality. For contrastive experiments, and for investigating the feasibility of unsupervised machine translation (MT) for low-resource distant language pairs, we also present unsupervised MT systems that only use for training the development data provided for these tasks and our monolingual data.

The remainder of this paper is organized as follows. In Section 2, we introduce the data preprocessing, including cleaning and normalization steps. In Section 3, we describe the details of our NMT and SMT systems. The back-translation of monolingual data used by some of our systems is described in Section 4. Then, the combination of NMT and SMT is described in Section 5. In Section 6, we present our unsupervised MT system. Empirical results achieved by all our systems are showed and analyzed in Section 7. Section 8 concludes this paper.

2 Data preprocessing

To train our systems, we used all the bilingual data provided by the organizers. The provided bilingual data comprises different types of corpora: the training data provided by the ALT project[2] and additional training data. These additional data are the UCSY corpus, constructed by the University of Computer Studies, Yangon (UCSY),[3] for the my-en task, and the ECCC corpus, collected by National Institute of Posts, Telecoms & ICT (NIPTICT)

---

[1] The team ID of our participation is "NICT-4".

[2] http://www2.nict.go.jp/astrec-att/member/mutiyama/ALT/index.html

[3] Note that this corpus is not the same as last year and has been further cleaned by the organizers.

Proceedings of the 6th Workshop on Asian Translation, pages 68–75
Hong Kong, China, November 4, 2019. ©2019 Association for Computational Linguistics

and cleaned by NICT, for the km-en task.

For English, we used the monolingual corpora provided by the WMT18 shared News Translation Task (Bojar et al., 2018). For Khmer, we experimented with a monolingual corpus extracted from Common Crawl.[4] As for Myanmar, we experimented with two monolingual corpora: Myanmar Wikipedia and Myanmar Common Crawl. During our last year's participation in the task, we only observed slight improvements, or even a significant drop of the translation quality with the Common Crawl corpus, when using these Myanmar monolingual corpora that we assumed to be the consequence of the extreme noisiness of the data. This year, we introduce a new cleaning and normalization process (Section 2.1) to better exploit the monolingual data. The Wikipedia corpus was created from the entire Myanmar Wikipedia dumped on 2017/06/01. The Khmer and Myanmar Common Crawl corpora consist of sentences in their respective languages[5] from the first quarter of the Common Crawl data crawled during April 2018 for Myanmar, and April 2019 for Khmer. These monolingual corpora, especially the Common Crawl corpora crawled from various websites, contain a large portion of useless data that necessitates cleaning and normalization as presented in the Sections 2.1 and 2.2.

We tokenized and truecased English data respectively with the tokenizer and truecaser of Moses[6] (Koehn et al., 2007). The truecaser was trained on all our English monolingual data. Truecasing was performed on all the tokenized data. For Myanmar, the provided bilingual data were already tokenized. However, for the sake of consistency with our tokenizer we chose to reverse it and tokenized the bilingual and monolingual data by ourselves with an in-house tokenizer. We did not apply truecasing to the Myanmar data. We performed the same procedure for Khmer.

For cleaning, after pre-processing the Myanmar and Khmer monolingual data as described in the Sections 2.1 and 2.2, we segmented the text into sentences and removed lines in both corpora that fulfill at least one of the following conditions:

- more than 25% of its tokens are numbers or punctuation marks.

- contains less than 4 tokens

- contains more than 80 tokens

For cleaning bilingual data, we only applied the Moses script `clean-n-corpus.perl` to remove lines in the parallel data containing more than 80 tokens and escaped characters forbidden by Moses. Note that we did not perform any punctuation normalization.

To tune/validate and evaluate our systems, we used the official development and test sets designated for the tasks: the ALT test data consisting of translations of English texts sampled from English Wikinews.

Tables 1 and 2 present the statistics of the parallel and monolingual data, respectively, after preprocessing.

2.1 Cleaning of Myanmar Data

Many lines in the Common Crawl corpus are made of long sequences of numbers and/or punctuation marks, and 80% of Myanmar lines are not written in a standard Unicode format. It also contains foreign languages, such as English, Thai, and Chinese sentences. In the Wikipedia corpus, a standard Unicode format is used but the text is also very noisy. The most common issues in these corpora are spelling errors. From these observations, we applied the following steps for cleanings:

- Encoding normalization

- Noisy sentence removal

- Spelling error correction

First, we used the UCSY encoding converter to convert Zawgyi font to Unicode.[7] Second, we manually removed 22% of noisy sentences in the Common Crawl corpus and 15% of noisy sentences in the Wikipedia corpus.

There are many spelling errors in the corpora. The spell and pronunciation of a word

---

[4] https://commoncrawl.org/

[5] We used **fasttext** and its pretrained models for language identification: https://fasttext.cc/blog/2017/10/02/blog-post.html

[6] https://github.com/moses-smt/mosesdecoder

[7] This step requires three minutes of computational time for processing one thousand sentences.

Data set	#sent. pairs (#tokens)	
	my-en	km-en
Train	221.1k (my: 4.1M, en: 3.2M)	122.7k (km: 4.1M, en: 3.3M)
Development	1,000 (my: 36,688, en: 25,538)	1,000 (km: 33,604, en: 25,538)
Test	1,018 (my: 37,519, en: 26,236)	1,018 (km: 34,238, en: 26,236)

Table 1: Statistics of our preprocessed parallel data.

Corpus	#lines	#tokens
WMT (English)	338.7M	7.5B
CommonCrawl (English)	2.0M	44.5M
Wikipedia (Myanmar)	268.7k	5.5M
CommonCrawl (Myanmar)	3.0M	67.5M
CommonCrawl (Khmer)	882.9k	30.1M

Table 2: Statistics of our preprocessed monolingual data.

Order	From	To	Graph
1	◌ៈ + ឌ	◌ៈ + គ	◌
2	◌̊ + ក	ក + ◌̇	ក̇
3	◌̣ + ក̇ ក̇ + ◌̣ ក̇ + ◌̈	◌̈ + ក̇	ក̇
4	V + S[S]	S[S] + V	-
5	WS + SS	SS + WS	-

Table 3: Khmer Text normalization rules, where "V" is Vowel, "S" is subscript (subscript sign + a consonant) and [S] refer to one or zero subscript, WS is west subscript, and SS is south subscript.

may lead to misspelling because there are complex orthographic rules and a large gap between the script and the pronunciation in the Myanmar language. One type of spelling errors results in words that do not exist in the Myanmar language. They can be detected easily by a spell checker and a dictionary look-up. Another type of errors happened when the writer uses existing words but wrongly or ambiguously in context. Those errors are difficult to automatically detect as these words exist in a Myanmar dictionary but are incorrect according to the context. There are two types of errors: phonetic errors and context errors. Context error is a subset of phonetic error (e.g., "I saw three trees in the park" as "I saw tree trees in the park").

We performed a dictionary[8] look-up to match the word in the given text with the word in the dictionary. If a word is not there then it is considered as an error. We also measured the Levenshtein distance at the character level to find the closest word in a large Myanmar dictionary. After generating a list of suggestions, we used a bigram language model to select and apply the best correction in context.

2.2 Cleaning of Khmer Data

We clean the Common Crawl corpus for Khmer in two steps, spelling disambiguation and over-tokenization recovery. In our context, over-tokenization refers to dependant

---

[8] We used a Myanmar dictionary that contains a list of unique 41,343 Myanmar words from `https://github.com/chanmratekoko/Awesome-Myanmar`.

characters that should never be separated by a space.

The Khmer corpus is in Unicode format and it is very common for spelling ambiguities where multiple character sequences can represent word with the same graphical representation. We solve this problem by replacing the spelling ambiguities into one form which basically follows the way of Khmer native speakers' spelling. The replacement rules are simply in the order as in Table 3.

As our in-house tokenizer works at character level, over-tokenization is unavoidable when out-of-vocabularies (OOVs) appear. We reverted the over-tokenization by removing spaces as follows:

- before `[U+17B6 - U+17D3]`

- before `.?[U+17CB - U+17CD]`

- before and after `U+17D2`

- after `[U+17A5 U+17A7 U+17AB U+17AD]`

However, recovering from over-tokenization did not result in improvements of translation quality according to BLEU. Consequently, for the sake of simplicity, we did not use this step when building our MT systems.

```
--type transformer --max-length 80
--mini-batch-fit --valid-freq 5000
--save-freq 5000 --workspace 10000
--disp-freq 500 --beam-size 12
--normalize 1 --valid-mini-batch
16 --overwrite --early-stopping
5 --cost-type ce-mean-words
--valid-metrics ce-mean-words
perplexity translation --keep-best
--enc-depth 4 --dec-depth 4
--transformer-dropout 0.1
--learn-rate 0.001 --dropout-src
0.1 --dropout-trg 0.1 --lr-warmup
16000 --lr-decay-inv-sqrt 16000
--lr-report --label-smoothing
0.1 --devices 0 1 2 3 4 5
6 7 --dim-vocabs 8000 8000
--optimizer-params 0.9 0.98
1e-09 --clip-norm 5 --sync-sgd
--exponential-smoothing
```

Table 4: Parameters of Marian used for training our NMT systems.

3 Supervised MT Systems

3.1 NMT

To build competitive NMT systems, we relied on the Transformer architecture (Vaswani et al., 2017). We chose Marian[9] (Junczys-Dowmunt et al., 2018) to train and evaluate our NMT systems. In order to limit the size of the vocabulary of the NMT models, we further segmented tokens in the parallel data into sub-word units via byte pair encoding (BPE) (Sennrich et al., 2016b) using 8k operations for each language. All our NMT systems were consistently trained on 8 GPUs,[10] with the parameters presented in Table 4.

3.2 SMT

We also trained SMT systems using Moses. Word alignments and phrase tables were trained on the tokenized parallel data using `mgiza`. Source-to-target and target-to-source word alignments were symmetrized with the `grow-diag-final-and` heuristic. We trained phrase-based SMT models and `MSLR` (monotone, swap, discontinuous-left, discontinuous-

right) lexicalized reordering models. We also used the default distortion limit of 6. We trained two 4-gram language models, one on the WMT monolingual data for English, on the Common Crawl corpus for Khmer, and on the Wikipedia data for Myanmar, concatenated to the target side of the parallel data, and another one on the target side of the parallel data, using `LMPLZ` (Heafield et al., 2013). To tune the SMT model weights, we used `kb-mira` (Cherry and Foster, 2012) and selected the weights giving the best BLEU score for the development data during 15 iterations.

4 Back-Translation of Monolingual Data for NMT

Parallel data for training NMT can be augmented with synthetic parallel data, generated through a so-called back-translation, to significantly improve translation quality (Sennrich et al., 2016a). We used an NMT system, trained on the parallel data provided by the organizers, to translate target monolingual sentences into the source language. Then, these back-translated sentences were simply mixed with the original parallel data to train from scratch a new source-to-target NMT system.

We back-translated 2M sentences randomly sampled from WMT18 English data for my→en and km→en, our Myanmar Wikipedia corpus for en→my, and our Khmer Common Crawl corpus for en→km.

5 Combination of NMT and SMT

Our primary submissions for the tasks were the results of a simple combination of NMT and SMT. As demonstrated by Marie and Fujita (2018a), and despite the simplicity of the method used, combining NMT and SMT makes MT more robust and can significantly improve translation quality, even when SMT greatly underperforms NMT. Following Marie and Fujita (2018a), our combination of NMT and SMT works as follows.

5.1 Generation of n-best Lists

We first independently generated the 100-best translation hypotheses with 7 NMT models, independently trained, and also with the ensemble of these 7 NMT models. We also generated 100-best translation hypotheses with our

---

[9]`https://marian-nmt.github.io/`, version 1.7.6
[10]NVIDIA® Tesla® V100 32Gb.

Feature	Description
L2R (7)	Scores given by each of the 7 left-to-right Marian models
LEX (4)	Sentence-level translation probabilities, for both translation directions
LM (2)	Scores given by the language models used by the Moses baseline systems
LEN (2)	Difference between the length of the source sentence and the length of the translation hypothesis, and its absolute value

Table 5: Set of features used by our reranking systems. The "Feature" column refers to the same feature name used in Marie and Fujita (2018a). The numbers between parentheses indicate the number of scores in each feature set.

SMT system. We then merged all these 9 lists generated by different systems, without removing duplicated hypotheses, which resulted in a list of 900 diverse translation hypotheses for each source sentence.

5.2 Reranking Framework and Features

We rescored all the hypotheses in the list with a reranking framework using features to better model the fluency and the adequacy of each hypothesis. This method can find a better hypothesis in these merged n-best lists than the one-best hypothesis originated by the individual systems. We chose `kb-mira` as a rescoring framework and used a subset of the features proposed in Marie and Fujita (2018a). All the following features we used are described in details by Marie and Fujita (2018a). As listed in Table 5, it includes the scores given by 7 left-to-right NMT models independently trained. We computed sentence-level translation probabilities using the lexical translation probabilities learned by `mgiza` during the training of our SMT systems. The two language models trained for SMT for each translation direction were also used. To account for hypotheses length, we added the difference, and its absolute value, between the number of tokens in the translation hypothesis and the source sentence.

The reranking framework was trained on n-best lists generated by decoding of the development data that we used to validate the training of NMT systems and to tune the weights of SMT models.

6 Unsupervised SMT

We also built an SMT system, without any supervision, i.e., using only our monolingual data for training. We chose unsupervised SMT (USMT) over unsupervised NMT (UNMT) since previous work (Lample et al., 2018) has shown that USMT significantly outperforms UNMT for distant languages.

We built USMT systems using a framework similar to the one proposed in Marie and Fujita (2018b). The first step of USMT is the induction of a phrase table from the monolingual corpora. We first collected phrases of up to six tokens from the monolingual corpora[11] using `word2phrase`.[12] As phrases, we also considered all the token types in the corpora. Then, we selected the 300k most frequent phrases in the monolingual corpora to be used for inducing a phrase table. All possible phrase pairs are scored, as in Marie and Fujita (2018b), using bilingual word embeddings, and the 300 target phrases with the highest scores were kept in the phrase table for each source phrase. As a result, the induced phrase table contains a total of 90M (300k×300) phrase pairs. For this induction, bilingual word embeddings of 300 dimensions were obtained using word embeddings trained with `fastText`[13] and aligned in the same space using unsupervised `Vecmap` (Artetxe et al., 2018a). This alignment is the most critical step for unsupervised MT since it is used for initializing the training. It is expected to be extremely difficult for distant languages such as Myanmar, Khmer, and English, as reported by previous work (Søgaard et al., 2018). For each phrase pair, a total of four scores, to be used as features in the phrase tables were computed to mimic phrase-

---

[11] Since our Myanmar Wikipedia corpus is significantly smaller than the Myanmar Common Crawl corpus, we concatenated both corpora and used the resulting corpus in all the subsequent steps of USMT training.

[12] https://code.google.com/archive/p/word2vec/

[13] https://github.com/facebookresearch/fastText

ID	System	my→en	en→my	km→en	en→km
1.	Moses	10.3	20.5	19.8	40.4
2.	Marian single	15.7	25.2	17.0	37.8
3.	Marian single w/ backtr.	19.1	28.8	24.9	42.9
4.	Marian ensemble of 4 w/ backtr.	22.4	29.7	25.9	43.0
5.	#1 + #4	24.8	31.3	27.5	43.9
6.	Unsupervised SMT	< 1.0	< 1.0	< 1.0	< 1.0

Table 6: Official BLEU scores for our MT systems on the official test set of the tasks. "backtr" denotes the use of back-translated monolingual data. #5 denotes our n-best list combination described in Section 5: a combination of the best SMT and the best NMT systems realized using monolingual data. We submitted systems #5 for human evaluation.

based SMT: forward and backward phrase and lexical translation probabilities. Finally, the phrase table and the language models were plugged into a Moses system that was tuned on the development data using KB-MIRA.

We performed four refinement steps to improve the system, using at each step synthetic parallel sentences generated from one third of the monolingual corpus, by the forward and backward translation systems, instead of using only either forward (Marie and Fujita, 2018b) or backward translations (Artetxe et al., 2018b). We report on the performance of the systems obtained after the fourth refinement step.

7 Results

Table 6 presents the results for different versions of our SMT and NMT systems. We can observe that NMT (#2) is significantly better than SMT (#1) for my-en while we can observe the reverse for km-en. Our assumption for explaining this difference is that my-en has a much larger training data while km-en may not have enough to train a better NMT systems. The extreme noisiness of the training data for km-en, that we assessed by a native Khmer speaker, may also explain the large gap between SMT and NMT since it is well-known that SMT is much more robust than NMT when trained on noisy data.

Exploiting monolingual data through back-translation (#3) consistently improves all our NMT systems by a large margin, from 3.4 (my→en) to 7.9 (km→en) BLEU points. This highlights the importance of using monolingual data in low-resource scenarios, even when the NMT system used for generating back-

translations deliver a translation of a low quality.

Our results are more contrasted when ensembling 7 NMT models during decoding (#4). While we observe an improvement of 3.3 BLEU points for (my→en), the improvements for the other directions were limited to 1.0 BLEU points or less. Considering the cost of independently training 7 NMT models and the cost of decoding with 7 models, ensembling does not seem to offer a cost-effective solution.

Finally, combining SMT and NMT (#5) provides the best results with improvements over #4 ranging from 0.9 (en→km) to 2.4 BLEU points (my→en).

Our results for unsupervised SMT (#6) follow the same trend as the results presented by Marie et al. (2019) for English-Gujarati and English-Kazakh at WMT19: while unsupervised MT has shown promising results for European languages, it is far from being useful for real-world applications, i.e., truly low-resource distant language pairs. We assume that training useful bilingual weakly-supervised/unsupervised bilingual word embeddings for initializing the system remains one of the main challenges.

8 Conclusion

In this paper, we showed that exploiting cleaned and normalized noisy monolingual data significantly helps in improving the translation quality for my-en and km-en. Furthermore, as in our previous participation in WAT2018, we showed that combining NMT and SMT can further improve the translation quality over a very strong NMT system. In order to allow participants to build state-of-the-art MT systems, we encourage, even more than last year, WAT organizers to provide monolingual data for future editions of the workshop.

References

Mikel Artetxe, Gorka Labaka, and Eneko Agirre. 2018a. A robust self-learning method for fully unsupervised cross-lingual mappings of word embeddings. In *Proceedings of the 56th Annual Meeting of the Association for Computational Linguistics (Volume 1: Long Papers)*, pages 789–798, Melbourne, Australia. Association for Computational Linguistics.

Mikel Artetxe, Gorka Labaka, and Eneko Agirre. 2018b. Unsupervised statistical machine translation. In *Proceedings of the 2018 Conference on Empirical Methods in Natural Language Processing*, pages 3632–3642, Brussels, Belgium. Association for Computational Linguistics.

Ondřej Bojar, Christian Federmann, Mark Fishel, Yvette Graham, Barry Haddow, Matthias Huck, Philipp Koehn, and Christof Monz. 2018. Findings of the 2018 conference on machine translation (WMT18). In *Proceedings of the Third Conference on Machine Translation, Volume 2: Shared Task Papers*, Brussels, Belgium. Association for Computational Linguistics.

Colin Cherry and George Foster. 2012. Batch tuning strategies for statistical machine translation. In *Proceedings of the 2012 Conference of the North American Chapter of the Association for Computational Linguistics: Human Language Technologies*, pages 427–436, Montréal, Canada. Association for Computational Linguistics.

Kenneth Heafield, Ivan Pouzyrevsky, Jonathan H. Clark, and Philipp Koehn. 2013. Scalable modified Kneser-Ney language model estimation. In *Proceedings of the 51st Annual Meeting of the Association for Computational Linguistics (Volume 2: Short Papers)*, pages 690–696, Sofia, Bulgaria. Association for Computational Linguistics.

Marcin Junczys-Dowmunt, Roman Grundkiewicz, Tomasz Dwojak, Hieu Hoang, Kenneth Heafield, Tom Neckermann, Frank Seide, Ulrich Germann, Alham Fikri Aji, Nikolay Bogoychev, André F. T. Martins, and Alexandra Birch. 2018. Marian: Fast neural machine translation in C++. In *Proceedings of ACL 2018, System Demonstrations*, pages 116–121, Melbourne, Australia. Association for Computational Linguistics.

Philipp Koehn, Hieu Hoang, Alexandra Birch, Chris Callison-Burch, Marcello Federico, Nicola Bertoldi, Brooke Cowan, Wade Shen, Christine Moran, Richard Zens, Chris Dyer, Ondřej Bojar, Alexandra Constantin, and Evan Herbst. 2007. Moses: Open source toolkit for statistical machine translation. In *Proceedings of the 45th Annual Meeting of the Association for Computational Linguistics Companion Volume Proceedings of the Demo and Poster Sessions*, pages 177–180, Prague, Czech Republic. Association for Computational Linguistics.

Guillaume Lample, Myle Ott, Alexis Conneau, Ludovic Denoyer, and Marc'Aurelio Ranzato. 2018. Phrase-based & neural unsupervised machine translation. In *Proceedings of the 2018 Conference on Empirical Methods in Natural Language Processing*, pages 5039–5049, Brussels, Belgium. Association for Computational Linguistics.

Benjamin Marie and Atsushi Fujita. 2018a. A smorgasbord of features to combine phrase-based and neural machine translation. In *Proceedings of the 13th Conference of the Association for Machine Translation in the Americas (Volume 1: Research Papers)*, pages 111–124, Boston, USA. Association for Machine Translation in the Americas.

Benjamin Marie and Atsushi Fujita. 2018b. Unsupervised neural machine translation initialized by unsupervised statistical machine translation. *CoRR*, abs/1810.12703.

Benjamin Marie, Atsushi Fujita, and Eiichiro Sumita. 2018. Combination of statistical and neural machine translation for Myanmar-English. In *Proceedings of the 32nd Pacific Asia Conference on Language, Information and Computation: 5th Workshop on Asian Translation: 5th Workshop on Asian Translation*, Hong Kong. Association for Computational Linguistics.

Benjamin Marie, Haipeng Sun, Rui Wang, Kehai Chen, Atsushi Fujita, Masao Utiyama, and Eiichiro Sumita. 2019. NICT's unsupervised neural and statistical machine translation systems for the WMT19 news translation task. In *Proceedings of the Fourth Conference on Machine Translation (Volume 2: Shared Task Papers, Day 1)*, pages 294–301, Florence, Italy. Association for Computational Linguistics.

Toshiaki Nakazawa, Chenchen Ding, Raj Dabre, Hideya Mino, Isao Goto, Win Pa Pa, Nobushige Doi, Yusuke Oda, Anoop Kunchukuttan, Shantipriya Parida, Ondřej Bojar, and Sadao Kurohashi. 2019. Overview of the 6th workshop on Asian translation. In *Proceedings of the 6th Workshop on Asian Translation*, Hong Kong. Association for Computational Linguistics.

Kishore Papineni, Salim Roukos, Todd Ward, and Wei-Jing Zhu. 2002. Bleu: a method for automatic evaluation of machine translation. In *Proceedings of 40th Annual Meeting of the Association for Computational Linguistics*, pages

311–318, Philadelphia, Pennsylvania, USA. Association for Computational Linguistics.

Rico Sennrich, Barry Haddow, and Alexandra Birch. 2016a. Improving neural machine translation models with monolingual data. In *Proceedings of the 54th Annual Meeting of the Association for Computational Linguistics (Volume 1: Long Papers)*, pages 86–96, Berlin, Germany. Association for Computational Linguistics.

Rico Sennrich, Barry Haddow, and Alexandra Birch. 2016b. Neural machine translation of rare words with subword units. In *Proceedings of the 54th Annual Meeting of the Association for Computational Linguistics (Volume 1: Long Papers)*, pages 1715–1725, Berlin, Germany. Association for Computational Linguistics.

Anders Søgaard, Sebastian Ruder, and Ivan Vulić. 2018. On the limitations of unsupervised bilingual dictionary induction. In *Proceedings of the 56th Annual Meeting of the Association for Computational Linguistics (Volume 1: Long Papers)*, pages 778–788, Melbourne, Australia. Association for Computational Linguistics.

Ashish Vaswani, Noam Shazeer, Niki Parmar, Jakob Uszkoreit, Llion Jones, Aidan N. Gomez, Łukasz Kaiser, and Illia Polosukhin. 2017. Attention is all you need. In *Proceedings of the 30th Neural Information Processing Systems Conference (NIPS)*, pages 5998–6008. Curran Associates, Inc.

NICT's participation to WAT 2019:
Multilingualism and Multi-step Fine-Tuning for Low Resource NMT

Raj Dabre   **Eiichiro Sumita**

National Institute of Information and Communications Technology

3-5 Hikaridai, Seika-cho, Soraku-gun, Kyoto, 619-0289, Japan

firstname.lastname@nict.go.jp

Abstract

In this paper we describe our submissions to WAT 2019 for the following tasks: English–Tamil translation and Russian–Japanese translation. Our team,"NICT-5", focused on multilingual domain adaptation and back-translation for Russian–Japanese translation and on simple fine-tuning for English–Tamil translation . We noted that multi-stage fine tuning is essential in leveraging the power of multilingualism for an extremely low-resource language like Russian–Japanese. Furthermore, we can improve the performance of such a low-resource language pair by exploiting a small but in-domain monolingual corpus via back-translation. We managed to obtain second rank in both tasks for all translation directions.

1   Introduction

Neural machine translation (NMT) (Cho et al., 2014; Sutskever et al., 2014; Bahdanau et al., 2015) has enabled end-to-end training of a translation system without needing to deal with word alignments, translation rules, and complicated decoding algorithms, which are the characteristics of phrase-based statistical machine translation (PBSMT) (Koehn et al., 2007). Although vanilla NMT is significantly better than PBSMT in resource-rich scenarios, PBSMT performs better in resource-poor scenarios (Zoph et al., 2016). By exploiting transfer learning techniques, the performance of NMT approaches can be improved substantially.

For WAT 2019, we participated as team "NICT-5" and worked on Russian–Japanese and English–Tamil translation. The techniques we focused on for each translation task can be summarized as below:

- For the Russian–Japanese translation task, we submitted the results of our work pre-

sented in Imankulova et al. (2019) where we focused on multilingual stage-wise tuning followed by back-translation.

- For the English–Tamil translation task, we observed that simply fine-tuning a Hindi–English model is enough to give high quality translations.

For additional details of how our submissions are ranked relative to the submissions of other WAT participants, kindly refer to the overview paper (Nakazawa et al., 2019).

2   NMT Models and Approaches

We will first describe the Transformer which is the state-of-the-art NMT model we used for our experiments.

2.1   The Transformer

The Transformer (Vaswani et al., 2017) is the current state-of-the-art model for NMT. It is a sequence-to-sequence neural model that consists of two components, the *encoder* and the *decoder*. The encoder converts the input word sequence into a sequence of vectors of high dimensionality. The decoder, on the other hand, produces the target word sequence by predicting the words using a combination of the previously predicted word and relevant parts of the input sequence representations. Due to lack of space, we briefly describe the encoder and decoder as follows. The reader is encouraged to read the Transformer paper (Vaswani et al., 2017) for a deeper understanding.

2.2   Fine-Tuning for Transfer Learning

We use fine-tuning for transfer learning. Zoph et al. (2016) proposed to train a robust L3→L1 parent model using a large L3–L1 parallel corpus and then fine-tune it on a small L2–L1 corpus to

Proceedings of the 6th Workshop on Asian Translation, pages 76–80
Hong Kong, China, November 4, 2019. ©2019 Association for Computational Linguistics

obtain a robust L2→L1 child model. The underlying assumption is that the pre-trained L3→L1 model contains prior probabilities for translation into L1. The prior information is divided into two parts: language modeling information (strong prior) and cross-lingual information (weak or strong depending on the relationship between L3 and L2). Dabre et al. (2017) have shown that linguistically similar L3 and L2 allow for better transfer learning. As such, we used Hindi as the helping language, L3 for which L2 is Tamil because both are Indian languages. In theory, Tamil should benefit more from Dravidian languages but there is no large helping corpus involving a Dravidian language.

It is reasonable to expect improvements in translation by fine-tuning a L3→L1 model on L2→L1 data because of the additional target language monolingual data that helps improve the decoder-side language model. However, previous research has shown that this works even if the translation direction is reversed (Kocmi and Bojar, 2018). As such, we also experiment with fine-tuning a L1→L3 model on L1→L2 data with the expectation that the encoder representations will be improved.

2.3 Multilingual Multi-stage Training with Back-translation

In Imankulova et al. (2019), we proposed leveraging multilingualism via multiple training stages. Although we explain the idea in detail below, we urge the readers to read this paper for minute details regarding implementation and data-preprocessing.

Assume that our language pair of interest is L1–L2 for which we have very little data. We have the following types of helping data: large L1–L3 and L2–L3 out-of-domain parallel corpora, small L1–L3 and L2–L3 in-domain parallel corpora and in-domain monolingual corpora that are slightly larger than the in-domain parallel corpora. In order to train robust NMT models we do the following:

1. Train a multilingual L1↔L3 and L2↔L3 model using the out-of-domain data.

2. Perform domain-adaptation by fine-tuning the previous model on in-domain and out-of-domain L1↔L3 and L2↔L3 data.

3. Introduce L1–L2 pair by fine-tuning the previous model on in-domain L1↔L2, L1↔L3 and L2↔L3 data.

4. Use robust multilingual model for back-translation and final model training:

    (a) Use the previous model to back-translate all in-domain monolingual corpora for L1, L2 and L3 into all other languages.

    (b) a. Train a multilingual model for L1↔L2, L1↔L3 and L2↔L3 using all in-domain parallel and pseudo-parallel corpora.

5. Repeat N^1 times:

    (a) Use the previous model to back-translate all in-domain monolingual corpora for L1, L2 and L3 into all other languages.

    (b) a. Fine-tune the previous model using all in-domain parallel and pseudo-parallel corpora.

This stage-wise division of training ensures that the model focuses on a specific domain per training step and relies on multilingualism to address the scarcity of data. The resultant model used for back-translation leads to an inflation in good quality in-domain data which should substantially increase translation performance. In our experiments, L1 is Russian, L2 is Japanese and L3 is English.

3 Model Training Details

For all our experiments, we used the tensor2tensor[2] version 1.6 implementation of the Transformer (Vaswani et al., 2017) model. We chose this implementation because it is known to give the state-of-the-art results for NMT. For Russian–Japanese, we use the same pre/post-processing steps as mentioned in Imankulova et al. (2019). Specifically, we processed the Russian and English text using the tokenizer[3] and detokenizer[4] in Moses. We tokenized the Japanese

---

[1]In practice we noticed that the performance stagnates after repeating this process 3 times

[2]https://github.com/tensorflow/tensor2tensor

[3]https://github.com/moses-smt/mosesdecoder/blob/master/scripts/tokenizer/tokenizer.perl

[4]https://github.com/moses-smt/mosesdecoder/blob/master/scripts/tokenizer/detokenizer.perl

Lang.pair	Partition	#sent.	#tokens	#types
Ja↔Ru	train	12,356	341k / 229k	22k / 42k
	development	486	16k / 11k	2.9k / 4.3k
	test	600	22k / 15k	3.5k / 5.6k
Ja↔En	train	47,082	1.27M / 1.01M	48k / 55k
	development	589	21k / 16k	3.5k / 3.8k
	test	600	22k / 17k	3.5k / 3.8k
Ru↔En	train	82,072	1.61M / 1.83M	144k / 74k
	development	313	7.8k / 8.4k	3.2k / 2.3k
	test	600	15k / 17k	5.6k / 3.8k

Table 1: Statistics on our in-domain parallel data for the Russian–Japanese task.

text using Mecab[5]. Note that the implementation we used for our experiments learns and performs sub-word segmentation on the tokenized text. In order to compute BLEU we unsub-worded and detokenized Russian translations whereas we only unsub-worded Japanese translations. For Tamil–English we do not perform any specific pre/post-processing like we did for Russian–Japanese. In order to train multilingual models we used the artificial token trick used for zero-shot NMT (Johnson et al., 2017). In order to avoid vocabulary mismatches during fine-tuning we use multilingual vocabularies learned from the concatenation of all data available for a particular task. We always oversample the smaller datasets to ensure that the training phase sees equal amounts of data from all datasets. We used the default hyperparameters in tensor2tensor for all our models with the exception of the number of training iterations. We use the "base" transformer model hyperparameter settings with a 32000 subword vocabulary which is learned using tensor2tensor's default subword segmentation mechanism. During training, a model checkpoint is saved every 1000 iterations. We train models till convergence of the development set. In our implementation we used the following setting: a model is said to convergence when the BLEU score does not vary by more than 0.1 BLEU for 20,000 iterations. We averaged the last 10 model checkpoints and used it for decoding the test sets.

4 Russian↔Japanese Task

We observed that Russian↔Japanese translation shows best performance when multilingual multi-stage training is performed in conjunction with back-translation.

4.1 Datasets

For the Russian↔Japanese task tasks we used the official data provided by the organizers. Refer to Table 1 for an overview of the in-domain parallel corpora and the data splits. In addition we used out-of-domain corpora involving Russian↔English and English↔Japanese and in-domain monolingual corpora for all 3 languages. All data used was the same as in Imankulova et al. (2019). The testing domain was News Commentary and hence is challenging given the scarce amount of in-domain data.

4.2 Results

For Japanese→Russian our submission had a BLEU score of 8.11 which is substantially lower than the best system's BLEU of 14.36. On the other hand, for Russian→Japanese our submission had a BLEU score of 12.09 (JUMAN segmentation) which is not that far from the best system whose BLEU score was 15.29. For both directions, we are much better than the organizer baseline which have BLEU scores of 0.69 and 1.97 respectively. We were 2nd out of 4 submissions to this task. The reason for being better than the baseline is rather simple: We exploit a large amount of data and use robust multi-stage training mechanisms.

We did not utilize large monolingual corpora for back-translation and instead focused on small in-domain corpora in order to avoid problems related to balancing large and extremely small (relatively speaking) corpora. Furthermore, we realized that it should be possible to fine-tune our models on Japanese–Russian data in order to obtain additional BLEU gains. We will pursue the use of larger monolingual data and additional fine-tuning in the future.

For additional results using other metrics, human as well as automatic, we refer the reader to the official website[67].

5 Tamil↔English Task

For Tamil↔English translation we used a simple fine-tuning based approach which manages to yield translations of reasonably good quality.

---

[5]https://github.com/taku910/mecab

[6]http://lotus.kuee.kyoto-u.ac.jp/WAT/evaluation/list.php?t=66&o=4

[7]http://lotus.kuee.kyoto-u.ac.jp/WAT/evaluation/list.php?t=67&o=1

Dataset	Sentences	English tokens	Tamil tokens
train	166,871	3,913,541	2,727,174
test	2,000	47,144	32,847
development	1,000	23,353	16,376
total	169,871	3,984,038	2,776,397
Domain	Sentences	English tokens	Tamil tokens
bible	26,792 (15.77%)	703,838	373,082
cinema	30,242 (17.80%)	445,230	298,419
news	112,837 (66.43%)	2,834,970	2,104,896
total	169,871	3,984,038	2,776,397

Table 2: Statistics on our in-domain parallel data for the Tamil–English task.

5.1 Datasets

The Tamil–English parallel corpus (Ramasamy et al., 2012) belongs to a mixed domain of bible, cinema and news. The corpora statistics and splits at the sentence and domain level are are described in Table 2. Additionally, we used the IITB Hindi–English parallel corpus for transfer learning via fine-tuning. This corpus consists of 1,561,840 lines. We do not use Hindi–English development set for tuning as we we pre-train for a fixed number of iterations.

5.2 Results

For Tamil→English translation we obtained a BLEU score of 27.81 which is approximately 2 BLEU below the best system wheres for the opposite direction we obtained a BLEU score of 12.74 which is only 0.31 BLEU below the best system. In the latter case, the difference is not statistically significant. Furthermore, for English→Tamil, we observed that we can obtain a statistically significant improvement over a baseline model that uses only the English–Tamil parallel corpus. We believe that this improvement comes from the strengthened encoder which is pretrained on the English–Hindi data. However, the improvement for the reverse direction using the same type of pretraining is approximately 3.5 BLEU. As such, we can conclude that fine-tuning a pre-trained model is more valuable when the target language is the same as compared to when the source language is the same. For Tamil→English our submission was ranked 3rd out of 7 submissions whereas our English→Tamil submission was ranked 2nd out of 6 submissions. In the future we will experiment with back-translation as well as mechanisms to improve the quality of transfer learning by fine-tuning. Perhaps, pre-training with multiple language pairs might give better results similar to what we observed when working on our Russian↔Japanese submission.

For additional results using other metrics, human as well as automatic, we refer the reader to the official website[89].

6 Conclusion

In this paper we have described our submissions to WAT 2019. We focused on multilingualism, transfer learning and back-translation for our submissions. For Russian↔Japanese we observed that our work on multilingual multi-stage training in conjunction with back-translating in-domain corpora leads to a competitive submission. On the other hand, for our Tamil↔English submissions we showed that simple transfer learning techniques such as fine-tuning can reliably improve translation quality especially for translation into English. Having noted the importance of multilingual pre-training, in the future, we will focus on fine-tuning extremely large multilingual models that use more parameters as well as layers. In particular we expect that fine-tuning multilingual BERT models (XLM) (Lample and Conneau, 2019) on parallel corpora will lead to the best translations.

Acknowledgments

We would like to thank the reviewers for their comments which helped improve the quality of this paper.

References

Dzmitry Bahdanau, Kyunghyun Cho, and Yoshua Bengio. 2015. Neural machine translation by jointly learning to align and translate. In *Proceedings of the 3rd International Conference on Learning Representations (ICLR 2015)*, San Diego, USA. International Conference on Learning Representations.

Kyunghyun Cho, Bart van Merriënboer, Çalar Gülçehre, Dzmitry Bahdanau, Fethi Bougares, Holger Schwenk, and Yoshua Bengio. 2014. Learning phrase representations using rnn encoder–decoder for statistical machine translation. In *Proceedings of the 2014 Conference on Empirical Methods in Natural Language Processing (EMNLP)*, pages 1724–1734, Doha, Qatar. Association for Computational Linguistics.

---

[8]http://lotus.kuee.kyoto-u.ac.jp/WAT/evaluation/list.php?t=72&o=4

[9]http://lotus.kuee.kyoto-u.ac.jp/WAT/evaluation/list.php?t=73&o=7

Raj Dabre, Tetsuji Nakagawa, and Hideto Kazawa. 2017. An empirical study of language relatedness for transfer learning in neural machine translation. In *Proceedings of the 31st Pacific Asia Conference on Language, Information and Computation*, pages 282–286. The National University (Phillippines).

Aizhan Imankulova, Raj Dabre, Atsushi Fujita, and Kenji Imamura. 2019. Exploiting out-of-domain parallel data through multilingual transfer learning for low-resource neural machine translation. In *Proceedings of Machine Translation Summit XVII Volume 1: Research Track*, pages 128–139, Dublin, Ireland.

Melvin Johnson, Mike Schuster, Quoc V. Le, Maxim Krikun, Yonghui Wu, Zhifeng Chen, Nikhil Thorat, Fernanda Viégas, Martin Wattenberg, Greg Corrado, Macduff Hughes, and Jeffrey Dean. 2017. Google's multilingual neural machine translation system: Enabling zero-shot translation. *Transactions of the Association for Computational Linguistics*, 5:339–351.

Tom Kocmi and Ondrej Bojar. 2018. Trivial transfer learning for low-resource neural machine translation. In *Proceedings of the Third Conference on Machine Translation: Research Papers, WMT 2018, Belgium, Brussels, October 31 - November 1, 2018*, pages 244–252.

Philipp Koehn, Hieu Hoang, Alexandra Birch, Chris Callison-Burch, Marcello Federico, Nicola Bertoldi, Brooke Cowan, Wade Shen, Christine Moran, Richard Zens, Chris Dyer, Ondrej Bojar, Alexandra Constantin, and Evan Herbst. 2007. Moses: Open source toolkit for statistical machine translation. In *Proceedings of the 45th Annual Meeting of the Association for Computational Linguistics Companion Volume Proceedings of the Demo and Poster Sessions*, pages 177–180, Prague, Czech Republic. Association for Computational Linguistics.

Guillaume Lample and Alexis Conneau. 2019. Cross-lingual language model pretraining. *CoRR*, abs/1901.07291.

Toshiaki Nakazawa, Chenchen Ding, Raj Dabre, Hideya Mino, Isao Goto, Win Pa Pa, Nobushige Doi, Yusuke Oda, Anoop Kunchukuttan, Shantipriya Parida, Ondej Bojar, and Sadao Kurohashi. 2019. Overview of the 6th workshop on Asian translation. In *Proceedings of the 6th Workshop on Asian Translation*, Hong Kong. Association for Computational Linguistics.

Loganathan Ramasamy, Ondřej Bojar, and Zdeněk Žabokrtský. 2012. Morphological processing for english-tamil statistical machine translation. In *Proceedings of the Workshop on Machine Translation and Parsing in Indian Languages (MTPIL-2012)*, pages 113–122.

Ilya Sutskever, Oriol Vinyals, and Quoc V. Le. 2014. Sequence to sequence learning with neural networks. In *Proceedings of the 27th International Conference on Neural Information Processing Systems*, NIPS'14, pages 3104–3112, Cambridge, MA, USA. MIT Press.

Ashish Vaswani, Noam Shazeer, Niki Parmar, Jakob Uszkoreit, Llion Jones, Aidan N Gomez, Łukasz Kaiser, and Illia Polosukhin. 2017. Attention is all you need. In I. Guyon, U. V. Luxburg, S. Bengio, H. Wallach, R. Fergus, S. Vishwanathan, and R. Garnett, editors, *Advances in Neural Information Processing Systems 30*, pages 5998–6008. Curran Associates, Inc.

Barret Zoph, Deniz Yuret, Jonathan May, and Kevin Knight. 2016. Transfer learning for low-resource neural machine translation. In *Proceedings of the 2016 Conference on Empirical Methods in Natural Language Processing, EMNLP 2016, Austin, Texas, USA, November 1-4, 2016*, pages 1568–1575.

KNU-HYUNDAI's NMT system for Scientific Paper and Patent Tasks on WAT 2019

**Cheoneum Park[1], Young-Jun Jung[1], Kihoon Kim[1], Geonyeong Kim[1],
Jae-Won Jeon[1], Seongmin Lee[2], Junseok Kim[2] and Changki Lee[1]**
[1]Kangwon National University, South Korea
[2]EDITH TFT, HYUNDAI MORTOR COMPANY, South Korea
`{parkce, kongjun, rlarlgnsu, gyk, jwj, leeck}@kangwon.ac.kr`
`{blueworm7, junseok.kim}@hyundai.com`

Abstract

In this paper, we describe the neural machine translation (NMT) system submitted by the Kangwon National University and HYUNDAI (KNU-HYUNDAI) team to the translation tasks of the 6th workshop on Asian Translation (WAT 2019). We participated in all tasks of ASPEC and JPC2, which included those of Chinese-Japanese, English-Japanese, and Korean→Japanese. We submitted our transformer-based NMT system with built using the following methods: a) relative positioning method for pairwise relationships between the input elements, b) back-translation and multi-source translation for data augmentation, c) right-to-left (r2l)-reranking model robust against error propagation in autoregressive architectures such as decoders, and d) checkpoint ensemble models, which selected the top three models with the best validation bilingual evaluation understudy (BLEU) . We have reported the translation results on the two aforementioned tasks. We performed well in both the tasks and were ranked first in terms of the BLEU scores in all the JPC2 subtasks we participated in.

1 Introduction

Owing to several studies on neural networks, the field of machine translation has significantly developed. Numerous methods have been attempted for machine translation, ranging from a simple approach such as an encoder-decoder of two recurrent neural networks (RNN) (Bahdanau et al., 2014), and to a transformer model (Vaswani et al., 2017) comprising multiple layers with multi-head attention. Furthermore, with the development of open sources such as OpenNMT[1] (Klein et al., 2017), anyone with a parallel corpus can easily challenge neural machine translation (NMT).

---

[1]http://opennmt.net/

We herein describe the KNU-HYUNDAI's NMT system, which uses a transformer model based on OpenNMT. We participated in the ASPEC (Nakazawa et al., 2016) and JPC2 tasks of WAT 2019 (Nakazawa et al., 2019). The ASPEC task consisted of English-Japanese and Chinese-Japanese parallel corpus, and the JPC2 task consisted of English-Japanese, Chinese-Japanese, and Korean-Japanese parallel corpus.

To solve open vocabulary problems, we preprocessed all the data into subword units called byte-pair-encoding (BPE) (Sennrich et al., 2015b). We encoded the source and target languages as shared dictionaries. The encoded subwords are subsequently converted to an embedding with relative position representations (Shaw et al., 2018) and transmitted to a transformer.

We attempted three methods to use other resources. 1) Training by blending distinct parallel corpora of the same language pair. 2) Back-translation (Sennrich et al., 2015a) of the monolingual corpus added to the current train set. 3) Augmentation of the dataset according to multi-source translation (Zoph and Knight, 2016) that trains two different pairs of sources with the same target as a model. When translating, we re-ranked (Liu et al., 2016) the generated text by training model decoded by the backward (Right-to-Left) technique, and the model decoded by the forward (Left-to-Right) technique.

2 System Overview

2.1 Transformer

Our base system is based on the transformer architecture (Vaswani et al., 2017) implemented in OpenNMT (Klein et al., 2017). This transformer comprises multi-head attention and a feed-forward neural network (FFNN). The multi-head attention such as $Mhead(Q, K, V)$ calculates the attention

Proceedings of the 6th Workshop on Asian Translation, pages 81–89
Hong Kong, China, November 4, 2019. ©2019 Association for Computational Linguistics

scores for the Q, K, and V matrices with scaled dot-product attention for each head and concatenates the attentions for all heads, the equations for which are as follows:

$$Mhead(Q, K, V) = concat(head_1, ..., head_h)\mathbf{W}^o \tag{1}$$

$$head_i = Attn(Q\mathbf{W}_i^Q, K\mathbf{W}_i^K, V\mathbf{W}_i^V) \tag{2}$$

$$Attn(Q_i, K_i, V_i) = softmax(Q_i K_i^T / \sqrt{d_k})V_i \tag{3}$$

The multi-head attention used here resembles self-attention and calculates the attention score by capturing its own structural information. The encoder of the transformer has the same encoding for Q, K, and V, and the number of dimensions of the hidden state is split by h and multiplied by $\mathbf{W}_i^Q, \mathbf{W}_i^K, \mathbf{W}_i^V$, respectively. Attention scores of the inputs Q_i, K_i, V_i are calculated using scaled dot-product attention, and therefore, the calculated attention score is $head_i$. The concatenation of all $head_i$ multiplied by $\mathbf{W}^O$ yields the hidden states of the multi-head attention. Subsequently, the output of the transformer block is generated by performing $max(0, x\mathbf{W}_1 + \mathbf{b}_1)\mathbf{W}_2 + \mathbf{b}_2$ which is a position-wise FFNN.

The performance of the transformer decoder is similar to that of the encoder but produces one word at a time from left to right through masking. The decoder consists of three sublayers: the first sublayer is a masked multi-head self-attention that forces the attention to only the previous word. The second layer is multi-head attention, followed by the encoder-decoder attention. The final sublayer is a position-wise feed-forward layer. The transformer model uses residual connection (He et al., 2016) and layer normalization (Ba et al., 2016) around each of the sublayers.

2.2 Relative Position Representation

In contrast to recurrent and convolutional neural networks, the transformer does not explicitly model relative or absolute positions to its inputs. The transformer adds positional encoding to the embedding to consider the positional information of words. This type of encoding conducts sequence modeling by adding an absolute positional representation for the input word. For relative positional encoding (Shaw et al., 2018), a self-attention extension model is used to consider the pairwise relationships between the input elements. By modeling the input as a connected graph, the relative positional encoding represents the edges between the inputs x_i and x_j by the vectors α_{ij}^V, α_{ij}^K. The vectors represent information on the relative difference of position between the input elements. Relative position information is incorporated by adding the embedding vectors α_{ij}^V, α_{ij}^K that can be trained to the self-attention layer as in Equation (4-6).

$$\mathbf{z}_i = \sum_{j=1}^{n} \alpha_{i,j}(x_j \mathbf{W}^V + \alpha_{i,j}^V) \tag{4}$$

$$\alpha_{i,j} = \exp(e_{i,j})/\sum_{k=1}^{n} \exp(e_{i,k}) \tag{5}$$

$$e_{i,j} = x_i \mathbf{W}^Q (x_j \mathbf{W}^K + \alpha_{i,j}^K)^{\mathrm{T}}/\sqrt{d_z} \tag{6}$$

2.3 Data Augmentation

In deep learning, a large amount of data is needed to achieve superior performances, however, data annotation is expensive. Data augmentation can be used to enhance the model efficiency by automatically increasing the amount of training data. In natural language processing, data is augmented by the use of external resources or back-translation or text generation.

We herein use some of the data supplied by WAT 2019 (ASPEC, JPC2) for performing data augmentation by back-translation and multi-source translation, which are frequently used in NMT.

2.3.1 Back-translation

Back-translation (Sennrich et al., 2015a) is an effective and widely used data augmentation technique in NMT monolingual data integration. In view of the source and target languages, training is done in reverse and subsequently the model is used to translate the new corpus corresponding to the target language. The corpus used for translation and translated sentences form an auto-generated parallel corpus, and the translation model is retrained in addition to the original corpus. We performed back-translation using the parallel corpus provided in WAT.

2.3.2 Multi-source Translation for Augmentation

The multi-source translation (Zoph and Knight, 2016) is a method of training by giving various source languages as input to the same target language to improve the quality of NMT. We used the same target language and different source languages when training the transformer model. For example, if the translation is Zh→Ja, we add En→Ja and Ko→Ja dataset to train together. The symbols Zh, En, Ko, and Ja denote the words Chinese, English, Korean, and Japanese, respectively.

2.4 Right-to-Left Re-ranking

The decoder of the sequence-to-sequence model is an autoregressive architecture that uses previous predictions as contextual information. If the previous prediction is incorrect, the error will act as noise that will degrade the quality of the next prediction. To address this, Liu et al. (2016) proposed a Right-to-Left (r2l) model, which reranks the n-best hypothesis generated by the Left-to-Right (l2r) model to the r2l model. The formula for the r2l reranking model is as follows (Morishita et al., 2018):

$$P(\tilde{y}) = arg\,max_{y \in Y} P(y|x; \theta_{l2r}) P(y^r|x; \theta_{r2l}) \tag{7}$$

3 Experiments

Subtasks of WAT 2019 (Nakazawa et al., 2019) include Scientific paper using Asian Scientific Paper Excerpt Corpus (ASPEC) (Nakazawa et al., 2016) and Patent task using Japan Patent Office Patent Corpus 2.0 (JPC2). We participated in both tasks. ASPEC consists of English-Japanese (En-Ja) and Chinese-Japanese (Zh-Ja), and JPC2 consists of English-Japanese (En-Ja), Chinese-Japanese (Zh-Ja), Korean-Japanese (Ko-Ja).

3.1 Dataset

Dataset statistics for each of the subtasks are presented in Table 1. Because similarity scores sorted the ASPEC En-Ja dataset, we used up to 1,000,000 (1M) parallel sentences for the training dataset and 2M sentences for back-translation.

3.2 Tokenization

We used a BPE-based algorithm for subword segmentation. Using this algorithm, it is possible to represent a sentence as a subword sequence through as fixed-size vocabulary and to solve the

Task	Dataset	Train	Dev	Test
ASPEC	En-Ja	3,008,500	1,790	1,812
	Zh-Ja	672,315	2,090	2,107
JPC2	En-Ja	1,000,000	2,000	5,668
	Ko-Ja	1,000,000	2,000	5,230
	Zh-Ja	1,000,000	2,000	5,204

Table 1: Statistics of parallel sentences (sentence)

problem of unknown words and rare words effectively. SentencePiece used the BPE application. SentencePiece performs sentence normalization with NFKC-based text normalization. The normalized sentence, such as '°C' in the generated translation sentence, was therefore changed to '°C'. We used 32,000 shared vocabularies for each language dataset. Japanese sentences were segmented using Juman++[2] (Tolmachev et al., 2018; Kurohashi, 2018), and the tokenization of Chinese dataset was performed using the Stanford Word Segmenter[3] (Chang et al., 2008). The English sentences were tokenized using Moses[4] and the Korean sentences were morphologically analyzed using Mecab[5] (Sim, 2014; Matsumoto et al., 1999).

3.3 Experimental Setup

We used the OpenNMT transformer for our experiments. The early-stopping method from OpenNMT was specifically used. The training stopped when the model did not reach the new maximum accuracy for ten savepoints (saved every 5,000 steps) with a validation accuracy. We selected the validation model with the highest BLEU score. When we trained the Zh-Ja dataset, we chose the validation model with the highest BLEU score among all the validation models except for the early-stopping method in OpenNMT. We optimized the hyperparameters to six layers, word embedding size to 512, FFNN dimension size to 2048, number of attention heads to eight, number of training steps to 200,000, dropout to 0.1, batch size to 4096, accum to 2, and learning rate to 2. We used the same hyperparameters for all the models for training, and set the decoding beam size to 12 for En-Ja, Zh-Ja, and to 2 for Ko→Ja.

---

[2] https://github.com/ku-nlp/jumanpp
[3] https://nlp.stanford.edu/software/segmenter.shtml
[4] https://github.com/moses-smt/mosesdecoder/blob/master/scripts/tokenizer/tokenizer.perl
[5] https://bitbucket.org/eunjeon/mecab-ko-dic/src/master/

Sub-task	BLEU	B rank	H rank
ASPEC (En→Ja)	44.08	4 of 5	5 of 5
ASPEC (Ja→En)	30.88	2 of 4	2 of 4
JPC2 (En→Ja)	47.38	1 of 2	None
JPC2 (Ja→En)	44.72	1 of 2	None

Table 2: BLEU score for English-Japanese tasks on leaderboard

Method	En→Ja	Ja→En
Baseline	40.34	29.08
+ relative position	40.85	29.31
+ back-translation	42.26	29.93
+ checkpoint ensemble	43.21	30.23
+ independent ensemble	43.78	30.47
+ r2l re-ranking	**44.08**	**30.88**

Table 3: Method ablation for ASPEC En-Ja sub-task

3.4 Evaluations

We measure Bilingual Evaluation Understudy (BLEU) (Papineni et al., 2002), Rank-based Intuitive Bilingual Evaluation Score (RIBES) (Isozaki et al., 2010), Adequacy-fluency metrics (AM-FM) (Banchs et al., 2015) on leaderboard. BLEU is computed as the geometric mean of unigram, bigram, trigram, and 4-gram precision multiplied by a brevity penalty. RIBES, which provides a value in the range of [0; 1], was proposed to address the shortcomings of BLEU, in particular, the distant language pairs, where changes in word order deteriorates the effectiveness of BLEU. We also submitted a manual evaluation, such as Pairwise Crowdsourcing evaluation and JPO Adequacy evaluation, which was performed in case of more than three submissions.

3.5 Experimental Results

3.5.1 English-Japanese

Table 2 indicates the BLEU score and rank of the system we submitted in the ASPEC and JPC2 subtasks of WAT 2019. We obtained 44.08 and 30.88 BLEU scores, respectively, in the ASPEC En→Ja and Ja→En tasks and were ranked fourth amongst the five teams and second out of the four teams who submitted their BLEU scores (B rank). At this time, we were ranked fifth out of the five teams and second out of the four teams in the case of human evaluation (H rank in table 2). In the JPC2 En→Ja, Ja→En tasks, our system recorded 47.38 and 44.72 scores, respectively, and thus, we were ranked first about the bilingual dataset.

English-Japanese for ASPEC dataset: Table 3 shows the cumulative feature ablation for the En-Ja for the ASPEC dataset. We used only the upper part of the training dataset comprising 1M parallel sentences (train-1) to train the baseline model as a transformer base model. We applied relative positioning to the baseline model to improve the BLEU scores by 0.51 and 0.23 in the cases of

En→Ja and Ja→En, respectively. We used the remaining training dataset comprising 2M sentences for back-translation, and the synthetic data generated by back-translation was added to train-1 parallel data and subsequently used for training. We oversampled the train-1 parallel data and used the parallel and composite data in a 1:1 ratio. We used the ⟨BT⟩ tag for training at the beginning of the sentences for back-translation (Caswell et al., 2019). By applying back-translation, our system improved by 1.41 and 0.62 in terms of BLEU scores in En→Ja, Ja→En, respectively.

Next, we performed the checkpoint ensemble and independency ensemble methods. The former was performed for the top three models with the best validation BLEU scores among the checkpoints created in the first round of training. Similarly, the latter was also used for training the top three models with the best validation BLEU scores. The checkpoint ensemble method led to a performance improvement by 0.95 and 0.30 of the BLEU score, and the independent to 1.52 and 0.54 of the BLEU score. Finally, the r2l model reranked the 12 best output (beam size 12) of the left-to-right model by a right-to-left ensemble model (similar to the l2r ensemble method). The best performance of our model was a BLEU score of 44.08 in the En→Ja dataset and 30.88 in the Ja→En dataset.

English-Japanese for JPC2 dataset: Using only the training dataset having 1M parallel sentence for the JPC2 dataset, the baseline model was trained using a transformer base model from the OpenNMT. In table 4, we demonstrated the performance when external resources were not used for the JPC2 dataset (En→Ja (a)) and when ASPEC En-Ja dataset was used as an external resource (En→Ja (b), Ja→En). The En→Ja (b) and Ja→En models were trained by adding ASPEC train-1 for En-Ja to the existing trainset for JPC2. This method improved the score by 1.86 and 1.43

Method	En→Ja (a)	En→Ja (b)	Ja→En
baseline	42.67	42.67	41.25
+ ASPEC data	None	44.53	42.68
+ relative position	42.95	44.90	43.14
+ back-translation	45.84	46.33	43.59
+ checkpoint en-semble	46.32	46.82	43.94
+ r2l re-ranking	**47.19**	**47.38**	**44.72**

Table 4: Method ablation for JPC2 En-Ja sub-task

Sub-task	BLEU	BLEU rank
ASPEC (Zh→Ja)	51.92	2 of 2
ASPEC (Ja→Zh)	36.77	2 of 2
JPC2 (Zh→Ja)	51.33	1 of 3
JPC2 (Ja→Zh)	43.30	1 of 3

Table 5: BLEU score for Chinese-Japanese tasks on leaderboard

over the baseline. By applying relative positioning, En→Ja (a) score improved by 0.28 from the baseline, and the En→Ja (b), Ja→En were 0.37 and 0.46 higher than in the case of the ASPEC data addition method, respectively.

In En→Ja (a, b), the back-translation process used 2M single sentences of the Japanese dataset in the JPC2 Zh-Ja and Ko-Ja datasets. Ja→En used the remaining training dataset of 2M sentences from the ASPEC Ja-En dataset for back-translation. En→Ja (a) and Ja→En oversampled the JPC2 parallel data to ensure that the ratio of data added with the parallel data and back-translation was 1:1. We also inserted a back-translation tag ⟨BT⟩ at the beginning of the sentences during back-translation. As a result of adding back-translation data, the BLEU scores improvement of En→Ja (a) was 2.89, En→Ja (b) was 1.43, and Ja→En was 0.45 as compared to that of the previous case (+relative position). Additionally, we verified the performance of BLEU to be 45.36, which is 0.44 higher than the previous step (+relative position), and for multi-source application using Zh-Ja parallel data instead of the back-translation in En→Ja (b).

We performed the checkpoint ensemble method. This improved the BLEU score over 0.3 by selecting the top three models from validation. Finally, we reranked the 12-best outputs (beam size 12) of the l2r model to a r2l model using the checkpoint ensemble method to improve their respective BLEU scores by 0.87, 0.56, and 0.78.

3.5.2 Chinese-Japanese

In this paper, we experimented by combining ASPEC and JPC2 dataset methods for each subtask: (1) Using only ASPEC or JPC2 dataset, (2) Using both data together, (3) Using 1:1 ratio of data. We used fast align tool to match the rate of the datasets. As the number of sentences in JPC2 is one million, which is larger than the ASPEC dataset, 1:1 ratio of dataset experiment does not experiment in the Patent task. The baseline is the transformer model with only ASPEC or JPC2 dataset. In both Ja→Zh and Zh→Ja subtasks in the Patent task, the method of using both the dataset performances is better than using only one dataset.

Table 5 presents the results of BLEU for each Zh→Ja subtask of the method used in this paper. The system we used scored 51.92 and 36.77 BLEU in the Zh→Ja and Ja→Zh subtasks of the ASPEC data set, respectively. The Zh→Ja and Ja→Zh subtasks of the JPC2 dataset scored 51.33 and 43.30 BLEU, respectively, and therefore, we were first amongst the three teams.

Chinese→Japanese for ASPEC dataset: The baseline performance of the ASPEC Zh→Ja subtask is a 47.24 BLEU score, which is the highest among all the combination experiments. The baseline is 0.1 score higher than the experiment when both the datasets were used, and 0.18 score higher than the experiment in which the datasets were in the ration of 1:1.

Relative positioning method leads to an improvement of 0.49 BLEU score. We applied back-translation using 700K sentences of the ASPEC En-Ja dataset. The existing dataset was added one more time to adjust the ratio of the existing dataset and back translation dataset to 2:1. This led to an increase of 0.37 F1 BLEU score. A 0.95 increase in the method was observed when 1M sentences of ASPEC En-Ja dataset were used in the multi-source experiment. r2l re-ranking leads to a 0.52 performance improvement.

The performance of nine checkpoint ensemble models for the six different models is a 51.92 BLEU score. The difference between the highest performing model of this task is the 2.35 BLEU score. The number of sentence pairs used to train the final model of this task is 3,044,630.

Japanese→Chinese for ASPEC dataset: AS-

Method	BLEU
Baseline (ASPEC)	**47.24**
ASPEC + JPC2	47.14
ASPEC + JPC2 (1:1)	47.06
+ relative position	47.55
+ back-translation	47.92
+ multi-source	48.87
+ r2l re-ranking	**49.39**
Ensemble	**51.92**

Table 6: Method ablation for ASPEC Zh→Ja sub-task

Method	BLEU
Baseline (ASPEC)	34.93
ASPEC + JPC2	34.91
ASPEC + JPC2 (1:1)	**35.03**
+ relative position	35.23
+ back-translation	35.23
+ r2l re-ranking	**35.69**
Ensemble	**36.77**

Table 7: Method ablation for ASPEC Ja→Zh sub-task

Method	BLEU
Baseline (JPC2)	40.04
+ JPC2 + ASPEC	41.54
+ relative positio	41.80
+ back-translation	41.97
+ r2l re-ranking	**42.92**
Ensemble	**43.30**

Table 8: Method ablation for JPC2 Zh→Ja sub-task

PEC Ja→Zh subtask showed a 34.93 F1 BLEU score in an experiment using only ASPEC dataset (baseline). The experiment in which the ratio of ASPEC and JPC2 was adjusted to be 1:1 showed the highest score among all the data combination experiments. The BLEU F1 score for this experiment was 35.03, which is 0.12 higher than that using both the datasets.

Relative positioning yielded a 0.2 score improvement. We applied back-translation method using 670K ASPEC En-Ja dataset, but no performance improvement was seen. The r2l re-ranking method lead to a 0.46 score increase.

The final performance was at 36.77, which is the BLEU score of the ensemble model. The ensemble method ensembled the eight checkpoints for the four different models. This performance differs from the highest performing model of this task with a 0.82 BLEU score. The number of sentence pairs used to train the final model was 2,014,630.

Chinese→Japanese for JPC2 dataset: The JPC2 Zh→Ja subtask requires one million sentences of JPC2 data and 672,315 sentences of AS-PEC data to conduct further experiments. The JPC2 Zh→Ja subtask 1.23 BLEU scores higher than the Baseline score.

We applied relative positioning, back-translation, multi-sourcing, and r2l re-ranking to increase the BLEU score by 0.1, 0.63, 1.14, and 1.32, respectively. In this task, the back translation method combines JPC2 Ja→Zh data 1M sentences and JPC2 Ko-Ja also comprising 1M sentences to generate new Zh-Ja data. The 1M sentences of the JPC2 Ja-En dataset was used during the application of the multi-source method. The total number of sentence pairs used in the final model in this task is 4,672,315.

As the ensemble method creates a new shared dictionary for the application of the multi-source, the ensemble system is applied to the seven checkpoints of the five independent models up to the multi-source system.

Japanese→Chinese for JPC2 dataset: JPC2 Ja→Zh subtasks are further experimented based on the model trained by combining the one million JPC2 dataset and 672,315 ASPEC dataset. The method using both the datasets is 1.5 BLEU higher than the baseline using only JPC2.

We applied relative positioning, back-translation, and r2l re-ranking to increase the BLEU scores by 0.26, 0.17, and 0.95 , respectively. Back-translation uses the one million existing dataset to generate the Ja→Zh dataset.

The ensemble method of this task performs an ensemble experiment on nine checkpoints of the baseline model, the additional relative position model, the other r2l re-ranking model, and the transformer big model . The number of sentence pairs of training data in the final model is 2,672,315, and the BLEU score is 43.3. This score differs from the second and third place models submitted to WAT2019, respectively, with 1.3 and 2.13 BLEU scores, respectively.

3.5.3 Korean-Japanese

Table 10 shows the translation performance of JPC2 dataset for Korean and Japanese as JPC2 Ko-Ja. We applied the methods proposed in this paper.

Method	BLEU
Baseline (JPC2)	46.31
+ JPC2 + ASPEC	47.54
+ relative position	47.64
+ back-translation	48.27
+ multi-source	49.41
+ r2l re-ranking	**50.73**
Ensemble	**51.33**

Table 9: Method ablation for JPC2 Ja→Zh sub-task

Sub-task	BLEU	BLEU rank
JPC2 (Ko→Ja)	73.04	1 of 3

Table 10: BLEU score for Korean→Japanese sub-tasks on leaderboard

The Ko-Ja translation task has only a paten sub-task as JPC2, and we only participated in tasks for Korean to Japanese (Ko→Ja). The final submission performance was 73.04 for BLEU and ranked first among the three teams competing.

Korean→Japanese for JPC2 dataset: Similarly, we used the OpenNMT transformer as the baseline for the JPC2 Ko→Ja dataset, with a BLEU of 70.90. In table 11, we added the baseline to the relative position, and then methods performed a method ablation until R2L re-ranking. When the relative position was added to the transformer, the BLEU performance improved from 0.62 to 71.52. We performed back-translation with JPC2's Japanese datasets (2M sentences) of Zh-Ja and En-Ja and measured the transformer using a relative position model with a total of 3M sentences in addition to JPC2 Ko-Ja.

Unlike other sub-tasks, JPC2 Ko-Ja showed a 71.23 BLEU performance, which is less by 0.3 from the previous method of the transformer with relative position. For back-translation, we trained the JPC2 Ja→Ko dataset as a transformer model, which showed a BLEU score of 68.53. Unlike back-translation, the multi-source training method by adding JPC2 En-Ja and Zh-Ja datasets to JPC2 Ko→Ja dataset showed a performance of 0.9 lower than the BLEU score of 70.62. When R2L reranking was applied, the BLEU score was 70.34, which is 1.18 less compared to the case of the transformer when relative positioning was applied.

Accordingly, we performed an ensemble method based on the model using the best performing transformer models with relative

Method	BLEU
Baseline (JPC2)	70.90
+ relative position	**71.52**
+ back-translation	71.23
+ multi-source	70.62
+ r2l re-ranking	70.34
Ensemble	**73.04**

Table 11: Method ablation for JPC2 Ko→Ja sub-task

Sub-task	Adequacy
ASPEC (Ja→En)	4.51
ASPEC (Zh→Ja)	4.63
ASPEC (Ja→Zh)	4.36
JPC2 (En→Ja)	4.50
JPC2 (Ja→En)	4.78
JPC2 (Zh→Ja)	4.65
JPC2 (Ja→Zh)	4.55
JPC2 (Ko→Ja)	4.65

Table 12: Adequacy Evaluation of Our Model

positioning. We ensembled the eight checkpoints generated when we trained by setting the learning rate to two and three checkpoints created when we trained by setting the learning rate to three. As a result of the ensemble experiments, the best performance was achieved with a BLEU score of 73.04.

3.6 Adequacy Evaluation Summary

WAT 2019 (Nakazawa et al., 2019) showed the evaluation summary of top systems. Table 12 shows the adequacy performance for the sub-tasks we participated in. In terms of adequacy performance, ASPEC Ja→En showed the best adequacy performance of 4.51. ASPEC Zh→Ja scored 4.59 and Ja→Zh scored 4.36 adequacy evaluation. JPC2's En→Ja, Ja→En, Zh→Ja, Ja→Zh, and Ko→Ja all performed well with adequacy scores of 4.50, 4.78, 4.65, 4.55, 4.65, respectively.

4 Conclusion

We participated in the ASPEC and JPC2 translation tasks of WAT 2019. We utilized several methods of the NMT system. Relative positioning was applied based on OpenNMT's transformer model, and the data was added to construct a model robust to error and back-translation, and multi-source methods were applied to address error propagation in the decoder, an autoregressive architecture, and the performance was further improved by performing the ensemble methods. Consequently, we were amongst the top ranks in the ASPEC En-Ja and Zh-Ja tasks and were ranked first in the JPC2 En-Ja, Zh-Ja, and Ko→Ja sub-tasks.

Acknowledgments

This work was supported by AIR Lab (AI Research Lab) in the Hyundai Motor Company.

References

Jimmy Lei Ba, Jamie Ryan Kiros, and Geoffrey E Hinton. 2016. Layer normalization. *arXiv preprint arXiv:1607.06450*.

Dzmitry Bahdanau, Kyunghyun Cho, and Yoshua Bengio. 2014. Neural machine translation by jointly learning to align and translate. *arXiv preprint arXiv:1409.0473*.

Rafael E Banchs, Luis F D'Haro, and Haizhou Li. 2015. Adequacy–fluency metrics: Evaluating mt in the continuous space model framework. *IEEE/ACM Transactions on Audio, Speech, and Language Processing*, 23(3):472–482.

Isaac Caswell, Ciprian Chelba, and David Grangier. 2019. Tagged back-translation. *arXiv preprint arXiv:1906.06442*.

Pi-Chuan Chang, Michel Galley, and Christopher D Manning. 2008. Optimizing chinese word segmentation for machine translation performance. In *Proceedings of the third workshop on statistical machine translation*, pages 224–232. Association for Computational Linguistics.

Kaiming He, Xiangyu Zhang, Shaoqing Ren, and Jian Sun. 2016. Deep residual learning for image recognition. In *Proceedings of the IEEE conference on computer vision and pattern recognition*, pages 770–778.

Hideki Isozaki, Tsutomu Hirao, Kevin Duh, Katsuhito Sudoh, and Hajime Tsukada. 2010. Automatic evaluation of translation quality for distant language pairs. In *Proceedings of the 2010 Conference on Empirical Methods in Natural Language Processing*, pages 944–952. Association for Computational Linguistics.

Guillaume Klein, Yoon Kim, Yuntian Deng, Jean Senellart, and Alexander M Rush. 2017. Opennmt: Open-source toolkit for neural machine translation. *arXiv preprint arXiv:1701.02810*.

Arseny Tolmachev Sadao Kurohashi. 2018. Juman++ v2: A practical and modern morphological analyzer.

Lemao Liu, Masao Utiyama, Andrew Finch, and Eiichiro Sumita. 2016. Agreement on target-bidirectional neural machine translation. In *Proceedings of the 2016 Conference of the North American Chapter of the Association for Computational Linguistics: Human Language Technologies*, pages 411–416.

Yuji Matsumoto, Akira Kitauchi, Tatsuo Yamashita, Yoshitaka Hirano, Hiroshi Matsuda, Kazuma Takaoka, and Masayuki Asahara. 1999. Japanese morphological analysis system chasen version 2.0 manual. *NAIST Techinical Report*.

Makoto Morishita, Jun Suzuki, and Masaaki Nagata. 2018. Ntt's neural machine translation systems for wmt 2018. In *Proceedings of the Third Conference on Machine Translation: Shared Task Papers*, pages 461–466.

Toshiaki Nakazawa, Chenchen Ding, Raj Dabre, Hideya Mino, Isao Goto, Win Pa Pa, Nobushige Doi, Yusuke Oda, Anoop Kunchukuttan, Shantipriya Parida, Ondřej Bojar, and Sadao Kurohashi. 2019. Overview of the 6th workshop on Asian translation. In *Proceedings of the 6th Workshop on Asian Translation*, Hong Kong. Association for Computational Linguistics.

Toshiaki Nakazawa, Manabu Yaguchi, Kiyotaka Uchimoto, Masao Utiyama, Eiichiro Sumita, Sadao Kurohashi, and Hitoshi Isahara. 2016. Aspec: Asian scientific paper excerpt corpus. In *Proceedings of the Tenth International Conference on Language Resources and Evaluation (LREC 2016)*, pages 2204–2208.

Kishore Papineni, Salim Roukos, Todd Ward, and Wei-Jing Zhu. 2002. Bleu: a method for automatic evaluation of machine translation. In *Proceedings of the 40th annual meeting on association for computational linguistics*, pages 311–318. Association for Computational Linguistics.

Rico Sennrich, Barry Haddow, and Alexandra Birch. 2015a. Improving neural machine translation models with monolingual data. *arXiv preprint arXiv:1511.06709*.

Rico Sennrich, Barry Haddow, and Alexandra Birch. 2015b. Neural machine translation of rare words with subword units. *arXiv preprint arXiv:1508.07909*.

Peter Shaw, Jakob Uszkoreit, and Ashish Vaswani. 2018. Self-attention with relative position representations. *arXiv preprint arXiv:1803.02155*.

Yanchuan Sim. 2014. A morphological analyzer for japanese nouns, verbs and adjectives. *arXiv preprint arXiv:1410.0291*.

Arseny Tolmachev, Daisuke Kawahara, and Sadao Kurohashi. 2018. Juman++: A morphological analysis toolkit for scriptio continua. In *Proceedings of the 2018 Conference on Empirical Methods in Natural Language Processing: System Demonstrations*, pages 54–59.

Ashish Vaswani, Noam Shazeer, Niki Parmar, Jakob Uszkoreit, Llion Jones, Aidan N Gomez, Łukasz Kaiser, and Illia Polosukhin. 2017. Attention is all you need. In *Advances in neural information processing systems*, pages 5998–6008.

Barret Zoph and Kevin Knight. 2016. Multi-source neural translation. *arXiv preprint arXiv:1601.00710*.

English-Myanmar Supervised and Unsupervised NMT: NICT's Machine Translation Systems at WAT-2019

Rui Wang[1]*, Haipeng Sun[2,1]*, Kehai Chen[1],
Chenchen Ding[1], Masao Utiyama[1], and Eiichiro Sumita[1]
[1] National Institute of Information and Communications Technology (NICT)
3-5 Hikaridai, Seika-cho, Souraku-gun, Kyoto, 619-0289, Japan
[2] Harbin Institute of Technology, Harbin, China
{wangrui, sun.haipeng, khchen, chenchen.ding, mutiyama, eiichiro.sumita}@nict.go.jp

Abstract

This paper presents the NICT's participation (team ID: NICT) in the 6th Workshop on Asian Translation (WAT-2019) shared translation task, specifically Myanmar (Burmese) - English task in both translation directions. We built neural machine translation (NMT) systems for these tasks. Our NMT systems were trained with language model pretraining. Back-translation technology is adopted to NMT. Our NMT systems rank the third in English-to-Myanmar and the second in Myanmar-to-English according to BLEU score.

1 Introduction

This paper describes the neural machine translation (NMT) systems[1] built for National Institute of Information and Communications Technology (NICT)'s participation in the the 6th Workshop on Asian Translation (WAT-2019) translation task(Nakazawa et al., 2019), specifically Myanmar (My) - English (En) for both translation directions.

The remainder of this paper is organized as follows. In Section 2, we present the data preprocessing. In Section 3, we introduce the details of our NMT systems. Empirical results obtained with our systems are analyzed in Section 4 and we conclude this paper in Section 5.

2 Data Preprocessing

As parallel data to train our systems, we used all the provided parallel data for all our targeted

translation directions, including the training corpus "ALT" and "UCSY", and the "ALT" dev/test data. The statistics of our preprocessed parallel data are illustrated in Table 1.

Corpus	#lines	#tokens (My/En)
train(ALT)	17.9K	1.0M / 410.2K
train(UCSY)	208.6K	5.8M / 2.6M
dev(ALT)	0.9K	57.4K / 22.1K
test(ALT)	1.0K	58.3K / 22.7K

Table 1: Statistics of our preprocessed parallel data.

In WAT2019, two Myanmar monolingual corpora consist of Myanmar Wikipedia and Myanmar Common Crawl. For English monolingual corpus, we randomly extracted 10 million sentences from WMT monolingual News Crawl datasets.[2] The statistics of our preprocessed monolingual data are illustrated in Table 2.

Corpus	#lines	#tokens
My	6.7M	125.6M
En	10.0M	229.8M

Table 2: Statistics of our preprocessed monolingual data.

We used `Moses` tokenizer and truecaser for English. The truecaser was trained on the English data, after tokenization. For Myanmar, we used the original tokens. For cleaning, we only applied the `Moses` script `clean-n-corpus.perl` to remove lines in the parallel data containing more than 80 tokens and replaced characters forbidden by `Moses`.

---

* Rui and Haipeng have equal contribution to this paper. This work was conductd when Haipeng visited NICT as an internship student.

[1]This system is based on our WMT-2019 system (Marie et al., 2019).

[2]`http://data.statmt.org/news-crawl/`

Proceedings of the 6th Workshop on Asian Translation, pages 90–93
Hong Kong, China, November 4, 2019. ©2019 Association for Computational Linguistics

3   MT Systems

To build competitive NMT systems, we chose to rely on the Transformer architecture (Vaswani et al., 2017) since it has been shown to outperform, in quality and efficiency, the two other mainstream architectures for NMT known as deep recurrent neural network (deep-RNN) and convolutional neural network (CNN). We chose to rely on the Transformer-based NMT initialized by a pretrained cross-lingual language model (Lample and Conneau, 2019) to train our NMT systems since it had been shown to be efficient in the low-resource language pairs. In order to limit the size of the vocabulary of the NMT model, we segmented tokens in the training data into sub-word units via byte pair encoding (BPE) (Sennrich et al., 2016b). We determined 60k BPE operations jointly on the training data for English and Myanmar, and used a shared vocabulary for both languages with 60k tokens based on BPE.

3.1   TLM

Before training NMT, we used all training corpora including parallel data and monolingual data to train a translation language model (TLM) using XLM[3] in order to pretrain the NMT model on 8 GPUs[4]. The parameters for training the language model were set as listed in Table 3.

```
--lgs 'en-my' --mlm_steps
'en,my,en-my,my-en'
--emb_dim 1024 --n_layers
6 --n_heads 8 --dropout
0.1 --attention_dropout
0.1 --gelu_activation true
--batch_size 32 --bptt 256
--optimizer adam,lr=0.0001
```

Table 3:   Parameters for training TLM.

3.2   NMT

We trained a Transformer-based NMT model with the pre-trained TLM using XLM toolkit. Our NMT system was consistently trained on 8 GPUs, with the following parameters listed in Table 4.

We performed NMT decoding with a single model according to the best BLEU (Papineni et al., 2002) and the perplexity scores.

---

[3]https://github.com/facebookresearch/XLM
[4]NVIDIA @ Tesla @ V100 32Gb.

```
--lgs 'en-my' --encoder_only
false --emb_dim 1024 --n_layers
6 --n_heads 8 --dropout
0.1 --attention_dropout
0.1 --gelu_activation
true --tokens_per_batch
2000 --batch_size 32
--bptt 256 --optimizer
adam_inverse_sqrt,beta1=0.9,
beta2=0.98,lr=0.0001
--eval_bleu true
```

Table 4:   Parameters for training NMT.

3.3   Back-translation

We also tried back-translation method (Sennrich et al., 2016a) to make use of monolingual corpora for English-to-Myanmar translation task. Parallel data for training NMT can be augmented with synthetic parallel data, generated through back-translation, to significantly improve translation quality. For back-translation generation, we used an NMT system, trained on the parallel data provided by the organizers, to translate target monolingual sentences into the source language to generate pseudo parallel corpora. Then, the pseudo parallel corpora were simply mixed with the original parallel data to train from scratch a new source-to-target NMT system.

3.4   UNMT

To the best of our knowledge, unsupervised NMT (UNMT) (Artetxe et al., 2018; Lample et al., 2018a; Yang et al., 2018; Lample et al., 2018b; Sun et al., 2019; Lample and Conneau, 2019) has achieved remarkable results on some similar language pairs. To obtain a better picture of the feasibility of UNMT, we also set up a UNMT system for one truly low-resource and distant language pair: En-My. We tried to train a Transformer-based UNMT model that relies solely on monolingual corpora, with the pre-trained cross-lingual language model using XLM toolkit. Note that this cross-lingual language model was trained solely on monolingual corpora shown in Section 2.

We used these monolingual corpora to train the UNMT model for 50000 iterations. The En-My UNMT system was trained on 8 GPUs, with the parameters listed in Table 6.

Systems	ALT	UCSY	MONO	My-En	En-My
UNMT			✓	0.81	0.31
NMT	✓			8.06	10.50
NMT	✓	✓		14.97	14.15
NMT+TLM	✓	✓		18.42	16.12
NMT+TLM	✓	✓	✓	21.33	**19.73**
NMT+TLM+back-translation	✓	✓	✓	**29.89**	19.01

Table 5: Results (BLEU-cased) of our MT systems on the test set. ALT denotes that ALT training data was used in this system; UCSY denotes that UCSY training data was used in this system; MONO denotes monolingual training data was used in this system. +TLM denotes that language model pretraining was used in this system; +back-translation denotes that back-translation was used in this system.

```
--lgs 'en-my' --ae_steps
'en,my' --bt_steps
'en-my-en,my-en-my'
--word_shuffle 3
--word_dropout 0.1
--word_blank 0.1 --lambda_ae
'0:1,100000:0.1,300000:0'
--encoder_only false
--emb_dim 1024 --n_layers
6 --n_heads 8 --dropout
0.1 --attention_dropout
0.1 --gelu_activation
true --tokens_per_batch
2000 --batch_size 32
--bptt 256 --optimizer
adam_inverse_sqrt,beta1=0.9,
beta2=0.98,lr=0.0001
--eval_bleu true
```

Table 6: Parameters for training UNMT.

4 Results

Our systems are evaluated on the ALT test set and the results[5] are shown in Table 5. Our observations from are as follows:

1) The results of UNMT are very low, highlighting that UNMT is still very far from exploitable for low-resource distant language pairs.

2) Language model pretraining showed significant improvement in the NMT systems for both translation directions. This demonstrates that language model pretraining is effective for low-resource machine translation.

3) For My-En translation direction, back-translation could further improve translation performance, achieving 8 BLEU scores improvement. However, back-translation for En-My translation direction was unable to improve or even harm the NMT performance since the My monolingual data was noisy.

5 Conclusion

We presented in this paper the NICT's participation in the WAT-2019 shared translation task. Our primary NMT submissions to the task performed the third in English-to-Myanmar and the second in Myanmar-to-English according to BLEU score. Our results also confirmed the positive impact of language model pretraining in NMT. Moreover, our results for UNMT highlighted that unsupervised machine translation is still very far from exploitable for low-resource distant language pairs.

References

Mikel Artetxe, Gorka Labaka, Eneko Agirre, and Kyunghyun Cho. 2018. Unsupervised neural machine translation. In *ICLR*, Vancouver, Canada.

Guillaume Lample and Alexis Conneau. 2019. Cross-lingual language model pretraining. *CoRR*, abs/1901.07291.

Guillaume Lample, Alexis Conneau, Ludovic Denoyer, and Marc'Aurelio Ranzato. 2018a. Unsupervised machine translation using monolingual corpora only. In *ICLR*, Vancouver, Canada.

Guillaume Lample, Myle Ott, Alexis Conneau, Ludovic Denoyer, and Marc'Aurelio Ranzato. 2018b. Phrase-based & neural unsupervised machine translation. In *EMNLP*, pages 5039–5049, Brussels, Belgium.

---

[5]The results of BLEU are based on our own evaluation. For the official results, please refer to http://lotus.kuee.kyoto-u.ac.jp/WAT/evaluation/index.html.

Benjamin Marie, Haipeng Sun, Rui Wang, Kehai Chen, Atsushi Fujita, Masao Utiyama, and Eiichiro Sumita. 2019. NICT's unsupervised neural and statistical machine translation systems for the WMT19 news translation task. In *WMT*, pages 294–301, Florence, Italy.

Toshiaki Nakazawa, Chenchen Ding, Raj Dabre, Hideya Mino, Isao Goto, Win Pa Pa, Nobushige Doi, Yusuke Oda, Anoop Kunchukuttan, Shantipriya Parida, Ondej Bojar, and Sadao Kurohashi. 2019. Overview of the 6th workshop on Asian translation. In *Proceedings of the 6th Workshop on Asian Translation*, Hong Kong. Association for Computational Linguistics.

Kishore Papineni, Salim Roukos, Todd Ward, and Wei-Jing Zhu. 2002. Bleu: a method for automatic evaluation of machine translation. In *ACL*, pages 311–318, Philadelphia, Pennsylvania, USA.

Rico Sennrich, Barry Haddow, and Alexandra Birch. 2016a. Improving neural machine translation models with monolingual data. In *ACL*, pages 86–96, Berlin, Germany.

Rico Sennrich, Barry Haddow, and Alexandra Birch. 2016b. Neural machine translation of rare words with subword units. In *ACL*, pages 1715–1725, Berlin, Germany.

Haipeng Sun, Rui Wang, Kehai Chen, Masao Utiyama, Eiichiro Sumita, and Tiejun Zhao. 2019. Unsupervised bilingual word embedding agreement for unsupervised neural machine translation. In *ACL*, pages 1235–1245, Florence, Italy.

Ashish Vaswani, Noam Shazeer, Niki Parmar, Jakob Uszkoreit, Llion Jones, Aidan N Gomez, Ł ukasz Kaiser, and Illia Polosukhin. 2017. Attention is all you need. In *NIPS*, pages 5998–6008, Long Beach, CA, USA.

Zhen Yang, Wei Chen, Feng Wang, and Bo Xu. 2018. Unsupervised neural machine translation with weight sharing. In *ACL*, pages 46–55, Melbourne, Australia.

UCSMNLP: Statistical Machine Translation for WAT 2019

Aye Thida, Nway Nway Han, Sheinn Thawtar Oo, Khin Thet Htar
AI Research Lab, University of Computer Studies, Mandalay, Myanmar
ayethida, nwaynwayhan, sheinthawtaroo, khinthethtar@ucsm.edu.mm

Abstract

This paper represents UCSMNLP's submission to the WAT 2019 Translation Tasks focusing on the Myanmar-English translation. Phrase based statistical machine translation (PBSMT) system is built by using other resources: Name Entity Recognition (NER) corpus and bilingual dictionary which is created by Google Translate (GT). This system is also adopted with listwise reranking process in order to improve the quality of translation and tuning is done by changing initial distortion weight. The experimental results show that PBSMT using other resources with initial distortion weight (0.4) and listwise reranking function outperforms the baseline system.

1 Introduction

Machine translation system can be formally defined as the task of translating text given in one natural language to others automatically (Koehn, P., et al., 2003). In Natural Language Processing (NLP), machine translation system is one of the important tasks to communicate one language to another. Developing high quality machine translation systems has been special interest in NLP research area. Many different preprocessing and post-processing tasks have also been studied in order to get high quality. In this work, both tasks are performed by building lexicons and reranking the translations. And translation quality is also observed by changing initial distortion weight.

For the preprocessing task, NER corpus and Bilingual lexicon which support the translation tasks, are built by Standford NER tagger and Google Translate (GT). These two resources are used to combine and retrain with existing ALT corpus for translation task. For the post-processing tasks, reranking is performed with the combination of baseline pointwise reranking and listwise reranking which takes into account the similarity score of each translation to all other

translations included in n-best list. And the initial distortion weight that gives better translation result is analyzed by changing various initial distortion weights.

This paper describes phrase based statistical machine translation (PBSMT) by building bilingual lexicons, changing distortion weight and reranking for English-Myanmar translation in both directions. Section 2 describes system description. PBSMT is described in Section 3 followed by building bilingual lexicons in Section 4 and Section 5 describe experimental results. Finally, Section 6 will conclude this report.

2 System Description

This system is built phrase based statistical machine translation (PBSMT) system using other resources: Name Entity Recognition (NER) corpus and bilingual dictionary which is created by Google Translate (GT). These two resources are combined with existing ALT corpus which is used as the training data. This system is also adopted with listwise reranking process in order to improve the quality of translation and tuning is done by changing initial distortion weight.

2.1 Phrase Based Statistical Machine Translation (PBSMT)

A PBSMT translation model strives to produce the best possible translations based on probabilistic models analyzing phrase units, sequences of words, extracted from sentence aligned Myanmar-English parallel corpus. A phrase based translation model typically gives better performance than word-based translation model because one word in one language may not be one word in other languages (Koehn, P., et al., 2003). Changing the initial distortion weights for tuning process and reranking are the

Proceedings of the 6th Workshop on Asian Translation, pages 94–98
Hong Kong, China, November 4, 2019. ©2019 Association for Computational Linguistics

crucial processes to acquire the better translation result.

2.1.1 Distortion

Distortion is one of phrase based models used to justify the placement of words in different orders in the output translation. Before tuning process, initial distortion weight value is needed to assign. This system performs tuning process by changing the initial weight of distortion model from 0.1 to 0.6. Table 1 shows BLEU scores by changing various initial distortion weights in Myanmar-English bidirectional translations.

Data Set	Initial Distortion Weight	BLEU	
		my-en	en-my
ALT	0.1	6.96	24.16
ALT	0.2	6.93	23.86
ALT	0.3	7.02	24.13
ALT	**0.4**	**7.15**	**24.24**
ALT	0.5	7.04	24.22
ALT	0.6	7.02	24.05

Table 1: BLEU scores by changing initial distortion weight in Myanmar-English bidirectional translations.

According to the experiments, the BLEU score result by changing the initial distortion weight (0.4) is better than other initial distortion weights for both Myanmar-English directions. Therefore, we choose the initial distortion weight (0.4) for tuning to get the better translation results.

2.1.2 Reranking

Reranking aims to consider the entire list of best possible translations as a whole through the adoption of a listwise ranking function, which calculates the reranking score by asking each translation to report its similarity to all other translations (Zhang, M. et al., 2016). Reranking is the combination of pointwise and listwise reranking score. Pointwise score is calculated based on 14 baseline features such as 4 translation models, a language model , a word penalty, a phrase penalty and 7 reordering models.

The listwise reranking process contains the two main functions, tuning and similarity calculation. In the similarity calculation, the translation scores of candidates correspond to the current candidate is also considered to get higher similarity between translations. In this system, two evaluation metrics, Bilingual Evaluation UnderStudy (BLEU) (Papineni et al., 2002) and Metric for Evaluation of Translation with Explicit Ordering (METEOR) (Denkowski, M. and Lavie, A., 2014), are used as two feature functions for reranking to measure the similarity between translations in n-best list. And then the weights of these two feature functions are tuned on development set using z-mert tuning (Zaidan, O., 2009). This system chooses the 100 translation candidates (N=100) which impact on reranking model because of consideration of similarity between translations in n-best list.

2.2 Building Bilingual Resources

In machine translation, bilingual resources are essential language resources to get the influent translations. Moreover, the areas concerned with NER are also needed to be developed for translation tasks from Myanmar language to other languages.

2.2.1 Name Entity Recognition (NER) Corpus

This system uses Stanford NER tagger[1] to make the tagging process for every English token e (in the parallel data). If e has any tag in tagging process, this system extracts the translation of e by using the Myanmar ALT Treebank. In order to decide whether the two tokens are correctly translated in extracting NER corpus, we manually checked if the two tokens have translation of each other. Finally, we added the translation pairs to the bilingual NER corpus one at a time. The data statistics of NER corpus is shown in Table 2.

Corpus	Translation pairs
ALT	230,240
NER (Raw)	14313
NER (clear)	14310

Table 2: Data statistics of the NER corpus.

---

[1]https://nlp.stanford.edu/software/CRF-NER.html#Download

2.2.2 Bilingual Lexicon

For bi-directional translation tasks of Myanmar-English, the system built bilingual lexicon to retrain the data with existing corpus to get the fluent translations. This bilingual corpus is built by using Google Translate (GT)[2]. When building the bilingual lexicon, distinct English and Myanmar tokens from ALT my-en corpus is used as input words for GT to get Myanmar-English translation pairs and then add these translations pairs to the bilingual lexicon. The data statistics of Bilingual lexicon is shown in Table 3.

Bilingual Lexicon	Translation pairs
English	54674
Myanmar	35532
Total	90206

Table 3: Data statistics of the Bilingual Lexicon.

3 Experiments

To evaluate the translation quality of baseline PBSMT and PBSMT with reranking, our analysis looked through the translation tasks of ALT corpus by adding bilingual lexicons. All experiments are trained on Dell PowerEdge R720.

3.1 Corpus Statistics

This system used ALT corpus for Myanmar-English translation tasks at WAT 2019. The

Data Set				#sentences
TRAIN	**ALT**	**NER**	**Bilingual**	112570
	18088	14310	80172	
DEV				1000
TEST				1018

Table 4: Statistics of data sets.

ALT corpus is one part from the Asian Language Treebank (ALT) Project, consists of twenty thousand Myanmar-English parallel sentences from news articles. In this experiment, the

---

[2] https://github.com/ssut/py-googletrans

training data was the combination of ALT corpus and two new resources, NER corpus and bilingual lexicon, which are built using ALT TreeBank, Standford NER tagger and Google Translate (GT).

3.2 Moses SMT system

We used the PBSMT system provided by the Moses toolkit (Philipp and Haddow, 2009) for training PBSMT statistical machine translation systems. The 5-grams language model was trained by KENLM (Heafield, 2011) with modified Knerser-Ney discounting (smoothing). The alignment process is implemented using GIZA++ (Och, F.J. and Ney, H., 2000). This system used grow-diag-final-and heuristic for symmetrized alignment and msd-bidirectional-fe (Koehn et al., 2003) option for the lexicalized reordering model was trained with. Although the sentences in test data are long, this system used (default 6) distortion limit in Moses. To tweak the parameters of decoding, Minimum Error Rate Training (MERT) (Och, F.J., 2003) is used by changing various initial distortion weights. Reranking is performed based on 100 (default) best possible target translations generated by Moses decoder.

4 Results and Discussion

This system reports the translation quality of those methods in terms of Bilingual Evaluation Understudy (BLEU), Rank-based Intuitive Bilingual Evaluation Measure (RIBIES) (Isozaki et al., 2010) and Adequacy-Fluency Metrics (AMFM) (Banchs et al., 2015) in Table. 5.

In our experiments, firstly the initial distortion weights are changed from 0.1 to 0.6 as shown in Table 1, we found that the translation result did not improve significantly compared with baseline. Second, we analyze with new reranking method (listwise) which is combined with pointwise. The translation quality is not good enough. Finally, two bilingual lexicons are added to the existing parallel data to reuse as the training data. In PBSMT without reranking model, the translation result is significantly improved from 7.15 to 10.70 in Myanmar-English and 24.24 to 28.20 in English to Myanmar translation. On the other hand, from Myanmar to English translation, the PBSMT with reranking is better than baseline PBSMT in

Source-Target	BLEU			RIBIES			AMFM		
	PBSMT	PBSMT (Without Reranking)	PBSMT (Reranking)	PBSMT	PBSMT (Without Reranking)	PBSMT (Reranking)	PBSMT	PBSMT (Without Reranking)	PBSMT (Reranking)
en-my	24.24	28.20	-	58.15	59.68	-	61.67	69.34	-
my-en	7.15	10.70	10.84	53.29	57.08	57.11	53.01	53.82	54.04

Table 5: BLEU, RIBES and AMFM scores for PBSMT, PBSMT with reranking.

Source	ပြည်ထဲရေး ဝန်ကြီး ဌာန နှင့် ထောက်လှမ်း ရေး အဖွဲ့အစည်း ၏ တာဝန် ရှိ သူ များ က သူမ ဆီသို့ ကောင်လေး ကို ပေး ခဲ့ ပြီးနောက် ဒေါက်တာ ဖာဇိယ က သတင်းထောက် များ ကို ပြောကြား ခဲ့ သည် ။
Reference	Dr. Fauzia told journalists after the boy had been given to her by officials of the interior ministry and intelligence agencies .
Baseline	Interior Ministry and intelligence officials of her towards the boy after the Dr. ဖာဇိယ told reporters .
Baseline with Reranking	Interior Ministry and Intelligence of officials said she was given to the boy after the Dr. ဖာဇိယ told reporters .
Baseline+NER+GT	Interior Ministry and intelligence agency in charge of the boy to her after Dr. **Fauzia** told reporters .
Baseline+NER+GT with Reranking	Interior Ministry and intelligence **agency 's** officials to her **after the boy** Dr. **Fauzia** told reporters .

Table 6: Comparison between my-en translation results.

terms of BLEU (7.15 to 10.84), RIBES (53.29 to 57.11) and AMFM (53.01 to 54.04) scores.

In table 6, the comparison between translation results of my-en is described. In this table, "Source" and "Reference" sentences are shown in the first two rows. The translation of "baseline" and the translation of baseline with reranking cannot translate the name "ဖာဇိယ". After using NER and GT, this name can translate as "**Fauzia**". The translation result is a slightly smooth after reranking. The result "agency in charge of the boy to her" to "agency 's officials to her" and "the boy to her after" has been changed to "after the boy". Even though the translation result is not definitely perfect, using resources with reranking can change to better translation is one of the worthy evidences.

According to our experiments, using resources with PBSMT model get better translation result significantly. Even though the translation result is better than the baseline, the current resources that we used in this system is not still covered for fluent translation, we need to extend the current resources and build new resources in future.

5   Conclusion

In this paper, we have described our submissions to WAT 2019. To improve the translation result, two bilingual resources were added to the training data and the result of our system was comparable to baseline PBSMT model. The reranking result of my-en is better than baseline system, however, our team can not submit PBSMT with reranking results of en-my because of time constraint. This is the initial learning of PBSMT model and still need to explore with other models to get the adequate and fulfilled translation results. In future, we would like to extend the existing Myanmar resources and investigate the better models for Myanmar to other language machine translation system.

References

Banchs, R.E., D'Haro, L.F. and Li, H., 2015. Adequacyfluency metrics: Evaluating MT in the continuous space model framework. *IEEE/ACM Transactions on Audio, Speech and Language Processing (TASLP), 23(3), pp.472-482.*

Chen, S.F. and Goodman, J., 1999. An empirical study of smoothing techniques for language modeling. *Computer Speech & Language, 13(4), pp.359-394.*

Cherry, C. and Foster, G., 2012, June. Batch tuning strategies for statistical machine translation. *In Proceedings of the 2012 Conference of the North*

American Chapter of the Association for Computational Linguistics: Human Language Technologies (pp. 427-436). Association for Computational Linguistics.

Denkowski, M. and Lavie, A., 2014, June. Meteor universal: Language specific translation evaluation for any target language. In *Proceedings of the ninth workshop on statistical machine translation* (pp. 376-380).

Finkel, J.R., Grenager, T. and Manning, C., 2005, June. Incorporating non-local information into information extraction systems by gibbs sampling. *In Proceedings of the 43rd annual meeting on association for computational linguistics 2005 Jun 25 (pp. 363-370). Association for Computational Linguistics.*

Gao, Q. and Vogel, S., 2008, June. Parallel implementations of word alignment tool. *In Software engineering, testing, and quality assurance for natural language processing (pp. 49-57). Association for Computational Linguistics.*

Heafield, K., 2011, July. KenLM : Faster and smaller language model queries. *In Proceedings of the Sixth Workshop on Statistical Machine Translation (pp. 187-197) . Association for Computational Linguistics.*

Heafield, K., Pouzyrevsky , I., Clark, J.H and Koehn, P., 2013. Scalable modified Kneser-Ney language model estimation. *In Proceedings of the 51st Annual Meeting of the Association for Computational Linguistic (Volume 2: Short Papers) (Vol. 2, pp. 690-696).*

Isozaki, H., Hirao, T., Duh, K., Sudoh, K. and Tsukada, H., 2010, October. Automatic evaluation of translation quality for distant language pairs. *In Proceedings of the 2010 Conference on Empirical Methods in Natural Language Processing (pp. 944952). Association for Computational Linguistics.*

Koehn, P. and Haddow, B., 2009, March. Edinburgh's submission to all tracks of the WMT2009 shared task with reordering and speed improvements to Moses. *In Proceedings of the Fourth Workshop on Statistical Machine Translation (pp. 160-164). Association for Computational Linguistics.*

Koehn, P., Hoang, H., Birch, A., Callison-Burch, C., Federico, M., Bertoldi, N., Cowan, B., Shen, W., Moran, C., Zens, R. and Dyer, C., 2007, June. Moses: Open source toolkit for statistical machine translation. In *Proceedings of the 45th annual meeting of the association for computational linguistics companion volume proceedings of the demo and poster sessions* (pp. 177-180).

Koehn, P., Och, F.J. and Marcu, D., 2003, May. Statistical phrase-based translation. *In Proceedings of the 2003 Conference of the North American Chapter of the Association for Computational Linguistics on Human Language Technology-*

Volume 1 (pp. 48-54). *Association for Computational Linguistics.*

Och, F.J. and Ney, H., 2000, October. Improved statistical alignment models. *In Proceedings of the 38th Annual Meeting on Association for Computational Linguistics (pp. 440-447). Association for Computational Linguistics.*

Och, F.J., 2003, July. Minimum error rate training in statistical machine translation. In *Proceedings of the 41st Annual Meeting on Association for Computational Linguistics-Volume 1 (pp. 160-167). Association for Computational Linguistics.*

Papineni, K., Roukos, S., Ward, T. and Zhu, W.J., 2002, July. BLEU: a method for automatic evaluation of machine translation. In *Proceedings of the 40th annual meeting on association for computational linguistics (pp. 311-318). Association for Computational Linguistics.*

Thida, A., Han, N.N. and Oo, S.T., 2018. Statistical Machine Translation Using 5-grams Word Segmentation in Decoding. In *Proceedings of the 32nd Pacific Asia Conference on Language, Information and Computation: 5th Workshop on Asian Translation: 5th Workshop on Asian Translation.*

Thu, Y.K., Pa, W.P., Sagisaka, Y. and Iwahashi, N., 2016. Comparison of grapheme-to-phoneme conversion methods on a myanmar pronunciation dictionary. *In Proceedings of the 6th Workshop on South and Southeast Asian Natural Language Processing (WSSANLP2016) (pp. 11-22).*

Tillmann, C., 2004, May. A unigram orientation model for statistical machine translation. *In Proceedings of HLT-NAACL 2004: Short Papers (pp. 101-104). Association for Computational Linguistics.*

Vilar, D., Leusch, G., Ney, H. and Banchs, R.E., 2007, June. Human evaluation of machine translation through binary system comparisons. *In Proceedings of the Second Workshop on Statistical Machine Translation (pp. 96-103). Association for Computational Linguistics.*

Zaidan, O., 2009. Z-MERT: A fully configurable open source tool for minimum error rate training of machine translation systems. *The Prague Bulletin of Mathematical Linguistics, 91*, pp.79-88.

Zhang, M., Liu, Y., Luan, H. and Sun, M., 2016. Listwise ranking functions for statistical machine translation. *IEEE/ACM Transactions on Audio, Speech and Language Processing (TASLP), 24*(8), pp.1464-1472.

NTT Neural Machine Translation Systems at WAT 2019

Makoto Morishita*, Jun Suzuki* and **Masaaki Nagata**
NTT Communication Science Laboratories, NTT Corporation
2-4 Hikaridai, Seika-cho, Soraku-gun, Kyoto, 619-0237, Japan
{makoto.morishita.gr, masaaki.nagata.et}@hco.ntt.co.jp
jun.suzuki@ecei.tohoku.ac.jp

Abstract

In this paper, we describe our systems that were submitted to the translation shared tasks at WAT 2019. This year, we participated in two distinct types of subtasks, a scientific paper subtask and a timely disclosure subtask, where we only considered English-to-Japanese and Japanese-to-English translation directions. We submitted two systems (En-Ja and Ja-En) for the scientific paper subtask and two systems (Ja-En, texts, items) for the timely disclosure subtask. Three of our four systems obtained the best human evaluation performances. We also confirmed that our new additional web-crawled parallel corpus improves the performance in unconstrained settings.

1 Introduction

We participated in a scientific paper subtask and a timely disclosure subtask at this year's shared translation tasks at WAT 2019 (Nakazawa et al., 2019). Since we only considered English-to-Japanese (**En-Ja**) and Japanese-to-English (**Ja-En**) translation directions, we submitted En-Ja and Ja-En systems for the scientific paper subtask and two Ja-En systems (texts, items) for the timely disclosure subtask. The base NMT model architecture that we employed is a widely used Transformer model, but we tried to explore a better set of hyper-parameters, leading to significant improvement. Three of our submissions were honored as the best human evaluation performances. As our new trial, we evaluated the usefulness of incorporating external data automatically collected from a wide variety of web pages to further improve the translation quality.

We independently developed two distinct systems for each subtask. Therefore, this paper separately explains the details; we first explain the systems developed for the scientific paper subtask in

Section 2. Then we describe the system developed for the timely disclosure subtask in Section 3.

Table 1: Numbers of sentences in ASPEC corpus

Set	# Sentences
Train	3,008,500
(bitext)	(1,500,000)
(synthetic)	(1,508,500)
Dev	1,790
Devtest	1,784
Test	1,812

2 Systems for Scientific Paper Subtask

2.1 Task Overview

For the scientific paper task, we participated in two translation directions: Japanese-to-English (Ja–En) and English-to-Japanese (En–Ja). We submitted two systems per direction in two different training settings: constrained and unconstrained settings.

2.2 Data and Data Preparation

2.2.1 Provided data: constrained setting

As training/dev/test data, the task organizer provided the Asian Scientific Paper Excerpt Corpus (ASPEC) (Nakazawa et al., 2016) whose statistics are shown in Table 1.

ASPEC was created by automatically aligning parallel documents and sentences, and the training sentences are ordered by sentence alignment scores. Thus, the previous participants generally removed the latter sentences (Neubig, 2014) or used them as synthetic data (Morishita et al., 2017). This year, we used the former 1.5M training sentences as bitext data and the latter 1.5M as monolingual data and created synthetic data (Sennrich et al., 2016).

*Equal contribution.

Proceedings of the 6th Workshop on Asian Translation, pages 99–105
Hong Kong, China, November 4, 2019. ©2019 Association for Computational Linguistics

2.2.2 JParaCrawl: unconstrained setting

The ParaCrawl[1] project is building parallel corpora by largely crawling the web. Their objective is to build parallel corpora for the 24 official languages of the European Union. They already released earlier versions of the corpora and they were used on the WMT 2018 news shared translation tasks (Bojar et al., 2018). The WMT shared task participants reported that this corpora boosted translation accuracy when used with careful corpus cleaning (Junczys-Dowmunt, 2018; Morishita et al., 2018).

Inspired by these previous works, we constructed a web-based Japanese-English parallel corpus. We followed almost the same procedure as ParaCrawl to make this corpus. First, we listed 100,000 candidate domains that might contain parallel Japanese and English sentences by analyzing the whole Common Crawl text data[2] on how each domain contains Japanese or English data with `extractor`[3].

We crawled the listed candidate domains and aligned parallel sentences using `bitextor`[4]. Then we filtered out noisy sentences with `bicleaner`[5] (Sánchez-Cartagena et al., 2018). After corpus cleaning, we retained 7.5M sentences.

We named this corpus "JParaCrawl" and we plan to release it publicly with a detailed corpus description paper.

2.2.3 Data Preprocessing

This year, we decided not to employ any external morphological analyzer like KyTea (Neubig et al., 2011). Instead we utilized `sentencepiece`[6] (Kudo and Richardson, 2018), which tokenizes a sentence into a sequence of subwords without requiring any other tokenizers. Note here that we did not apply any filtering method, such as sentence length filtering.

2.3 System Details

We selected the Transformer model (Vaswani et al., 2017) as our base NMT model. We also incorporated two techniques to further improve the performance: (1) model ensembling and (2) Right-to-Left (R2L) re-ranking.

2.3.1 Ensembling

We independently trained four models with different random seeds and simultaneously utilized them for model ensembling to boost the translation performance.

2.3.2 Right-to-left (R2L) re-ranking

The NMT model has auto-regressive architecture in its decoder that uses previously generated tokens for predicting the next token. In other words, we normally decode a sentence from the beginning-of-the-sentence (BOS), which is its left side, to the end-of-the-sentence (EOS), which is on the right. Here we call this normal decoding process as Left-to-Right (L2R) decoding. However, Liu et al. (2016) pointed out that L2R decoding lacks reliability near the EOS tokens because if the previous tokens contain errors, the next prediction might have error as well. To alleviate this problem, Liu et al. (2016) proposed a method that generates the n-best hypotheses with the L2R model and re-ranks them with the R2L model, which decodes the sentences from the EOS tokens to the BOS tokens. By R2L re-ranking, we can exploit both the advantages of the L2R and R2L models and improve their performance.

2.3.3 Model incorporation with JParaCrawl

The JParaCrawl domain basically differs from the scientific paper task. To effectively incorporate with the JParaCrawl, we first pre-trained the model with the mixed data of ASPEC and JParaCrawl.[7] Then we fine-tuned the pre-trained model using only ASPEC.

2.4 Hyper-parameter

As a base NMT model, we selected the Transformer model with the "big" hyper-parameter setting. During training, we used mixed-precision training (Micikevicius et al., 2018) that can boost the training speed and reduce the memory consumption. We saved the model each epoch and used the average of the last ten models for decoding. We set the beam size to six and normalized the scores by their length. All implementations are based on `fairseq` toolkit (Ott et al., 2019). Table 2 shows the selected set of the

---

[1] `http://paracrawl.eu/`
[2] `https://commoncrawl.org/`
[3] `https://github.com/paracrawl/extractor`
[4] `https://github.com/bitextor/bitextor`
[5] `https://github.com/bitextor/bicleaner`
[6] `https://github.com/google/sentencepiece`

[7] We mixed ASPEC and JParaCrawl by upsampling ASPEC twice.

Hyper-parameter	Selected Value
Subword (vocabulary) size	src:4000, trg:4000
Gradient clipping	1.0
Dropout rate	0.3
Mini-batch size	4K tokens
Update frequency	128 batches
Beam search (n-best)	6 best

Table 2: Hyper-parameters for the scientific paper task: Our basic hyper-parameters are identical to Transformer "big" setting.

Subword size	En-Ja	Ja-En
w/o synthetic data	44.2	29.9
Back-translation	**45.6**	29.5
Forward-translation	–	**30.1**

Table 3: Comparison of translation performance on changing subword size. Scores here were calculated by `sacreBLEU`.

Subword size	En-Ja	Ja-En
4000	**45.6**	**30.1**
8000	45.3	29.9
16000	45.2	29.6
32000	45.0	29.7

Table 4: Comparison of translation performance on changing the methods of building synthetic data. Scores here were calculated by `sacreBLEU`.

Mini-batch size	En-Ja	Ja-En
16 × 4,000 tokens	45.1	29.7
32 × 4,000 tokens	45.3	29.9
64 × 4,000 tokens	45.4	29.8
128 × 4,000 tokens	**45.6**	**30.1**
256 × 4,000 tokens	45.4	29.9

Table 5: Comparison of translation performance on changing mini-batch size (update frequency) for each update in NMT training. Scores here were calculated by `sacreBLEU`.

hyper-parameters we used for the final submission. In our preliminary experiments, we evaluated extensive combinations of hyper-parameters and we found that this setting was optimal in our hyper-parameter search. Hereafter, the reported performance in the rest of this paper was obtained using this setting unless otherwise specified.

2.4.1 Back- and forward-translation for building synthetic data

We first investigated the effectiveness of incorporating synthetic data generated by the back-translation technique. Table 3 shows the results. We significantly improved the performance of the En-Ja translation setting by adding the synthetic data. However surprisingly, the performance was significantly degraded (29.9 → 29.5) in the Ja-En translation setting. We observed that the quality of the English sentences in the latter half of the provided data looks somewhat awful (not very well). Therefore, we then tried to make synthetic data by using forward-translation instead of the standard back-translation. This means that we used the synthetic data for the En-Ja translation setting as the synthetic data of the Ja-En translation setting. This slightly improved the performance of the Ja-En translation setting.

2.4.2 Subword size/Vocabulary size

Table 4 shows the BLEU scores when we changed the number of subwords obtained from `sentencepiece`. Note that we evaluated the

performance using `sacreBLEU` (Post, 2018) for all the results shown in this section.

We clearly observe a tendency that the fewer subwords got better performance. This observation is actually a bit surprising since many recent previous studies in the NMT community often employed a larger amount of subwords like 16,000 or 32,000.

2.4.3 Mini-batch size/Update frequency

According to a previously introduced finding, Transformer models tend to provide better results with a larger mini-batch size (Ott et al., 2018). Based on this observation, we explored the effectiveness of the mini-batch size in our setting.

Table 5 shows the results. We found that an overly large mini-batch, i.e., 512, degraded the performance. In our experiments, an update frequency of 128, which means $128 \times 4,000 = 512,000$ tokens per mini-batch, was an appropriate value.

2.4.4 Ensemble and R2L re-ranking

Ensembling and re-ranking are currently the standard techniques for further improving the translation quality in the NMT models. Following this public knowledge, we also applied standard ensembling and right-to-left (R2L) re-ranking techniques to our models.

Table 6 shows the effectiveness of these techniques. Ensembling and R2L re-ranking offered

Model type	En-Ja	Ja-En
Single model (equivalent to 1)	45.6	30.1
Ensemble (4)	46.2	30.8
Ensemble (4) + R2L (4)	46.8	**31.2**
Ensemble (6) + R2L (4)	**46.9**	**31.2**

Table 6: Results of incorporating ensembling and R2L re-ranking techniques. The numbers in brackets shows the number of models for ensembling, e.g., (4) masn four model ensembling. Scores here were calculated by `sacreBLEU`.

Data	En-Ja	Ja-En
Ensemble (4) + R2L (4)		
(ASPEC only)	46.8	31.2
(ASPEC+JParaCrawl)	**47.4**	**31.6**

Table 7: Translation performance comparison when we incorporate additional training data JParaCrawl. Scores here were calculated by `sacreBLEU`.

significant improvements.

2.4.5 Unconstrained setting

Table 7 shows the "Ensemble (4) + R2L (4)" results that were trained by ASPEC or AS-PEC+JParaCrawl.

Incorporating JParaCrawl consistently and significantly improved performance . This fact indicates that using more data improves better performance; even the additional data (JParaCrawl) domain slightly differs from the target domain.

2.5 Official Result

We first planned to submit the *unconstrained setting* results (the second row in Table 7) as our primary results. Unfortunately, we failed to finish training for all the models (four L2R and four R2L models) by the submission deadline. Therefore, we submitted the *constrained setting* results (the first row in Table 7) as our primary results.

Table 8 shows the official results of our submissions computed in the evaluation server. Our system achieved the best BLEU score for the En-Ja subtask, but slightly lower than the best system for the Ja-En subtask. For pairwise crowd-sourcing evaluations, our system successfully obtained the best assessments for both the En-Ja and Ja-En subtasks. Our system also achieved the best performance in terms of adequacy for the En-Ja subtask. Although our Ja-En system ranked second, the gap between both systems is quite small (0.02).

2.6 Post-evaluation

As described in the previous section, since we could not finish training the unconstrained setting by the submission deadline, we evaluated the results of the unconstrained setting in the evaluation server as a post-evaluation. Table 9 shows the results. We further improved the official best scores for both the En-Ja and Ja-En subtasks: +0.74 for En-Ja and +0.67 for Ja-En.

3 Systems for Timely Disclosure Subtask

3.1 Task Overview

The new timely disclosure task focuses on translating Japanese company's announcements for investors into English. It is challenging because the documents contain many figures and proper nouns that are critical but difficult to translate.

The provided corpus sizes are shown in Table 10. This task has two sub-tasks: *texts* and *items*. The *texts* task contains the sentences whose Japanese side ends with ". " (Japanese period), and the *items* includes subjects, table titles, and bullet points.

Note that the data provider releases a detailed corpus description[8] that includes the corpus characteristics, the text normalization rules, and how they separate the data into *texts* and *items*. This description was quite useful when we tackled the task.

3.2 System Details

Our submission includes three features: (1) task-specific fine-tuning, (2) right-to-left re-ranking, and (3) model ensembles.

As mentioned in Section 3.1, this task has been separated into two categories: *texts* and *items*. Although the provided training data were not split, we easily separated them into sub-categories by just checking whether the Japanese sentence ends with ". " or not. To achieve the best performance, we first pre-trained the model with all of the provided training data and fine-tuned it with the specific parts of the training data. We also use the ensembling and R2L re-ranking techniques, as described in Sections 2.3.1 and 2.3.2. During the R2L re-ranking, we ensembled the R2L models in addition to the L2R models for better performance.

---

[8]`http://lotus.kuee.kyoto-u.ac.jp/`
`WAT/Timely_Disclosure_Documents_Corpus/`
`specifications_en.html`

| Lang. | Auto Eval | | Human Eval | | |
pair	BLEU	(Rank)	Pairwise	(Rank)	Adequacy	(Rank)
En-Ja	45.83	(1)	47.75	(1)	4.50	(1)
Ja-En	30.56	(5)	14.00	(1)	4.49	(2)

Table 8: Official results of our submitted systems for ASPEC subtask: For En-Ja direction, we show BLEU scores with JUMAN tokenizer.

Training data	En-Ja	Ja-En
ASPEC	45.83	30.56
ASPEC+JParaCrawl	**46.57**	**31.23**

Table 9: Performance comparison when we incorporate additional training data JParaCrawl: Scores here were obtained from evaluation server.

Set	Category	# Sentences
Train	texts	448,472
	items	955,523
Dev	texts	1,153
	items	2,845
Devtest	texts	1,114
	items	2,900
Test	texts	1,148
	items	2,129

Table 10: Number of sentences in timely disclosure document corpus: We split training set into two categories. See Section 3.2 for details.

3.3 Experimental Settings

For preprocessing, we only relied on `sentencepiece` (Kudo and Richardson, 2018), which tokenizes a sentence into subwords without requiring any other tokenizers. We set the vocabulary size to 32k[9]. The provided training data were split by their released years, but we concatenated them without distinguishing them.

As an NMT model, we used the Transformer (Vaswani et al., 2017) with big hyper-parameter settings and dropout (Srivastava et al., 2014) with a probability of 0.3. We trained the model with eight RTX 2080 Ti GPUs and set a batch size of 2,500 tokens. We accumulated 128 mini-batches per update (Ott et al., 2018), resulting in a per-update batch size around $128 \times 2,500 = 320,000$ tokens. Based on the validation perplexity, we stopped the training when the update count reached 5,000 and fine-tuned

	Texts	Items
Baseline model	55.26	54.58
+ Fine-tune	58.91	56.14
+ Ensemble (4 models)	60.48	56.93
+ R2L re-ranking (4 models)	**61.19**	**57.34**

Table 11: Case-sensitive BLEU scores of provided blind test sets: All scores were calculated by official evaluation server.

the model for 800 updates. During training, we used mixed-precision training (Micikevicius et al., 2018), like the scientific paper subtasks. We saved the model every 100 updates and used the average of the last eight models for decoding. We set the beam size to six and normalized the scores by length. All implementations are based on `fairseq` toolkit (Ott et al., 2019).

3.4 Experimental Results and Analysis

Table 11 shows the case-sensitive BLEU scores (Papineni et al., 2002) of the provided blind test sets. All the reported BLEU scores were calculated on the organizers' submission website.

3.4.1 Baseline model

We set the baseline system as a single NMT model trained with all the training data. Note that we used the same model for both categories in the baseline setting. Even the baseline system achieved around 55 points in both categories. This means that the model already outputs quite similar hypotheses as references.

3.4.2 Fine-tuning with a specific category

We found that fine-tuning with specific category data significantly increased the BLEU scores: +3.65 points for texts and +1.56 points for the items categories. Table 13 shows the example translations of the baseline and fine-tuned systems[10]. The fine-tuned system perfectly gener-

---

[9] In contrast to the scientific paper subtasks, we did not see improvement with a smaller vocabulary in the preliminary experiments.

[10] For finding good examples, we used `compare-mt` (Neubig et al., 2019), which is a toolkit that compares two MT outputs.

| Task | Auto Eval | | Human Eval | | | |
	BLEU	(Rank)	Pairwise	(Rank)	Adequacy	(Rank)
Texts	61.19	(1)	55.50	(1)	4.46	(1)
Items	57.34	(1)	34.00	(2)	4.47	(1)

Table 12: Official results of our submitted systems for timely disclosure subtask: Shown rank is only ordered among constrained submissions.

Input	実績値、類似建物の修繕費水準、エンジニアリング・レポートの修繕更新費等を考慮し査定
Reference	Based on historical data, comparable assets and estimates in the engineering report
Baseline	Assessed by taking into account the actual results, the level of repair expenses of similar buildings, the level of repair expenses in the engineering report, etc.
Fine-tuned	Based on historical data, comparable assets and estimates in the engineering report

Table 13: Example translations of baseline and fine-tuned system: Example was picked from devtest set.

Japanese	実績値、類似建物の修繕費水準、ER の修繕更新費等を考慮し査定
English	Based on historical data, comparable assets and estimates in the engineering report

Table 14: Example of sentence pair contained in the training set.

ated the same sentence as the reference. Although the baseline's hypothesis is also understandable, it does not match the *items* context. We further investigated why the fine-tuned system works so well, and we suspected that the sentences in the dev/test set mostly overlap with the training set; i.e. it might be possible to find almost the same sentence from the training set. Table 14 shows the sentence pair in the training set that was the most similar to the previous example. We found a sentence pair on the English side that is identical as the reference in Table 13, and the Japanese side is also quite similar. By fine-tuning, the model is somewhat over-fitted to the specific categories and memorized more training sentences. Thus, in this case, fine-tuning provides a large gain.

3.4.3 Ensemble and R2L re-ranking

Model ensembling and R2L re-ranking also improved the scores. Additional gains from both are +2.28 points for texts and +1.20 points for items compared with the fine-tuned models.

3.4.4 Submissions and human evaluations

Table 12 shows our submissions and their human evaluation scores. We achieved the best scores in terms of BLEU for both subtasks among the constrained submissions. By pairwise evaluation, our submission to the text subtask ranked first and the items subtask ranked second. However, in the adequacy evaluations, our system achieved top performance in both the texts and items subtasks.

4   Conclusion

We described the systems we submitted to the WAT 2019 shared translation tasks. We submitted the systems for scientific translation subtasks and timely disclosure subtasks and three of four systems won the best human evaluation performance. We also confirmed that an additional web-crawled based parallel corpus increased the performance on the scientific paper subtasks.

Acknowledgement

We thank the ParaCrawl project for their contribution and releasing the software, which we used for creating JParaCrawl.

References

Ondřej Bojar, Christian Federmann, Mark Fishel, Yvette Graham, Barry Haddow, Matthias Huck, Philipp Koehn, and Christof Monz. 2018. Findings of the 2018 conference on machine translation (WMT18). In Proceedings of the 3rd Conference on Machine Translation (WMT), pages 272–303.

Marcin Junczys-Dowmunt. 2018. Microsoft's submission to the WMT2018 news translation task: How I learned to stop worrying and love the data. In Proceedings of the 3rd Conference on Machine Translation (WMT), pages 425–430.

Taku Kudo and John Richardson. 2018. Sentence-Piece: A simple and language independent subword tokenizer and detokenizer for neural text processing. In Proceedings of the Conference on Empirical Methods in Natural Language Processing (EMNLP), pages 66–71.

Lemao Liu, Masao Utiyama, Andrew Finch, and Eiichiro Sumita. 2016. Agreement on target-bidirectional neural machine translation. In Proceedings of the 2016 Conference of the North American Chapter of the Association for Computational Linguistics: Human Language Technologies (NAACL HLT), pages 411–416.

Paulius Micikevicius, Sharan Narang, Jonah Alben, Gregory F. Diamos, Erich Elsen, David García, Boris Ginsburg, Michael Houston, Oleksii Kuchaiev, Ganesh Venkatesh, and Hao Wu. 2018. Mixed precision training. In Proceedings of the 6th International Conference on Learning Representations (ICLR).

Makoto Morishita, Jun Suzuki, and Masaaki Nagata. 2017. NTT neural machine translation systems at WAT 2017. In Proceedings of the 4th Workshop on Asian Translation (WAT), pages 89–94.

Makoto Morishita, Jun Suzuki, and Masaaki Nagata. 2018. NTT's neural machine translation systems for WMT 2018. In Proceedings of the 3rd Conference on Machine Translation (WMT), pages 461–466.

Toshiaki Nakazawa, Chenchen Ding, Raj Dabre, Hideya Mino, Isao Goto, Win Pa Pa, Nobushige Doi, Yusuke Oda, Anoop Kunchukuttan, Shantipriya Parida, Ondřej Bojar, and Sadao Kurohashi. 2019. Overview of the 6th workshop on Asian translation. In Proceedings of the 6th Workshop on Asian Translation (WAT).

Toshiaki Nakazawa, Manabu Yaguchi, Kiyotaka Uchimoto, Masao Utiyama, Eiichiro Sumita, Sadao Kurohashi, and Hitoshi Isahara. 2016. ASPEC: Asian scientific paper excerpt corpus. In Proceedings of the 10th International Conference on Language Resources and Evaluation (LREC), pages 2204–2208.

Graham Neubig. 2014. Forest-to-string SMT for asian language translation: NAIST at WAT2014. In Proceedings of the 1st Workshop on Asian Translation (WAT), pages 20–25.

Graham Neubig, Zi-Yi Dou, Junjie Hu, Paul Michel, Danish Pruthi, and Xinyi Wang. 2019. compare-mt: A tool for holistic comparison of language generation systems. In Proceedings of the 2019 Conference of the North American Chapter of the Association for Computational Linguistics: Human Language Technologies (NAACL HLT), pages 35–41.

Graham Neubig, Yosuke Nakata, and Shinsuke Mori. 2011. Pointwise prediction for robust, adaptable

Japanese morphological analysis. In Proceedings of the 49th Annual Meeting of the Association for Computational Linguistics (ACL), pages 529–533.

Myle Ott, Sergey Edunov, Alexei Baevski, Angela Fan, Sam Gross, Nathan Ng, David Grangier, and Michael Auli. 2019. fairseq: A fast, extensible toolkit for sequence modeling. In Proceedings of the 2019 Conference of the North American Chapter of the Association for Computational Linguistics: Human Language Technologies (NAACL HLT), pages 48–53.

Myle Ott, Sergey Edunov, David Grangier, and Michael Auli. 2018. Scaling neural machine translation. In Proceedings of the 3rd Conference on Machine Translation (WMT), pages 1–9.

Kishore Papineni, Salim Roukos, Todd Ward, and Wei-Jing Zhu. 2002. BLEU: a method for automatic evaluation of machine translation. In Proceedings of the 40th Annual Meeting of the Association for Computational Linguistics (ACL), pages 311–318.

Matt Post. 2018. A call for clarity in reporting BLEU scores. In Proceedings of the 3rd Conference on Machine Translation (WMT), pages 186–191.

Víctor M. Sánchez-Cartagena, Marta Bañón, Sergio Ortiz-Rojas, and Gema Ramírez-Sánchez. 2018. Prompsit's submission to WMT 2018 parallel corpus filtering shared task. In Proceedings of the 3rd Conference on Machine Translation (WMT), pages 955–962.

Rico Sennrich, Barry Haddow, and Alexandra Birch. 2016. Improving neural machine translation models with monolingual data. In Proceedings of the 54th Annual Meeting of the Association for Computational Linguistics (ACL), pages 86–96.

Nitish Srivastava, Geoffrey Hinton, Alex Krizhevsky, Ilya Sutskever, and Ruslan Salakhutdinov. 2014. Dropout: A simple way to prevent neural networks from overfitting. Journal of Machine Learning Research, 15:1929–1958.

Ashish Vaswani, Noam Shazeer, Niki Parmar, Jakob Uszkoreit, Llion Jones, Aidan N. Gomez, Lukasz Kaiser, and Illia Polosukhin. 2017. Attention is all you need. In Proceedings of the 31st Annual Conference on Neural Information Processing Systems (NIPS), pages 6000–6010.

Neural Machine Translation System using a Content-equivalently Translated Parallel Corpus for the Newswire Translation Tasks at WAT 2019

Hideya Mino [1,3]   Hitoshi Ito [1]   Isao Goto [1]   Ichiro Yamada [1]
Hideki Tanaka [2]   Takenobu Tokunaga [3]

[1]NHK Science & Technology Research Laboratories
[2]NHK Engineering System
[3] Tokyo Institute of Technology

{mino.h-gq,itou.h-ce,goto.i-es,yamada.i-hy}@nhk.or.jp,
tanaka.hideki@nes.or.jp, take@c.titech.ac.jp

Abstract

This paper describes NHK and NHK Engineering System (NHK-ES)'s submission to the newswire translation tasks of WAT 2019 in both directions of Japanese→English and English→Japanese. In addition to the JIJI Corpus that was officially provided by the task organizer, we developed a corpus of 0.22M sentence pairs by manually, translating Japanese news sentences into English content-equivalently. The content-equivalent corpus was effective for improving translation quality, and our systems achieved the best human evaluation scores in the newswire translation tasks at WAT 2019.

1 Introduction

We participated in the newswire translation tasks with JIJI Corpus, one of the tasks in WAT 2019 (Nakazawa et al., 2019). JIJI Corpus, a Japanese-English news corpus, comes from Jiji Press news, which has various categories including politics, economy, nation, business, markets, and sports. The newswire official tasks of WAT started in 2017, and some participants and organizer had already submitted their translation results before WAT 2019. Their quality, however, has not been equivalent with that in other tasks, such as scientific paper tasks and patent tasks. This is because of not only the small size (0.20M) of the JIJI Corpus but also a significant amount of noise for the neural machine translation (NMT) system training. The English news articles, which are generated as news-writing, not as translating, are mainly targeted at native English speakers, so information is often omitted or added. Figure 1 shows an example from JIJI Corpus. The omitted and added phrases become noise for the NMT training, and we consider this is one of the reasons for the low translation quality. To solve this problem and improve the translation quality of an NMT system,

Figure 1: Example of a Japanese-English parallel sentence pair in JIJI Corpus. Contents of the underlined parts are not contained in the other language.

we are making a corpus with content-equivalent English translations of Japanese Jiji Press news, i.e. translations that do not omit and add information. We called the corpus Equivalent-JIJI Corpus[1].

In this system description paper, we focus on these two styles of news parallel data, called the JIJI Corpus and the Equivalent-JIJI Corpus, and we named their styles the JIJI-style and the Equivalent-style, respectively. For WAT 2019, we submitted two translation results using translation systems adapted to the JIJI-style. In addition, to confirm the effectiveness of the content-equivalent translation, we submitted two more translation results using translation systems adapted to the Equivalent-style. Results showed that although our NMT systems adapted to the Equivalent-style scored lower than that adapted to the JIJI-style in the automatic evaluation, their scores reversed in the human evaluation.

---

[1]Equivalent-JIJI Corpus is still under construction and will be completed at the end of March 2021.

Proceedings of the 6th Workshop on Asian Translation, pages 106–111
Hong Kong, China, November 4, 2019. ©2019 Association for Computational Linguistics

Corpus name	Construction method	External data	Japanese	English	Size
JIJI Corpus	Alignment	No	Jiji Press news	Jiji Press news	0.20 M
Equivalent-JIJI Corpus	Manual translation	Yes	Jiji Press news	Content-equivalent translation	0.22 M
Aligned-JIJI Corpus	Alignment	Yes	Jiji Press news	Jiji Press news	0.29 M
BT-JIJI Corpus	Back translation	Yes	NMT output	Jiji Press news	0.53 M
Aligned-Yomiuri Corpus	Alignment	Yes	Yomiuri Shimbun	Yomiuri Shimbun	0.61 M

Table 1: Dataset.

2 Corpus Description

JIJI Corpus, which is extracted from Japanese and English Jiji Press news, is relatively small compared with those used in other Japanese→English or English→Japanese tasks of WAT 2019. To alleviate this low-resource translation problem, Morishita et al. (2017) used other resources for pre-training and fine-tuned with JIJI Corpus. We also used the external resources to improve the translation quality of the newswire tasks. For this purpose, we developed four types of corpora apart from JIJI Corpus. The first one was constructed through content-equivalent manual translation of Japanese Jiji Press news into English and is named Equivalent-JIJI Corpus. The second one was obtained through automatic sentence alignment between Japanese and English Jiji Press news using a sentence similarity score and is named Aligned-JIJI. The official JIJI Corpus is constructed in the same way. JIJI Corpus and Aligned-JIJI Corpus include noise as training data for an NMT system. The third corpus was constructed by back-translating monolingual English news sentences into Japanese (Sennrich et al., 2016b). This corpus is used for Japanese→English translation only. We named this parallel data BT-JIJI Corpus. For the back-translation, we used our best English→Japanese system adapted to the JIJI-style. Finally, we used another newspaper parallel corpus originating from the Yomiuri Shimbun, which we named Aligned-Yomiuri Corpus. Aligned-Yomiuri Corpus is made with a parallel sentence similarity score, as is the case of JIJI Corpus. Table 1 summarizes the detail of each corpus.

3 Domain Adaptation Techniques

In this paper, we used a domain-adaptation technique to train a model adapted to the JIJI- and Equivalent-style. The multi-domain method (Chu et al., 2017; Sennrich et al., 2016a) is one of the most effective approaches to leverage out-of-domain data. Chu et al. (2017) proposed training an NMT system with multi-domain parallel corpora using domain tags such as "<domain-name>" attached to the respective corpora. We used domain adaptations with the names of the styls as domain tags. We used a "<JIJI-style>" tag for the JIJI, Aligned-JIJI, and BT-JIJI corpora and a "<Equivalent-style>" tag for Equivalent-JIJI Corpus. In addition, we used a "<YOMIURI-style>" tag for Aligned-Yomiuri Corpus because it comes from a newspaper other than Jiji Press news.

4 Experiments

In this study, we verified the effectiveness of the Equivalent-style translation through the following procedures. Firstly, we trained the multiple NMT models with different combinations of five corpora as shown in Table 1, and evaluated these NMT models with an official test-set, in which the number of data was 2000. Then, we evaluated these NMT models with a further test-set, in which the number of data was 1764, extracted from Equivalent-JIJI Corpus of Equivalent-style in contrast to the official test-set extracted JIJI Corpus in JIJI-style. Finally, we evaluated the effectiveness of the Equivalent-style translation.

4.1 Data Processing and System Setup

All of the datasets were preprocessed as follows. We used the Moses toolkit [2] to clean and tokenize the English data and used KyTea (Neubig et al., 2011) to tokenize the Japanese data. Then, we used a vocabulary of 32K units based on a joint source and target byte-pair encoding (BPE) (Sennrich et al., 2016c). For the translation model,

---

[2] https://github.com/moses- smt/ mosesdecoder

Training corpus	Num. of data	Domain adaptation	Tag (Style)	JIJI-style test-set	Equivalent-style test-set
JIJI (Official data)	0.2M	No	-	18.14	7.76
Equivalent-JIJI	0.22M	No	-	9.15	21.36
JIJI, Equivalent-JIJI	0.42M	No	-	20.56	20.8
JIJI, Equivalent-JIJI	0.42M	Yes	JIJI-style	21.69	12.65
JIJI, Equivalent-JIJI	0.42M	Yes	Equivalent-style	12.01	23.16
JIJI, Equivalent-JIJI, Aligned-JIJI, Aligned-Yomiuri	1.32M	No	-	23.44	20.95
JIJI, Equivalent-JIJI, Aligned-JIJI, Aligned-Yomiuri	1.32M	Yes	JIJI-style	24.50	14.65
JIJI, Equivalent-JIJI, Aligned-JIJI, Aligned-Yomiuri	1.32M	Yes	Equivalent-style	13.40	24.78
JIJI, Equivalent-JIJI, Aligned-JIJI, Aligned-Yomiuri, BT-JIJI	1.85M	Yes	JIJI-style	25.54	15.03
JIJI, Equivalent-JIJI, Aligned-JIJI, Aligned-Yomiuri, BT-JIJI	1.85M	Yes	Equivalent-style	13.47	24.80

Table 2: BLEU scores for Japanese→English translation tasks.

Training corpus	Num. of data	Domain adaptation	Tag (Style)	JIJI-style test-set	Equivalent-style test-set
JIJI (Official data)	0.20M	No	-	18.46	15.9
Equivalent-JIJI	0.22M	No	-	17.92	36.67
JIJI, Equivalent-JIJI	0.42M	No	-	25.07	39.97
JIJI, Equivalent-JIJI	0.42M	Yes	JIJI-style	24.63	36.75
JIJI, Equivalent-JIJI	0.42M	Yes	Equivalent-style	24.52	39.93
JIJI, Equivalent-JIJI, Aligned-JIJI, Aligned-Yomiuri	1.32M	No	-	28.49	43.52
JIJI, Equivalent-JIJI, Aligned-JIJI, Aligned-Yomiuri	1.32M	Yes	JIJI-style	28.14	43.82
JIJI, Equivalent-JIJI, Aligned-JIJI, Aligned-Yomiuri	1.32M	Yes	Equivalent-style	27.77	43.68

Table 3: BLEU scores for English→Japanese translation tasks.

we used the encoder and decoder of the transformer model (Vaswani et al., 2017), which is a state of the art NMT model. The transformer model uses a multi-headed attention mechanism applied as self-attention and a position-wise fully connected feed-forward network. The encoder converts the received source language sentence into a sequence of continuous representations, and the decoder generates the target language sentence. We implemented our systems with the Sockeye toolkit (Hieber et al., 2018), and trained them on one Nvidia P100 Tesla GPU. While training our models, we used the stochastic gradient descent (SGD) with Adam (Kingma and Ba, 2015) as the optimizer, using a learning rate of 0.0002, multiplied by 0.7 after every eight checkpoints. We set the batch size to 5000 tokens and maximum sentence length to 99 BPE units. For the other hyperparameters of our models, we used the default parameter values of Sockeye. We used early stopping with a patience of 32. Decoding was performed with a beam search with a beam size of 5, and we did not apply an ensemble decoding with multiple models, although this could possibly improve the translation quality, though we used a beam search with a beam size of 30 and an ensemble of ten models when submitting the official results. To evaluate translation quality, we used BLEU (Papineni et al., 2002). BLEU is calculated using multi-bleu.perl [3]. We report case-sensitive scores.

4.2 Results

Tables 2 and 3 show the experimental results. The Training corpus column shows the corpora used for training. The Style column shows the tag used for translation, i.e. the JIJI- or Equivalent-style. The JIJI-style test-set is equal to the official test-set in the newswire task of WAT 2019.

4.2.1 Trained with Different Combinations of Five Corpora

The JIJI-style test-set column of Tables 2 and 3 shows the translation quality of the JIJI-style test-sets with the BLEU metric for different combinations of the five corpora. For the models without domain adaptation, where Domain adaptation column is "No," the BLEU scores are improved by adding the other domains' data into the JIJI

[3]https://github.com/moses-smt/mosesdecoder/blob/master/scripts/generic/multi-bleu-detok.perl

Task	Tag (Style)	BLEU	Rank	RIBES	Rank	AMFM	Rank	Pairwise	Rank	Adequacy	Rank
JIJI-JE	JIJI-style	26.83	1/4	0.70	1/4	0.55	1/4	72.00	2/4	-	-
	Equivalent-style	14.23	4/4	0.61	4/4	0.53	3/4	89.00	1/4	4.55	1/2
JIJI-EJ	JIJI-style	29.76	1/4	0.74	1/4	0.65	2/4	81.25	2/4	-	-
	Equivalent-style	28.75	2/4	0.73	2/4	0.66	1/4	87.75	1/4	4.11	1/2

Table 4: Official results for the newswire translation tasks of WAT 2019: For JIJI-EJ task, we show the BLEU, RIBES, and AMFM scores with KyTea tokenizer.

Corpus. For the JIJI-style Japanese→English test-set, the BLEU scores are higher with the use of tags for the domain adaptation. However, the use of the domain adaptation is not effective for the JIJI-style English→Japanese test-set. This seems to be due to the different origins of the target-side sentences in the Equivalent-JIJI Corpus. Japanese sentences in the Equivalent-JIJI Corpus come from the Japanese Jiji Press news, the same as for JIJI Corpus. In contrast, the English sentences in Equivalent-JIJI Corpus does not come from Jiji Press news. It appears that the use of different domain tags is less effective when using the same-origin data for the target-side as shown in the fourth and fifth columns of Table 1. In the case of Japanese→English task with JIJI Corpus and Equivalent-JIJI Corpus, the origin of the target-side English sentences differs between the two corpora (JIji Press news and Content-equivalent translation) despite the origin of the source-side is being the same (Jiji Press news), so the NMT system cannot decide which style, JIJI- or Equivalent-style, should be output. In contrast, no choice is necessary for the English→Japanese task because the target-side Japanese sentences is the same origin (Jiji Press news).

The Equivalent-style test-set column in Tables 2 and 3 shows translation quality of the Equivalent-style test-sets. For the models without domain adaptation, the BLEU scores are not improved by adding the other domains' data into the Equivalent-JIJI Corpus in case of the Japanese→English task. The domain adaptation using tags is extremely effective for the Japanese→Engish task. Although the amount of Equivalent-style data is much smaller than that of JIJI-style data, the BLEU scores for the Equivalent-style test-set are higher than those for the JIJI-style test-set. In particular, the BLEU scores of the Equivalent-style test-set for the English→Japanese are over 43. It appears that it is more difficult to improve the translation quality

for the JIJI-style test-set than for the Equivalent-style test-set because the JIJI-style test-set includes noise for training the NMT system.

4.2.2 Translation with Different Types of Systems

Supposing that JIJI Corpus includes noise, the NMT system adapted to the Equivalent-style seems to be a better system to translate news generally. However, the BLEU scores for the JIJI-style test-set trained with Equivalent-JIJI Corpus are 9.15 for Japanese→English and 17.92 for English→Japanese and they are lower than the scores for the test-set trained with JIJI Corpus, as shown in Tables 2 and 3. To determine whether or not the translation systems adapted to the Equivalent-style are better for human evaluation than those adapted to the JIJI-style, we submitted the translated results with both of the translation systems adapted to JIJI- and Equivalent-style.

4.3 Official Results

We used the bottom translation systems of Tables 2 and 3 for submitting to WAT 2019. These systems can be adapted to each style by attaching domain tags, "<JIJI-style>" for JIJI-style translation and "<Equivalent-style>" for Equivalent-style translation, at the top of the source sentence. To improve the translation quality further, we submitted the translation results with an ensemble decode of ten models and a beam search with a beam size of 30. Table 4 shows the official results of our submission to WAT 2019. Our systems adapted to JIJI-style achieved the best BLEU and RIBES scores. In contrast, for the pairwise crowdsourcing evaluation and the JPO adequacy evaluation[4], our systems adapted to the Equivalent-style achieved the best evaluation. For the AMFM, our system

---

[4]WAT 2019 organizer selected submissions for JPO adequacy evaluation, and only one submission for each task was evaluated.

	Example sentence	BLEU
Source	終了後、赤松氏は記者団に「公平、公正な形で国民の意見を聴く」と強調し、 江田氏は「客観的に調査した結果をそのまま受け入れる」と語った。	
Content-equivalent translation	After the meeting, Akamatsu emphasized to the press, "We will hear opinions of the public in a fair and equitable manner," and Eda said, "We will accept the results of the objective investigation."	
Reference (JIJI Corpus)	After the meeting, Akamatsu told reporters, "We will seek the views of the public in a fair and equitable manner."	
NMT output adapted to JIJI-style	After the meeting, Akamatsu told reporters that he will listen to public opinions in a fair and equitable manner.	51.61
NMT output adapted to Equivalent-style	After the meeting, Akamatsu emphasized to the press, "We will listen to the opinions of the people in a fair and fair manner," and Eda said, "We will accept the results of the investigation objectively."	22.70
Source	同日午後の参院本会議で可決、成立する見通し。	
Content-equivalent translation	It is expected to be passed and enacted at a plenary session of the House of Councilors in the afternoon of the same day.	
Reference (JIJI Corpus)	The House of Councillors, the upper chamber of the Diet, approved the spending program at a plenary meeting on Monday afternoon after the House of Representatives, the lower chamber, passed it earlier in the day.	
NMT output adapted to JIJI-style	The House of Councillors, the upper chamber, is expected to approve the bill at a plenary meeting later in the day.	26.33
NMT output adapted to Equivalent-style	It is expected to be passed and enacted at the plenary session of the House of Councilors in the afternoon of the same day.	0.00

Table 5: Example results of JIJI-JE tasks translated with JIJI- and Equivalent-style NMT

Task	Tag (Style)	Omitted-words	Added-words
JIJI-JE	JIJI-style	18.40	9.39
	Equivalent-style	4.27	1.44
JIJI-EJ	JIJI-style	28.19	13.16
	Equivalent-style	8.22	2.55

Table 6: Further human evaluation results, which is the average number of words per 100 words.

adapted to the JIJI-style achieved the best evaluation for the Japanese→English task, whereas our system adapted to the Equivalent-style achieved the best evaluation for the English→Japanese task. These results show that the NMT systems adapted to the Equivalent-style are generally better systems for translating the news. The overview paper for WAT 2019 gives the details of our submission including the other WAT participants' results.

4.4 Further Human Evaluation

Apart from the official pairwise crowdsourcing evaluation and JPO adequacy evaluation, we also evaluated our official submission independently with a translation company to analyze deeply the official results. We randomly selected 300 and 50 sentences from the Japanese→English and English→Japanese official test-sets respectively, and three evaluators counted the number of omitted and added words in the NMT outputs adapted to the JIJI- and Equivalent-styles. Table 6 shows the average number of words per 100 words of the three evaluators. These results indicate that the NMT systems adapted to the Equivalent-style can prevent the omission and addition of information. Table 5 shows the examples of NMT outputs adapted to the JIJI- and Equivalent-styles in the official tasks. The first example shows omitted information, and the second example shows added information in the NMT output adapted to the JIJI-style. The references also include omitted and added information. The NMT output adapted to the Equivalent-style is translated without omitted and added information. The sentence BLEU scores of outputs adapted to the JIJI-style NMT are higher than those of outputs adapted to the Equivalent-style NMT. These results indicate that NMT outputs adapted to the JIJI-style often include the omission and addition of information, and these cause the worse human evaluation. This seems to be a reason that our systems adapted to the Equivalent-style, which prevent the omission and addition of information, achieved the best human evaluation in spite of the lower BLEU scores.

5 Conclusions

In this description paper, we presented our NMT systems adapted to the JIJI- and the Equivalent-styles. In addition to the JIJI Corpus in the JIJI-style that was officially provided by the WAT 2019 organizer, we developed a corpus of 0.22M sentence pairs in the Equivalent-style by manually, content-equivalently translating Japanese news sentences into English. We obtained the state-of-the-art results for the newswire tasks of WAT 2019. In our four submissions, the translation models adapted to the JIJI-style achieved the best results for the BLEU evaluation. In contrast, the translation models adapted to the Equivalent-style achieved the best results for the pairwise crowdsourcing evaluation and JPO adequacy evaluation. We showed that the content-equivalently translated data is effective for the widespread news translation from the perspective of a human evaluation.

Acknowledgments

These research results have been achieved by "Research and Development of Deep Learning Technology for Advanced Multilingual Speech Translation," the Commissioned Research of National Institute of Information and Communications Technology (NICT), Japan.

References

Chenhui Chu, Raj Dabre, and Sadao Kurohashi. 2017. An empirical comparison of domain adaptation methods for neural machine translation. In *Proceedings of the 55th Annual Meeting of the Association for Computational Linguistics (Volume 2: Short Papers)*, pages 385–391, Vancouver, Canada. Association for Computational Linguistics.

Felix Hieber, Tobias Domhan, Michael Denkowski, David Vilar, Artem Sokolov, Ann Clifton, and Matt Post. 2018. The sockeye neural machine translation toolkit at AMTA 2018. In *Proceedings of the 13th Conference of the Association for Machine Translation in the Americas (Volume 1: Research Papers)*, pages 200–207, Boston, MA. Association for Machine Translation in the Americas.

Diederick P Kingma and Jimmy Ba. 2015. Adam: A method for stochastic optimization. In *International Conference on Learning Representations (ICLR)*.

Makoto Morishita, Jun Suzuki, and Masaaki Nagata. 2017. NTT neural machine translation systems at WAT 2017. In *Proceedings of the 4th Workshop on Asian Translation (WAT2017)*, pages 89–94, Taipei, Taiwan. Asian Federation of Natural Language Processing.

Toshiaki Nakazawa, Chenchen Ding, Raj Dabre, Hideya Mino, Isao Goto, Win Pa Pa, Nobushige Doi, Yusuke Oda, Anoop Kunchukuttan, Shantipriya Parida, Ondej Bojar, and Sadao Kurohashi. 2019. Overview of the 6th workshop on Asian translation. In *Proceedings of the 6th Workshop on Asian Translation*, Hong Kong. Association for Computational Linguistics.

Graham Neubig, Yosuke Nakata, and Shinsuke Mori. 2011. Pointwise prediction for robust, adaptable japanese morphological analysis. In *Proceedings of the 49th Annual Meeting of the Association for Computational Linguistics: Human Language Technologies*, pages 529–533, Portland, Oregon, USA. Association for Computational Linguistics.

Kishore Papineni, Salim Roukos, Todd Ward, and Wei-Jing Zhu. 2002. Bleu: a method for automatic evaluation of machine translation. In *Proceedings of the 40th Annual Meeting of the Association for Computational Linguistics*, pages 311–318, Philadelphia, Pennsylvania, USA. Association for Computational Linguistics.

Rico Sennrich, Barry Haddow, and Alexandra Birch. 2016a. Controlling politeness in neural machine translation via side constraints. In *Proceedings of the 2016 Conference of the North American Chapter of the Association for Computational Linguistics: Human Language Technologies*, pages 35–40, San Diego, California. Association for Computational Linguistics.

Rico Sennrich, Barry Haddow, and Alexandra Birch. 2016b. Improving neural machine translation models with monolingual data. In *Proceedings of the 54th Annual Meeting of the Association for Computational Linguistics (Volume 1: Long Papers)*, pages 86–96, Berlin, Germany. Association for Computational Linguistics.

Rico Sennrich, Barry Haddow, and Alexandra Birch. 2016c. Neural machine translation of rare words with subword units. In *Proceedings of the 54th Annual Meeting of the Association for Computational Linguistics (Volume 1: Long Papers)*, pages 1715–1725, Berlin, Germany. Association for Computational Linguistics.

Ashish Vaswani, Noam Shazeer, Niki Parmar, Jakob Uszkoreit, Llion Jones, Aidan N Gomez, Ł ukasz Kaiser, and Illia Polosukhin. 2017. Attention is all you need. In I. Guyon, U. V. Luxburg, S. Bengio, H. Wallach, R. Fergus, S. Vishwanathan, and R. Garnett, editors, *Advances in Neural Information Processing Systems 30*, pages 5998–6008. Curran Associates, Inc.

Facebook AI's WAT19 Myanmar-English Translation Task Submission

Peng-Jen Chen[*1] **Jiajun Shen**[*1] **Matt Le**[1] **Vishrav Chaudhary**[2]
Ahmed El-Kishky[2] **Guillaume Wenzek**[1] **Myle Ott**[1] **Marc'Aurelio Ranzato**[1]

[1]Facebook AI Research [2]Facebook AI Applied Research

```
{pipibjc,jiajunshen,mattle,vishrav,
  ahelk,guw,myleott,ranzato}@fb.com
```


Abstract

This paper describes Facebook AI's submission to the WAT 2019 Myanmar-English translation task (Nakazawa et al., 2019). Our baseline systems are BPE-based transformer models. We explore methods to leverage monolingual data to improve generalization, including self-training, back-translation and their combination. We further improve results by using noisy channel re-ranking and ensembling. We demonstrate that these techniques can significantly improve not only a system trained with additional monolingual data, but even the baseline system trained exclusively on the provided small parallel dataset. Our system ranks first in both directions according to human evaluation and BLEU, with a gain of over 8 BLEU points above the second best system.

1 Introduction

While machine translation (MT) has proven very successful for high resource language pairs (Ng et al., 2019; Hassan et al., 2018), it is still an open research question how to make it work well for the vast majority of language pairs which are low resource. In this setting, relatively little parallel data is available to train the system and the translation task is even more difficult because the language pairs are usually more distant and the domains of the source and target language match less well (Shen et al., 2019).

English-Myanmar is an interesting case study in this respect, because i) the language of Myanmar is morphologically rich and very different from English, ii) Myanmar language does not bear strong similarities with other high-resource languages and therefore does not benefit from multilingual training, iii) there is relatively little parallel data available and iv) even monolingual data in Myanmar language is difficult to gather due to the multiple encodings of the language.

Motivated by this challenge, we participated in the 2019 edition of the competition on Myanmar-English, organized by the Workshop on Asian Translation. This paper describes our submission, which achieved the highest human evaluation and BLEU score (Papineni et al., 2002) in the competition.

Following common practice in the field, we used back-translation (Sennrich et al., 2015) to leverage target side monolingual data. However, the domain of Myanmar monolingual data is very different from the test domain, which is English originating news (Shen et al., 2019). Since this may hamper the performance of back-translation, we also explored methods that leverage monolingual data on the source side, which is in-domain with the test set when translating from English to Myanmar. We investigated the use of self-training (Yarowski, 1995; Ueffing, 2006; Zhang and Zong, 2016; He et al., 2019) which augments the original parallel data with synthetic data where sources are taken from the original source monolingual dataset and targets are produced by the current machine translation system. We show that self-training and back-translation are often complementary to each other and yield additional improvements when applied in an iterative fashion.

In fact, back-translation and self-training can also be applied when learning from the parallel dataset alone, greatly improving performance over the baseline using the original bitext data. We also report further improvements by swapping beam search decoding with noisy channel re-ranking (Yee et al., 2019) and by ensembling.

We will start by discussing the data preparation process in §2, followed by our model details in §3 and results in §4. We conclude with some final remarks in §5. In Appendix A we report training details and describe the methods that have not proved useful for this task in Appendix B.

---

[*]Equal contribution.

Proceedings of the 6th Workshop on Asian Translation, pages 112–122
Hong Kong, China, November 4, 2019. ©2019 Association for Computational Linguistics

2 Data

In this section, we describe the data we used for training and the pre-processing we applied.

2.1 Parallel Data

The parallel data was provided by the organizers of the competition and consists of two datasets. The first dataset is the Asian Language Treebank (ALT) corpus (Thu et al., 2016; Ding et al., 2018, 2019) which consists of 18,088 training sentences, 1,000 validation sentences and 1,018 test sentences from English originating news articles. In this dataset, there is a space character separating each Myanmar morpheme (Thu et al., 2016).

The second dataset is the UCSY dataset[1] which contains 204,539 sentences from various domains, including news articles and textbooks. The originating language of these sentences is not specified. Unlike the ALT dataset, Myanmar text in the UCSY dataset is not segmented and contains very little spacing as it is typical in this language.

The organizers of the competition evaluate submitted systems on the ALT test set.

We denote the parallel dataset by $\mathcal{P} = \{X, Y\}$.

2.2 Monolingual Data

We gather English monolingual data by taking a subset of the 2018 Newscrawl dataset provided by WMT (Barrault et al., 2019), which contains approximately 79 million unique sentences. We choose Newscrawl data to match the domain of the ALT dataset, which primarily contains news originating from English sources.

For Myanmar language, we take five snapshots of the Commoncrawl dataset and combine them with the raw data from Buck et al. (2014). After de-duplication, this resulted in approximately 28 million unique lines. This data is not restricted to the news domain.

We denote by $\mathcal{M}_S$ the source monolingual dataset and by $\mathcal{M}_T$ target monolingual dataset.

2.3 Data Preprocessing

The Myanmar monolingual data we collect from Commoncrawl contains text in both Unicode and Zawgyi encodings. We use the `myanmar-tools`[2] library to classify and convert all Zawgyi text to Unicode. Since text classification is performed at the document level, the corpus is left with many embedded English sentences, which we filter by running the fastText classifier (Joulin et al., 2017) over individual sentences.

We tokenize English text using Moses (Koehn et al., 2007) with aggressive hyphen splitting. We explored multiple approaches for tokenizing Myanmar text, including the provided tokenizer and several open source tools. However, initial experiments showed that leaving the text untokenized yielded the best results. When generating Myanmar translations at inference time, we remove separators introduced by BPE, remove all spaces from the generated text, and then apply the provided tokenizer[3].

Finally, we use SentencePiece (Kudo and Richardson, 2018) to learn a BPE vocabulary of size 10,000 over the combined English and Myanmar parallel text corpus.

3 System Overview

Our architecture is a transformer-based neural machine translation system trained with `fairseq`[4] (Ott et al., 2019). We tuned model hyper-parameters via random search over a range of possible values (see Appendix A for details). We performed early stopping based on perplexity on the ALT validation set, and final model hyper-parameter selection based on the BLEU score on the same validation set. We never used the ALT test set during development, and only used it for the final reporting at submission time.

Next, we describe several enhancements to this baseline model (§3.1) and to the decoding process (§3.2). We also describe several methods for leveraging monolingual data, including our final iterative approach (§3.3).

3.1 Improvements to the Baseline Model

We improve our baseline neural machine translation system with: tagging (Sennrich et al., 2016; Kobus et al., 2016; Caswell et al., 2019), fine-tuning and ensembling.

Tagging: Since our test set comes from the ALT corpus and our training set is composed by sev-

---

[1] `http://lotus.kuee.kyoto-u.ac.jp/WAT/my-en-data/`

[2] `https://github.com/google/myanmar-tools`

[3] `myseg.py` can be found in the parallel dataset file on the page `http://lotus.kuee.kyoto-u.ac.jp/WAT/my-en-data/`

[4] `https://github.com/pytorch/fairseq`

eral datasets from different domains, we prepend to the input source sentence a token specifying the domain of the input data. We have a total of four domain tokens, indicating whether the input source sentence comes from the ALT dataset, the UCSY dataset, the source monolingual data or if it is a back-translation of the target monolingual data (see §3.3 for more details).

Fine-tuning: The models submitted for final evaluation have also been fine-tuned to the training set of the ALT dataset, as a way to better adapt to the domain of the test set. Fine-tuning is early-stopped based on BLEU on the validation set.

Ensembling: Finally, since we tune our model hyper-parameters via randomized grid search, we are able to cheaply build an ensemble model from the top k best performing hyper-parameter choices. Ensembling yielded consistent gains of about 1 BLEU point.

3.2 Improvements to Decoding

Neural machine translation systems typically employ beam search decoding at inference time to find the most likely hypothesis for a given source sentence. In this work, we improve upon beam search through noisy-channel reranking (Yee et al., 2019). This approach was a key component of the winning submission in the WMT 2019 news translation shared task for English-German, German-English, English-Russian and Russian-English (Ng et al., 2019).

More specifically, given a source sentence x and a candidate translation y, we compute the following score:

$$\log P(y|x) + \lambda_1 \log P(x|y) + \lambda_2 \log P(y) \quad (1)$$

where $\log P(y|x)$, $\log P(x|y)$ and $\log P(y)$ are the forward model, backward model and language model scores, respectively. This combined score is used to rerank the n-best target hypotheses produced by beam search. In our experiments we set n to 50 and output the highest-scoring hypothesis from this set as our translation. The weights λ_1 and λ_2 are tuned via random search on the validation set. The ranges of values for λ_1 and λ_2 are reported in Appendix A.

Throughout this work we use noisy channel reranking every time we decode, whether it is to generate forward or backward translations or to generate translations from the final model for evaluation purposes.

Model	My→En	En→My
$\mathcal{P}$ — beam	25.1	35.9
$\mathcal{P}$ — reranking	26.3	36.9
$\mathcal{P} \cup \mathcal{M}_\mathcal{T}$, beam — beam	32.2	38.8
$\mathcal{P} \cup \mathcal{M}_\mathcal{T}$, reranking — beam	32.5	38.9
$\mathcal{P} \cup \mathcal{M}_\mathcal{T}$, reranking — reranking	35.2	39.4

Table 1: Effect of noisy channel reranking when evaluating on the validation set. On the left of the "—" symbol there is the dataset used to train the system and the decoding process used to generate back-translated data (if any). On the right of the "—" symbol there is the decoding process used to generate hypotheses from the forward model. $\mathcal{P}$ refers to the parallel dataset and $\mathcal{M}_\mathcal{T}$ refers to the target monolingual dataset.

Our language models are also based on the transformer architecture and follow the same setup as Radford et al. (2018). The English language model is trained on the CC-News dataset (Liu et al., 2019) and consists of 12 transformer layers and a total of 124M parameters. The Myanmar language model is first trained on the Commoncrawl monolingual data and then fine-tuned on the Myanmar portion of the ALT parallel training data; it consists of 6 transformer layers and 70M parameters. For our constrained submission, which does not make use of additional data, we trained smaller transformer language models for each language (5 transformer layers, 8M parameters) using each side of the provided parallel corpus. For both directions, we observed gains when applying noisy channel reranking, as shown in Table 1.

3.3 Leveraging Monolingual Data

In this section we describe basic approaches to leverage monolingual data. Notice however that these methods also improve system performance in the absence of additional monolingual data (i.e., by reusing the available parallel data), see §4.1.

We denote by $\overrightarrow{f}$ and $\overleftarrow{g}$ the forward (from source to target) and the backward (from target to source) machine translation systems.

Back-translation (BT) (Sennrich et al., 2015) is an effective data augmentation method leveraging target side monolingual data. To perform back-translation, we first train $\overleftarrow{g}$ on $\{Y, X\}$ and use it to translate $\mathcal{M}_\mathcal{T}$ to produce synthetic source side data, denoted by $\overleftarrow{g}(\mathcal{M}_\mathcal{T})$. We then concatenate the original bitext data $\{X, Y\}$ with the back-translated data $\{\overleftarrow{g}(\mathcal{M}_\mathcal{T}), \mathcal{M}_\mathcal{T}\}$ and train the forward translation model from scratch. We typi-

Model	My→En	En→My
BT	33.1	39.5
ST	33.2	39.9
BT + ST	34.1	40.3

Table 2: Combining BT and ST yields better BLEU score than BT and ST.

cally upsample the original parallel data, with the exact rate tuned together with the other hyper-parameters on the validation set (see Appendix A for the upsample ratio range).

Self-Training (ST) (Ueffing, 2006; Zhang and Zong, 2016; He et al., 2019) instead augments the original parallel dataset $\mathcal{P} = \{X, Y\}$ with synthetic pairs composed by a sentence from the source monolingual dataset with the corresponding forward model translation as target, $\{(\mathcal{M}_\mathcal{S}, \overrightarrow{f}(\mathcal{M}_\mathcal{S})\}$. The potential advantage of this method is that the source side monolingual data can be more in-domain with the test set, which is the case for the English to Myanmar direction. The shortcoming is that synthetic targets are often incorrect and may deteriorate performance.

Combining BT + ST: Self-training and back-translation are complementary to each other. The former is better when the source monolingual data is in-domain while the latter is better when the target monolingual data is in-domain, relative to the domain of the test set.

In Table 2, we show that these two approaches can be combined and yield better performance than either method individually. Specifically, we combine bitext data together with self-trained and back-translated data, $\{X, Y\} \cup \{\overleftarrow{g}(\mathcal{M}_\mathcal{T}), \mathcal{M}_\mathcal{T}\} \cup \{(\mathcal{M}_\mathcal{S}, \overrightarrow{f}(\mathcal{M}_\mathcal{S})\}$. As for BT, we upsample the bitext data, concatenate it with the forward and backward translations and train a new forward model from scratch. The upsample ratios for each dataset are tuned via hyper-parameter search on the validation set.

3.3.1 Final Iterative Algorithm

The final algorithm proceeds in rounds as described in Alg. 1. At each round, we are provided with a forward model $\overrightarrow{f}$ and a backward model $\overleftarrow{g}$. The forward model translates source side monolingual data (line 6). This is used as forward-translated data to improve the forward model, and as back-translated data to improve the backward model. Similarly, the backward model is used

1 **Data:** Given a parallel dataset $\{X, Y\}$, a source monolingual dataset $\mathcal{M}_\mathcal{S}$ and a target monolingual dataset $\mathcal{M}_\mathcal{T}$;

2 Given an initial forward model $\overrightarrow{f}$ and backward model $\overleftarrow{g}$ trained on $\{X, Y\}$;

3 Let N be the number of hyper-parameter configurations evaluated during random search;

4 Let k be the number of models used in the ensemble;

5 **for** t **in** $[1 \ldots T]$ **do**

6   forward-translated data: $\mathcal{F} \longleftarrow \overrightarrow{f}(\mathcal{M}_\mathcal{S})$;

7   back-translated data: $\mathcal{B} \longleftarrow \overleftarrow{g}(\mathcal{M}_\mathcal{T})$;

8     $\{\overrightarrow{f}_i\}_{i=1\ldots N} \longleftarrow$ random search using: $\{X, Y\} \cup \{\mathcal{M}_\mathcal{S}, \mathcal{F}\} \cup \{\mathcal{B}, \mathcal{M}_\mathcal{T}\}$;

9     $\{\overleftarrow{g}_i\}_{i=1\ldots N} \longleftarrow$ random search using: $\{Y, X\} \cup \{\mathcal{F}, \mathcal{M}_\mathcal{S}\} \cup \{\mathcal{M}_\mathcal{T}, \mathcal{B}\}$;

10   **if** $t == T$ **then**

11   Fine-tune $\{\overrightarrow{f}_i\}_{i=1\ldots N}$ and $\{\overleftarrow{g}_i\}_{i=1\ldots N}$ on the in-domain ALT dataset;

    end

12     $\overrightarrow{f} \longleftarrow$ ensemble of top k best models from $\{\overrightarrow{f}_i\}_{i=1\ldots N}$;

13     $\overleftarrow{g} \longleftarrow$ ensemble of top k best models from $\{\overleftarrow{g}_i\}_{i=1\ldots N}$;

end

Result: Forward MT system $\overrightarrow{f}$ and backward MT system $\overleftarrow{g}$

Algorithm 1: Iterative Learning Algorithm

to back-translate target monolingual data (line 7). This data is then used to improve the forward model via back-translation, but also the backward model via self-training. All these datasets are concatenated and weighted to train new forward and backward models (see lines 8 and 9). At the very last iteration, models are fine-tuned on the ALT training set (line 11 and 12), and either way, the best models from the random search are combined into an ensemble to define the new forward and backward models (line 13 and 14) to be used at the next iteration. This whole process of generation and training then repeats as many times as desired. In our experiments we iterated at most three times.

4   Results

In this section we report validation BLEU scores for the intermediate iterations and ablations, and test BLEU scores only for our final submission. Details of the model architecture, data processing and optimization algorithm are reported in Appendix A.

Our baseline system is trained on the provided parallel datasets with the modeling extensions described in §3.1. According to our hyper-parameter search, the optimal upsampling ratio of the smaller in-domain ALT dataset is three and the best for-

	Description	My → En	En → My
1	Baseline (single)	23.3	34.9
2	Baseline (ensemble)	25.1	35.9
3	2 + reranking	26.3	36.9
4	3 + ST	26.4	38.2
5	3 + BT	26.5	36.9
6	3 + (ST + BT)	27.0	38.1

Table 3: BLEU scores of systems trained only on the provided parallel datasets.

Description	My → En	En → My
Baseline (ensemble)	25.1	35.9
+ reranking	27.7	36.9
+ iter. 1 of ST + BT	35.5	40.1
+ iter. 2 of ST + BT	36.9	40.4
+ iter. 3 of ST + BT	37.9	40.6

Table 4: BLEU scores of systems trained using additional monolingual data.

ward and backward model have 5 encoder and 5 decoder transformer layers, where the number of attention heads, embedding dimension and inner-layer dimension are 4, 512, 2048, respectively. Each single model is trained on 4 Volta GPUs for 1.4 hours. We refer to this model as the "Baseline" in our result tables.

4.1 System Trained on Parallel Data Only

We submitted a machine translation system that only uses the provided ALT and UCSY parallel datasets, without any additional monolingual data, results are reported in Tab. 3. The baseline system achieves 23.3 BLEU points for My→En and 34.9 for En→My . Ensembling 5 models yields +1.8 BLEU points gain for My→En and +1.0 point for En→My . To apply noisy channel reranking, we train language models *using data from the ALT and UCSY training set*. The language model architectures are the same for both languages, each has 5 transformer layers, 4 attention heads, 256 embedding dimensions and 512 inner-layer dimensions. Noisy channel ranking yields a gain of +1.2 BLEU points for My→En and +1.0 points for En→My on top of the ensemble models.

To further improve generalization, we also translated the source and target portion of the parallel dataset using the baseline system in order to collect forward-translations of source sentences and back-translations of target sentences. Based on our grid search, we then train a different model architecture than the baseline system, consisting of 4 layers in encoder and decoder, 8 attention heads, 512 embedding dimensions and 2048 inner-layer dimensions. Each model is trained on 4 Volta GPUs for 2.8 hours. In this case, we train only for one iteration and we ensemble 5 models for each direction followed by reranking.

By applying back-translation and self-training

to the parallel data we obtain an additional gain of +0.7 points for My→En and +1.2 points for En→My over the baseline model. We also find that combining back-translation and self-training is beneficial for My→En direction, where we attain an increase of +0.5 BLEU compared to applying each method individually. The final BLEU scores on test set are 26.8 for My→En and 36.8 for En→My .

4.2 System Using Also Monolingual Data

The results using additional monolingual data are reported in Tab. 4. Starting from the ensemble baseline of the previous section, noisy channel reranking now yields a bigger gain for My→En , +2.64 points, since the language model is now trained on much more in-domain target monolingual data.

Using the ensemble and the additional monolingual data, we apply back-translation and self-training for three iterations. For each iteration, we use the best model from the previous iteration to translate monolingual data with noisy channel reranking. As before, we combine the original parallel data with the two synthetic datasets, and train models from random initialization. We search over hyper-parameters controlling the model architecture whenever we add more monolingual data.

At the first iteration we back-translate 18M English sentences from Newscrawl and 23M Myanmar sentences from Commoncrawl. The best model architecture has 6 layers in the encoder and decoder, where the number of attention heads, embedding dimension and inner-layer dimension are 1024, 4096, 8, respectively. Each model is trained on 4 Volta GPUs for 17 hours. Ensembling two models for My→En and three models for En→My strikes a good trade-off between translation quality and decoding efficiency to generate data for the next iteration. The re-ranked

Description (My → En)	BLEU	Adequacy
FBAI	38.6	4.4
Team1	30.2	4.0
FBAI	26.8	-
Team2	24.8	2.8
Team3	19.6	1.3
Team4	18.5	-
Team5	14.9	-
Team6	10.7	-

Table 5: My→En leaderboard[5]. The values are BLEU score (second column) and Adequacy scores (third column). Rows highlighted in yellow identify systems that make use of additional monolingual data. Our system is tagged as FBAI.

Description (En → My)	BLEU	Adequacy
FBAI	39.3	3.9
FBAI	36.8	-
Team A	31.3	2.4
Team B	30.8	2.7
Team C	30.8	-
Team D	28.2	-
Team F	25.9	-
Team G	22.5	-
Team H	20.9	1.1
Team I	19.9	-

Table 6: En→My leaderboard[6]. The values are BLEU score (second column) and Adequacy scores (third column). Rows highlighted in yellow identify systems that make use of additional monolingual data. Our system is tagged as FBAI.

ensemble improves by +7.78 BLEU points for My→En compared to best supervised model, and +3.18 points for En→My .

At the second iteration, we use the same amount of monolingual data of iteration 1 and repeat the same exact process. The model architecture is the same as in the first iteration. We ensemble two models for My→En and use a single model for En→My . We further improve upon the previous iteration by +1.41 points for My→En and +0.27 points for En→My .

At the third and last iteration, we use more monolingual data for both languages, 28M Myanmar sentences and 79M English sentences. We found beneficial (Ng et al., 2019) at this iteration to increase FFN dimension to 8192 and the number of heads to 16. Each model is trained on 8 Volta GPUs for 30 hours. After training models on the parallel and synthetic datasets, we fine-tune each of them on the ALT training set, followed by ensembling. We ensemble 5 models for both directions and apply noisy channel re-ranking as our final submission. Compared to iteration 2 models, the final models yield +0.94 points gain for My→En and +0.26 points for En→My . The BLEU scores of this system on the test set are 38.59 for My→En and 39.25 for En→My .

4.3 Final Evaluation

Tables 5 and 6 report the leaderboard results provided by the organizers of the competition. For each direction, they selected the best system of

the four teams that scored the best according to BLEU, and they performed a JPO adequacy human evaluation (Nakazawa et al., 2018). These evaluations are conducted by professional translations who assign a score between 1 and 5 to each translation based on its adequacy. A score equal to 5 points means that all the important information is correctly reported while a score equal to 1 point means that almost all the important information is missing or incorrect.

First, we observe that our system achieves the best BLEU and adequacy score in both directions, with a gain of more than 8 BLEU points over the second best entry for both directions. The average adequacy score is 0.4 point and 1.2 point higher than the second best entry for My→En and En→My , respectively. Among the rated sentences, more than 30% of sentences translated by our system are rated with 5 points in En→My , compared to 6.3% of the second best system. For My→En , 48% of our translated sentences are rated with 5 points while the second best system has only 24.5%. See Fig 1 for the percentage of each score obtained by the best systems which participated in the competition.

Second, our submission which does not use additional monolingual data is even stronger than all the other submissions in En→My in terms of BLEU score, including those that do make use of additional monolingual data (see second row of Tab. 6).

If we consider submissions that only use the provided parallel data (see rows that are not highlighted), our submission improves upon the sec-

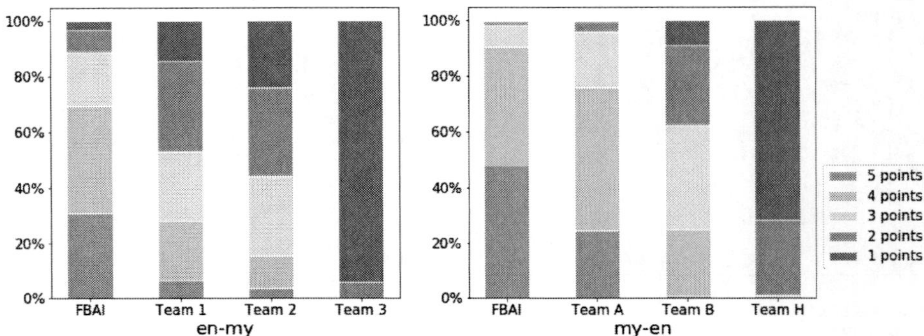

Figure 1: Percentage of each adequacy score obtained by the best systems which participated in the competition. Our system is tagged as FBAI.

ond best system by 7.2 BLEU in My→En and 10.9 BLEU in En→My . This suggests that our baseline system is very strong and that applying ST and BT to the parallel dataset is a good way to build even stronger baselines, as demonstrated also in Tab. 3.

Finally, the gains brought by monolingual datasets is striking only in My→En (+11.8 BLEU points in My→En compared to only +2.5 BLEU points in En→My , for our submissions). The reason is because the ALT test set originates from English news and the target English monolingual data is high quality and in-domain with the test set. Moreover, the source originating Myanmar sentences are translationese of English news sentences, a setting which is particularly favorable to BT. Instead, Myanmar monolingual data is out-of-domain and noisy which makes BT much less effective. ST helps improving BT performance as shown in Tab. 2 but the gains are still limited.

5   Conclusion

We described the approach we used in our submission to the WAT 2019 Myanmar-English machine translation competition. Our approach achieved the best performance both with and without the use of additional monolingual data. It is based on several methods which we combine together. First, we use back-translation to help regularizing and adapting to the test domain, particularly in the Myanmar to English direction. Second, we use self-training as a way to better leverage in-domain source-side monolingual data, particularly in the English to Myanmar direction. Third, given the complementary nature of these two approaches we combined them in an iterative fashion. Fourth,

we improve decoding by using noisy-channel re-ranking and ensembling.

We surmise that there is still quite some room for improvement by better leveraging noisy parallel data resources, by better combining together these different sources of additional data, and by designing better approaches to leverage source side monolingual data.

Acknowledgements

The Authors wish to thank Sergey Edunov for sharing precious insights about his experience participating in WMT competitions and Htet Linn for feedback on how spacing is used in Burmese and for checking a handful of translations during early development.

References

Mikel Artetxe and Holger Schwenk. 2018. Massively Multilingual Sentence Embeddings for Zero-Shot Cross-Lingual Transfer and Beyond. *arXiv preprint arXiv:1812.10464*.

Loïc Barrault, Ondřej Bojar, Marta R. Costa-jussà, Christian Federmann, Mark Fishel, Yvette Graham, Barry Haddow, Matthias Huck, Philipp Koehn, Shervin Malmasi, Christof Monz, Mathias Müller, Santanu Pal, Matt Post, and Marcos Zampieri. 2019. Findings of the 2019 conference on machine translation (WMT19). In *Proceedings of the Fourth Conference on Machine Translation (Volume 2: Shared Task Papers, Day 1)*, pages 1–61, Florence, Italy. Association for Computational Linguistics.

Peter F. Brown, Stephen A. Della-Pietra, Vincent J. Della-Pietra, and Robert L. Mercer. 1993. The mathematics of statistical machine translation. *Computational Linguistics*, 19(2):263–313.

Christian Buck, Kenneth Heafield, and Bas van Ooyen. 2014. N-gram counts and language models from the common crawl. In *Proceedings of the Language Resources and Evaluation Conference*, Reykjavik, Iceland.

Christian Buck and Philipp Koehn. 2016. Quick and reliable document alignment via tf/idf-weighted cosine distance. In *Proceedings of the First Conference on Machine Translation: Volume 2, Shared Task Papers*, pages 672–678.

Isaac Caswell, Ciprian Chelba, and David Grangier. 2019. Tagged back-translation. *arXiv preprint arXiv:1906.06442*.

Vishrav Chaudhary, Yuqing Tang, Francisco Guzmán, Holger Schwenk, and Philipp Koehn. 2019. Low-resource corpus filtering using multilingual sentence embeddings. In *Proceedings of the Fourth Conference on Machine Translation (WMT)*.

Chenchen Ding, Hnin Thu Zar Aye, Win Pa Pa, Khin Thandar Nwet, Khin Mar Soe, Masao Utiyama, and Eiichiro Sumita. 2019. Towards Burmese (Myanmar) morphological analysis: Syllable-based tokenization and part-of-speech tagging. *ACM Transactions on Asian and Low-Resource Language Information Processing (TALLIP)*, 19(1):5.

Chenchen Ding, Masao Utiyama, and Eiichiro Sumita. 2018. NOVA: A feasible and flexible annotation system for joint tokenization and part-of-speech tagging. *ACM Transactions on Asian and Low-Resource Language Information Processing (TALLIP)*, 18(2):17.

Francisco Guzmán, Peng-Jen Chen, Myle Ott, Juan Pino, Guillaume Lample, Philipp Koehn, Vishrav Chaudhary, and Marc'Aurelio Ranzato. 2019. Two new evaluation datasets for low-resource machine translation: Nepali-english and sinhala-english. *arXiv preprint arXiv:1902.01382*.

Hany Hassan, Anthony Aue, Chang Chen, Vishal Chowdhary, Jonathan Clark, Christian Federmann, Xuedong Huang, Marcin Junczys-Dowmunt, William Lewis, Mu Li, Shujie Liu, Tie-Yan Liu, Renqian Luo, Arul Menezes, Tao Qin, Frank Seide, Xu Tan, Fei Tian, Lijun Wu, Shuangzhi Wu, Yingce Xia, Dongdong Zhang, Zhirui Zhang, and Ming Zhou. 2018. Achieving human parity on automatic chinese to english news translation. In *arXiv:1803.05567*.

Junxian He, Jiatao Gu, Jiajun Shen, and Marc'Aurelio Ranzato. 2019. Revisiting self-training for neural sequence generation. *arXiv:1909.13788*.

Armand Joulin, Edouard Grave, Piotr Bojanowski, and Tomas Mikolov. 2017. Bag of tricks for efficient text classification. In *Proceedings of the 15th Conference of the European Chapter of the Association for Computational Linguistics: Volume 2, Short Papers*, pages 427–431. Association for Computational Linguistics.

Catherine Kobus, Josep Maria Crego, and Jean Senellart. 2016. Domain control for neural machine translation. *CoRR*, abs/1612.06140.

Philipp Koehn, Francisco Guzmán, Vishrav Chaudhary, and Juan M. Pino. 2019. Findings of the wmt 2019 shared task on parallel corpus filtering for low-resource conditions. In *Proceedings of the Fourth Conference on Machine Translation, Volume 2: Shared Task Papers*, Florence, Italy. Association for Computational Linguistics.

Philipp Koehn, Hieu Hoang, Alexandra Birch, Chris Callison-Burch, Marcello Federico, Nicola Bertoldi, Brooke Cowan, Wade Shen, Christine Moran, Richard Zens, Chris Dyer, Ondřej Bojar, Alexandra Constantin, and Evan Herbst. 2007. Moses: Open source toolkit for statistical machine translation. In *Proceedings of the 45th Annual Meeting of the ACL on Interactive Poster and Demonstration Sessions*, ACL '07, pages 177–180. Association for Computational Linguistics.

Taku Kudo and John Richardson. 2018. Sentencepiece: A simple and language independent subword tokenizer and detokenizer for neural text processing. *Proceedings of the 2018 Conference on Empirical Methods in Natural Language Processing: System Demonstrations*.

G. Lample, A. Conneau, L. Denoyer, and M. Ranzato. 2018a. Unsupervised machine translation using monolingual corpora only. In *International Conference on Learning Representations (ICLR)*.

Guillaume Lample and Alexis Conneau. 2019. Cross-lingual language model pretraining. *CoRR*, abs/1901.07291.

Guillaume Lample, Myle Ott, Alexis Conneau, Ludovic Denoyer, and Marc'Aurelio Ranzato. 2018b. Phrase-based & neural unsupervised machine translation. In *Empirical Methods in Natural Language Processing (EMNLP)*.

Yinhan Liu, Myle Ott, Naman Goyal, Jingfei Du, Mandar Joshi, Danqi Chen, Omer Levy, Mike Lewis, Luke Zettlemoyer, and Veselin Stoyanov. 2019. Roberta: A robustly optimized bert pretraining approach. *arXiv preprint arXiv:1907.11692*.

Toshiaki Nakazawa, Chenchen Ding, Raj Dabre, Hideya Mino, Isao Goto, Win Pa Pa, Nobushige Doi, Yusuke Oda, Anoop Kunchukuttan, Shantipriya Parida, Ondej Bojar, and Sadao Kurohashi. 2019. Overview of the 6th workshop on Asian translation. In *Proceedings of the 6th Workshop on Asian Translation*, Hong Kong. Association for Computational Linguistics.

Toshiaki Nakazawa, Katsuhito Sudoh, Shohei Higashiyama, Chenchen Ding, Raj Dabre, Hideya Mino, Isao Goto, Win Pa Pa, Anoop Kunchukuttan, and Sadao Kurohashi. 2018. Overview of the

5th workshop on Asian translation. In *Proceedings of the 32nd Pacific Asia Conference on Language, Information and Computation: 5th Workshop on Asian Translation: 5th Workshop on Asian Translation*, Hong Kong. Association for Computational Linguistics.

Nathan Ng, Kyra Yee, Alexei Baevski, Myle Ott, Michael Auli, and Sergey Edunov. 2019. Facebook fair's wmt19 news translation task submission. *arXiv preprint arXiv:1907.06616*.

Myle Ott, Sergey Edunov, Alexei Baevski, Angela Fan, Sam Gross, Nathan Ng, David Grangier, and Michael Auli. 2019. fairseq: A fast, extensible toolkit for sequence modeling. In *Proceedings of NAACL-HLT 2019: Demonstrations*.

K. Papineni, S. Roukos, T. Ward, and W.J. Zhu. 2002. Bleu: a method for automatic evaluation of machine translation. In *Proceedings of the 40th Annual Meeting of the Association for Computational Linguistics*.

Alec Radford, Karthik Narasimhan, Tim Salimans, and Ilya Sutskever. 2018. Improving language understanding by generative pre-training. *URL https://s3-us-west-2. amazonaws. com/openai-assets/researchcovers/languageunsupervised/language understanding paper. pdf*.

Rico Sennrich, Barry Haddow, and Alexandra Birch. 2015. Improving neural machine translation models with monolingual data. In *Proceedings of the 54th Annual Meeting of the Association for Computational Linguistics*, pages 86–96.

Rico Sennrich, Barry Haddow, and Alexandra Birch. 2016. Controlling politeness in neural machine. In *Proceedings of NAACL-HLT*.

Jiajun Shen, Peng-Jen Chen, Matt Le, Junxian He, Jiatao Gu, Myle Ott, Michael Auli, and Marc'Aurelio Ranzato. 2019. The source-target domain mismatch problem in machine translation. *arXiv:1909.13151*.

Ye Kyaw Thu, Win Pa Pa, Masao Utiyama, Andrew Finch, and Eiichiro Sumita. 2016. Introducing the asian language treebank (alt). In *LREC*.

Nicola Ueffing. 2006. Using monolingual source-language data to improve mt performance. In *IWSLT*.

P. Vincent, H. Larochelle, Y. Bengio, and P.A. Manzagol. 2008. Extracting and composing robust features with denoising autoencoders. In *Proceedings of the 25th international conference on Machine learning*.

David Yarowski. 1995. Unsupervised word sense disambiguation rivaling supervised methods. In *Annual Meeting of the Association for Computational Linguistics*.

Kyra Yee, Nathan Ng, Yann N. Dauphin, and Michael Auli. 2019. Simple and effective noisy channel modeling for neural machine translation. *arXiv:1908.05731*.

Jiajun Zhang and Chengqing Zong. 2016. Exploiting source-side monolingual data in neural machine translation. In *Empirical Methods in Natural Language Processing*.

A Hyper-Parameter Search

In this section we report the set of hyper-parameters and range of values that we used in our random hyper-parameter search. For each experiment we searched using $N = 30$ hyper-parameter configurations.

Notice that the actual range of hyper-parameters searched in each experiment may be smaller than reported below; for instance, if a model shows signs of overfitting we may search up to 5 layers as opposed to 6 at the next iteration.

- Layers: $\{4, 5, 6\}$

- Embedding dim: $\{128, 256, 512, 1024\}$

- FFN dim: $\{128, 256, 512, 1024, 2048, 4096, 8192\}$

- Attention heads: $\{1, 2, 4, 8, 16\}$

- Dropout: $\{0.1, 0.2, 0.3, 0.4, 0.5\}$

- Batch size (number of tokens): $\{1, 2, 4, 8, 12, 16, 24, 32\}$ (multiply by 16000)

- Label smoothing: $\{0.1, 0.2, 0.3\}$

- Learning rate: $\{1, 3, 5, 7, 10, 30, 50, 100, 300, 500\}$ (multiply by 1e-4)

- Seed: $\{1, 2, 3, \dots, 30\}$

- Data upsampling ratio
  - bitext: $\{1, 2, 3, 4, 6, 8, 12, 16, 20, 32, 40, 64\}$
  - forward-translated: $\{1, 2, 3, 4, 6, 8, 9\}$
  - back-translated: $\{1, 2, 3, 4, 6, 8, 9\}$

When applying noisy-channel reranking, we tune the hyper-parameters λ_1 and λ_2 on the validation set. The ranges of the two hyper-parameters are between 0 and 3.

B Things We Tried But Did Not Use

This section details attempts that did not significantly improve the overall performance of our translation system and which were therefore left out of the final system.

B.1 Out-of-domain parallel data

Similarly to Guzmán et al. (2019) we added out-of-domain parallel data from various sources of the OPUS repository[7], namely GNOME/Ubuntu, QED and GlobalVoices. This provides an additional 38,459 sentence pairs. We also considered two versions of Bible translations from the bible-corpus[8] resulting in additional 61,843 sentence pairs. Adding this data improved the baseline system by +0.17 BLEU for My→En and +0.26 BLEU for En→My .

B.2 Pre-training

We pre-trained our translation system using a cross-lingual language modeling task (Lample and Conneau, 2019) as well as a Denoising Auto-Encoding (DAE) task (Vincent et al., 2008). They both did not provide significant improvements; in the following, we report our results using DAE.

In this setting, we have a single encoder-decoder model which takes a batch of monolingual data, encodes it with the model's encoder, prepends the encoded representation with a language-specific token, and then tries to reconstruct the original input using the model's decoder. Additionally, the source sentences are corrupted using three different types of noise: word dropping, word blanking, and word swapping (Lample et al., 2018a,b). The goal is to encourage the model to learn some kind of common representation for both languages.

We found some gains, particularly for the En→My direction, however, doing backtranslation on top of DAE pretraining did worse or did not improve compared to backtranslation without DAE pretraining. For this reason, we decided to leave this technique out of our final system.

B.3 PBSMT

We also train a phrase based system using Moses with a default setting. We preprocessed the data using moses tokenizer for English sentences. For Myanmar sentences, we use BPE instead. We train a count-based 5-gram English and Myanmar language models on the monolingual data we collect. We tune the system using MERT on the ALT validation set. However, the phrase based system does not perform as good as our NMT baseline.

---

[7]http://opus.nlpl.eu/
[8]https://github.com/christos-c/bible-corpus/

The phrase based system we train on the parallel data only yields 10.98 BLEU for My→En and 21.89 BLEU for En→My , which are 12.32 and 13.05 BLEU points lower than our supervised single NMT model.

B.4 Weak Supervision

For augmenting the original training data with a noisy set of parallel sentences, we mine bitexts from Commoncrawl. This is achieved by first aligning the webpages in English and Myanmar and then extracting parallel sentences from them. To align webpages, we perform sentence alignment using the IBM1 sentence alignment algorithm (Brown et al., 1993), trained on the provided parallel data to obtain bilingual dictionaries from English to Myanmar and Myanmar to English. Using these dictionaries, unigram-based Myanmar translations are added to the English web documents and Myanmar translations are added to the English documents. The similarity score of a document pair a and b is computed as:

$$sim(a, b) = Lev(url_a, url_b) \times Jaccard(a, b)$$

(2)

where $Lev(url_a, url_b)$ is the Levenshtein similarity between the url_a and url_b and $Jaccard(a, b)$ is the Jaccard similarity between documents a and b. Finally, a one-to-one matching between English and Myanmar documents is enforced by applying a greedy bipartite matching algorithm as described in Buck and Koehn (2016). The set of matched aligned documents is then mined for parallel bitexts.

We align sentences within two comparable webpages by following the methods outlined in the parallel corpus filtering shared task for low-resource languages (Koehn et al., 2019). One of the best performing methods for this task used the LASER model (Artetxe and Schwenk, 2018) to gauge similarity between sentence pairs (Chaudhary et al., 2019). Since the open-source LASER model is only trained with 2,000 Myanmar-English bitexts, we retrained the model using the provided UCSY and ALT corpora. For tuning, we use similarity error on the ALT validation dataset and observe that the model performs rather poorly as the available training data was substantially lower than the original setup.

Combining Translation Memory with Neural Machine Translation

Akiko Eriguchi
Microsoft

Spencer Rarrick
Microsoft

Hitokazu Matsushita
Microsoft

One Microsoft Way, Redmond, WA 98052 USA
{akikoe, spencer, himatsus}@microsoft.com

Abstract

In this paper, we report our submission systems (geoduck) to the Timely Disclosure task on the 6th Workshop on Asian Translation (WAT) (Nakazawa et al., 2019). Our system employs a combined approach of translation memory and Neural Machine Translation (NMT) models, where we can select final translation outputs from either a translation memory or an NMT system, when the similarity score of a test source sentence exceeds the predefined threshold. We observed that this combination approach significantly improves the translation performance on the Timely Disclosure corpus, as compared to a standalone NMT system. We also conducted source-based direct assessment on the final output, and we discuss the comparison between human references and each system's output.

1   Introduction

One of the desired features in automatic translation systems is the ability to flexibly make use of a translation memory to translate known sentences and phrase, while still allowing a more flexible Machine Translation (MT) model to translate less-familiar phrases and sentences without sacrificing quality. Koehn and Senellart (2010) explored methods of combining translation memories with statistical machine translation, and proposed a method to apply phrase fixing on the translation candidate retrieved from the translation memory. As for statistical machine translation models, Neural Machine Translation (NMT) models have been nowadays employed in large-scale production MT systems (Johnson et al., 2017; Hassan et al., 2018) due to its state-of-the-art performance in many languages.

There are several studies that combine translation memories with NMT models. Cao and Xiong (2018) introduced the idea of using a trans-

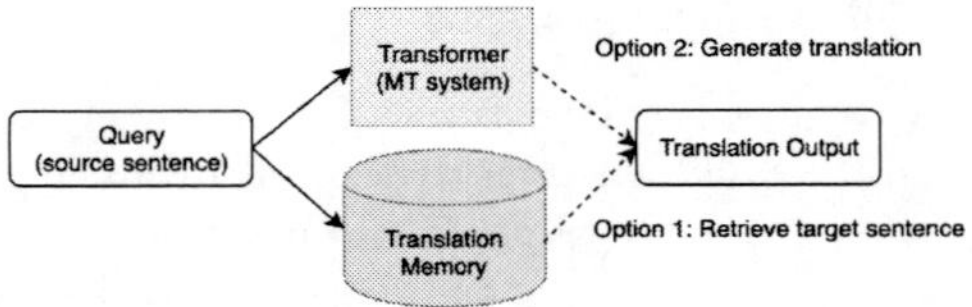

Figure 1: Overview of our proposed approach combining translation memory and NMT models.

lation memory gating network with NMT models in a multi-encoder fashion so that the model can make full use of both training data and the retrieved data. Zhao et al. (2018) created phrase tables as recommendation memory and let the NMT models select the better translation. In Gu et al. (2018), the authors proposed a search-engine-guided NMT model, where a search engine first collects a small subset of relevant training translation pairs from the translation memory and NMT models are trained on the subset as well.

In this paper, we combine a translation memory with an NMT model, simply choosing either the translation memory output or NMT output at inference time, depending on a similarity score of a given source sentence, and then investigate the effectiveness of this strategy. Figure 1 illustrates an overview of our proposed architecture. In Section 2, we first conduct an analysis of the Timely Disclosure task data set and report interesting characteristics. In Section 3, we explain our approach of combining a translation memory with an NMT model. We describe our experimental design in Section 4, and we report experimental results, human evaluation analyses, and discussion in Section 5. In Section 6, we conclude by summarizing our findings on the task and contributions of the paper.

Proceedings of the 6th Workshop on Asian Translation, pages 123–130
Hong Kong, China, November 4, 2019. ©2019 Association for Computational Linguistics

	size	# (Ja)	# (En)
Train.	1,403,995	583,805	709,358
Dev.	3,998	3,518	3,752
Devtest	4,014	3,753	3,483
Test	3,277	2,898	——

Table 1: Data statistics of Timely Disclosure Documents Corpus. # denotes the number of unique sentences in each language.

2 Analysis of Timely Disclosure Documents Corpus

We first analyzed the data set for the Timely Disclosure Task[1] to better understand trends in the data set. The corpus consists of past years' timely disclosure documents, and contains about 1.4 million Japanese-English sentence pairs. Table 1 reports the statistics of the full corpus. Here, we show the total size of parallel corpora, as well as the number of unique Japanese (Ja) and English (En) sentences in each data set. From this table, we can observe a large number of duplicated training examples on both the source and target sides. We also checked for duplicates between training data (Train.), development (Dev.) and devtest (Devtest), and found respectively 1,047 and 1,117 duplicated translation pairs between Train. and Dev. / Devtest data sets. Note that unique hash values are given to all translation pairs, which guarantees that these sentence-level translation pairs are independently sampled from the original documents. This finding is our motivation for combining translation memory retrieval with NMT models, and we investigate if this leads to an improvement in translation quality.

3 Combining Translation Memory with Neural Machine Translation

As observed in Section 2, approximately 26% of the development data set and 28% of the devtest data set are exact duplicates on both source and target of a sentence pair in the training data set. Considering this characteristic of the evaluation data sets, we use the entire training data set as a translation memory and allow the system to directly retrieve a translation candidate for each test sentence based on the best similarity score. If there is no translation candidates in the translation memory whose similarity score exceeds the threshold, we let the NMT models generate a translation and use it as a final output. We would like to mention that this kind of translation scenario is not specific to this task data set but also is common in other domain text translations like a software manual. We aim at investigating when to and when not to translate from scratch in such scenarios.

3.1 Retrieval Approaches on Translation Memory

The retrieval approach on the translation memory is useful, since it is well known that NMT models are data-hungry and it is difficult to control the translation outputs generated by NMT models. At inference time, we calculate a sentence-level similarity score between a query, i.e. a given source sentence, and all the source sentences stored in the translation memory. If there exists a source sentence in the translation memory whose similarity score is above the threshold, we employ its target sentence as a final output. In our systems, we provide two types of retrieval approaches: 1) Edit-distance-based retrieval and 2) Inverse document frequency(IDF)-based retrieval.

Edit-distance-based retrieval The edit-distance-based retrieval is a widely-used method in work that investigates using translation memories to enhance NMT models (Gu et al., 2018; Cao and Xiong, 2018). We calculate the similarity score between two source sentences (S_1 and S_2) using the character-based Levenshtein distance as follows:

$$\text{Sim}_{edit}(S_1, S_2) = 1 - \frac{\Delta_{dist}(S_1, S_2)}{\max(|S_1|, |S_2|)}, \quad (1)$$

where Δ_{dist} indicates the Levenshtein distance of sentences S_1 and S_2. $|S|$ denotes the length of a sentence S.

IDF-based retrieval An IDF-based retrieval approach was investigated by Bapna and Firat (2019). Following the previous work, we calculate a sentence-level similarity score by using an IDF score f_t of a token t as follows:

$$\text{Sim}_{idf}(S_1, S_2) = 2 \times \sum_{t \in (S_1 \bigcup S_2)} f_t \\ - \sum_{t \in (S_1 \bigcap S_2)} f_t, \quad (2)$$

[1]http://lotus.kuee.kyoto-u.ac.jp/WAT/
Timely_Disclosure_Documents_Corpus/

$$f_t = \log \frac{|C_{TM}|}{n_t}, \qquad (3)$$

where $|C_{TM}|$ is the number of sentence pairs in the translation memory. n_t denotes the number of occurrences of a token t in the corpus. In our preliminary experiments, we found that using sub-words for a token unit t is better than characters. We also tried IDF-based n-gram retrieval proposed in (Bapna and Firat, 2019); however, the two above-mentioned retrieval methods always worked better.

3.2 Neural Machine Translation

We employ a Transformer (base) model (Vaswani et al., 2017) as a default NMT system in our proposed approach. Transformer is modeled as an encoder-decoder network architecture, where an input sentence $x = (x_1, x_2, \ldots, x_n)$ is encoded into a fixed vector space and decoded from the fixed vector to the output sequence $y = (y_1, y_2, \ldots, y_m)$. Following Vaswani et al. (2017), the inputs are mapped into the 512-dimensional embedding space with positional embedding. Both the encoder and decoder networks map the vectors through 6-layer 2048-dimensional feed-forward networks with 8-head self-attention and layer-normalization (Ba et al., 2016), and the decoder has an 8-head attention layer before the feed-forward network layer between the target hidden state and the source hidden states. We shared the parameters across the target embeddings and a softmax layer in the decoder (Inan et al., 2017; Hashimoto and Tsuruoka, 2017). To avoid overfitting, we use dropout with the rate of 0.1 and introduce the label-smoothed cross entropy loss with the coefficient of 0.1 (Pereyra et al., 2017). We use Adam (Kingma and Ba, 2015) to optimize all model parameters. We apply warm-up learning rate scheduling, increasing the learning rate linearly during predefined warm-up updates and applying learning rate decay based on the inverse square root of the update number (Vaswani et al., 2017).

4 Experimental Design

Data Preparation All of the training corpora provided for ITEM and TEXT data are concatenated into a single training corpus. We also use the 1M Japanese-English Wikipedia parallel corpus provided by Asai et al. (2018) as an additional training resource. The corpus is automatically created by crawling multilingual Wikipedia pages and applying a sentence aligner. Because the parallel data in that corpus are pre-tokenized, we applied a detokenization script on both sides. In preliminary experiments, we confirmed that using the additional Wikipedia training data improved translation accuracy on the task.

All of the data sets are tokenized using `SentencePiece` (Kudo and Richardson, 2018), and we set the vocabulary size to 32k. To determine the optimal sentence-similarity threshold in the retrieval approaches, we evaluated the systems based on `sacreBLEU` score (Post, 2018) with thresholds varying within $\{80, 100\}$ and $\{10, 25\}$ for THRESHOLD$_{edit}$ and THRESHOLD$_{IDF}$, respectively. The best thresholds for each NMT system are determined based on the development results. When tuning our submission systems, we perform the threshold optimization on the devtest data, and the development data is added into the translation memory.

System Description A (Marian) We use a codebase of *Marian* (Junczys-Dowmunt et al., 2018) to train the Transformer model described in Subsection 3.2. In System A, we set the mini-batch size to 1,000. The initial learning rate and warm-up steps are set to 0.0002 and 8,000. The maximum length of the training examples is set to 100, and 0.4% training data are discarded during the training. We trained the system for 200k updates with 8 GPUs. Regarding data preprocessing, we create a joint vocabulary with the size of 32k. We refer System A as "Marian" after this.

System Description B (Fairseq) We use a vocabulary set separately created in the source and target languages, and each vocabulary size is set to 32k. We fill a mini-batch with up to 6,000 tokens, and we use the initial learning rate of $1e-07$ and warm-up updates of 2,000. We trained the model for 80k updates with 4 GPUs. We use a codebase of *Fairseq* (Ott et al., 2019). We refer System B as "Fairseq" in the following sections. At inference time, we use the beam-search decoding with the size of $\{4, 8, 12\}$ and select the best beam size based on the development results for both systems.

Large-scale Black-box MT systems To verify the effectiveness of using translation memory on the task, we experiment by using three types of production-level black-box MT systems, i.e.

	Dev.	Devtest
Marian	48.6	50.6
Fairseq	40.9	42.2
Online A	24.8	24.8
Online B	24.5	24.4
Online C	24.5	24.5

Table 2: General translation accuracy of each system on the concatenated data (ITEM+TEXT).

Google Translate[2], Microsoft Bing Translator[3], and Mirai Translate[4]. More concretely, we replace our MT outputs with those of the production MT systems and evaluate the translation performance. These online MT systems are anonymized into Online A, Online B and Online C in a random order after this section.

5 Results and Discussion

5.1 Experimental Results

First of all, we evaluate the overall translation accuracy of each NMT system and production system on the concatenated data (ITEM+TEXT). Table 2 reports the case-sensitive `sacreBLEU` scores of the NMT systems and the production systems without translation memory. Marian shows the best BLEU score on both development and devtest datasets. The reason for this can be that Marian as an over-trained model translates better on the duplicates. We also see huge gaps between our white-box NMT systems and online black-box MT systems at least by 16.1 and 17.4 BLEU scores on development and devtest data sets, respectively. The three online systems show equivalent accuracy with each other due to lacking the training examples of the task.

Table 3 shows the experimental results of our proposed approach using the translation memory, reporting the sacreBLEU scores on the ITEM and TEXT evaluation data sets. The best retrieval approach is different for those two data sets. We found that in general, edit-distance-based retrieval produces better results for ITEM data, while the IDF-based retrieval works better for TEXT data. The only exception to this was Online C on

[2]`https://translate.google.com/`, as of July, 2019.
[3]`https://www.bing.com/translator`, as of July, 2019.
[4]`https://miraitranslate.com/en/` as of July, 2019.

		threshold	Dev.	Devtest
ITEM	Marian	89	54.1	58.1
	Fairseq	89	53.3	57.0
	Online A	83	51.2	55.6
	Online B	80	51.8	55.8
	Online C	83	51.6	55.6
TEXT	Marian	18	57.7	57.9
	Fairseq	14	57.1	57.6
	Online A	15	55.9	56.7
	Online B	10	55.6	56.4
	Online C	80	55.7	56.8

Table 3: BLEU results of our proposed approach on the evaluation data sets (ITEM and TEXT).

		threshold	Devtest.	Test
ITEM	Marian	95	57.5	54.27
	Fairseq	89	56.6	50.90
TEXT	Marian	21	58.0	61.38
	Fairseq	18	57.7	51.08

Table 4: BLEU results on the evaluation data sets (ITEM and TEXT). We employed edit-distance-based and IDF-based retrieval approaches for evaluation on the ITEM and TEXT data sets, respectively. The BLEU scores on the test set are cited from the official leader board (`http://lotus.kuee.kyoto-u.ac.jp/WAT/evaluation/`).

TEXT. Higher sentence-similarity thresholds were selected for Marian and Fairseq with the ITEM data, indicating that the outputs generated by these systems show better quality than those by the online systems. Introducing the translation memory to the systems outputs, however, we can largely fill the gaps between our systems and the online systems by around 1-2 BLEU scores on both evaluation data sets.

Table 4 shows the results of our submission systems on the devtest and test data sets, where Fairseq provides the result of an ensemble with 4 replicas. We include the development translation pairs in the translation memory, and selected the threshold to use on the test data based on scores on the devtest data set.

5.2 Human Evaluation

We used source-based direct assessment for human evaluation, as described in Cettolo et al.

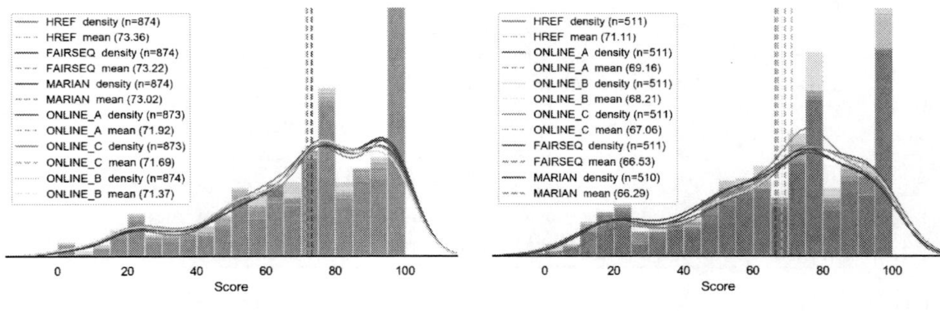

(a) ITEM Score Distribution   (b) TEXT Score Distribution

Figure 2: Human Evaluation Score Distributions

(2017). For the annotation process, we used an updated version of Appraise (Federmann, 2012), the human evaluation tool used for the Conference on Machine Translation (WMT)[5], and we followed the evaluation campaign setup as specified in Hassan et al. (2018). In source-based direct assessment, annotators are shown source text and a candidate translation and are asked the question "How accurately does the above candidate text convey the semantics of the source text?", answering this using a slider ranging from 0 (Not at all) to 100 (Perfectly).

In this campaign we examined five systems: Marian, Fairseq, Online A, Online B and Online C. We also added human reference (HREF) to the campaign for comparison. Table 5 shows the evaluation campaign parameters. We hired 25 bilingual crowd-sourced annotators and assigned two tasks to each. We collected a single score for each of the randomly selected translations on each system. There were no overlapping annotation items among annotators. For the ITEM testset, we obtained at least 873 assessments for each system[6]. Likewise we obtained 511 assessments for the TEXT testset. We collected a total of 8,308 annotation data points.

Table 6 shows the mean scores for ITEM, TEXT and ALL (ITEM+TEXT) for each system. A boldfaced number indicates that the mean score is indistinguishable from HREF in the same category (ITEM, TEXT or ALL) using the Mann-Whitney U Test at p-level $p < 0.05$. Figures 2a and 2b show the evaluation score distributions for ITEM and TEXT, respectively.

[5]http://www.statmt.org/wmt19/
[6]We obtained 874 assessments for some systems.

Testset:	Devtest
Annotators:	25
Tasks:	50
Redundancy:	1
Task per Annotator:	2
Data points:	8308

Table 5: Human Evaluation Campaign Parameters

	ITEM	TEXT	ALL
HREF	73.4	71.0	72.5
Fairseq	**73.2**	66.5	70.8
Marian	**73.0**	66.3	70.5
Online A	**71.9**	69.2	**70.9**
Online B	**71.4**	68.2	70.2
Online C	**71.7**	67.1	70.0

Table 6: Human Evaluation results. The boldfaced numbers indicate that they are indistinguishable from HREF at p-level $p < 0.05$.

5.3 Discussion

The human evaluation results indicate that the translation quality of each system is comparable with human reference for the ITEM testset while the differences were statistically significant for the TEXT testset. One possible reason for this is that the retrieval approach using the translation memory works better for shorter sentence translation in the ITEM dataset but not for longer sentence translation in the TEXT dataset. The average English sentence length of the ITEM devtest is 7.7, whereas that of the TEXT devtest is 25.6. Regarding the number of unique words, the ITEM data contains 22,453 vocabulary items,

	#	ITEM
Source	—	依頼者提示資料に基づき査定
HREF	28	Based on materials provided by IIA
Fairseq	99	Assessed based on documents presented by the requester.
Marian	99	Assessed based on documents presented by the requester.
Online A	99	Assessed based on documents presented by the requester.
Online B	99	Assessed based on documents presented by the requester.
Online C	99	Assessed based on documents presented by the requester.

Table 7: Translation examples of each system on the devtest data set (ITEM) that obtain a higher evaluation score than the human reference. "#" denotes the human evaluation score. All the translations are retrieved from the translation memory.

	#	TEXT
Source	—	なお、当社は平成31年3月期の配当予想を年間配当金62円00銭といたしました。
HREF	97	In addition, the Company made an annual dividend of 62.00 yen for the fiscal year ending March 31, 2019.
Fairseq	96	The dividend forecast for the fiscal year ending March 31, 2019 is 62.00 yen per share.
Marian	95	The Company's dividend forecast for the fiscal year ending March 31, 2019 is projected to be ¥62.00 per share.

Table 8: Translation examples of each system on the devtest data set (TEXT) that are highly evaluated by human annotators. The column of "#" reports the human evaluation score of each output. Both translation outputs are generated by the NMT models.

while the TEXT datasets does 28,507. These different trends between the ITEM and TEXT data suggest that the systems are required to translate relatively fixed phrases or sentences more in the ITEM data set, which is a suitable scenario for translation memories. On the other hand, it also suggests that MT is more desirable in the cases where long sentences with a variety of expressions need to be translated. However, this is not always the case for the TEXT translations with our systems because longer sentences which may contain major semantic errors can be chosen due to their high similarity scores. Tables 7 and 8 show each system's translation outputs and its human evaluation score on the devtest data set (ITEM and TEXT).

Our approach of combining a translation memory with MT systems is evaluated lower than the human reference by human annotators on the TEXT data, whereas the online systems are more highly evaluated among all the systems. It is because those production systems are better at translating longer sentences due to much larger training corpora. For instance, Google Translate is trained on three or four orders of magnitudes larger training data (Johnson et al., 2017), and such a system should cover a variety of expressions and domains. Thus, it is still important to improve the translation quality of NMT models on longer sentences, which has been actively studied in the context of document-level translation (Jean et al., 2017; Tiedemann and Scherrer, 2017; Junczys-Dowmunt, 2019).

6 Conclusion

This paper describes our submission systems to WAT'19 Timely Disclosure task. The system is a combination approach of translation memory and NMT model. First, we observed that 26-28% of data are duplicated between training data and test sets. The system enables us to directly retrieve a translation candidate from the translation memory. Any MT model can be applied to our approach, and we confirmed its effectiveness even when using black-box MT production systems. Results from the human evaluation campaign demonstrate that translation on a fixed form or short expressions can be covered well with translation memory, while NMT is much more robust especially when flexible translation on longer sentences is required.

References

Akari Asai, Akiko Eriguchi, Kazuma Hashimoto, and Yoshimasa Tsuruoka. 2018. Multilingual extractive reading comprehension by runtime machine translation. In *arXiv preprint arXiv:1809.03275*.

Jimmy Lei Ba, Jamie Ryan Kiros, and Geoffrey E. Hinton. 2016. Layer normalization. In *arXiv preprint arXiv:1607.06450*.

Ankur Bapna and Orhan Firat. 2019. Non-parametric adaptation for neural machine translation. In *Proceedings of the 2019 Conference of the North American Chapter of the Association for Computational Linguistics: Human Language Technologies, Volume 1 (Long and Short Papers)*, pages 1921–1931, Minneapolis, Minnesota. Association for Computational Linguistics.

Qian Cao and Deyi Xiong. 2018. Encoding gated translation memory into neural machine translation. In *Proceedings of the 2018 Conference on Empirical Methods in Natural Language Processing, Brussels, Belgium, October 31 - November 4, 2018*, pages 3042–3047.

Mauro Cettolo, Marcello Federico, Luisa Bentivogli, Niehues Jan, Stüker Sebastian, Sudoh Katsuitho, Yoshino Koichiro, and Federmann Christian. 2017. Overview of the IWSLT 2017 evaluation campaign. In *International Workshop on Spoken Language Translation*, pages 2–14.

Christian Federmann. 2012. Appraise: an open-source toolkit for manual evaluation of MT output. *The Prague Bulletin of Mathematical Linguistics*, 98:25–35.

Jiatao Gu, Yong Wang, Kyunghyun Cho, and Victor O. K. Li. 2018. Search engine guided neural machine translation. In *Proceedings of the Thirty-Second AAAI Conference on Artificial Intelligence, (AAAI-18), the 30th innovative Applications of Artificial Intelligence (IAAI-18), and the 8th AAAI Symposium on Educational Advances in Artificial Intelligence (EAAI-18)*, pages 5133–5140.

Kazuma Hashimoto and Yoshimasa Tsuruoka. 2017. Neural machine translation with source-side latent graph parsing. In *Proceedings of the 2017 Conference on Empirical Methods in Natural Language Processing*, pages 125–135, Copenhagen, Denmark.

Hany Hassan, Anthony Aue, Chang Chen, Vishal Chowdhary, Jonathan Clark, Christian Federmann, Xuedong Huang, Marcin Junczys-Dowmunt, William Lewis, Mu Li, et al. 2018. Achieving human parity on automatic Chinese to English news translation. *arXiv preprint arXiv:1803.05567*.

Hakan Inan, Khashayar Khosravi, and Richard Socher. 2017. Tying word vectors and word classifiers: A loss framework for language modeling. *In 7th International Conference on Learning Representations*.

Sebastien Jean, Stanislas Lauly, Orhan Firat, and Kyunghyun Cho. 2017. Does neural machine translation benefit from larger context? *arxiv preprint arXiv:1704.05135*.

Melvin Johnson, Mike Schuster, Quoc V. Le, Maxim Krikun, Yonghui Wu, Zhifeng Chen, Nikhil Thorat, Fernanda Viégas, Martin Wattenberg, Greg Corrado, Macduff Hughes, and Jeffrey Dean. 2017. Google's multilingual neural machine translation system: Enabling zero-shot translation. *Transactions of the Association for Computational Linguistics*, 5:339–351.

Marcin Junczys-Dowmunt. 2019. Microsoft translator at WMT 2019: Towards large-scale document-level neural machine translation. In *Proceedings of the Fourth Conference on Machine Translation (Volume 2: Shared Task Papers, Day 1)*, pages 225–233, Florence, Italy. Association for Computational Linguistics.

Marcin Junczys-Dowmunt, Roman Grundkiewicz, Tomasz Dwojak, Hieu Hoang, Kenneth Heafield, Tom Neckermann, Frank Seide, Ulrich Germann, Alham Fikri Aji, Nikolay Bogoychev, André F. T. Martins, and Alexandra Birch. 2018. Marian: Fast neural machine translation in C++. In *Proceedings of ACL 2018, System Demonstrations*, pages 116–121, Melbourne, Australia. Association for Computational Linguistics.

Diederick P Kingma and Jimmy Ba. 2015. Adam: A method for stochastic optimization. In *International Conference on Learning Representations (ICLR)*.

Philipp Koehn and Jean Senellart. 2010. Convergence of translation memory and statistical machine translation. In *Proceedings of AMTA Workshop on MT Research and the Translation Industry*, pages 21–31.

Taku Kudo and John Richardson. 2018. SentencePiece: A simple and language independent subword tokenizer and detokenizer for neural text processing. In *Proceedings of the 2018 Conference on Empirical Methods in Natural Language Processing: System Demonstrations*, pages 66–71, Brussels, Belgium. Association for Computational Linguistics.

Toshiaki Nakazawa, Chenchen Ding, Raj Dabre, Hideya Mino, Isao Goto, Win Pa Pa, Nobushige Doi, Yusuke Oda, Anoop Kunchukuttan, Shantipriya Parida, Ondřej Bojar, and Sadao Kurohashi. 2019. Overview of the 6th workshop on Asian translation. In *Proceedings of the 6th Workshop on Asian Translation*, Hong Kong. Association for Computational Linguistics.

Myle Ott, Sergey Edunov, Alexei Baevski, Angela Fan, Sam Gross, Nathan Ng, David Grangier, and Michael Auli. 2019. fairseq: A fast, extensible toolkit for sequence modeling. In *Proceedings of NAACL-HLT 2019: Demonstrations*.

Gabriel Pereyra, George Tucker, Jan Chorowski, Lukasz Kaiser, and Geoffrey E. Hinton. 2017. Regularizing neural networks by penalizing confident output distributions. In *In Proceedings of International Conference on Learning Representation Workshop*.

Matt Post. 2018. A call for clarity in reporting BLEU scores. In *Proceedings of the Third Conference on Machine Translation: Research Papers*, pages 186–191, Belgium, Brussels. Association for Computational Linguistics.

Jörg Tiedemann and Yves Scherrer. 2017. Neural machine translation with extended context. In *Proceedings of the Third Workshop on Discourse in Machine Translation*, pages 82–92, Copenhagen, Denmark. Association for Computational Linguistics.

Ashish Vaswani, Noam Shazeer, Niki Parmar, Jakob Uszkoreit, Llion Jones, Aidan N Gomez, L ukasz Kaiser, and Illia Polosukhin. 2017. Attention is all you need. In I. Guyon, U. V. Luxburg, S. Bengio, H. Wallach, R. Fergus, S. Vishwanathan, and R. Garnett, editors, *Advances in Neural Information Processing Systems 30*, pages 5998–6008. Curran Associates, Inc.

Yang Zhao, Yining Wang, Jiajun Zhang, and Chengqing Zong. 2018. Phrase table as recommendation memory for neural machine translation. In *Proceedings of the Twenty-Seventh International Joint Conference on Artificial Intelligence, IJCAI-18*, pages 4609–4615. International Joint Conferences on Artificial Intelligence Organization.

CVIT's Submissions to WAT-2019

Jerin Philip [*†]
IIIT Hyderabad

Shashank Siripragada[*‡]
IIIT Hyderabad

Upendra Kumar
IIIT Hyderabad

Vinay P. Namboodiri
IIT Kanpur

C.V. Jawahar
IIIT Hyderabad

Abstract

This paper describes the Neural Machine Translation systems used by IIIT Hyderabad (CVIT-MT) for the translation tasks part of WAT-2019. We participated in tasks pertaining to Indian languages and submitted results for English-Hindi, Hindi-English, English-Tamil and Tamil-English language pairs. We employ Transformer architecture experimenting with multilingual models and methods for low-resource languages.

1 Introduction

Neural Machine Translation (NMT) has emerged as the de-facto standard for language translation following the success of deep learning. Recurrent Neural Networks (Sutskever et al., 2014), Convolutional sequence to sequence (Gehring et al., 2017) and pure attention based Transformer (Vaswani et al., 2017) architectures have incrementally improved translation numbers over the years.

Recent works demonstrate success in training multiway among several languages while sharing parameters and learning across languages (Aharoni et al., 2019; Artetxe and Schwenk, 2018). Multiway models enable few-shot learning among several pairs of languages for which parallel data does not exist in training by being able to implicitly pivot (Johnson et al., 2017) through parameter sharing across languages.

Despite the success of NMT and surrounding research in neural methods in other languages around the world, not many successful NMT systems or trained models for Indian languages are available for public use at the time of writing this paper. Indian languages pose a challenge for NMT due to scarcity of parallel corpora across many languages.

In this edition of Workshop on Asian Translation (WAT) (Nakazawa et al., 2019), we explore multiway-models for Indian Languages, improving upon our WAT 2018 submissions in the IIT-Bombay Hindi-English tasks. We pursue two approaches to the UFAL English-Tamil tasks, one training from scratch (cold-start) and fine-tuning an already trained model from a pretrained model on a different dataset (warm-start).

The rest of this document is organized as follows: Section 2 outlines ideas used in the task. Section 3 details the implementation and in Section 4 we summarize our findings.

2 System Components

NMT is commonly formulated in literature within an encoder-decoder framework. An encoder consumes the source-side sequence and provides representations rich in context across the sentence. The decoder along with an attention module looks at the encoded-representations of the source-sequence and generated target-language tokens to predict the token at the current time-step.

In our experiments, we use the Transformer architecture (Vaswani et al., 2017) which is state-of-the-art in several natural language tasks such as Translation, Language modelling (Lample and Conneau, 2019) and Language understanding (Devlin et al., 2019). The transformer is used in both the encoder and decoder.

2.1 Multiway Translation Models

Recent advances and extensive studies (Aharoni et al., 2019; Johnson et al., 2017) suggest using multilingual models to get best results and robust translation systems. A single model is trained here to translate across several languages sharing parameters. We use a shared encoder and decoder for multiway training, switching between target lan-

---

*Equal contribution.

[†] `jerin.philip@research.iiit.ac.in`

[‡] `shashank.siripragada@alumni.iiit.ac.in`

Proceedings of the 6th Workshop on Asian Translation, pages 131–136
Hong Kong, China, November 4, 2019. ©2019 Association for Computational Linguistics

guages by use of a special token (`__t2xx__`) following Johnson et al. (2017).

2.2 Backtranslation

One widely successful method to exploit monolingual data to improve the NMT systems is backtranslation proposed by Sennrich et al. (2016) wherein an NMT system trained from target to source is used to translate the monolingual data. The synthetic parallel data thus obtained is used to augment the source to target NMT system. We employ backtranslation in both the multiway model and the model trained from scratch.

2.3 Low-Resource settings

It has been shown that the performance of neural machine translation (NMT) drops in low-resource conditions, underperforming statistical machine translation (SMT). Sennrich and Zhang (2019) argue that this is due to lack of system adaptation to low-resource settings. They demonstrate that with suitable choice of parameters in low-data setting NMT systems can outperform Phrase Based SMT (PBSMT). To this end they propose reduction of subword vocabulary size, aggressive dropout, label smoothing and some more set of best practices. Following their settings for our English Tamil model, we restrict the subword vocabulary size of English and Tamil to 2000 each. We also use layer normalization after every encoder and decoder layers and label smoothing.

3 Experimental Setup

In this section, we describe our setup in detail. In 3.1, we describe the multiway system which gave the best numbers for the Hindi-English tasks provided by the IIT-Bombay Hindi-English corpus, followed by the setup for UFAL English-Tamil task in 3.2. 3.3 discusses evaluation metrics common to both tasks.

3.1 Indian Language Multiway System

We use The IIT-Bombay English-Hindi (IITB-hi-en) (Kunchukuttan et al., 2018) corpus provided by the organizers. This dataset supplies parallel corpus for English-Hindi as well as monolingual Hindi corpus. We use noisy backtranslated Hindi-English corpus obtained through our previous models for the same task translating Hindi monolingual data provided by IITB-hi-en to English. In addition to this, we use the Indian Language Corpora Initiative Corpus (ILCI) (Jha, 2010) and the Indian Language Multi Parallel Corpus (WAT-ILMPC) (Nakazawa et al., 2018) consisting of subtitles provided as training data for WAT-2018.

Source	#pairs	type
IITB-hi-en	1.5M	en-hi
Backtranslated-Hindi	2.5M	en-hi
WAT-ILMPC	188K	xx-en
ILCI	50K	xx-yy
Backtranslated-wiki	10.4M	mono

Table 1: Training dataset used for ilmulti model. xx-yy indicates parallel sentences aligned across multiple languages. xx-en indicates bilingual corpora with English in one direction.

We use pairs obtained among Hindi (hi), English (en), Tamil (ta), Malayalam (ml), Telugu (te) and Urdu (ur) from the datasets mentioned in Table 1 in training our model hereafter referred to as `ilmulti`.

We use sentences extracted from Wikipedia dumps of the respective languages, monolingual data provided by WAT-ILMPC and some additionally crawled news-articles for further backtranslation to obtain more training samples across languages. We backtranslate only to Hindi and English from other low-resource languages since the BLEU scores for the other directions were not promising. We refer the reader to Philip et al. (2019) for comprehensive information on the data used in training this model and multilingual comparisons on other test-sets.

Preprocessing and Filtering We use trained SentencePiece (Kudo, 2018)[1] models to tokenize the sentences in all languages and source to target token count ratio to filter sentences. We chose sentences whose source to target ratio is between 0.8 and 1.2. In addition to this, we use a threshold of 98% language match through `langid.py` (Lui and Baldwin, 2012) to remove sentences that did not belong to the language the parallel corpus was provided for. These methods are applied on both the original training data and the backtranslated corpus added to augment training data.

Training and Inference We use the default configuration provided by `transformer` model in `fairseq` (Ott et al., 2019).[2] Embedding layers of

---

[1]https://github.com/google/sentencepiece
[2]https://github.com/pytorch/fairseq

No	Model	BLEU		RIBES		AM-FM		Human	
		en-hi	hi-en	en-hi	hi-en	en-hi	hi-en	en-hi	hi-en
1	`ilmulti`	20.17	22.62	0.761061	0.766180	0.701670	0.637230	-	-
2	1 + backtranslation	20.46	**22.91**	0.765422	**0.768324**	0.702380	**0.641730**	-	-
		en-ta	ta-en	en-ta	ta-en	en-ta	ta-en	en-ta	ta-en
3	2 (out of the box inference)	0.80	4.68						
4	2 + UFAL warm-start	10.91	27.14	0.671850	0.770024	0.795160	0.693750	-	-
5	UFAL cold-start	**13.05**	**30.04**	**0.698482**	**0.788588**	**0.801570**	**0.707060**	-	-

Table 2: Translation evaluation scores on IIT-Bombay Hindi-English and UFAL English-Tamil test sets. 3 and 4 indicate BLEU obtained during ilmulti inference out-of-box and warm-start respectively. Bold indicates best values among all submissions at the time of writing this paper.

dimension 512 are in place and are shared among the encoder and decoder (also known in literature as tied embeddings) along with the parameters. Stacked 6 Multi-Head-Attention layers were used to realize both the encoder and decoder. The model is trained with Adam optimizer with the token-wise negative log-likelihood objective. We trained on 4 nodes with 4 NVIDIA 1080Ti GPUs. We used beam-search with beam-size of 10 for generating the translations at test time.

3.2 UFAL English-Tamil Tasks

For UFAL English-Tamil tasks, we explore training single direction models from scratch and fine-tuning our ilmulti model.

Source	#pairs	type
UFAL EnTam	160K	en-ta
Leipzig Newscrawl	300K	ta mono
Kaggle Indian Politics News	300K	en mono

Table 3: Training dataset used for UFAL English-Tamil task.

Dataset For the UFAL English-Tamil translation task we used the EnTam v2.0 dataset (Ramasamy et al., 2012). This parallel corpora covers texts from bible, cinema and news domains. Additional Tamil monolingual data was obtained by sampling a subset of 300K sentences from Leipzig Tamil Newscrawl[3] data to avoid deterioration from noise per Edunov et al. (2018). For English monolingual data, we used a subset of 300K sentences randomly sampled from Kaggle Indian Politics News data[4] which contains 15346 news articles along with their headlines. We have restricted to use of only 300K additional English and Tamil monolingual sentences in order to maintain a appropriate ratio of original and synthetic parallel data after

back-translation. Adding too much synthetic parallel data introduces more than feasible noise in already brittle model trained in low-resource settings.

Preprocessing and Filtering We used SentencePiece to restrict the vocabulary size while being able to cover the full text. For the UFAL English-Tamil task we have trained a SentencePiece model separately on English and Tamil corpus restricting the Vocabulary size to 2000 tokens in each language. Pairs with length ratio of target to source sentences less than 0.7 were filtered out from both original as well as backtranslated data.

Backtranslation For backtranslation experiments, we augmented training corpus with additional data comprising of 300K sentences. We obtained the noisy synthetic data for augmentation by translating monolingual data in both en→ta and ta→en directions, using the data described in Table 3. For obtaining synthetic data, beam search with beam size of 5 was used. Edunov et al. (2018) demonstrate that the original parallel data provides much richer training signal as compared to synthetic data generated by beam search. Hence we upsample the original data by a factor of 2 which results in the ratio of UFAL EnTam(∼150K) to synthetic data(∼300K) being 1:1.

Training We used the Transformer-Base implementation available in `fairseq`. The encoder and decoder have 5 layers each with and embedding dimension of 512 and 8 attention heads. The inner-layer dimension is 2048. We apply layer normalization (Ba et al., 2016) before each encoder and decoder layer. We use dropout, weight decay and label smoothing to regularize the model. The model is trained to minimize the label smoothed cross entropy loss using Adam optimizer with label smoothing of 0.2. We run the training on 4

---

[3] `http://cls.corpora.uni-leipzig.de/en/tam_newscrawl_2011`

[4] `https://www.kaggle.com/xenomorph/indian-politics-news-2018`

Source	A room was arranged for him at Sun Towers Lodge.
Hypothesis	இவருக்கு சன் டோர்ஸ் லோட்ஜில் ஒரு அறை ஏற்பாடு செய்யப்பட்டிருந்தது.
Target	அங்குள்ள சன் டவர்ஸ் லாட்ஜில் அவருக்கு அறை ஏற்பாடாகியிருந்தது.
Source	His administration, however, has been regarded as untenable in the eyes of substantial sections of the ruling class.
Hypothesis	ஆனால் அவருடைய நிர்வாகம் ஆளும் வர்க்கத்தின் கணிசமான பிரிவுகளின் பார்வையில் தக்-கவைத்துக் கொள்ள முடியாதது என்று கருதப்படுகிறது.
Target	எவ்வாறாயினும், அவரது நிர்வாகம், ஆளும் வர்க்கத்தின் கணிசமான பிரிவினரது கண்களுக்கு ஏற்புடையதாகத் தோன்றவில்லை.
Source	பிரெஞ்சு முதலாளித்துவத்திற்கு மற்றொரு முண்டுகோல் தேவை
Hypothesis	French capitalism needs another prop.
Target	French capitalism needs another prop
Source	இந்த சூழ்நிலையில் Lufthansa விமானிகளுக்கு சலுகைகளைக் கொடுக்கத் தயாராக இருக்காது.
Hypothesis	Under these conditions, Lufthansa would not be prepared to make concessions to pilots.
Target	Under these circumstances, Lufthansa will hardly be prepared to make any concessions to the pilots.

Table 4: Examples from the test set of correctly translated samples.

NVIDIA 1080Ti GPUs with mini-batches of maximum size of 4K tokens. The model described above is referred to hereafter as Transformer-base.

We further extend the existing `ilmulti` + backtranslation model to UFAL English-Tamil training data domain by warm-starting and training for a few epochs.

Inference and decoding Decoding was performed with beam size of 5 for generation of hypotheses for both en→ta and ta→en tasks. For UFAL-3 and UFAL-5, ensembles of models were used in inference by test time averaging outputs from last 5 checkpoints saved at interval of 10 epochs. In experiment UFAL-6, for generating hypotheses, length penalty of 1.5 for en→ta task and 2.0 for ta→en task was enforced.

3.3 Evaluation

We primarily use Bilingual Evaluation Understudy (BLEU) (Papineni et al., 2002) scores for comparisons. BLEU is an automatic evaluation metric widely use for translation and is based on precision. N-grams of sizes 1-4 are used to compute precision and the geometric mean of the same is multiplied by a brevity-penalty (BP) to obtain the final score. For aggregate value over a corpus, micro averaging is performed. In addition to BLEU, we report AM-FM, RIBES (Isozaki et al., 2010) and Human Evaluation scores from the submission site, when available.

4 Results and Discussion

Since IITB-hi-en has been widely discussed in the past, we focus on UFAL English Tamil in this pa-per. We provide both qualitative and quantitative analyses of the results obtained below.

4.1 Quantitative Results

IITB-en-hi The automated evaluation scores for both directions in IITB-hi-en are reported in Table 2. For hi→en, the `ilmulti` model provides BLEU scores higher than past submissions, and the additional augmentation through backtranslation gives an extra +0.39 increase in BLEU. A similar increase in en→hi direction with respect to the `ilmulti` model was observed through addition of backtranslated data. Both provide competitive numbers, although not the best in the category[5].

UFAL English-Tamil With no further training on the `ilmulti` model with backtranslation, we evaluate for BLEU scores on the test-set of UFAL English Tamil task. However, the non-adapted model leads to poor BLEU scores. On warm-starting and training with UFAL English-Tamil dataset further for a few epochs, we obtain better scores in both directions. These numbers are reported in Table 2.

However, the warm-started multiway model underperforms compared to model trained from scratch described below. Table 6 indicates the incremental improvements along with the numbers which got us to the best scores on the test set, training from scratch using only UFAL English Tamil training data to begin with. We refer to BLEU scores obtained in UFAL-1 as base-

---

[5]The same model performs reasonably well for the WAT-ILMPC tasks from WAT-2018.

Source	Or you could leave and return to your families as men instead of murderers.
Hypothesis	அல்லது கொலைகாரர்களுக்குப் பதிலாக உங்களது குடும்பங்களுக்குத் திரும்பிப் போகலாம்.
Target	அல்லது நீங்கள் வெளியேறி, கொலைகாரர்களுக்குப் பதிலாக ஆண்களாக உங்கள் குடும்பங்களுக்குத் திரும்பலாம்.
Source	Srinivasan has his hand in the original of 'Vellithirai' currently under production in Tamil.
Hypothesis	'வெள்ளித்திரை'யின் ஒரிஜினலில் ஸ்ரீனிவாசன் கைவசம் வைத்துள்ளார்.
Target	தற்போது தமிழில் தயாராகிக் கொண்டிருக்கும் 'வெள்ளித்திரை'யின் ஒரிஜினல், 'உதயனானு தாரம்' படத்திலும் ஸ்ரீனிவாசனின் பங்களிப்பு உண்டு.
Source	அங்குள்ள சன் டவர்ஸ் லாட்ஜில் அவருக்கு அறை ஏற்பாடாகியிருந்தது.
Hypothesis	In the Sun Dawers lodged there, he had a slap.**
Target	A room was arranged for him at Sun Towers Lodge.
Source	முதன்முறையாக காதல் படமொன்றை இயக்குகிறேன்.
Hypothesis	I am directing a romantic film for the first time.**
Target	Vikraman is confident that this love story will appeal to the youth.

Table 5: Failure cases among translated samples. Red colored words in source text do not have corresponding translation in generated hypothesis. Generated hypotheses marked with ** are fluent but don't preserve meaning of source sentence.

Id	Model	BLEU	
		en-ta	ta-en
UFAL-1	Transformer-base	11.59	27.31
UFAL-2	UFAL-1 + filtered	11.73	27.58
UFAL-3	UFAL-2 + ensemble	11.96	28.05
UFAL-4	UFAL-3 + backtranslation	12.63	29.21
UFAL-5	UFAL-4 + ensemble	12.87	29.75
UFAL-6	UFAL-5 + length penalty	13.14	30.10
	UFAL-5 + length penalty	**13.05†**	**30.04†**

Table 6: Automated evaluation scores on the UFAL En-Tam v2.0 test set. This table demonstrates incremental improvements which got us to the final submission in Table 2. † indicates numbers from the submission site, others were computed locally and have minor differences.

line BLEU scores for English-Tamil and Tamil-English tasks. Using filtered data to warm-start the UFAL-1 model provided only marginal increments in BLEU for translation in both directions. In UFAL-4, significant improvements in BLEU scores were obtained by doing warm-start of English to Tamil and Tamil to English model on filtered UFAL EnTam train data augmented with additional back-translated data. Further, based on observation that length ratio of generated hypotheses to reference sentence in UFAL-5 was less than 1.0 on validation data for both tasks, we found that enforcing appropriate length penalty for both tasks gave better BLEU scores on validation data. These settings of length penalty parameters were used for obtaining best evaluation BLEU scores in UFAL-6.

4.2 Qualitative Samples

The qualitative samples from Table 4 indicate en→ta comparable to ta→en, despite the imbalance in BLEU scores. We attribute this to be due to the tokenization in place while determining n-grams for BLEU computation. Whitespace and punctuation based tokenization fails to recognize multiple words conjoined to obtain newer words in Tamil, being an agglutinative language.

Table 5 indicates failure cases, many of which shows under-translation phenomenon, when all source tokens do not have corresponding translated tokens in generated translation.

5 Conclusion and Future Work

In this paper, we built and demonstrated that a practical translation system is feasible in low-resource settings with improvements in performance of models obtained from pre-processing and filtering, augmentation with additional training corpus using back-translation and simple intuitive tuning of hyper-parameters like length-penalty. Along with this system description paper, we release the trained models and associated code for tokenization and inference[6]. A live web-interface is hosted on the web and available at preon.iiit.ac.in/babel.

There is an increasing interest in unsupervised methods for NMT (Lample et al., 2017; Artetxe et al., 2018) and also to obtain parallel-pairs from sources which provide same content in different

---

[6] github.com/jerinphilip/ilmulti/

languages (Schwenk et al., 2019; Schwenk, 2018).
We intend to tap into increasing monolingual data
online across major languages of the country to
collectively improve multilingual models in the future.

Acknowledgements

We thank the multilingual milieu at our lab which
enable us to worry less about the challenges in interpreting the results which comes with the many
languages involved – special thanks to Prajwal
Renukanand, Kiran Devraj, Rudrabha Mukhapodhyay.
We thank the organizers for hosting the tasks including Indian languages curating the platform and
providing compiled resources.

References

Roee Aharoni, Melvin Johnson, and Orhan Firat. 2019. Massively multilingual neural machine translation. *arXiv preprint arXiv:1903.00089*.

Mikel Artetxe, Gorka Labaka, and Eneko Agirre. 2018. Unsupervised statistical machine translation. In *EMNLP*.

Mikel Artetxe and Holger Schwenk. 2018. Massively multilingual sentence embeddings for zero-shot cross-lingual transfer and beyond. *arXiv preprint arXiv:1812.10464*.

Jimmy Lei Ba, Jamie Ryan Kiros, and Geoffrey E Hinton. 2016. Layer normalization. *arXiv preprint arXiv:1607.06450*.

Jacob Devlin, Ming-Wei Chang, Kenton Lee, and Kristina Toutanova. 2019. Bert: Pre-training of deep bidirectional transformers for language understanding. In *NAACL*.

Sergey Edunov, Myle Ott, Michael Auli, and David Grangier. 2018. Understanding Back-Translation at Scale. In *EMNLP*.

Jonas Gehring, Michael Auli, David Grangier, Denis Yarats, and Yann N Dauphin. 2017. Convolutional sequence to sequence learning. In *ICML*.

Hideki Isozaki, Tsutomu Hirao, Kevin Duh, Katsuhito Sudoh, and Hajime Tsukada. 2010. Automatic evaluation of translation quality for distant language pairs. In *EMNLP*.

Girish Nath Jha. 2010. The TDIL Program and the Indian Language Corpora Intitiative (ILCI). In *LREC*.

Melvin Johnson, Mike Schuster, Quoc V Le, Maxim Krikun, Yonghui Wu, Zhifeng Chen, Nikhil Thorat, Fernanda Viégas, Martin Wattenberg, Greg Corrado, et al. 2017. Google's multilingual neural machine translation system: Enabling zero-shot translation. *Transactions of ACL*.

Taku Kudo. 2018. Subword regularization: Improving neural network translation models with multiple subword candidates. In *Proceedings of ACL*.

Anoop Kunchukuttan, Pratik Mehta, and Pushpak Bhattacharyya. 2018. The IIT Bombay English-Hindi Parallel Corpus. In *LREC*.

Guillaume Lample and Alexis Conneau. 2019. Cross-lingual language model pretraining. *arXiv preprint arXiv:1901.07291*.

Guillaume Lample, Alexis Conneau, Ludovic Denoyer, and Marc'Aurelio Ranzato. 2017. Unsupervised machine translation using monolingual corpora only. *arXiv preprint arXiv:1711.00043*.

Marco Lui and Timothy Baldwin. 2012. langid. py: An off-the-shelf language identification tool. In *ACL (System Demonstrations)*.

Toshiaki Nakazawa, Chenchen Ding, Raj Dabre, Hideya Mino, Isao Goto, Win Pa Pa, Nobushige Doi, Yusuke Oda, Anoop Kunchukuttan, Shantipriya Parida, Ondřej Bojar, and Sadao Kurohashi. 2019. Overview of the 6th workshop on Asian translation. In *Proceedings of the 6th Workshop on Asian Translation*, Hong Kong. ACL.

Toshiaki Nakazawa, Katsuhito Sudoh, Shohei Higashiyama, Chenchen Ding, Raj Dabre, Hideya Mino, Isao Goto, Win Pa Pa, Anoop Kunchukuttan, and Sadao Kurohashi. 2018. Overview of the 5th workshop on asian translation. In *WAT*.

Myle Ott, Sergey Edunov, Alexei Baevski, Angela Fan, Sam Gross, Nathan Ng, David Grangier, and Michael Auli. 2019. fairseq: A fast, extensible toolkit for sequence modeling. In *NAACL (Demonstrations)*.

Kishore Papineni, Salim Roukos, Todd Ward, and Wei-Jing Zhu. 2002. Bleu: a method for automatic evaluation of machine translation. In *ACL*.

Jerin Philip, Vinay P Namboodiri, and CV Jawahar. 2019. A baseline neural machine translation system for indian languages. *arXiv preprint arXiv:1907.12437*.

Loganathan Ramasamy, Ondřej Bojar, and Zdeněk Žabokrtský. 2012. Morphological processing for english-tamil statistical machine translation. In *Proceedings of the Workshop on Machine Translation and Parsing in Indian Languages (MTPIL-2012)*, pages 113–122.

Holger Schwenk. 2018. Filtering and mining parallel data in a joint multilingual space. In *ACL (Short Papers)*.

Holger Schwenk, Vishrav Chaudhary, Shuo Sun, Hongyu Gong, and Francisco Guzmán. 2019. Wikimatrix: Mining 135m parallel sentences in 1620 language pairs from wikipedia. *arXiv preprint arXiv:1907.05791*.

Rico Sennrich, Barry Haddow, and Alexandra Birch. 2016. Improving neural machine translation models with monolingual data. In *ACL*.

Rico Sennrich and Biao Zhang. 2019. Revisiting low-resource neural machine translation: A case study. *ACL*.

Ilya Sutskever, Oriol Vinyals, and Quoc V Le. 2014. Sequence to sequence learning with neural networks. In *NIPS*.

Ashish Vaswani, Noam Shazeer, Niki Parmar, Jakob Uszkoreit, Llion Jones, Aidan N Gomez, Łukasz Kaiser, and Illia Polosukhin. 2017. Attention is all you need. In *NIPS*.

LTRC-MT Simple & Effective Hindi-English Neural Machine Translation Systems at WAT 2019

Vikrant Goyal
IIIT Hyderabad
`vikrant.goyal@research.iiit.ac.in`

Dipti Misra Sharma
IIIT Hyderabad
`dipti@iiit.ac.in`

Abstract

This paper describes the Neural Machine Translation systems of IIIT-Hyderabad (LTRC-MT) for WAT 2019 Hindi-English shared task. We experimented with both Recurrent Neural Networks & Transformer architectures. We also show the results of our experiments of training NMT models using additional data via backtranslation.

1 Introduction

Neural Machine Translation (Luong et al., 2015; Bahdanau et al., 2014; Johnson et al., 2017; Wu et al., 2017; Vaswani et al., 2017) has been receiving considerable attention in the recent years, given its superior performance without the demand of heavily hand crafted engineering efforts. NMT often outperforms Statistical Machine Translation (SMT) techniques but it still struggles if the parallel data is insufficient like in the case of Indian languages. Hindi being one of the most common spoken Indian languages, continue to remain as a low resource language demanding further attention from the research community. The Hindi-English pair has limited availability of sentence level aligned bitext as parallel corpora.

This paper describes an overview of the submission of IIIT Hyderabad (LTRC) in WAT 2019 (Nakazawa et al., 2019) Hindi-English Machine Translation shared task. We experimented with both attention-based LSTM encoder-decoder architecture & the recently proposed Transformer architecture. We used Byte Pair Encoding (BPE) to enable open vocabulary translation. We then leveraged synthetic data generated by our own models to improve the translation performance.

2 Neural MT Architecture

In this section, we briefly discuss the attention-based LSTM encoder-decoder architecture & the Transformer model.

2.1 Attention-based encoder-decoder

In this architecture, the NMT model consists of an encoder and a decoder, each of which is a Recurrent Neural Network (RNN) as described in (Luong et al., 2015). The model directly estimates the posterior distribution $P_\theta(y|x)$ of translating a source sentence $x = (x_1, .., x_n)$ to a target sentence $y = (y_1, .., y_m)$ as:

$$P_\theta(y|x) = \prod_{t=1}^{m} P_\theta(y_t|y_1, y_2, .., y_{t-1}, x) \quad (1)$$

Each of the local posterior distribution $P(y_t|y_{1,2}, .., y_{t-1}, x)$ is modeled as a multinomial distribution over the target language vocabulary which is represented as a linear transformation followed by a softmax function on the decoder's output vector $\tilde{h}_t^{dec}$:

$$c_t = AttentionFunction(h_{1:n}^{enc}; h_t^{dec}) \quad (2)$$

$$\tilde{h}_t^{dec} = tanh(W_o[h_t^{dec}; c_t]) \quad (3)$$

$$P(y|y_1, y_2, .., y_{t-1}, x) = softmax(W_s\tilde{h}_t^{dec}; \tau) \quad (4)$$

where c_t is the context vector, h^{enc} and h^{dec} are the hidden vectors generated by the encoder and decoder respectively, AttentionFunction(. , .) is the attention mechanism as shown in (Luong et al., 2015) and [. ; .] is the concatenation of two vectors.

An RNN encoder first encodes x to a continuous vector, which serves as the initial hidden vector for the decoder and then the decoder performs recursive updates to produce a sequence of hidden vectors by applying the transition function f as:

$$h_t^{dec} = f(h_{t-1}^{dec}, [\tilde{h}_{t-1}^{dec}; e(y_t)]) \quad (5)$$

where e(.) is the word embedding operation. Popular choices for mapping f are Long-Short-Term

Proceedings of the 6th Workshop on Asian Translation, pages 137–140
Hong Kong, China, November 4, 2019. ©2019 Association for Computational Linguistics

Memory (LSTM) units and Gated Recurrent Units (GRU), the former of which we use in our models.

An NMT model is typically trained under the maximum log-likelihood objective:

$$\max_\theta J(\theta) = \max_\theta \mathrm{E}_{(x,y)\sim D}[\log P_\theta(y|x)] \quad (6)$$

where D is the training set. Our NMT model uses a bi-directional LSTM as an encoder and a uni-directional LSTM as a decoder with global attention (Luong et al., 2015) .

2.2 Transformer Model

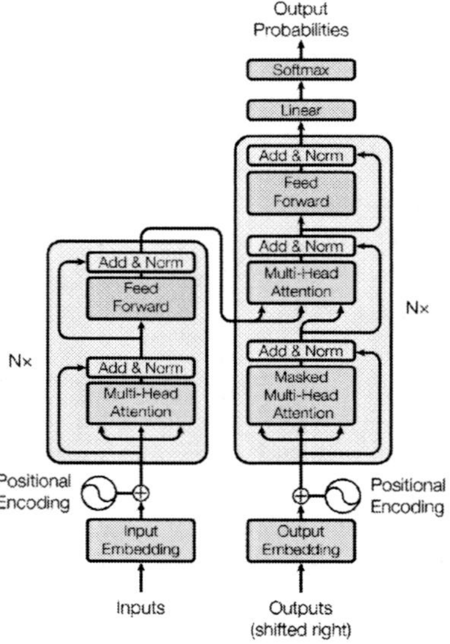

Figure 1: Transformer model architecture from Vaswani et al. (2017)

The Transformer (Vaswani et al., 2017) model is the first NMT model relying completely on self-attention mechanism to compute representations of its input and output without using recurrent neural networks (RNN) or convolutional neural networks (CNN). RNNs read one word at a time, having to perform multiple steps before generating an output that depends on words that are far away. But it has been shown that the more steps required, the harder it is for the network to learn to make these decisions (Bahdanau et al., 2014). RNNs being sequential in nature, do not effectively exploit the modern computing devices such as GPUs which rely on parallel processing. The Transformer is also an encoder-decoder model that

was conceived to solve these problems. The encoder is composed of three stages. In the first stage input words are projected into an embedded vector space. In order to capture the notion of token position within the sequence, a positional encoding is added to the embedded input vectors. The second stage is a multi-headed self-attention. Instead of computing a single attention, this stage computes multiple attention blocks over the source, concatenates them and projects them linearly back onto a space with the initial dimensionality. The individual attention blocks compute the scaled dot-product attention with different linear projections. Finally a position-wise fully connected feed-forward network is used, which consists of two linear transformations with a ReLU activation (Nair and Hinton, 2010) in between.

The decoder operates similarly, but generates one word at a time, from left to right. It is composed of five stages. The first two are similar to the encoder: embedding and positional encoding and a masked multi-head self-attention, which unlike in the encoder, forces to attend only to past words. The third stage is a multi-head attention that not only attends to these past words, but also to the final representations generated by the encoder. The fourth stage is another position-wise feed-forward network. Finally, a softmax layer allows to map target word scores into target word probabilities. For more specific details about the architecture, refer to the original paper (Vaswani et al., 2017).

2.3 Subword Segmentation for NMT

Neural Machine Translation relies on first mapping each word into the vector space, and traditionally we have a word vector corresponding to each word in a fixed vocabulary. Addressing the problem of data scarcity and the hardness of the system to learn high quality representations for rare words, (Sennrich et al., 2015b) proposed to learn subword units and perform translation at a subword level. With the goal of open vocabulary NMT, we incorporate this approach in our system as a preprocessing step. In our early experiments, we note that Byte Pair Encoding (BPE) works better than UNK replacement techniques & also aids in better translation performance. For all of our systems, we learn separate vocabularies for Hindi and English each with 32k merge operations. With the help of BPE, the vocabulary size is reduced drastically and we no longer need to prune the vocabularies. After the translation, we do an extra post processing step to convert the target language subword units back to normal words. We found this approach to be very helpful in handling rare word representations.

2.4 Synthetic Training Data

To utilize monolingual data along with IITB corpus, we employ back translation. Backtranslation (Sennrich et al., 2015a) is a widely used data augmentation technique for aiding Neural Machine Translation for languages low on parallel data. The method works by generating synthetic data on the source side from target side monolingual data using a target-to-source NMT model. The synthetic parallel data thus formed is combined with the actual parallel data to train a new NMT model. We used around 10M English sentences and backtranslated them into Hindi using a English-Hindi NMT model.

3 Experimental Setup

3.1 Dataset

In our experiments, we used IIT-Bombay (Kunchukuttan et al., 2017) Hindi-English parallel data provided by the organizers. The training corpus provided by the organizers, consists of data from mixed domains. There are roughly 1.5M samples in training data from diverse sources, while the development and test sets are from news domains. In addition to this, around 10M English monolingual data from WMT14 newscrawl articles is used in our backtranslation enabled attempts at training an NMT system.

Table 1: Statistics of our processed parallel data.

Dataset	Sentences	Tokens
IITB Train	15,28,631	21.5M / 20.3M
IITB Test	2,507	62.3k / 55.8k
IITB Dev	520	9.7k / 10.3k

3.2 Data Processing

We used Moses (Koehn et al., 2007) toolkit for tokenization and cleaning the English side of the data. Hindi side of the data is first normalized with Indic NLP library[1] followed by tokenization with the same library. As our preprocessing step, we removed all the sentences of length greater than 80 from our training corpus. We used BPE segmentation with 32k merge operations. During training, we lowercased all of our training data & used truecase[2] as a truecaser during testing.

3.3 Training Details

For all of our experiments, we used OpenNMT-py (Klein et al., 2018) toolkit. We used both attention-based LSTM models and Transformer models in our submissions.

We used an LSTM based Bi-directional encoder and a unidirectional decoder along with global attention mechanism. We kept 4 layers in both the encoder & decoder with embedding size set to 512. The batch size was set to 64 and a dropout rate of 0.3. We used Adam optimizer (Kingma and Ba, 2014) for all our experiments.

For our transformer model, we used 6 layers in both encoder and decoder with 512 hidden units in each layer. The word embedding size was set to 512 with 8 heads. The training is run in batches of maximum 4096 tokens at a time with dropout set to 0.3. The model parameters are optimized using Adam optimizer.

4 Results

In table 2, we report Bilingual Evaluation Understudy (BLEU) (Papineni et al., 2002) score, Rank-based Intuitive Bilingual Evaluation Score (RIBES) (Isozaki et al., 2010), Adequacy-fluency metrics (AM-FM) (Banchs et al., 2015) and the Human Evaluation results provided by WAT 2019 for all our attempts. The results show that our NMT system based on Transformer & backtranslation is ranked 2nd among all the constraint submissions made in WAT 2019 Hindi-English shared task & is ranked 3rd overall.

5 Conclusion Future Work

We believe that NMT is indeed a promising approach for Machine Translation of low resource languages. In this paper, we showed the effectiveness of Transformer models on a low resource languages pair Hindi-English. Additionally we show, how synthetic data can help improving the NMT systems for Hindi-English.

---

[1]https://anoopkunchukuttan.github.io/indic_nlp_library/

[2]https://pypi.org/project/truecase/

Table 2: This table describes the results of WAT 2019 evaluation of our submitted systems & compared with the best system submissions of WAT 2019 & the previous year. 'BT' stands for backtranslation.

Architecture	BLEU	RIBES	AM-FM	Human
Transformer	16.32	0.729072	0.563590	-
LSTM with global attention + BT	17.07	0.729059	0.587060	-
Transformer + BT	**18.64**	**0.735358**	**0.594770**	**3.43**
2018 Best	17.80	0.731727	0.611090	2.96
2019 Best (Constraint)	19.06	0.741197	0.566490	3.83
2019 Best (Unconstraint)	22.91	0.768324	0.641730	4.14

References

Dzmitry Bahdanau, Kyunghyun Cho, and Yoshua Bengio. 2014. Neural machine translation by jointly learning to align and translate. *arXiv preprint arXiv:1409.0473*.

Rafael E Banchs, Luis F DHaro, and Haizhou Li. 2015. Adequacy–fluency metrics: Evaluating mt in the continuous space model framework. *IEEE/ACM Transactions on Audio, Speech, and Language Processing*, 23(3):472–482.

Hideki Isozaki, Tsutomu Hirao, Kevin Duh, Katsuhito Sudoh, and Hajime Tsukada. 2010. Automatic evaluation of translation quality for distant language pairs. In *Proceedings of the 2010 Conference on Empirical Methods in Natural Language Processing*, pages 944–952. Association for Computational Linguistics.

Melvin Johnson, Mike Schuster, Quoc V Le, Maxim Krikun, Yonghui Wu, Zhifeng Chen, Nikhil Thorat, Fernanda Viégas, Martin Wattenberg, Greg Corrado, et al. 2017. Googles multilingual neural machine translation system: Enabling zero-shot translation. *Transactions of the Association for Computational Linguistics*, 5:339–351.

Diederik P Kingma and Jimmy Ba. 2014. Adam: A method for stochastic optimization. *arXiv preprint arXiv:1412.6980*.

Guillaume Klein, Yoon Kim, Yuntian Deng, Vincent Nguyen, Jean Senellart, and Alexander M Rush. 2018. Opennmt: Neural machine translation toolkit. *arXiv preprint arXiv:1805.11462*.

Philipp Koehn, Hieu Hoang, Alexandra Birch, Chris Callison-Burch, Marcello Federico, Nicola Bertoldi, Brooke Cowan, Wade Shen, Christine Moran, Richard Zens, et al. 2007. Moses: Open source toolkit for statistical machine translation. In *Proceedings of the 45th annual meeting of the association for computational linguistics companion volume proceedings of the demo and poster sessions*, pages 177–180.

Anoop Kunchukuttan, Pratik Mehta, and Pushpak Bhattacharyya. 2017. The iit bombay english-hindi parallel corpus. *arXiv preprint arXiv:1710.02855*.

Minh-Thang Luong, Hieu Pham, and Christopher D Manning. 2015. Effective approaches to attention-based neural machine translation. *arXiv preprint arXiv:1508.04025*.

Vinod Nair and Geoffrey E Hinton. 2010. Rectified linear units improve restricted boltzmann machines. In *Proceedings of the 27th international conference on machine learning (ICML-10)*, pages 807–814.

Toshiaki Nakazawa, Chenchen Ding, Raj Dabre, Hideya Mino, Isao Goto, Win Pa Pa, Nobushige Doi, Yusuke Oda, Anoop Kunchukuttan, Shantipriya Parida, Ondej Bojar, and Sadao Kurohashi. 2019. Overview of the 6th workshop on Asian translation. In *Proceedings of the 6th Workshop on Asian Translation*, Hong Kong. Association for Computational Linguistics.

Kishore Papineni, Salim Roukos, Todd Ward, and Wei-Jing Zhu. 2002. Bleu: a method for automatic evaluation of machine translation. In *Proceedings of the 40th annual meeting on association for computational linguistics*, pages 311–318. Association for Computational Linguistics.

Rico Sennrich, Barry Haddow, and Alexandra Birch. 2015a. Improving neural machine translation models with monolingual data. *arXiv preprint arXiv:1511.06709*.

Rico Sennrich, Barry Haddow, and Alexandra Birch. 2015b. Neural machine translation of rare words with subword units. *arXiv preprint arXiv:1508.07909*.

Ashish Vaswani, Noam Shazeer, Niki Parmar, Jakob Uszkoreit, Llion Jones, Aidan N Gomez, Łukasz Kaiser, and Illia Polosukhin. 2017. Attention is all you need. In *Advances in Neural Information Processing Systems*, pages 5998–6008.

Lijun Wu, Yingce Xia, Li Zhao, Fei Tian, Tao Qin, Jianhuang Lai, and Tie-Yan Liu. 2017. Adversarial neural machine translation. *arXiv preprint arXiv:1704.06933*.

Long Warm-up and Self-Training:
Training Strategies of NICT-2 NMT System at WAT-2019

Kenji Imamura and **Eiichiro Sumita**

National Institute of Information and Communications Technology

3-5 Hikaridai, Seika-cho, Soraku-gun, Kyoto 619-0289, Japan

{kenji.imamura,eiichiro.sumita}@nict.go.jp

Abstract

This paper describes the NICT-2 neural machine translation system at the 6th Workshop on Asian Translation. This system employs the standard Transformer model but features the following two characteristics. One is the long warm-up strategy, which performs a longer warm-up of the learning rate at the start of the training than conventional approaches. Another is that the system introduces self-training approaches based on multiple back-translations generated by sampling. We participated in three tasks—ASPEC.en-ja, ASPEC.ja-en, and TDDC.ja-en—using this system.

1 Introduction

This paper describes the NICT-2 neural machine translation (NMT) system at the 6th Workshop on Asian Translation (WAT-2019) (Nakazawa et al., 2019). This system employs Vaswani et al. (2017)'s Transformer base model but improves translation quality by applying the following training strategies and hyperparameters.

- We investigated the relationship between the learning rate, warm-up, and model perplexity, and found that a long warm-up allows high learning rates, and consequently the translation quality improves. According to this finding, we applied the long warm-up.

- We applied the self-training strategy, which uses multiple back-translations generated by sampling (Imamura et al., 2018) to increase the robustness of the encoder and improve the translation quality.

The remainder of this paper is organized as follows. Section 2 summarizes the system, including its settings. We describe the characteristics

Corpus	Set		# Sents.	Note
ASPEC	Train		3,007,754	$\leq$ 128 tokens
	Dev.		1,790	
	Test		1,812	
TDDC	Train		1,398,184	$\leq$ 128 tokens
	Dev.	Items	2,845	
		Texts	1,153	
	DevTest	Items	2,900	
		Texts	1,114	
	Test	Items	2,129	
		Texts	1,148	

Table 1: Corpus sizes.

of our system—the long warm-up and the self-training based on multiple back-translations by sampling—in Sections 3 and 4, respectively. The results are presented in Section 5. Finally, Section 6 concludes the paper.

2 System Summary

We participated in three tasks, namely English-to-Japanese and Japanese-to-English of ASPEC (abbreviated to ASPEC.en-ja and ASPEC.ja-en, respectively), and Japanese-to-English of the TDDC (TDDC.ja-en).

The corpus used in the ASPEC tasks is Asian Scientific Paper Excerpt Corpus (Nakazawa et al., 2016), which is a collection of scientific papers. In the TDDC task, the Timely Disclosure Documents Corpus (TDDC) was used. The development and test sets of TDDC are divided into items and texts sets, which are collections of titles and body texts, respectively. The sizes of the corpora are shown in Table 1.

All corpora were divided into sub-words using the byte-pair encoding rules (Sennrich et al., 2016b) acquired from the training sets of each corpus. The rules were independently acquired from the source and target languages, to give a vocabulary size around 16K.

Proceedings of the 6th Workshop on Asian Translation, pages 141–146

Hong Kong, China, November 4, 2019. ©2019 Association for Computational Linguistics

	Attribute	Value
Model	# Layers	6
	d_{model}	512
	d_{ff}	2,048
	# Heads	8
Training	Optimizer	Adam ($\beta_1 = 0.9$, $\beta_2 = 0.99$)
	Loss function	Label-smoothed cross-entropy
	Label smoothing	0.1
	Batch size	Approx. 500 sentences
	Learning rate	0.0004
	Warm-up	Linear, approx. 5 epochs
	Cool-down	Inverse square root
	Dropout	Selected from {0.1, 0.15, 0.2}
	Clip norm	5
	Etc.	Early stopping Checkpoint averaging of 10 models
Test	Beam	10
	Length penalty	Tuned by Dev. set
	Etc.	Ensemble of 4 models

Table 2: Summary of system settings.

We used fairseq[1] as a basic translator. The model used here is the Transformer base model (six layers). Table 2 shows the hyperparameters of the model, training, and test.

Training was performed on Volta 100 GPUs (two GPUs for the ASPEC dataset and one GPU for the TDDC dataset) using 16-bit floating point computation. The training was stopped when the loss of the development set was minimized (i.e., early stopping). We also used checkpoint averaging: using the best checkpoint and the next nine checkpoints (10 checkpoints in total).

During testing, we used 32-bit floating point computation. For the final submission, four models, which were trained using different random seeds, were ensembled (Imamura and Sumita, 2017).

3 Long Warm-up

The warm-up is a technique that gradually increases the learning rate at the beginning of training. The most general strategy is to increase the learning rate linearly. Using the warm-up, the model parameters are updated toward convergence, even if they were randomly initialized. This allows us to obtain stable models.

We generally use a fixed time for the warm-up. For example, Vaswani et al. (2017) used 4,000 updates in their experiments. However, the warm-up

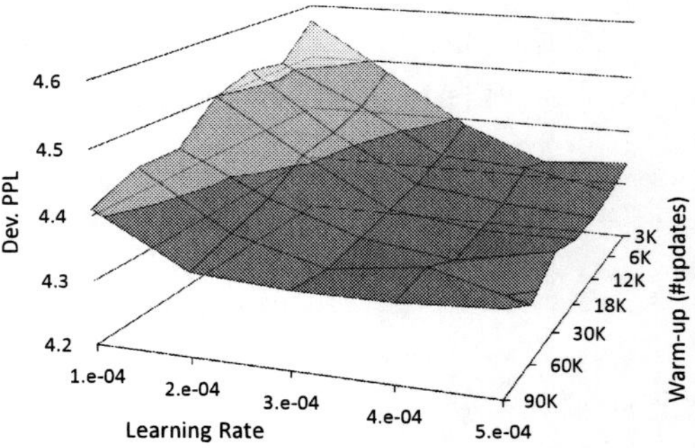

Figure 1: Relationship between learning rate, warm-up, and perplexity of development set in ASPEC.ja-en task.

time influences the final quality of models.

Figure 1 shows how the development set perplexity (Dev. PPL) changes as the learning rate and warm-up time vary, using the ASPEC.ja-en dataset (as explained in Section 5). Lower perplexity indicates a better model. We can observe that both the learning rate and the warm-up time influence the perplexity. When we use a long warm-up, we can apply high learning rates and consequently obtain low-perplexity models. We observed a similar tendency in the TDDC.ja-en task.

Based on the above experiment, we used 0.0004 as the learning rate and set the warm-up time to 30K updates for ASPEC datasets and 14K updates for TDDC datasets.[2] These values almost minimize the development perplexity.

Recently, a variant of Adam optimization (called RAdam), which automatically adapts the learning rate and does not require any warm-up, has been proposed (Liu et al., 2019). To confirm the relationship between the warm-up and RAdam is our future work.

4 Self-Training Based on Back-Translation

Back-translation is a technique to enhance neural machine translators (NMT), particularly the decoder part of NMT, using monolingual corpora (Sennrich et al., 2016a). It translates sentences of the target language into those of the source language. A forward translator is trained using this pseudo-parallel corpus with corpora that are cre-

---

[1]https://github.com/pytorch/fairseq

[2]The warm-up time is around five epochs because the mini-batch size is approximately 500 sentences.

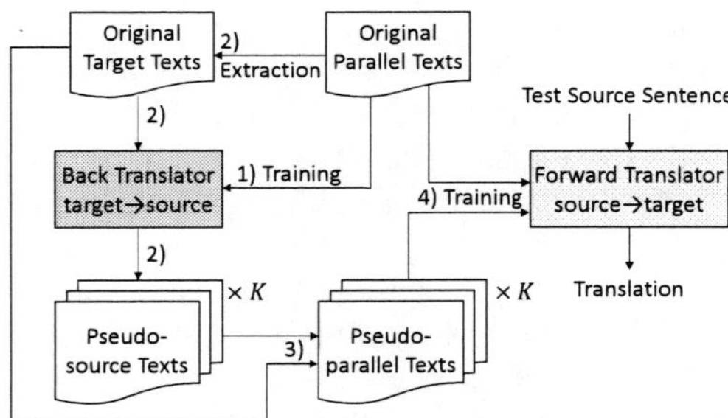

Figure 2: Data flow of self-training based on back-translation.

ated manually. The back-translation can be applied to self-training if the pseudo-parallel corpora are created from the manually created corpora that will be used for training the forward translator (Figure 2).

4.1 Back-Translation with Sampling Generation

A problem with back-translation is that the pseudo-parallel sentences become less varied than those created manually, because of machine translation. This characteristic makes it difficult for the back-translation method to enhance the encoder, in contrast to the decoder.

To solve this problem, Imamura et al. (2018) proposed a method that combines the following two methods.

- To generate diverse pseudo-parallel sentences, words are generated by sampling based on the word probability distribution (Eq. 1) instead of the maximum likelihood during the back-translation.

$$\hat{y}_t \sim \frac{\Pr(y|\boldsymbol{y}_{<t}, \boldsymbol{x})^{1/\tau}}{\sum_{y'} \Pr(y'|\boldsymbol{y}_{<t}, \boldsymbol{x})^{1/\tau}}, \quad (1)$$

  where $\hat{y}_t$, $\boldsymbol{y}_{<t}$, and $\boldsymbol{x}$ denote the generated word at time t, the history until time t, and the input word sequence, respectively. τ denotes the temperature parameter, which is used to control the diversity, but we use $\tau = 1.0$ in this paper.

- Multiple pseudo-source sentences, for a target sentence, are used for training.

Both methods are intended to enhance the encoder by increasing the diversity of source sentences, while fixing the target sentences.

4.2 Training Procedure

The training procedure is summarized as follows (Figure 2).

1) Train a back-translator from the target language to the source language, using the original parallel corpus.

2) Translate the target side of the original corpus to the source language, using the back-translator. During the back-translation, K pseudo-source sentences are generated for each target sentence, using sampling.

3) Construct K sets of pseudo-parallel sentences by pairing the target and pseudo-source sentences.

4) Build the training set by mixing the original and pseudo-parallel corpora, and train the forward translator from the source language to the target language.

4.3 Static and Dynamic Self-Training

There are two types of self-training based on back-translation, depending on the pseudo-parallel sentences and the structure of mini-batches: the static self-training (Imamura et al., 2018) and dynamic self-training (Imamura and Sumita, 2018). Steps 3 and 4 of Section 4.2 are different for each type.

Static self-training constructs a training set by combining K_{static} pseudo-parallel sentences with each of the original sentences. In this paper, we set $K_{static} = 4$. During training, the training set is fixed.

In static self-training, the number of pseudo-parallel sentences is K_{static} times larger than the number of original sentences. If we simply mix these sentences, the ratio of pseudo-parallel sentences to original sentences would be too high. To avoid this problem, we oversample the original sentences by a factor of K_{static}, instead of changing the learning rate depending on the sentence (Imamura et al., 2018). Therefore, the total size of the training set is $2K_{static}$ times larger than the size of the original corpus.

In contrast, dynamic self-training constructs $K_{dynamic}$ training sets. A training set includes one pseudo-parallel set and one original set. For each epoch, a set is randomly selected from the $K_{dynamic}$ training sets, and the model is trained using the set. In this paper, we set $K_{dynamic} = 20$.

In dynamic self-training, the size of a training set is twice the size of the original corpus. Therefore, the training time for an epoch is shorter than that for static self-training. However, a greater number of epochs are required until convergence, because diverse training sets are used.

5 Results of ASPEC and TDDC Tasks

The results of ASPEC and TDDC are shown in Tables 3 and 4, respectively. Both tables show the translation quality (BLEU) and the perplexity of the development set (Dev. PPL), depending on the model type and training method. The effect of the long warm-up has already been shown in Section 3.

5.1 Notes of Experimental Settings

The BLEU scores (Papineni et al., 2002) in the tables were computed based on the tokenizers MeCab (for Japanese (Kudo et al., 2004)) and Moses (for English (Koehn et al., 2007)). We trained four models with different random seeds. The single model rows of the tables show the average score of four models, and the ensemble rows show the score of the ensemble of four models.

The length penalty for testing was set to maximize the BLEU score of the development set. However, in the TDDC task, we used different penalties for the items and texts sets, and independently optimized according to the set.

Finally, we submitted the ensemble models for which the BLEU scores of the development set (in the single model cases) were the highest.

5.2 Results

First, we focus on the ASPEC.en-ja task. In the single model cases, the BLEU scores improved around +0.20 to +0.58 by adding static self-training to the base model. In the case of dynamic self-training, the improvements were between +0.46 and +0.60. The ensemble models have a similar tendency, and we can conclude that self-training is effective because the BLEU scores significantly improved in many cases. Comparing static and dynamic self-training, there were no significant differences, even though the scores of dynamic self-training were higher than those of static self-training.

In contrast, for the ASPEC.ja-en task, the BLEU scores of static self-training were worse than those of the base model, in both the single model and ensemble cases. However, for dynamic self-training, some BLEU scores significantly improved. Dynamic self-training tends to be more effective for the ASPEC tasks.

In terms of the training time, the number of epochs of the static self-training was lower than that of the dynamic self-training in both ASPEC.en-ja and ASPEC ja-en tasks. However, conversely, the total number of updates of the dynamic self-training was lower. As the training data size increased, the total training time increased in the static self-training. The dynamic self-training was more efficient from the perspective of training time.

For the TDDC.ja-en task, the items and texts sets have a different tendency. For the items set, the BLEU scores improved by applying static self-training, but became worse for the texts set.

Self-training based on back-translation is not always effective; that is, there are effective and ineffective datasets. Investigating the conditions that influence translation quality is our future work. Note that this phenomenon is only observed for self-training; the back-translation of additional monolingual corpora has different features.

6 Conclusions

This paper explained the NICT-2 NMT system at WAT-2019. This system employs the Transformer model and applies the following two training strategies.

- We employed the long warm-up strategy and trained the model using a high learning rate.

- We also employed the self-training strategy, which uses multiple back-translations generated by sampling.

Acknowledgments

This work was supported by the "Research and Development of Enhanced Multilingual and Multipurpose Speech Translation Systems" a program of the Ministry of Internal Affairs and Communications, Japan.

References

Kenji Imamura, Atsushi Fujita, and Eiichiro Sumita. 2018. Enhancement of encoder and attention using target monolingual corpora in neural machine translation. In *Proceedings of the 2nd Workshop on Neural Machine Translation and Generation*, pages 55–63, Melbourne, Australia.

Task /Lang		Model	Dev. PPL $\downarrow$	Dev.	DevTest	Test	Remark
				BLEU $\uparrow$			
ASPEC en-ja	Single	Base	3.21	43.80	43.05	44.11	392K updates (65 epochs)
		Static ST	3.12	44.38 (+)	43.25	44.54 (+)	2,162K updates (45 epochs)
		Dynamic ST	3.14	**44.40** (+)	**43.51** (+)	**44.71** (+)	810K updates (71 epochs)
	Ensemble (4 Models)	Base	–	45.14	44.01	45.13	
		Static ST	–	**45.53**	44.41 (+)	45.64 (+)	
		Dynamic ST	–	45.39	**44.58** (+)	**45.66** (+)	Submitted model
ASPEC ja-en	Single	Base	4.42	27.90	26.12	28.40	161K updates (27 epochs)
		Static ST	4.31	27.05 (-)	25.97	27.39 (-)	798K updates (16 epochs)
		Dynamic ST	4.26	**28.24** (+)§	**26.62** (+)§	**28.57** §	502K updates (42 epochs)
	Ensemble (4 Models)	Base	–	28.94	27.31	**29.41**	
		Static ST	–	28.47	26.73 (-)	28.25 (-)	
		Dynamic ST	–	**29.19** §	**27.59** §	29.40 §	Submitted model

Table 3: Results of ASPEC tasks.
The bold values indicate the highest score among base, static self-training (ST), and dynamic ST. The (+) and (-) symbols denote significant improvement and degradation, respectively, from the base model ($p \leq 0.05$). The § symbol indicates that there is a significant difference between static and dynamic ST cases.

Task /Lang		Model / Training	Dev. PPL	Dev.		DevTest		Remark
				BLEU $\uparrow$				
				Items	Texts	Items	Texts	
TDDC ja-en	Single	Base	2.76	52.75	**52.45**	54.28	**52.76**	115K updates (42 epochs)
		Static ST	2.74	52.94	51.78 (-)	**54.99** (+)§	51.92 (-)	335K updates (15 epochs)
		Dynamic ST	2.68	**52.95**	51.35 (-)	54.41	51.82 (-)	239K updates (43 epochs)
	Ensemble (4 Models)	Base	–	**54.35**	**54.74**	55.56	**54.98**	Submitted text model
		Static ST	–	54.34	53.53 (-)	**56.60** (+)§	53.81 (-)	Submitted item model
		Dynamic ST	–	54.29	53.04 (-)	55.92	53.97 (-)	

Table 4: Results of TDDC task.
The bold values indicate the highest score among base, static self-training (ST), and dynamic ST. The (+) and (-) symbols denote significant improvement and degradation, respectively, from the base model ($p \leq 0.05$). The § symbol indicates that there is a significant difference between static and dynamic ST cases.

Kenji Imamura and Eiichiro Sumita. 2017. Ensemble and reranking: Using multiple models in the NICT-2 neural machine translation system at WAT2017. In *Proceedings of the 4th Workshop on Asian Translation (WAT2017)*, pages 127–134, Taipei, Taiwan. Asian Federation of Natural Language Processing.

Kenji Imamura and Eiichiro Sumita. 2018. NICT self-training approach to neural machine translation at NMT-2018. In *Proceedings of the 2nd Workshop on Neural Machine Translation and Generation*, pages 110–115, Melbourne, Australia.

Philipp Koehn, Hieu Hoang, Alexandra Birch, Chris Callison-Burch, Marcello Federico, Nicola Bertoldi, Brooke Cowan, Wade Shen, Christine Moran, Richard Zens, Chris Dyer, Ondrej Bojar, Alexandra Constantin, and Evan Herbst. 2007. Moses: Open source toolkit for statistical machine translation. In *Proceedings of the 45th Annual Meeting of the Association for Computational Linguistics Companion Volume Proceedings of the Demo and Poster Sessions*, pages 177–180, Prague, Czech Republic.

Taku Kudo, Kaoru Yamamoto, and Yuji Matsumoto. 2004. Applying conditional random fields to Japanese morphological analysis. In *Proceedings of EMNLP 2004*, pages 230–237, Barcelona, Spain.

Liyuan Liu, Haoming Jiang, Pengcheng He, Weizhu Chen, Xiaodong Liu, Jianfeng Gao, and Jiawei Han. 2019. On the variance of the adaptive learning rate and beyond. *ArXiv*, abs/1908.03265.

Toshiaki Nakazawa, Chenchen Ding, Raj Dabre, Hideya Mino, Isao Goto, Win Pa Pa, Nobushige Doi, Yusuke Oda, Anoop Kunchukuttan, Shantipriya Parida, Ondřej Bojar, and Sadao Kurohashi. 2019. Overview of the 6th workshop on Asian translation. In *Proceedings of the 6th Workshop on Asian Translation*, Hong Kong.

Toshiaki Nakazawa, Manabu Yaguchi, Kiyotaka Uchimoto, Masao Utiyama, Eiichiro Sumita, Sadao Kurohashi, and Hitoshi Isahara. 2016. ASPEC: Asian scientific paper excerpt corpus. In *Proceedings of the Tenth International Conference on Language Resources and Evaluation (LREC 2016)*, pages 2204–2208, Portorož, Slovenia.

Kishore Papineni, Salim Roukos, Todd Ward, and Wei-Jing Zhu. 2002. Bleu: a method for automatic evaluation of machine translation. In *Proceedings of the 40th Annual Meeting of the Association for Computational Linguistics (ACL)*, pages 311–318, Philadelphia, Pennsylvania, USA.

Rico Sennrich, Barry Haddow, and Alexandra Birch. 2016a. Improving neural machine translation models with monolingual data. In *Proceedings of the 54th Annual Meeting of the Association for Computational Linguistics (ACL-2016, Volume 1: Long Papers)*, pages 86–96, Berlin, Germany.

Rico Sennrich, Barry Haddow, and Alexandra Birch. 2016b. Neural machine translation of rare words with subword units. In *Proceedings of the 54th Annual Meeting of the Association for Computational Linguistics (Volume 1: Long Papers)*, pages 1715–1725, Berlin, Germany.

Ashish Vaswani, Noam Shazeer, Niki Parmar, Jakob Uszkoreit, Llion Jones, Aidan N. Gomez, Lukasz Kaiser, and Illia Polosukhin. 2017. Attention is all you need. *CoRR*, abs/1706.03762.

Supervised neural machine translation based on data augmentation and improved training & inference process

Yixuan Tong   Liang Liang   Boyan Liu   Shanshan Jiang   Bin Dong
Ricoh Software Research Center Beijing Co., Ltd.
{ yixuan.tong, liang.liang, boyan.liu, shanshan.jiang, bin.dong}@srcb.ricoh.com

Abstract

This is the second time for SRCB to participate in WAT. This paper describes the neural machine translation systems for the shared translation tasks of WAT 2019. We participated in ASPEC tasks and submitted results on English-Japanese, Japanese-English, Chinese-Japanese, and Japanese-Chinese four language pairs. We employed the Transformer model as the baseline and experimented relative position representation, data augmentation, deep layer model, ensemble. Experiments show that all these methods can yield substantial improvements.

1   Introduction

The advent of neural networks in machine translation has brought great improvement on translation quality over traditional statistical machine translation (SMT) in recent years (Kalchbrenner and Blunsom, 2013; Sutskever et al., 2014; Cho et al., 2014; Bahdanau et al., 2014). A lot of research efforts have been attracted to investigate neural networks in machine translation. This paper describes the Neural Machine Translation systems of Ricoh Software Research Center Beijing (SRCB) for the shared translation tasks of WAT 2019 (Nakazawa et al., 2019). We participated in ASPEC tasks, and submitted results on four language pairs, including English-Japanese, Japanese-English, Japanese-Chinese and Chinese-Japanese.
In the ASPEC tasks, we employed Transformer (Vaswani et al., 2018) as our baseline model and built our translation system based on OpenNMT (Klein et al., 2017) open source toolkit. To enhance the performance of the model, we made

the following changes: 1) We proposed data augmentation method (Yihan et al., 2018) and back translation algorithm (Sennrich et al., 2015), which was observed to be useful in Japanese-English and Japanese-Chinese corpus. 2) We incorporated weighted loss function and Sentence-wise regularization method (Gong et al., 2019) into Transformer model. 3) We used deep layer (Wang et al., 2019) technique to further improve translation quality. 4) We used ensemble techniques and model stabilization to further improve translation quality.
The remainder of this paper is organized as follows: Section 2 describes our NMT system and algorithms. Section 3 describes the processing of the data and all experimental results and analysis. Finally, we conclude in section 4.

2   Systems

2.1   Base Model

Our system is based on the Transformer model. Transformer model is a paradigm model for neural machine translation which can achieve start-of-the-art translation quality.

2.2   Data augmentation and back translation

We use data augmentation algorithm (Yihan et al., 2018) to select the parallel sentences that original model cannot train well, then retrain the model using the new dataset to improve the translation quality. However, data augmentation algorithm is mutual exclusion with back translation algorithm (Sennrich et al., 2015). Back translation algorithm translates monolingual sentences to corresponding predictions to generate parallel sentences, which can augment the training set. In the real translation model, we use both data augmentation and back translation to train different models, then combine the models by ensemble learning.

2.3 Weighted loss function

The loss function of the neural network is a standard to judge whether it is convergent. When calculating the cross-entropy between predicted words with the original references, there is no consideration about words' length. So we add the length influence weight to the loss function which can represent the real loss score more accurately.

2.4 Sentence-wise smooth Regularization

Sentence-wise regularization method (Gong et al., 2019) is used in our system, which aims to output smooth prediction probabilities for all tokens in the target sequence. Compared with maximum-likelihood estimation, this method could adjust the weights and gradients in the target sequence automatically to ensure the predictions in a sequence uniformly. We implement grid search to find the best parameters for smooth regularization in different subtasks.

2.5 Deep layer model

Wang et al. (2019) showed that the location of layer normalization played a vital role when training deep Transformer. They also proved that pre-norm Transformer is more efficient for training than post-norm (vanilla Transformer) when the model goes deeper. Dynamic linear combination of previous layers was introduced which improves the translation quality as well. Note that we built our deep layer model in pre-norm way as default. In the state of practice, we find that more layers in decoders could enhance the ability of our real model. We use grid search to find proper parameters to achieve a balance between efficiency and performance

2.6 Ensemble

It has been investigated that ensembling different model can yield significant improvement in translation quality (Denkowski and Neubig, 2017). In our systems, we adopted two ensembling schemes. For one configured translation model, once the model finishes training, the last 8 checkpoints of the model are averaged to get one trained model. Then, we make different configurations and train several models independently. After averaging checkpoints for each model, we do step-wise ensembling. Specifically, these models are run at each time step and an arithmetic mean of predicted probability is obtained, which is used to determine the next word.

2.7 Model Stabilization

We observed unneglectable level of instability in the Transformer models (up to 0.4 BLEU diverse for models with the same settings).
The first remedy to fight against instability is by introducing noise (Devlin et al., 2018). We randomly deletes tokens from the source side in the training dataset. It turns out this method would bring marginal improvement. We believe that by introducing noise, models would turn from over confident, thus result in better stability and generalization.
The other strategy is batch filtering. In our experiments, there are special batches of training which lead to considerable up going of training loss. We believe the outliers are to be blame. Thus batch filtering mechanism (Chen et al., 2018) is hired which eliminate bathes with gradient norm exceeding certain threshold.

3 Experiments

We experimented our NMT system on Japanese-English, English-Japanese, Chinese-Japanese, and Japanese-Chinese scientific paper translation subtasks.

3.1 Datasets

We used Asian Scientific Paper Excerpt Corpus (ASPEC) (Nakazawa et al., 2014) as parallel corpora for all language pairs. For Japanese-English subtask and English-Japanese subtask, we used the first 1M sentences with augmented the second 1M sentences. Furthermore, for Japanese-English subtask, we augmented training data to nearly 2M by data augmentation. And, we also trained back translation models using the second 1M and the third 1M sentences as difference training datasets. For Chinese-Japanese subtask, all the sentences in ASPEC corpora are used as training data. And, we also trained back translation models using the first 1M Japanese sentences in Japanese-English subtask as difference training datasets.

For all corpora, Japanese sentences were segmented by the morphological analyzer Juman[1] and English sentences were tokenized by tokenizer.perl of Moses[2], while Chinese sentences were segmented by KyTea[3]. Sentences with more than 100 words were excluded. We used the subword unit, that is Joint Byte Pair Encoding (BPE) (Sennrich et al., 2016c) scheme, to encoder vocabulary for both source and target sentences.

3.2 Results

As shown in Table 1, we rank 1st in the direction of Japanese-English, Japanese-Chinese and Chinese-Japanese, and 2nd in one English-Japanese.

	Ja-En	En-Ja	Ja-Zh	Zh-Ja
Rank	1st	2nd	1st	1st
BLEU	30.92	45.71	38.63	52.37

Table 1: Results of subtasks

Japanese-English subtask:

The baseline model is a vanilla Transformer model with the first 1M data. Using the second 1M sentences to do data augmentation, the BLEU score has increased 1.34 to 30.20 which is the biggest improvement in this direction. What's more, the relative position representation has improved more than 1 BLEU score in WAT 2018 system. However, there is only more than a 0.2 increase in 2019's model. Changing the loss function weight with length, the new BLEU score become 30.78. Besides, the re-ranking algorithm using max function has 0.16 improvement.

System	BLEU
Baseline	28.86
Data augmentation	30.20
Relative position	30.42
Weighted loss function	30.78
Re-ranking	30.92

Table 2: Technical point contributions

English-Japanese subtask:

As for this subtask, this is our first time to participate in that we tried many other algorithms. As for the training data, we tried four kinds of combinations shown in Table 3. The baseline model is the big Transformer model with the first 1M parallel sentences. For data augmentation and back translation is mutual exclusion, we trained different models and did ensemble to combine all the features. The BLEU score of first 1M data with the second 1M data using data augmentation is 43.33. The first 1M data with the second 1M data or the remaining 2M data using back translation is 43.32 and 43.66, respectively. The best combination rate for original data and back translation data is 1:4. So the results meet the exception. The last category is the 1M data with the second 1M data using back translation and the third 1M data using data augmentation which BLEU score is 43.57. It's lower than the model with back translation only. In practice, we choose different kinds of combination for model ensemble.

System	BLEU
Baseline	42.57
1M + Da 1M	43.33
1M + Bt 1M	43.32
1M + Bt 2M	43.66
1M + Bt 1M + Da 1M	43.57

Table 3: Results of different data combination. 'Da' is the abbreviation of data augmentation, 'Bt' is the abbreviation of back-translation.

The baseline model is a vanilla Transformer model with the first 1M data. Using the relative position representation has improved 0.56 BLEU score. Using the last 2M sentences to do data augmentation, the BLEU score has increased 0.53 to 43.66. Besides, the sentence-wise smooth has improved 0.12 BLEU score in WAT 2019 system. There is a 0.14 increase in 2019's model when introducing deep layer model. Finally, the model ensemble algorithm has 1.79 improvement.

System	BLEU
Baseline	42.57
Relative position	43.13
Data augmentation	43.66
Sentence-wise smooth	43.78

[1] http://nlp.ist.i.kyoto-u.ac.jp/EN/index.php?JUMAN
[2] http://www.statmt.org/moses/
[3] http://www.phontron.com/kytea/index.html

Deep layer model	43.92
Ensemble	45.71

Table 4: Technical point contributions

Japanese-Chinese subtask:

For this subtask, we utilized only the data in ASPEC, no data augmentation was used. We implemented the system based on OpenNMT 1.22.0, and adapted the beam search bug fix in the afterwards versions. We hired sentence-wise smooth, encoder side token deletion and batch filtering. The hyper parameters were searched with respect to the devtest.txt dataset. After generating 8 models (with BLEU above 37.0), we ensembled those models with step-wise ensemble system. The results of applying thus technologies was in Table 5 (results after averaging of last 8 checkpoints, best in two models).

System	BLEU
Baseline	35.92
Relative position	36.71
Sentence-wise smooth	36.98
Encoder side token deletion & batch filtering	37.21
Ensemble of 8 models	38.63

Table 5: Technical point contributions

Chinese-Japanese subtask:

The baseline model is a vanilla Transformer model with all ASPEC data. We using the first 1M sentences in English-Japanese subtask to do data augmentation, the BLEU score has increased 0.81 to 50.46. What's more, the relative position representation has improved 0.59 BLEU score in WAT 2019 system. Sentence-wise smooth increases 0.19. Besides, deep layer model algorithm has 0.57 improvement. Finally, the model ensemble algorithm has 0.56 improvement.

System	BLEU
Baseline	49.65
Data augmentation	50.46
Relative position	51.05
Sentence-wise smooth	51.24
Deep layer model	51.81
Ensemble	52.37

Table 6: Technical point contributions

4 Conclusion

In this paper, we described our NMT system, which is based on Transformer model. We made several changes to original Transformer model, including relative position representation, deep layer model, ensembling and other technical points. We evaluated our Transformer system on Japanese-English, English-Japanese, Japanese-Chinese and Chinese-Japanese scientific paper translation subtasks at WAT 2019.The results show that the implementation of these points can effectively improve the translation quality.

In our future work, we plan to explore more vocabulary encoding schemes and compare with byte pair encoding (BPE) (Sennrich et al., 2016). In addition, we will attempt to implement other transformer structures, which combine other advanced technologies.

References

Nal Kalchbrenner and Phil Blunsom. 2013. Recurrent continuous translation models. In Proceeding of the ACL Conference on Empirical Methods in Natural Language Processing (EMNLP), 1700-1709.

Ilya Sutskever, Oriol Vinyals,and Quoc Le. 2014. Sequence to sequence learning with neural networks. In Advances in Neural Information Processing Systems (NIPS 2014), December.

Kyunghyun Cho, Bart Van and et al. 2014. Learning phrase representations using RNN encoder-decoder for statistical machine translation. In Proceedings of the Empirical Methods in Natural Language Processing (EMNLP 2014), October.

Dzmitry Bahdanau, Kyunghyun Cho, and Yoshua Bengio. 2014. Neural machine translation by jointly learning to align and translate. arXiv preprint arXiv:1409.0473.

Nakazawa, Toshiaki and Ding, Chenchen and Dabre, Raj and Mino, Hideya and Goto, Isao and Pa, Win Pa and Doi, Nobushige and Oda, Yusuke and Kunchukuttan, Anoop and Parida, Shantipriya and Bojar, Ondřej and Kurohashi, Sadao. 2019. Overview of the 6th Workshop on Asian Translation. In Proceedings of the 6th Workshop on Asian Translation (WAT2019).

Vaswani A, Shazeer N, Parmar N, et al. 2017 Attention is all you need. Advances in Neural Information Processing Systems, 5998-6008.

Guillaume Klein, Yoon Kim, Yuntian Deng, Jean Senellart, and Alexander M. Rush. 2017. Open-NMT: Open-Source Toolkit for Neural Machine Translation. arXiv preprint arXiv:1701.02810.

Li Y, Liu B, Tong Y, et al. SRCB Neural Machine Translation Systems in WAT 2018[C]//Proceedings of the 32nd Pacific Asia Conference on Language, Information and Computation: 5th Workshop on Asian Translation: 5th Workshop on Asian Translation. 2018.

Sennrich R, Haddow B, Birch A. Improving neural machine translation models with monolingual data[J]. arXiv preprint arXiv:1511.06709, 2015.

Michael Denkowski and Graham Neubig. 2017. Stronger baselines for trustable results in neural machine translation. In Proceedings of the First Workshop on Neural Machine Translation (WNMT), pages 18–27.

Toshiaki Nakazawa, Manabu Yaguchi, Kiyotaka Uchimoto, Masao Utiyama, Eiichiro Sumita, Sadao Kurohashi, and Hitoshi Isahara. 2014. ASPEC : Asian Scientific Paper Excerpt Corpus. In Proceedings of the Tenth International Conference on Language Resources and Evaluation (LREC), pages 2204–2208.

Gong C, Tan X, He D, et al. Sentence-wise smooth regularization for sequence to sequence learning[C]//Proceedings of the AAAI Conference on Artificial Intelligence. 2019, 33: 6449-6456.

Qiang Wang, Bei Li, Tong Xiao, and Jingbo Zhu. 2019. Learning deep transformer models for machine translation. In Proceedings of the 57th Annual Meeting of the Association for Computational Linguistics (Volume 1: Long Papers), Italy, Florence. Association for Computational Linguistics

Rico Sennrich, Barry Haddow, and Alexandra Birch. 2016c. Neural machine translation of rare words with subword units. In Proceedings of ACL, pages 1715–1725.

Devlin J, Chang M W, Lee K, et al. Bert: Pre-training of deep bidirectional transformers for language understanding[J]. arXiv preprint arXiv:1810.04805, 2018.

Chen M X, Firat O, Bapna A, et al. The best of both worlds: Combining recent advances in neural machine translation[J]. arXiv preprint arXiv:1804.09849, 2018.

Sarah's Participation in WAT 2019

Raymond Hendy Susanto, Ohnmar Htun, Liling Tan
Rakuten Institute of Technology
Rakuten, Inc.
{first.last}@rakuten.com

Abstract

This paper describes our MT systems' participation in the WAT 2019. We participated in the (i) Patent, (ii) Timely Disclosure, (iii) Newswire and (iv) Mixed-domain tasks. Our main focus is to explore how similar Transformer models perform on various tasks. We observed that for tasks with smaller datasets, our best model setup are shallower models with lesser number of attention heads. We investigated practical issues in NMT that often appear in production settings, such as coping with multilinguality and simplifying pre- and post-processing pipeline in deployment.

1 Introduction

This paper describes our machine translation systems' participation in the 6th Workshop on Asian Translation (WAT-2019) translation task (Nakazawa et al., 2019). We participated in the (i) Patent, (ii) Timely Disclosure, (iii) Newswire, and (iv) Mixed-domain tasks. We trained our systems under a constrained setting, meaning that no additional resources were used other than those provided by the shared task organizer. We built all MT systems based on the Transformer architecture (Vaswani et al., 2017). Our main findings for each task are summarized in the following:

- **Patent task:** We built several translation systems for six translation directions. We also explored a multilingual approach and compared it with the unidirectional models.

- **Timely disclosure task:** We tried a simplified data processing such that the model is trained directly on raw texts without requiring language-specific pre/post-processing.

- **Newswire task:** We explored fine-tuning the hyperparameters of a Transformer model on a relatively small dataset and found that a compact model is able to achieve a competitive performance.

- **Mixed-domain task:** We explored low-resource translation approaches for Myanmar-English.

2 JPO Patent Task

2.1 Task Description

For the patent translation task, we used the JPO Patent Corpus (JPC) version 4.3, which is constructed by the Japan Patent Office (JPO). Similar to previous WAT tasks (Nakazawa et al., 2015, 2016, 2017, 2018), the task includes patent description translations for Chinese-Japanese, Korean-Japanese, and English-Japanese. Each language pair's training set consists of 1M parallel sentences. We used the official training, validation, and test split provided by the organizer without any external resources. We trained individual unidirectional models for each language pair. Additionally, we explored multilingual NMT approaches for this task.

2.2 Data Processing

We used SentencePiece (Kudo and Richardson, 2018) for training subword units based on byte-pair encoding (BPE). We pre-tokenized the data using the following tools:

- Juman version 7.01[1] for Japanese,

- Stanford Word Segmenter version 2014-06-16[2] with Peking University (PKU) model for Chinese,

- Mecab-ko[3] for Korean, and

- Moses tokenizer for English.

Source and target sentences are merged for training a joint vocabulary. We set the vocabulary size to 100,000 and removed subwords that occur less than 10 times from the vocabulary, following similar pre-processing steps for the baseline NMT system released by the organizer.[4]

---

[1] http://nlp.ist.i.kyoto-u.ac.jp/EN/index.php?JUMAN
[2] https://nlp.stanford.edu/software/segmenter.shtml
[3] https://bitbucket.org/eunjeon/mecab-ko/
[4] http://lotus.kuee.kyoto-u.ac.jp/WAT/WAT2019/baseline/dataPreparationBPE.html

Proceedings of the 6th Workshop on Asian Translation, pages 152–158
Hong Kong, China, November 4, 2019. ©2019 Association for Computational Linguistics

Embedding dim.	1024
Tied embeddings	Yes
Transformer FFN dim.	4096
Attention heads	8
En/Decoder layers	6
Label smoothing	0.1
Dropout	0.3
Attention weight dropout	0.1
Transformer FFN dropout	0.1
Learning rate	0.001
Batch size in tokens	4000
Update frequency	1

Table 1: JPO model settings

2.3 Model

Our NMT model is based on the Transformer (Vaswani et al., 2017) implementation in the Fairseq toolkit (Ott et al., 2019). The details of the parameters used for our experiments are summarized in Table 1. Encoder's input embedding, decoder's input and output embedding layers were tied together (Press and Wolf, 2017), which saves significant amounts of parameters without impacting performance. The model was optimized with Adam (Kingma and Ba, 2015) using $\beta_1 = 0.9$, $\beta_2 = 0.98$, and $\epsilon = $ 1e-8. We used the same learning rate schedule as (Ott et al., 2018) and run the experiments on 4 Nvidia V100 GPUs, enabling mixed-precision training in Fairseq (`--fp16`). The best performing model on the validation set was chosen for decoding the test set. We trained 4 independent models with different random seeds to perform ensemble decoding.

2.4 Results

Table 2 shows our model performance for the patent task. For brevity, we only reported the results on the JPCN test set, which is a union of JPCN{1,2,3}, and the Expression Pattern task (JP-CEP) for zh-ja. For the detailed breakdown for each test set, we would like to refer readers to the overview paper. Since human evaluation result is not available as the time of this writing, we only present the results in terms of BLEU scores. It is clear that ensemble decoding significantly outperforms single model decoding. Under the constrained settings, our best submissions obtain the first place in the WAT leaderboard[5] for zh-ja, ja-

[5] `http://lotus.kuee.kyoto-u.ac.jp/WAT/evaluation/index.html`

Task	Model	BLEU
JPCN zh-ja	Unidirectional, single	46.77
JPCN zh-ja	Unidirectional, ensemble	48.68
JPCN zh-ja	Multilingual, single*	45.98
JPCN ja-zh	Unidirectional, single	40.78
JPCN ja-zh	Unidirectional, ensemble	42.22
JPCN ja-zh	Multilingual, single*	39.57
JPCN ko-ja	Unidirectional, single	71.41
JPCN ko-ja	Unidirectional, ensemble	72.55
JPCN ko-ja	Multilingual, single*	69.80
JPCN ja-ko	Unidirectional, single	69.81
JPCN ja-ko	Unidirectional, ensemble	70.94
JPCN ja-ko	Multilingual, single*	67.87
JPCN en-ja	Unidirectional, single	44.14
JPCN en-ja	Unidirectional, ensemble	44.97
JPCN en-ja	Multilingual, single*	43.82
JPCN ja-en	Unidirectional, single	41.74
JPCN ja-en	Unidirectional, ensemble	43.34
JPCN ja-en	Multilingual, single*	39.82
JPCEP zh-ja	Unidirectional, single	35.41
JPCEP zh-ja	Unidirectional, ensemble	36.73
JPCEP zh-ja	Multilingual, single*	34.45

Table 2: JPO task results. Note that we did not submit our multilingual model output (marked with *) and it serves as comparative purposes.

zh, and ja-en. Interestingly, our model did not perform well on ja-ko translation, where the performance was behind the organizer's baseline system which is based on a sequence-to-sequence LSTM. More careful investigation could help us understand which component in our training pipeline (e.g., data processing or tokenization) could possibly cause this difference.

2.5 Multilingual Experiments

Given that multiple language pairs are involved for this task, we further experimented with multilingual NMT approaches after the submission period. We followed the approach in (Johnson et al., 2017), which adds an artificial token in each source sentence for indicating the target translation language (`--encoder-langtok tgt` in Fairseq). Encoder and decoder parameters are shared among all the language pairs. We merged all training data from all four languages for training a joint subword vocabulary of size 100,000 approximately. As a result, we can share the embedding layer in the encoder and decoder. Since the number of training examples for each direction is the same, we iterate round-robin over batches from the six language pairs.

As shown in Table 2, our multilingual result did not show improvement in the NMT systems, falling behind the unidirectional model by not more than 2 BLEU points for single decoding. Nonetheless, parameter sharing in multilingual model reduces the total number of parameters to approximately the same as that of one unidirectional model. In practice, this can potentially simplify production deployment for multiple language translation. Effectively, the model is able to perform a zero-shot translation for language pairs not included in this task (such as Chinese-Korean), although we left this for future investigation.

3 JPX Timely Disclosure Task

3.1 Task Description

The timely disclosure task evaluated Japanese to English translations from the Timely Disclosure Document Corpus (TDDC), which is constructed by the Japan Exchange Group (JPX). The corpus consists of 1.4M parallel Japanese-English sentences made from past timely disclosure documents between 2016 and 2018. The validation and test sets are further split into two sub data sets: 1) nouns and phrases ("X_ITEMS") and 2) complete texts ("X_TEXTS"). We used the official data split given by the organizer with no additional external resources. For this task, we did a brief study on the effect of different pre-processing procedures on model performance.

3.2 Data Processing

MT systems typically include complicated pre/post-processing pipeline, which is often language-specific. This usually forms a long chain in the pipeline: *tokenization/segmentation → truecasing → translation → detruecasing → detokenization.*

While tools like Moses (Koehn et al., 2007), Experiment Management System[6] and SacreMoses[7] simplify the data processing pipeline, handling various languages produces significant technical debt in maintaining language specific resources and rules. Although there are language agnostic approaches to tokenization/truecasing, (e.g. Evang et al., 2013; Susanto et al., 2016), the errors from

---

[6] http://www.statmt.org/moses/?n=FactoredTraining.EMS
[7] https://github.com/alvations/sacremoses

Embedding dim.	1024
Tied embeddings	Yes
Transformer FFN dim.	4096
Attention heads	8
En/Decoder layers	6
Label smoothing	0.1
Dropout	0.1
Attention weight dropout	0.1
Transformer FFN dropout	0.1
Learning rate	0.001
Batch size in tokens	14336
Update frequency	2

Table 3: JPX model settings

various components in the pipeline are propagated. Instead we propose to use a single step pre-processing using SentencePiece subword tokenizer.

SentencePiece is an unsupervised tokenizer that can learn directly on raw sentences, and pre-tokenization is an optional step. This greatly simplifies the training process as we can feed the data directly into SentencePiece to produce subword tokens based on BPE. We merged source and target sentences for training a shared vocabulary of 32,000 tokens with 100% character coverage and no further filtering. We removed empty lines and sentences exceeding 250 subword tokens from the training set. Both items and texts sub data sets were processed in the same manner. We concatenated the items and texts development data sets together for model validation.

3.3 Model

For the timely disclosure task, we used a 6-layer Transformer with 8 heads as shown in Table 3. The overall model is similar to the JPO model, except a couple differences: 1) Smaller dropout probability, 2) Larger number of tokens per batch, and 3) Delayed updates. Particularly, gradients for multiple sub-batches on each GPU were accumulated, which reduces variance in processing time and reduces communication time (Ott et al., 2019). With `--update-freq 2`, this effectively doubles the batch size. We trained 4 independent models with different random seeds to perform ensemble decoding on both the items and texts test sets. Every model was trained for 40 epochs and the best performing checkpoint on validation set was chosen.

Task	Model	Tokenization	BLEU	Human
TDDC Item ja-en	Single	None	52.77	29.25
TDDC Item ja-en	Ensemble	None	54.25	36.75
TDDC Item ja-en	Single	Juman*	52.83	-
TDDC Text ja-en	Single	None	54.84	37.75
TDDC Text ja-en	Ensemble	None	58.38	49.50
TDDC Text ja-en	Single	Juman*	57.34	-

Table 4: JPX task results. Note that we did not submit the output from our model that includes Japanese word segmentation (marked with *) and it serves as comparative purposes.

3.4 Results

Table 4 shows our model performance for the timely disclosure task. Human evaluation ranks our best submissions in the first place for the "Item" test set and second place for the "Text" test set. After the submission period has ended, we did a further study on the effect of including Japanese segmentation in data pre-processing. We tokenized the Japanese text using Juman and re-trained our model. Comparing their BLEU scores on single decoding, we observe that tokenization slightly improves on Item data, while it significantly improves on Text data by 2.5 BLEU points, which might have boosted our scores in the leaderboard. Nonetheless, a single step pre-processing greatly simplifies our training and translation pipeline. This is particularly helpful in deploying MT systems for several languages in production settings because it allows us to build an end-to-end system that does not rely on language-specific pre/post-processing.

4 JIJI Newswire Task

4.1 Task Description

The newswire task evaluated Japanese-English translations on the JIJI corpus. The corpus was created by Jiji Press in collaboration with National Institute of Information and Communications Technology (NICT). The data set contains 200,000 parallel sentences for training, 2,000 for validation and 2,000 for testing. We did not use any external resources other than the provided corpus. For this task, we investigated the importance of choosing a suitable Transformer network size with respect to the size of our training set.

4.2 Data Processing

We ran Juman version 7.01 for Japanese word segmentation but English sentences were not tokenized. After tokenization, both Japanese and En-

Embedding dim.	512
Tied embeddings	Yes
Transformer FFN dim.	2048
Attention heads	2
En/Decoder layers	5
Label smoothing	0.2
Dropout	0.4
Attention weight dropout	0.2
Transformer FFN dropout	0.2
Learning rate	0.001
Batch size in tokens	4000
Update frequency	1

Table 5: JIJI model settings

glish sentences were combined and fed into SentencePiece for training BPE subword units. The subword vocabulary size is 32,000 with 100% character coverage and no further filtering. We further removed empty lines and sentences exceeding 250 subword tokens from the training set. We also tried feeding the sentences directly into SentencePiece without pre-tokenization for Japanese but we observed a weaker performance on the JIJI task by doing so.

4.3 Model

Sennrich and Zhang (2019) adapted RNN-based NMT systems in low-resource settings by reducing vocabulary size and careful hyperparameter tuning. Similarly, we applied system adaptation techniques to Transformer-based NMT systems for this task, given that the JIJI corpus is a relatively small data set. As shown in Table 5, we chose to scale down our Transformer model so as to prevent overfitting. We made the following adjustments: (i) Halving embedding and hidden dimension, (ii) Reducing the number of attention heads and encoder/decoder layers, and (iii) Increasing regularization through

Task	Model	BLEU	Human
JIJI en-ja	BASE (Single)*	16.70	-
JIJI en-ja	MINI (Single)	21.80	55.25
JIJI en-ja	MINI (Ensemble)	22.65	63.25
JIJI ja-en	BASE (Single)*	15.91	-
JIJI ja-en	MINI (Single)	21.34	44.75
JIJI ja-en	MINI (Ensemble)	21.84	50.75

Table 6: JIJI task results. Note that we did not submit the BASE model output (marked with *) and it serves for comparative purposes.

dropout and weight decay (`--weight-decay 0.0001`). We used the same model set up for both directions. Considering the size of this data set, we were able to run longer epochs for JIJI tasks: 150 epochs for Japanese→English and 100 for English→Japanese. We compare the performance of this downsized model (MINI) to the previous model setup used for the JPX task (BASE).

4.4 Results

Table 6 shows our model performance on the newswire task. We can observe that the MINI model significantly outperforms the BASE model by around 5 BLEU points on single decoding. These results affirm our hypothesis that it is possible to improve NMT performance in low-resource settings by more careful hyperparameter tuning without relying too much on auxiliary resources. Overall, our submissions for both translation directions ranked the first in the leaderboard in terms of BLEU scores and under the constrained settings. Unfortunately, our system output are the only constrained submissions that were humanly evaluated and thus we are not able to do a comparative evaluation.

5 Mixed-domain Task

5.1 Task Description

The mix-domain task evaluated Myanmar-English translations from the University of Computer Studies, Yangon (UCSY) (Ding et al., 2018) and the Asian Language Treebank (ALT) corpora (Ding et al., 2019). The models were trained on the UCSY corpus, then validated and tested on the ALT corpus. The UCSY corpus contains approximately 200,000 sentences, ALT validation and test sets had 1,000 sentences each. No other resources were used to train our models for the task participation.

5.2 Data Processing

For the mix-domain task, no special pre-processing steps were taken to handle the data; sentences were fed directly to the SentencePiece to produce subwords tokens. We experimented with two Transformer models of varying sizes using the Marian[8] toolkit (Junczys-Dowmunt et al., 2018).

5.3 Model

Using similar models settings as (i) JPX model in Table 3 with 32,000 subwords tokens at 100% character coverage (BASE) and (ii) the JIJI model in Table 5 with 10,000 subwords tokens at 100% character coverage (MINI), we train one model each to compare (i) vs (ii) in the Mixed-domain Task. We only participated in the English to Myanmar task.

5.4 Results

Task	Model	BLEU
ALT2 en-my	BASE (Single)	12.55
ALT2 en-my	MINI (Single)	19.64
ALT2 en-my	MINI (Ensemble)	19.94

Table 7: Mixed-domain Task Results

Table 7 shows the result of our English to Myanmar models. Due to the low resource nature of the Myanmar-English language pair and the added difficulty of domain adaptation, for future work, we will explore extending language resources in the generic domain to further improve translation quality in this language pair.

We have compiled the *Myth Corpus*[9] with various Myanmar-English datasets that researchers can use to improve Myanmar-English models. The datasets created ranges from manually cleaned dictionaries to synthetically translated data using

---

[8] `https://marian-nmt.github.io`
[9] `https://github.com/alvations/myth`

commercial translation API and unsupervised machine translation algorithms.

6 Conclusion

In this paper we presented our submissions to the WAT 2019 translation shared task. We trained similar Transformer-based NMT systems across different tasks. We found that shallower Transformers with a small number of heads perform better on smaller data sets. We also found a trade-off between simplifying data processing pipeline and model performance. Finally, we attempted simple techniques for training a multilingual NMT system and we will continue our investigation along this direction in future work.

References

Chenchen Ding, Hnin Thu Zar Aye, Win Pa Pa, Khin Thandar Nwet, Khin Mar Soe, Masao Utiyama, and Eiichiro Sumita. 2019. Towards Burmese (Myanmar) morphological analysis: Syllable-based tokenization and part-of-speech tagging. *ACM Transactions on Asian and Low-Resource Language Information Processing (TALLIP)*, 19(1):5.

Chenchen Ding, Masao Utiyama, and Eiichiro Sumita. 2018. NOVA: A feasible and flexible annotation system for joint tokenization and part-of-speech tagging. *ACM Transactions on Asian and Low-Resource Language Information Processing (TALLIP)*, 18(2):17.

Kilian Evang, Valerio Basile, Grzegorz Chrupała, and Johan Bos. 2013. Elephant: Sequence labeling for word and sentence segmentation. In *Proceedings of the 2013 Conference on Empirical Methods in Natural Language Processing*, pages 1422–1426, Seattle, Washington, USA. Association for Computational Linguistics.

Melvin Johnson, Mike Schuster, Quoc V. Le, Maxim Krikun, Yonghui Wu, Zhifeng Chen, Nikhil Thorat, Fernanda Viégas, Martin Wattenberg, Greg Corrado, Macduff Hughes, and Jeffrey Dean. 2017. Google's multilingual neural machine translation system: Enabling zero-shot translation. *Transactions of the Association for Computational Linguistics*, 5:339–351.

Marcin Junczys-Dowmunt, Roman Grundkiewicz, Tomasz Dwojak, Hieu Hoang, Kenneth Heafield, Tom Neckermann, Frank Seide, Ulrich Germann, Alham Fikri Aji, Nikolay Bogoychev, André F. T. Martins, and Alexandra Birch. 2018. Marian: Fast neural machine translation in C++. In *Proceedings of ACL 2018, System Demonstrations*, pages 116–121, Melbourne, Australia. Association for Computational Linguistics.

Diederick P Kingma and Jimmy Ba. 2015. Adam: A method for stochastic optimization. In *International Conference on Learning Representations (ICLR)*.

Philipp Koehn, Hieu Hoang, Alexandra Birch, Chris Callison-Burch, Marcello Federico, Nicola Bertoldi, Brooke Cowan, Wade Shen, Christine Moran, Richard Zens, et al. 2007. Moses: Open source toolkit for statistical machine translation. In *Proceedings of the 45th annual meeting of the ACL on interactive poster and demonstration sessions*, pages 177–180.

Taku Kudo and John Richardson. 2018. Sentence-Piece: A simple and language independent subword tokenizer and detokenizer for neural text processing. In *Proceedings of the 2018 Conference on Empirical Methods in Natural Language Processing: System Demonstrations*, pages 66–71, Brussels, Belgium. Association for Computational Linguistics.

Toshiaki Nakazawa, Chenchen Ding, Raj Dabre, Hideya Mino, Isao Goto, Win Pa Pa, Nobushige Doi, Yusuke Oda, Anoop Kunchukuttan, Shantipriya Parida, Ondej Bojar, and Sadao Kurohashi. 2019. Overview of the 6th workshop on Asian translation. In *Proceedings of the 6th Workshop on Asian Translation*, Hong Kong. Association for Computational Linguistics.

Toshiaki Nakazawa, Shohei Higashiyama, Chenchen Ding, Hideya Mino, Isao Goto, Hideto Kazawa, Yusuke Oda, Graham Neubig, and Sadao Kurohashi. 2017. Overview of the 4th workshop on Asian translation. In *Proceedings of the 4th Workshop on Asian Translation (WAT2017)*, pages 1–54, Taipei, Taiwan. Asian Federation of Natural Language Processing.

Toshiaki Nakazawa, Hideya Mino, Isao Goto, Graham Neubig, Sadao Kurohashi, and Eiichiro Sumita. 2015. Overview of the 2nd workshop on Asian translation. In *Proceedings of the 2nd Workshop on Asian Translation (WAT2015)*, Kyoto, Japan.

Toshiaki Nakazawa, Hideya Mino, Isao Goto, Graham Neubig, Sadao Kurohashi, and Eiichiro Sumita. 2016. Overview of the 3rd workshop on Asian translation. In *Proceedings of the 3rd Workshop on Asian Translation (WAT2016)*, Kyoto, Japan.

Toshiaki Nakazawa, Katsuhito Sudoh, Shohei Higashiyama, Chenchen Ding, Raj Dabre, Hideya Mino, Isao Goto, Win Pa Pa, Anoop Kunchukuttan, and Sadao Kurohashi. 2018. Overview of the 5th workshop on Asian translation. In *Proceedings of the 32nd Pacific Asia Conference on Language, Information and Computation: 5th Workshop on Asian Translation: 5th Workshop on Asian Translation*, Hong Kong. Association for Computational Linguistics.

Myle Ott, Sergey Edunov, Alexei Baevski, Angela Fan, Sam Gross, Nathan Ng, David Grangier, and Michael Auli. 2019. fairseq: A fast, extensible toolkit for sequence modeling. In *Proceedings of the 2019 Conference of the North American Chapter of the Association for Computational Linguistics (Demonstrations)*, pages 48–53, Minneapolis, Minnesota. Association for Computational Linguistics.

Myle Ott, Sergey Edunov, David Grangier, and Michael Auli. 2018. Scaling neural machine translation. In *Proceedings of the Third Conference on Machine Translation: Research Papers*, pages 1–9, Belgium, Brussels. Association for Computational Linguistics.

Ofir Press and Lior Wolf. 2017. Using the output embedding to improve language models. In *Proceedings of the 15th Conference of the European Chapter of the Association for Computational Linguistics: Volume 2, Short Papers*, pages 157–163, Valencia, Spain. Association for Computational Linguistics.

Rico Sennrich and Biao Zhang. 2019. Revisiting low-resource neural machine translation: A case study. In *Proceedings of the 57th Annual Meeting of the Association for Computational Linguistics*, pages 211–221, Florence, Italy. Association for Computational Linguistics.

Raymond Hendy Susanto, Hai Leong Chieu, and Wei Lu. 2016. Learning to capitalize with character-level recurrent neural networks: An empirical study. In *Proceedings of the 2016 Conference on Empirical Methods in Natural Language Processing*, pages 2090–2095, Austin, Texas. Association for Computational Linguistics.

Ashish Vaswani, Noam Shazeer, Niki Parmar, Jakob Uszkoreit, Llion Jones, Aidan N Gomez, Ł ukasz Kaiser, and Illia Polosukhin. 2017. Attention is all you need. In I. Guyon, U. V. Luxburg, S. Bengio, H. Wallach, R. Fergus, S. Vishwanathan, and R. Garnett, editors, *Advances in Neural Information Processing Systems 30*, pages 5998–6008. Curran Associates, Inc.

AISTAI Neural Machine Translation Systems for WAT 2019

Wei Yang
Artificial Intelligence Research Center,
National Institute of Advanced Industrial
Science and Technology (AIST),
Tsukuba 305-8560, Japan
wei.yang@aist.go.jp

Jun Ogata
Artificial Intelligence Research Center,
National Institute of Advanced Industrial
Science and Technology (AIST),
Tsukuba 305-8560, Japan
jun.ogata@aist.go.jp

Abstract

In this paper, we describe our Neural Machine Translation (NMT) systems for the WAT 2019 translation tasks we focus on. This year we participate in scientific paper tasks and focus on the language pair between English and Japanese. We use Transformer model through our work in this paper to explore and experience the powerful of the Transformer architecture relying on self-attention mechanism. We use different NMT toolkit/library as the implementation of training the Transformer model. For word segmentation, we use different subword segmentation strategies while using different toolkit/library. We not only give the translation accuracy obtained based on absolute position encodings that introduced in the Transformer model, but also report the the improvements in translation accuracy while replacing absolute position encodings with relative position representations. We also ensemble several independent trained Transformer models to further improve the translation accuracy.

1 Introduction

Machine translation (MT) is a specific task of natural language processing (NLP). It is used to automatically translate speech or text from one natural language to another natural language using translation system. In neural machine translation (NMT), different from statistical machine translation (SMT), deep learning is done using neural network technology. In the last five years, statistical machine translation is gradually fading out in favor of neural machine translation. Google translate supports over 100 languages. In November 2016, Google has switched to a neural machine translation engine for 8 languages firstly between English (to and from) and Chinese, French, German, Japanese, Korean, Portuguese, Spanish

and Turkish[1]. By July 2017 all languages support translation to and from English by GNMT (Wu et al., 2016).

In our work, we focus on the NMT system constructed based on the Transformer model (Vaswani et al., 2017). The Transformer model use a different neural network architecture with self-attention mechanism. Different from sequence-aligned recurrent neural networks (RNNS) or convolution, the Transformer model computes representations of a sequence by considering different positions of the sequence relying on self-attention mechanism. All NMT experiments in our work are performed by using this state-of-the-art new network architecture.

"Tensor2Tensor[2]" (Vaswani et al., 2018) is a library for deep learning models that is widely used for NMT recently and includes the implementation of the Transformer model (Vaswani et al., 2017). It is used to train Transformer models and obtain the state-of-the-art translation accuracy for WMT[3] shared tasks: English-to-German and English-to-French on newstest2014 tests.

An open source for NMT and neural sequence learning, "OpenNMT[4]" has been released by the Harvard NLP group (Klein et al., 2017), and it provides implementations in 2 popular deep learning frameworks: PyTorch[5] (OpenNMT-py[6]) and TensorFlow[7] (Abadi et al., 2016) (OpenNMT-tf[8]). It has been extended to support many additional models and features including the Transformer

---

[1] https://en.wikipedia.org/wiki/Google_
Neural_Machine_Translation
[2] https://github.com/tensorflow/
tensor2tensor
[3] http://www.statmt.org/wmt19/
[4] http://opennmt.net/
[5] https://github.com/pytorch/pytorch
[6] https://github.com/OpenNMT/OpenNMT-py
[7] https://www.tensorflow.org/
[8] https://github.com/OpenNMT/OpenNMT-tf

Proceedings of the 6th Workshop on Asian Translation, pages 159–164
Hong Kong, China, November 4, 2019. ©2019 Association for Computational Linguistics

model, each implementation has its own set of features[9]. According to the needs in our experiments such as "Relative position representations" in model configuration and "Ensemble" in decoding, we choose to use "OpenNMT-py". We give the description of these two terms ("Relative position representations" and "Ensemble") in the following section.

In the last five years, two parallel corpora were released in the domain of scientific papers and patents. They are provided to promote machine translation research, including the condition of participating in the open evaluation campaign Workshop on Asian Translation (WAT) (Nakazawa et al., 2018, 2019). The first parallel corpus which provided for WAT from 2014 is the Asian Scientific Paper Excerpt Corpus (ASPEC) (Nakazawa et al., 2016). It contains 680,000 Japanese–Chinese parallel sentences used for training and approximately 3,000,000 English–Japanese training data extracted from scientific papers. The second parallel corpus provided for WAT from 2015 is the JPO corpus, created jointly, based on an agreement between the Japan Patent Office (JPO) and NICT. In our work, we propose to train several NMT systems between English and Japanese by leveraging a part of ASPEC-JE training data and several techniques. We also compare the translation accuracy between these systems so as to significantly improve the performance of NMT in scientific and technical domain.

Section 2 further introduces the background of our NMT systems and some related work. In section 3, we present the experiments and report the results by adding each technique or combine several techniques which are described in Sec. 2. Section 4 gives the conclusion and some future work.

2 Translation systems

2.1 Subword segmentation

Word segmentation (tokenization), i.e., breaking sentences down into individual words (tokens), is normally treated as the first step of preprocessing for natural language processing (NLP). For English and Japanese, in our experiments, we use scripts in Moses (Koehn et al., 2007) and Juman[10] as the basic segmentation toolkits for word segmentation (tokenization), and then we perform subword segmentation to further segment words for preparing the final experimental data. Because some previous work has used subwords as a way for addressing unseen word or rare word problems in machine translation (Sennrich et al., 2016b), reducing model size (Wu et al., 2016), or as one of the performance of training a independent translation model (Denkowski and Neubig, 2017) so as to obtain a stronger translation system. The investigation in the relationship between the choice of using "word-based" or "subword-based" segmentation strategy and the improvement of machine translation (MT) is conducted. It is conclude that the "subword-based" segmented data and the byte pair encoding (BPE) compression algorithm (Gage, 1994) that the segmenter relied on is effective and affects MT performance (Sennrich et al., 2016b).

In our experiments, we also examine the impact of "subword-based" strategy in technical and scientific domain. Because as we known, there exist a large amount technical words/terms in scientific paper and this may lead to some rare word or unknown word problems in MT. Thus, "subword-based" segmentation strategy can be very helpful for the translation of these words. We use BPE in "OpenNMT-py" and "wordpieces" (Schuster and Nakajima, 2012; Wu et al., 2016) in "Tensor2Tensor".

2.2 Relative position representations

Due to the Transformer is a different neural network architecture compare with recurrent neural network (RNN) and convolutional neural network (CNN), adding position information to its inputs is necessary and crucial important in model construction. In (Shaw et al., 2018), it is demonstrated that the way of introducing relative position representations, and instead of using absolute position encodings, using relative position representations in self-attention mechanism of the Transformer yields improvements of 1.3 BLEU and 0.3 BLEU respectively on the WMT 2014 English-to-German and English-to-French translation tasks.

In our experiments, we shall use a similar idea on ASPEC-JE tasks. In other words, we try to use absolute position encodings or relative position representations independently for training our Transformer models, but for WAT 2019 ASPEC translation tasks: English-to-Japanese and Japanese-to-English. There exist several previous

---

[9]http://opennmt.net/features/
[10]http://nlp.ist.i.kyoto-u.ac.jp/index.php?JUMAN

work for WAT using this method for improving translation accuracy on scientific paper tasks such as (Li et al., 2018). Different from their experiments, we use different size of the training data and development data at least and obtain better results in English-to-Japanese translation sub-task.

2.3 Ensemble technique

Some previous work shows improvements in BLEU scores for model ensembles (Sutskever et al., 2014; Sennrich et al., 2016a). The basic idea of ensemble technique is that training and decoding with multiple translation models. We propose to follow the idea given in (Denkowski and Neubig, 2017), combine several techniques and imply them in ASPEC-JE shared tasks. Thus, the final technique we explore is the ensemble of multiple independently trained, averaged translation models in prediction of the test set.

2.4 Evaluation

The main metric used in our experiments for automatically evaluating the translation outputs is BLEU (Papineni et al., 2002) method. All evaluation BLEU scores for translation results given in this paper are evaluated by WAT 2019 automatic evaluation system[11].

3 Experiments

We train and evaluate our model on the WAT 2019 scientific paper tasks, using the ASPEC-JE dataset consisting of approximately 3,000,000 lines of sentence pairs. It worth noticing that the data contained in the ASPEC-JE training corpus are not all perfect aligned. Thus, we use the first 1,500,000 pairs of sentences with higher similarity scores which are calculated using the method given in (Utiyama and Isahara, 2007) as our training data (Train). We do not do any filtering for these sentences by length in words/tokens. All development data (Dev) and test data (Test) sets are used in performing experiments. Statistics on our experimental data sets are given in Table 1.

First of all, we use the "Tensor2Tensor" library for training and evaluating the Transformer models. We train translation models using "transformer (big)" hyperparameter setting. For the two experiments (English-to-Japanese and Japanese-to-English) 32k "wordpieces" are broken from

	ASPEC-JE	English	Japanese
Train	sentences (lines)	1,500,000	1,500,000
	length in words (avg. ± std.dev.)	26.01 ± 11.76	28.20 ± 12.32
Dev	sentences (lines)	3,574	3,574
	length in words (avg. ± std.dev.)	24.65 ± 11.50	26.72 ± 11.87
Test	sentences (lines)	1,812	1,812
	length in words (avg. ± std.dev.)	24.49 ± 11.28	26.32 ± 11.50

Table 1: Statistics on our experimental data sets (after tokenizing and lowercasing). Here, 'avg ± std.dev.' gives the average length of the sentences in words.

words. We train for 300,000 steps on 4 GPUs, it costs only about 27 hours for each experiment. During training, we save checkpoints every 1,000 steps. We average the last 8, 10 and 20 checkpoints for decoding the test set and report the best one. For evaluation, we use beam search with a beam size of 4 and length penalty α=0.6 (Wu et al., 2016). On the English-to-Japanese and Japanese-to-English subtasks, our "Transformer (big)" models achieve BLEU scores of 42.92 (average the last 20 models) and 29.01 (average the last 10 model) respectively. Compare with the result for English-to-Japanese sub-task (BLEU=42.87) given in WAT official evaluation[12], we obtained the similar result (BLEU=42.92) to a certain extend. But we also give the translation result for Japanese-to-English direction (BLEU=29.01) which is not given in WAT official evaluation[13].

Except this two experiments, the following, a series of experiments are all performed using "OpenNMT-py" as shown in Table 2, thus, we do not mention it every time.

We then measure the effect of BPE by training "word-based" and "subword-based" systems using "OpenNMT-py" with the same 1,500,000 training data (without any cleaning). All options and parameters used in "OpenNMT-py" are set refer to "transformer (big)" hyperparameter setting in "Tensor2Tensor". These two systems ("word-based" and "subword-based") are considered as two baselines ("weak baseline" and "stronger baseline") of the following experiments. The only difference from the "weak baseline", the "stronger baseline" use BPE segmentation with 32k vocabulary both for English and Japanese. Scores for

---

[11]http://lotus.kuee.kyoto-u.ac.jp/WAT/
evaluation/index.html

[12]http://lotus.kuee.kyoto-u.ac.jp/WAT/
evaluation/list.php?t=1&o=1

[13]http://lotus.kuee.kyoto-u.ac.jp/WAT/
evaluation/list.php?t=2&o=4

Toolkit/library	System opts.	En-Ja	Ja-En
Tensor2Tensor	wordpieces + transformer (big)	42.92	29.01
OpenNMT-py	word-based + dropout=0.3 + warm-up=8,000 (weak baseline)	38.73	26.70
OpenNMT-py (1)	BPE + dropout=0.3 + warm-up=8,000 (stronger baseline)	41.91	28.92
OpenNMT-py (2)	BPE + Relative Position + dropout=0.1 + warm-up=8,000	42.06	28.64
OpenNMT-py (3)	BPE + Relative Position + dropout=0.3 + warm-up=8,000	42.83	28.86
OpenNMT-py (4)	BPE + Relative Position + dropout=0.3 + warm-up=16,000	42.63	28.32
OpenNMT-py	Ensemble (1) and (3)	43.15	29.36
OpenNMT-py	Ensemble (1), (2) and (3)	**43.76**	29.54
OpenNMT-py	Ensemble (1), (2) , (3) and (4)	43.60	**29.71**

Table 2: BLEU scores for ASPEC-JE test set using the Transformer (model) based NMT.

single models are averaged after training step. For using "OpenNMT-py", we average 4-6 saved models (models are saved per 10,000 steps, each experiments are trained for 160,000 steps.) with higher validation accuracy. Because we found that this may lead to better translation accuracy. As the results, compare with our "weak baseline", we improved translation accuracy by 3.2 and 2.2 BLEU points for both directions (English↔Japanese) by directly applying BPE subword segmentation strategy for English and Japanese.

But we found that the big transformer model (Transformer (big) in Table 2) training by "Tensor2Tensor" outperforms the reported models training by "OpenNMT-py" (the fourth line in Table 2), especially for English-to-Japanese (42.92 vs. 41.91).

After that, we compare our models using absolute position (sinusoidal position encodings) to using relative position representation instead. For English-to-Japanese, this approach improved nearly 1 BLEU points (41.91→42.83) compare with the "stronger baseline". In this experiment, for Japanese-to-English, there is no improvement in BLEU even slightly decreased compare with the "stronger baseline" system (28.92 →28.86).

For English-to-Japanese, "dropout" setting, we begin with 0.3 and then change it with 0.1, for "warm-up" setting, we begin with 8,000 and then change it with 16,000, we apply the same changing for Japanese-to-English. In other words, we do not touch any other settings and perform another two groups of experiments with the same data for both directions by only modifying the "dropout" value ("dropout=0.3" ⇒ "dropout=0.1" ("warm-up=8,000")) and "warm-up" value ("warm-up=8,000" ⇒ "warm-up=16,000" ("dropout=0.3"). As the results in both direc-

tions, "BPE + Relative position + dropout=0.3 + warm-up=8,000" allow us to obtain better BLEU scores compare with our "stronger baseline" system, especially for English-to-Japanese. In our experiments, translation accuracy are negatively affected by whatever changing "dropout" from 0.3 to 0.1 or "warm-up" form 8,000 to 16,000.

However, ensemble these models allow us to obtain our best BLEU scores for English-to-Japanese and Japanese-to-English sub-tasks. Again, all of these models are independent trained, averaged models. In Table 2, we show that combing these techniques can lead to significant improvements of over 1.85 BLEU score for English-to-Japanese by ensembling 3 independent models, 0.79 BLEU points for Japanese-to-English translation by ensembling 4 independent models. Boldface indicates the best BLEU scores over the two baseline systems. If we compare our final results with the "weak baseline" systems, combine using the Transformer model and several introduced efficient techniques, we obtained even more significant improvements by 5 and 3 BLEU points for English-to-Japanese and Japanese-to-English respectively in scientific domain.

As we mentioned in Sec. 2.4, all evaluation BLEU scores given in Table 2 are evaluated by WAT 2019 official automatic evaluation system[14]. We published the best two BLEU scores (43.76 and 29.71 for English-to-Japanese and Japanese-to-English) obtained by ensembling models using "OpenNMT-py", as well as another two BLEU scores (42.92 and 29.01 for English-to-Japanese and Japanese-to-English) obtained by "Tensor2Tensor" (transformer (big)).

---

[14] http://lotus.kuee.kyoto-u.ac.jp/WAT/evaluation/index.html

The translation result (BLEU=42.64)[15] submitted to WAT 2019 (Nakazawa et al., 2019) for both automatic evaluation and human evaluation obtained by an English-to-Japanese translation system using "Tensor2Tensor" (transformer (big)). We do not mention that system too much because it is only a test and very first system in our experiments with "transformer (big)" setting except the "train_steps" is only 131,000 (not 300,000 which allowed us to obtain BLEU=42.92).

4 Conclusion

The main focus of this paper is to exploit ASPEC-JE linguistic resources in technical and scientific domain and some existing technical methods to improve the translation accuracy between English and Japanese. In our experiments, we improved translation accuracy for WAT 2019 scientific paper tasks by using subword segmentation strategy, relative position representations and ensemble techniques, and tried to use the training data as small as possible without the use of any additional lexicon or additional corpus. We combined and applied several approaches and further improved the translation accuracy of English-to-Japanese and Japanese-to-English NMT by 1.85 and 0.79 BLEU scores compare with our "stronger baseline" systems, at the same time, we obtained 5 and 3 BLEU point improvements compare with our "weak baseline" systems. We found that we may obtain better translation accuracy by ensembling several independent models, even these models do not work very well independently. In future work, we propose to give in-depth analysis of where improvements obtained for translation results and give some statistics of them.

References

Martín Abadi, Paul Barham, Jianmin Chen, Zhifeng Chen, Andy Davis, Jeffrey Dean, Matthieu Devin, Sanjay Ghemawat, Geoffrey Irving, Michael Isard, Manjunath Kudlur, Josh Levenberg, Rajat Monga, Sherry Moore, Derek G. Murray, Benoit Steiner, Paul Tucker, Vijay Vasudevan, Pete Warden, Martin Wicke, Yuan Yu, and Xiaoqiang Zheng. 2016. Tensorflow: A system for large-scale machine learning. In *Proceedings of the 12th USENIX Conference on Operating Systems Design and Implementation*, OSDI'16, pages 265–283.

Michael Denkowski and Graham Neubig. 2017. Stronger baselines for trustable results in neural machine translation. In *Proceedings of the First Workshop on Neural Machine Translation*, pages 18–27, Vancouver.

Philip Gage. 1994. A new algorithm for data compression. *C Users J.*, 12(2):23–28.

Guillaume Klein, Yoon Kim, Yuntian Deng, Jean Senellart, and Alexander Rush. 2017. OpenNMT: Open-source toolkit for neural machine translation. In *Proceedings of ACL 2017, System Demonstrations*, pages 67–72.

Philipp Koehn, Hieu Hoang, Alexandra Birch, Chris Callison-Burch, Marcello Federico, Nicola Bertoldi, Brooke Cowan, Wade Shen, Christine Moran, Richard Zens, Chris Dyer, Ondřej Bojar, Alexandra Constantin, and Evan Herbst. 2007. Moses: Open source toolkit for statistical machine translation. In *Proceedings of the 45th Annual Meeting of the Association for Computational Linguistics Companion Volume Proceedings of the Demo and Poster Sessions*, pages 177–180.

Yihan Li, Boyan Liu, Yixuan Tong, Shanshan Jiang, and Bin Dong. 2018. SRCB neural machine translation systems in WAT 2018. In *Proceedings of the 32nd Pacific Asia Conference on Language, Information and Computation: 5th Workshop on Asian Translation: 5th Workshop on Asian Translation*, Hong Kong.

Toshiaki Nakazawa, Chenchen Ding, Raj Dabre, Hideya Mino, Isao Goto, Win Pa Pa, Nobushige Doi, Yusuke Oda, Anoop Kunchukuttan, Shantipriya Parida, Ondřej Bojar, and Sadao Kurohashi. 2019. Overview of the 6th workshop on Asian translation. In *Proceedings of the 6th Workshop on Asian Translation*, Hong Kong. Association for Computational Linguistics.

Toshiaki Nakazawa, Katsuhito Sudoh, Shohei Higashiyama, Chenchen Ding, Raj Dabre, Hideya Mino, Isao Goto, Win Pa Pa, Anoop Kunchukuttan, and Sadao Kurohashi. 2018. Overview of the 5th workshop on Asian translation. In *Proceedings of the 32nd Pacific Asia Conference on Language, Information and Computation: 5th Workshop on Asian Translation: 5th Workshop on Asian Translation*, Hong Kong.

Toshiaki Nakazawa, Manabu Yaguchi, Kiyotaka Uchimoto, Masao Utiyama, Eiichiro Sumita, Sadao Kurohashi, and Hitoshi Isahara. 2016. ASPEC: Asian scientific paper excerpt corpus. In *Proceedings of the Tenth International Conference on Language Resources and Evaluation (LREC 2016)*, pages 2204–2208, Portorož, Slovenia.

Mike Schuster and Kaisuke Nakajima. 2012. Japanese and Korean voice search. In *International Conference on Acoustics, Speech and Signal Processing, IEEE (2012)*, pages 5149–5152.

---

[15]`http://lotus.kuee.kyoto-u.ac.jp/WAT/evaluation/list.php?t=1&o=1`

Rico Sennrich, Barry Haddow, and Alexandra Birch. 2016a. Edinburgh neural machine translation systems for WMT 16. In *Proceedings of the First Conference on Machine Translation: Volume 2, Shared Task Papers*, pages 371–376, Berlin, Germany.

Rico Sennrich, Barry Haddow, and Alexandra Birch. 2016b. Neural machine translation of rare words with subword units. In *Proceedings of the 54th Annual Meeting of the Association for Computational Linguistics (Volume 1: Long Papers)*, pages 1715–1725, Berlin, Germany.

Peter Shaw, Jakob Uszkoreit, and Ashish Vaswani. 2018. Self-attention with relative position representations. In *Proceedings of the 2018 Conference of the North American Chapter of the Association for Computational Linguistics: Human Language Technologies, Volume 2 (Short Papers)*, pages 464–468, New Orleans, Louisiana.

Ilya Sutskever, Oriol Vinyals, and Quoc V Le. 2014. Sequence to sequence learning with neural networks. pages 3104–3112.

Masao Utiyama and Hitoshi Isahara. 2007. A Japanese-English patent parallel corpus. In *In proceedings of the Machine Translation Summit XI*.

Ashish Vaswani, Samy Bengio, Eugene Brevdo, Francois Chollet, Aidan Gomez, Stephan Gouws, Llion Jones, Łukasz Kaiser, Nal Kalchbrenner, Niki Parmar, Ryan Sepassi, Noam Shazeer, and Jakob Uszkoreit. 2018. Tensor2Tensor for neural machine translation. In *Proceedings of the 13th Conference of the Association for Machine Translation in the Americas (Volume 1: Research Papers)*, pages 193–199.

Ashish Vaswani, Noam Shazeer, Niki Parmar, Jakob Uszkoreit, Llion Jones, Aidan N. Gomez, Lukasz Kaiser, and Illia Polosukhin. 2017. Attention is all you need. In *NIPS'17 Proceedings of the 31st International Conference on Neural Information Processing Systems*, pages 6000–6010, Long Beach, CA, USA.

Yonghui Wu, Mike Schuster, Zhifeng Chen, Quoc V. Le, Mohammad Norouzi, Wolfgang Macherey, Maxim Krikun, Yuan Cao, Qin Gao, Klaus Macherey, Jeff Klingner, Apurva Shah, Melvin Johnson, Xiaobing Liu, Lukasz Kaiser, Stephan Gouws, Yoshikiyo Kato, Taku Kudo, Hideto Kazawa, Keith Stevens, George Kurian, Nishant Patil, Wei Wang, Cliff Young, Jason Smith, Jason Riesa, Alex Rudnick, Oriol Vinyals, Gregory S. Corrado, Macduff Hughes, and Jeffrey Dean. 2016. Google's neural machine translation system: Bridging the gap between human and machine translation. *ArXiv preprint arXiv*, 1609.08144.

Japanese-Russian TMU Neural Machine Translation System using Multilingual Model for WAT 2019

Aizhan Imankulova   Masahiro Kaneko   Mamoru Komachi
Tokyo Metropolitan University
6-6 Asahigaoka, Hino, Tokyo 191-0065, Japan
{imankulova-aizhan, kaneko-masahiro}@ed.tmu.ac.jp
komachi@tmu.ac.jp

Abstract

We introduce our system that is submitted to the News Commentary task (Japanese↔Russian) of the 6th Workshop on Asian Translation. The goal of this shared task is to study extremely low resource situations for distant language pairs. It is known that using parallel corpora of different language pair as training data is effective for multilingual neural machine translation model in extremely low resource scenarios. Therefore, to improve the translation quality of Japanese↔Russian language pair, our method leverages other in-domain Japanese-English and English-Russian parallel corpora as additional training data for our multilingual NMT model.

1 Introduction

News Commentary shared task of the 6th Workshop on Asian Translation (Nakazawa et al., 2019) addresses Japanese↔Russian (Ja↔Ru) news translation. It is a very challenging task considering: (a) extremely low resource setting, the size of parallel data is only 12k parallel sentences; (b) how distant given language pair is, in terms of different writing system, phonology, morphology, grammar, and syntax; (c) difficulty of translating news from various topics which leads to large presence of unknown tokens in such extremely low-resource scenario.

Usually, neural machine translation (NMT) (Cho et al., 2014; Sutskever et al., 2014; Bahdanau et al., 2015; Vaswani et al., 2017) enables end-to-end training of a translation system requiring a large amount of training parallel data (Koehn and Knowles, 2017). Therefore, there are different techniques of involving other pivot languages to increase the accuracy of low-resource MT such as pivot-based SMT (Utiyama and Isahara, 2007),

transfer learning (Zoph et al., 2016; Kocmi and Bojar, 2018), and multilingual modeling (Firat et al., 2016). Recently, a simple multilingual modeling (MultiNMT) was proposed by Johnson et al. (2017) which translates between multiple languages using a single model and an artificial token indicating a target language, taking advantage of multilingual data to improve NMT for all languages involved. Imankulova et al. (2019) showed that incorporating MultiNMT (Johnson et al., 2017) provided better BLEU scores than unidirectional and pivot-based PBSMT approaches and that domain mismatch had a negative effect on low-resource NMT.

Therefore, we use MultiNMT modeling for an extremely low-resource Ja↔Ru translation involving English (En) as the pivoting third language (Utiyama and Isahara, 2007). Considering the importance of domain matching, we focus on only news domain of additional Ja↔En and Ru↔En auxiliary parallel corpora, which we will refer as pivot parallel corpora. And we investigate how translation results are improved by using in-domain pivot parallel corpora (Ja↔En and Ru↔En) in MultiNMT modeling. As a result, in-domain pivot parallel corpora increases the coverage of Ja and Ru vocabulary, and it is clarified that the new tokens introduced from in-domain pivot corpora could be translated successfully.

2 Related Work

The existing state-of-the-art NMT model known as the Transformer (Vaswani et al., 2017) works well on different scenarios (Lakew et al., 2018; Imankulova et al., 2019). MultiNMT using the artificial token approach (Johnson et al., 2017) is known to help the language pairs with relatively lesser data (Lakew et al., 2018; Rikters et al., 2018)

Proceedings of the 6th Workshop on Asian Translation, pages 165–170
Hong Kong, China, November 4, 2019. ©2019 Association for Computational Linguistics

Lang.pair	Source	Partition	#sent.	#tokens	#types
	Global Voices	train	12,356	341k / 229k	22k / 42k
Ja↔Ru	News Commentary	development	486	16k / 11k	2.9k / 4.3k
	News Commentary	test	600	22k / 15k	3.5k / 5.6k
	Global Voices	train	47,082	1.27M / 1.01M	48k / 55k
Ja↔En	Jiji	train	200,000	5.84M / 5.11M	45k / 78k
	News Commentary	development	589	21k / 16k	3.5k / 3.8k
	Global Voices	train	82,072	1.61M / 1.83M	144k / 74k
Ru↔En	News Commentary	train	279,307	7.00M / 7.41M	214k / 89k
	News Commentary	development	313	7.8k / 8.4k	3.2k / 2.3k

Table 1: Statistics on our in-domain parallel data.

and outperform bi-directional and uni-directional translation approaches (Imankulova et al., 2019). Similarly, we exploit MultiNMT approach with Transformer architecture.

Our work is heavily based on Imankulova et al. (2019). They proposed a multi-stage fine-tuning approach that combines multilingual modeling and domain adaptation. They utilize out-of-domain pivot parallel corpora to perform domain adaptation on in-domain pivot parallel corpora and then perform multilingual transfer for a language pair of interest. However, instead of utilizing out-of-domain pivot parallel corpora, we investigate the impact of other in-domain pivot parallel corpora.

Pseudo-parallel data can be used to augment existing parallel corpora for training, and previous work has reported that such data generated by so-called back-translation can substantially improve the quality of NMT (Sennrich et al., 2016). However, this approach requires base MT systems that can generate somewhat accurate translations (Imankulova et al., 2017). Therefore, instead of creating noisy pseudo-parallel corpora, we take advantage of other in-domain pivot parallel corpora.

3 Experimental Settings

3.1 Data

To train MultiNMT systems we used the news domain data provided by WAT2019[1]. More specifically, we used Global Voices[2] as a training data for Ja↔Ru, Ja↔En and Ru↔En, and manually aligned, cleaned and filtered News Commentary data was used as development and test sets.[3] Additionally, we utilized Jiji[4] and News Commentary[5] data for Ja↔En and Ru↔En, respectively. Table 1 summarizes the size of train/development/test splits used in our experiments.

We tokenized English and Russian sentences using *tokenizer.perl* of Moses (Koehn et al., 2007).[6] To tokenize Japanese sentences, we used MeCab[7] with the IPA dictionary. After tokenization, we eliminated duplicated sentence pairs and sentences with more than 100 tokens for all the languages.

3.2 Systems

This section describes our system TMU and our baseline which based on the same MultiNMT architecture (Johnson et al., 2017) but trained on different training corpora (Table 1). Here, MultiNMT translates from multiple source languages into different target languages within a single model. To realize such translation, an artificial token is introduced at the beginning of the input sentence to indicate the target language the model should translate to. Since we have 3 language pairs, we concatenate all pairs in both directions with oversampling to match the biggest parallel data. We add a target language token to the source side of each pair and treat it like a single language-pair case.

We experiment with the following systems:

- **TMU**: Our system is trained on a balanced concatenation of Global Voices, Jiji and News Commentary corpora on 6 translation directions.

- **Only GV**: This is our baseline system which is trained on only Global Voices data on

---

[1]http://lotus.kuee.kyoto-u.ac.jp/WAT/WAT2019/index.html
[2]https://globalvoices.org/
[3]https://github.com/aizhanti/JaRuNC
[4]http://lotus.kuee.kyoto-u.ac.jp/WAT/jiji-corpus/
[5]http://lotus.kuee.kyoto-u.ac.jp/WAT/News-Commentary/news-commentary-v14.en-ru.filtered.tar.gz
[6]https://github.com/moses-smt/mosesdecoder
[7]http://taku910.github.io/mecab, version 0.996.

6 translation directions, the same as in Imankulova et al. (2019).

Only GV is used as a comparative model to investigate the effect of additional pivot corpora.

3.3 Implementation

We used the open-source `tensor2tensor` implementation of the Transformer model.[8]

Table 2 contains some specific hyper-parameters. The hyper-parameters not mentioned in this table used the default values in `tensor2tensor`. We over-sampled Ja→Ru and Ja→En training data so that their sizes match the largest Ru→En data for each model. However, the development set was created by concatenating those for the individual translation directions without any over-sampling. We also used `tensor2tensor`'s internal sub-word segmentation mechanism. The size of the shared sub-word vocabularies was set to 32k. By default, `tensor2tensor` truncates sentences longer than 256 sub-words to prevent out-of-memory errors during training. We incorporated early-stopping by stopping training if BLEU score for the development set was not improved for 10,000 updates (10 check-points).

At inference time, we averaged the last 10 check-points and decoded the test sets with beam size and a length penalty which were tuned by a linear search on the BLEU score for the development set. Length penalty for Ja→Ru was 1.0 and for Ru→Ja 1.1. Beam size was set to 12 and 3 for Ja→Ru and Ru→Ja, respectively. Although we train our models on 6 translation directions, we only report the BLEU scores on Ja→Ru and Ru→Ja test sets.

4 Results

Table 3 demonstrates the BLEU scores of our baseline Only GV model and proposed TMU model on News Commentary Ja→Ru[9] and Ru→Ja[10] test data for News Commentary shared task. Our TMU system trained on additional pivot parallel corpora exceeded the baseline Only GV

<hr>

[8]https://github.com/tensorflow/tensor2tensor, version 1.6.6.

[9]http://lotus.kuee.kyoto-u.ac.jp/WAT/evaluation/list.php?t=66o=4

[10]http://lotus.kuee.kyoto-u.ac.jp/WAT/evaluation/list.php?t=67o=1

Parameter	Value
Word Embedding size	512
Multi-Head number	8
Layer size	6
Hidden size	512
Optimizer	Adam
Adam β_1	0.9
Adam β_2	0.997
Warmup steps	16,000
Learning rate	0.2
Dropout	0.2
Weight decay	0.0
Label smoothing	0.1
Batch size	6144

Table 2: Hyper parameter values of transformer models.

Models	Ja→Ru	Ru→Ja
Only GV	3.66	8.79
TMU	**6.59**	**11.00**

Table 3: Evaluation results: BLEU scores. **Bold** indicates the best BLEU score for each translation direction.

model trained without additional pivot parallel corpora by approximately 3 BLEU points on both Ja→Ru and Ru→Ja.

5 Discussion

We investigate the effect of adding Jiji and News Commentary corpora as pivot parallel corpora to original Global Voices training data. In extremely low-resource machine translation in the news domain, unknown tokens become a serious issue due to vocabulary coverage. Adding the pivot parallel corpora to training data can be expected to increase vocabulary coverage.

Therefore, we investigate how much vocabulary coverage was improved by using pivot parallel corpora. For that purpose, we investigate the following vocabulary sets $\mathcal{A}$ and $\mathcal{B}$:

$$\mathcal{A} = \mathcal{T} \cap \mathcal{G} \tag{1}$$
$$\mathcal{B} = \mathcal{T} \cap (\mathcal{G} \cup \mathcal{P}) \tag{2}$$

$\mathcal{T}$ is a set of unknown tokens from test data not included in the direct Ja↔Ru 12k training data, $\mathcal{G}$ is pivot Gloval Voices vocabulary set and $\mathcal{P}$ is Jiji and News Commentary training vocabulary set. $\mathcal{A}$ is the test data unknown tokens set covered by pivot Global Voices training data. $\mathcal{B}$ is the test data unknown tokens set covered by concatenated vocabulary of Jiji and News Commentary pivot paral-

	Ja→Ru				Ru→Ja			
	$\mathcal{A}$ (Only GV)		$\mathcal{B}$ (TMU)		$\mathcal{A}$ (Only GV)		$\mathcal{B}$ (TMU)	
	#tokens	#types	#tokens	#types	#tokens	#types	#tokens	#types
Coverage in data	1,467	1,220	2,072	1,751	481	362	596	450
Correctly translated	85	65	191	147	26	21	31	24

Table 4: The coverage of tokens from additional pivot parallel data and the number of correctly translated tokens and types of distinct words by each system calculated for test set.

(a)	**Source**	Должны ли акционеры быть королями ?	
	Target	[株主] が、王様 に なる べき か? (Should [shareholders] be kings ?)	
	Only GV	この акционер が 社会 の 中心 と なっ てい る の だろ う か? (Is this акционер the center of society?)	
	TMU	[株主] は 王 を 持つ べき な の か? (Should [shareholders] have a king?)	
(b)	**Source**	Преемственность всегда оставалась сугубо семейным делом , и все споры оставались за закрытыми дверями .	
	Target	これ まで、継承 者 は、厳格 に 首長 家 から 選ば れる もの と され、いかなる 論 争 も [表立つ] て される こと は なかっ た。 (The succession was always strictly a family affair , and no disputes have [emerged].)	
	Only GV	家族 経営 の ドライクリーニング店 で、常習 的 な 商事 に は 至っ てい ない。 (It is a family-run dry cleaning shop, and it has not become a regular business.)	
	TMU	この よう な 虐待 は 日々 くり 返さ れ てい た。 (Such abuse was repeated every day.)	

Table 5: Examples of translating [unknown tokens] included in pivot parallel data $\mathcal{C}$ from Russian into Japanese.

lel corpora added to $\mathcal{A}$. By comparing the number of tokens and types of distinct words of $\mathcal{A}$ and $\mathcal{B}$, you can see how much the coverage has increased. In addition, we investigate how correctly the tokens added by Jiji corpus and News Commentary are translated. If a token from vocabulary set of $\mathcal{A}$ or $\mathcal{B}$ appeared in both the gold sentence and the translated sentence of the system, it was counted as being correctly translated.

Table 4 shows token and type coverage and correctly translated tokens and types of distinct words on test data for $\mathcal{A}$ and $\mathcal{B}$, respectively. It can be seen that both Ru and Ja have improved $\mathcal{B}$ coverage compared to $\mathcal{A}$. In particular, the coverage of Ru is greatly improved. And by adding Jiji corpus and News Commentary to the training data, you can see that the number of correctly translated tokens has increased. This shows that vocabulary coverage has increased and translation accuracy has improved. On the other hand, the number of correctly translated tokens is few compared to increased coverage from additional parallel data. This is considered to be due to difficulty of directly learning Ja↔Ru translation from added indirect Ja↔En and Ru↔En pivot corpora.

Furthermore, in order to deepen the knowledge about the tokens covered using pivot corpora, we analyze the cases where the newly added tokens by Jiji and News Commentary corpora are translated correctly and incorrectly. By adding Jiji and News Commentary corpora, we define the vocabulary set newly covered by the test data vocabulary as $\mathcal{C}$ as follows:

$$\mathcal{C} = (\mathcal{T} \cap \mathcal{P}) - \mathcal{G} \tag{3}$$

Table 5 shows translation examples of only GV and TMU systems. The [unknown tokens] in each sentence belong to $\mathcal{C}$. The first sentence is an example (a) where TMU was able to correctly translate "株主" compared to Only GV. On the other hand, the second example shows that neither TMU nor Only GV could correctly translate an unknown token "表立つ" included in pivot parallel corpora. It is considered that it cannot be translated because the whole sentence was translated incorrectly.

6 Conclusion

In this paper, we introduced our system submitted to the News Commentary task (Ja↔Ru) of the 6th Workshop on Asian Translation. The difficult part of this shared task is unknown tokens due to difficult news domain covering various topics and extremely low-resource available parallel data. To address this issue, we investigated the coverage of translatable tokens by training MultiNMT using an in-domain pivot parallel corpora. As a result, we found out that our system can translate more tokens by taking advantage of additional pivot parallel corpora. In the future, we will explore whether translation results improve by using other Ja↔Ru (e.g. Tatoeba) and Ru↔En (e.g. UN) corpora.

In the news domain, there is also a problem of completely new tokens, which is a type of unknown tokens, that cannot be dealt by simply increasing training data coverage since new information is out every day. Therefore, we plan to tackle the problem of new tokens that cannot be introduced by using additional corpora.

References

Dzmitry Bahdanau, Kyunghyun Cho, and Yoshua Bengio. 2015. Neural Machine Translation by Jointly Learning to Align and Translate. In *Proceedings of the 3rd International Conference on Learning Representations*.

Kyunghyun Cho, Bart van Merriënboer, Çaglar Gülçehre, Dzmitry Bahdanau, Fethi Bougares, Holger Schwenk, and Yoshua Bengio. 2014. Learning Phrase Representations using RNN Encoder–Decoder for Statistical Machine Translation. In *Proceedings of the 2014 Conference on Empirical Methods in Natural Language Processing*, pages 1724–1734.

Orhan Firat, Kyunghyun Cho, and Yoshua Bengio. 2016. Multi-Way, Multilingual Neural Machine Translation with a Shared Attention Mechanism. In *The 2016 Conference of the North American Chapter of the Association for Computational Linguistics: Human Language Technologies*, pages 866–875.

Aizhan Imankulova, Raj Dabre, Atsushi Fujita, and Kenji Imamura. 2019. Exploiting Out-of-Domain Parallel Data through Multilingual Transfer Learning for Low-Resource Neural Machine Translation. In *Proceedings of Machine Translation Summit XVII Volume 1: Research Track*, pages 128–139.

Aizhan Imankulova, Takayuki Sato, and Mamoru Komachi. 2017. Improving Low-resource Neural Machine Translation with Filtered Pseudo-parallel Corpus. In *Proceedings of the 4th Workshop on Asian Translation*, pages 70–78.

Melvin Johnson, Mike Schuster, Quoc Le, Maxim Krikun, Yonghui Wu, Zhifeng Chen, Nikhil Thorat, Fernanda Viégas, Martin Wattenberg, Greg Corrado, Macduff Hughes, and Jeffrey Dean. 2017. Google's Multilingual Neural Machine Translation System: Enabling Zero-Shot Translation. *Transactions of the Association for Computational Linguistics*, 5:339–351.

Tom Kocmi and Ondřej Bojar. 2018. Trivial Transfer Learning for Low-Resource Neural Machine Translation. In *Proceedings of the Third Conference on Machine Translation: Research Papers*, pages 244–252.

Philipp Koehn, Hieu Hoang, Alexandra Birch, Chris Callison-Burch, Marcello Federico, Nicola Bertoldi, Brooke Cowan, Wade Shen, Christine Moran, Richard Zens, Chris Dyer, Ondrej Bojar, Alexandra Constantin, and Evan Herbst. 2007. Moses: Open Source Toolkit for Statistical Machine Translation. In *Proceedings of the 45th Annual Meeting of the Association for Computational Linguistics Companion Volume Proceedings of the Demo and Poster Sessions*, pages 177–180.

Philipp Koehn and Rebecca Knowles. 2017. Six Challenges for Neural Machine Translation. In *Proceedings of the First Workshop on Neural Machine Translation*, pages 28–39.

Surafel M Lakew, Mauro Cettolo, and Marcello Federico. 2018. A Comparison of Transformer and Recurrent Neural Networks on Multilingual Neural Machine Translation. In *Proceedings of the 27th International Conference on Computational Linguistics*, pages 641–652.

Toshiaki Nakazawa, Chenchen Ding, Raj Dabre, Hideya Mino, Isao Goto, Win Pa Pa, Nobushige Doi, Yusuke Oda, Anoop Kunchukuttan, Shantipriya Parida, Ondřej Bojar, and Sadao Kurohashi. 2019. Overview of the 6th workshop on Asian translation. In *Proceedings of the 6th Workshop on Asian Translation*, Hong Kong. Association for Computational Linguistics.

Matīss Rikters, Mārcis Pinnis, and Rihards Krišlauks. 2018. Training and Adapting Multilingual NMT for Less-resourced and Morphologically Rich Languages. In *Proceedings of the 11th International Conference on Language Resources and Evaluation*, pages 3766–3773.

Rico Sennrich, Barry Haddow, and Alexandra Birch. 2016. Controlling Politeness in Neural Machine Translation via Side Constraints. In *Proceedings of the 2016 Conference of the North American Chapter of the Association for Computational Linguistics: Human Language Technologies*, pages 35–40.

Ilya Sutskever, Oriol Vinyals, and Quoc V. Le. 2014. Sequence to Sequence Learning with Neural Networks. In *Proceedings of the 27th International Conference on Neural Information Processing Systems*, pages 3104–3112.

Masao Utiyama and Hitoshi Isahara. 2007. A Comparison of Pivot Methods for Phrase-Based Statistical Machine Translation. In *Human Language Technologies 2007: The Conference of the North American Chapter of the Association for Computational*

Linguistics; Proceedings of the Main Conference, pages 484–491.

Ashish Vaswani, Noam Shazeer, Niki Parmar, Jakob Uszkoreit, Llion Jones, Aidan N. Gomez, Łukasz Kaiser, and Illia Polosukhin. 2017. Attention is All you Need. In *Proceedings of 30th Advances in Neural Information Processing Systems*, pages 5998–6008.

Barret Zoph, Deniz Yuret, Jonathan May, and Kevin Knight. 2016. Transfer Learning for Low-Resource Neural Machine Translation. In *Proceedings of the 2016 Conference on Empirical Methods in Natural Language Processing*, pages 1568–1575.

Transformer-based Neural Machine Translation System for Tamil – English

Amit Kumar, Anil Kumar Singh
Department of Computer Science & Engineering
Indian Institute of Technology (B.H.U.)
Varanasi, India
{amitkumar.rs.cse17, aksingh.cse}@iitbhu.ac.in

Abstract

This paper describes the Machine Translation (MT) system submitted by the NLPRL team for the Tamil – English Indic Task at WAT 2019. We presented the Neural Machine Translation (NMT) system based on the Transformer approach. Training and performance of the model are evaluated on the En-Tam corpus (An English-Tamil Parallel Corpus) collected by researchers at UFAL (Institute of Formal and Applied Linguistics). The evaluation of the model done using Adequacy, BLEU, RIBES, and AM-FM scores, and the model improves translation in terms of Adequacy, RIBES and AM-FM as compared to the baseline.

1   Introduction

Asia[1] is home to billions of people who speaks about 2,300 languages. The population of the continent is about six times that of Europe. A majority of Asians speak languages which are, in terms of language resources and tools, low to medium resource languages. The causes of this may be historical, economic, social and political, but this fact has technical implications. There is a need to develop Machine Translation (MT) systems to bridge the communication gap between peoples of Asian countries, not just between Asian and European countries. There are continued efforts in this direction, but the lack of resources poses a challenge, which requires innovative solutions. The work presented here is not very innovative, but can be treated as an incremental step in this direction.

We discuss here our submission to the Indic Task for Tamil – English language pair (Ramasamy et al., 2012a) at the 6th workshop on Asian Translation or WAT 2019 (Nakazawa et al., 2019). Neural Machine Translation (NMT)

---

[1] https://www.worldatlas.com/

(Sutskever et al., 2014) has been revolutionary for MT in the past few years.

Tamil comes under the family of Dravidian languages, spoken mostly in a southern state (Tamil Nadu) of India. If we consider a standard sentence in Tamil, the order is usually subject-object-verb (SOV), but object-subject-verb (OSV) is also common. While English follows subject-verb-object (SVO), therefore, Tamil-English language pairs can be considered distant language pairs. The two have very different word order, apart from other differences. Therefore, a major requirement of MT system for this language pair is to handle word order better.

2   Related work

In the last few decades, a number of works have been done on Machine Translation (MT), the initial attempt was made in the 1950s (Booth, 1955). A number of approaches have been tried out by researchers, for example, rule-based MT (Poornima et al., 2011), hybrid-based MT (Salunkhe et al., 2016), and data-driven MT (Wong et al., 2006). All of these approaches have their own advantages and disadvantages.

Rule-based approaches (Kasthuri and Kumar, 2013) cover rules based on linguistic knowledge about source and target languages in the form of dictionaries and grammars, and it covers the morphological, syntactic and semantic characteristics of each language, respectively.

Data-driven approaches rely on corpus analysis and processing. It covers Statistical Machine Translation (SMT) (Ramasamy et al., 2012b), Example-based Machine Translation (EBMT) (Carl and Way, 2003) and Neural Machine Translation (NMT) (Sutskever et al., 2014). SMT works on a large parallel corpus and does translation based on a statistical model. It relies on a combi-

Proceedings of the 6th Workshop on Asian Translation, pages 171–174
Hong Kong, China, November 4, 2019. ©2019 Association for Computational Linguistics

nation of language model as well as a translation model with decoding algorithms. On the the other hand, EBMT uses available translated examples to perform translation based on analogies. This is executed by detecting examples that coincide with the input. Then the alignment is performed to locate those parts of the translation that can be reused. Neural Machine Translation (NMT) (Sutskever et al., 2014) came into the prominence around 2014. (Choudhary et al., 2018) train an NMT model using pre-trained word-embedding (Al-Rfou' et al., 2013) along with subword units using Byte-Pair-Encoding (BPE) (Sennrich et al., 2015). Several models have been trained on various datasets and have given promising results.

Hybrid-based MT (Simov et al., 2016) is the combination of rule-based methods and any of the data-driven approaches.

Our paper describes experiments on using the transformer architecture (Vaswani et al., 2017) that we tried with English and Tamil language pair and it achieves a better result than the shared task baseline.

3 System Description

This section covers the dataset, preprocessing, and the experimental setup required for our systems.

3.1 Datasets

For the Indic Task, we use the EnTam Corpus collected by researchers at UFAL (Ramasamy et al., 2012a). EnTam Corpus contains development, training, and test data. The training data includes around 160,000 lines of parallel corpora. The data belongs to three domains: Cinema, News, and the Bible. The development and test data contain 1000 and 2000 lines of parallel corpora, respectively. Before performing training, we preprocess the data using SentencePiece library[2].

3.2 Preprocessing

NMT models usually operate on a fixed size vocabulary. Unlike most unsupervised word segmentation algorithms, which assume an infinite vocabulary, SentencePiece trains the segmentation model such that the final vocabulary size is fixed, e.g. 8000 (8K), 16k, or 32k. We tried SentencePiece on vocabulary sizes of 50,000 and 5,000 symbols. Indic sentences have a large vocabulary

due to complex morphology, but size of the training data is limited. Hence, to deal with Indic corpora, we decided to use a vocabulary size of 5,000 symbols for source and target byte-pair encoding, respectively.

3.3 Experimental Setup

We trained two models, namely, Tamil – English and English – Tamil. For training the model, We use fairseq, a sequence modelling toolkit [3]. Our models are based on Transformer network. The number of encoder and decoder layers is set to 5. Encoder and decoder have embedding dimensions of 512. Embeddings are shared between encoder, decoder, and output, i.e., our model requires shared dictionary and embedding space. The embedding dimensions of encoder and decoder in the feed-forward network are set to 2048. The number of encoder and decoder attention heads are set to 2. The models are regularized with dropout, label smoothing and weight decay, with the corresponding hyper-parameters being set to 0.4, 0.2 and 0.0001, respectively. Models are optimized with Adam using $\beta_1 = 0.9$ and $\beta_2 = 0.98$. We perform the experiments on an Nvidia Titan Xp GPU.

4 Results and Analysis

RIBES (Isozaki et al., 2010), BLEU (Papineni et al., 2002), and AM-FM (Banchs et al., 2015) scores of our submitted systems are shown in Table 1, Table 2, and Table 3 resepectively. WAT 2019 organizers evaluate all the submitted system using Adequacy, BLEU, RIBES, and AM-FM scores, as shown in Figure 1 and Figure 2. It is known that Tamil and English follow different word orders, therefore we have to focus on word order for translation. On considering word order, our system performs well on RIBES metric, as shown in Figure 2. If we go through AM-FM score in Figure 2, our system still works well, keeping in view the preservation of semantic meaning and syntactic structure. Overall, if we consider Adequacy score, System beats the baseline model and top performer for English-to-Tamil among all the submitted systems as shown in Figure 1 and Figure 2.

5 Conclusion

In this paper, we report our submitted system. We train our system for Tamil-to-English and English-

---

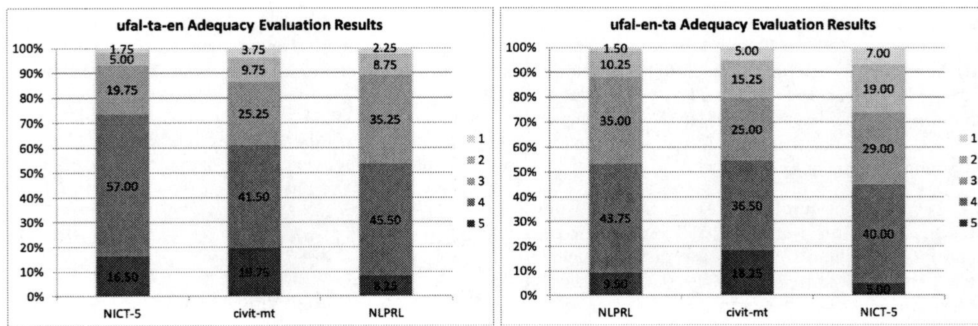

Figure 1: Official bar chart showing Adequacy Evaluation for Tamil–English and English–Tamil Indic languages shared task at WAT 2019.

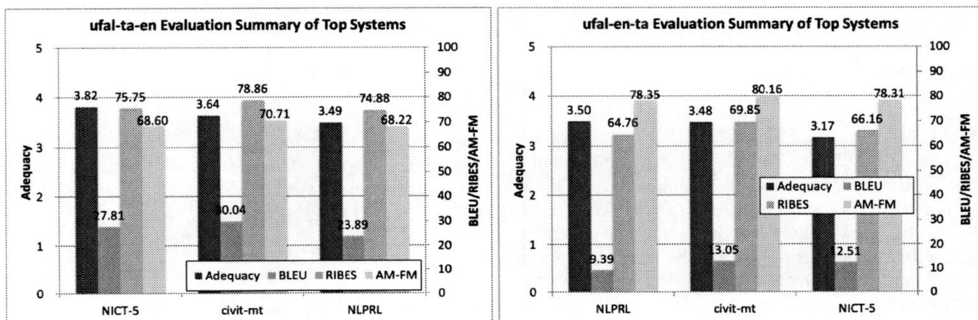

Figure 2: Official bar chart showing Adequacy, BLEU, RIBES and AM-FM scores of top systems submitted in the Tamil–English and English–Tamil Indic languages shared task at WAT 2019.

System	Baseline	Our System
Tamil–English	0.728999	0.748829
English–Tamil	0.634551	0.647579

Table 1: RIBES score of Tamil–English and English–Tamil System submitted by our team at WAT 2019.

System	Baseline	Our System
Tamil–English	24.46	23.89
English–Tamil	11.73	9.39

Table 2: BLEU score of Tamil–English and English–Tamil System submitted by our team at WAT 2019.

System	Baseline	Our System
Tamil–English	0.663930	0.682170
English–Tamil	0.769600	0.783550

Table 3: AM-FM score of Tamil–English and English–Tamil System submitted by our team at WAT 2019.

to-Tamil language pairs. The system is based on Transformer-based Neural Machine Translation. We evaluate our system using Adequacy, BLEU, RIBES, and AM-FM. Based on the official scores of Adequacy released by WAT 2019, We found that our system performs well on preserving word order and semantic-syntactic features on translation and performs better than the baseline.

References

Rami Al-Rfou', Bryan Perozzi, and Steven Skiena. 2013. Polyglot: Distributed word representations for multilingual NLP. In *Proceedings of the Seventeenth Conference on Computational Natural Language Learning*, pages 183–192, Sofia, Bulgaria. Association for Computational Linguistics.

Rafael E Banchs, Luis F DHaro, and Haizhou Li. 2015. Adequacy–fluency metrics: Evaluating mt in the continuous space model framework. *IEEE/ACM Transactions on Audio, Speech, and Language Processing*, 23(3):472–482.

Andrew Donald Booth. 1955. Machine translation of languages, fourteen essays.

Michael Carl and Andy Way. 2003. *Recent advances in example-based machine translation*, volume 21. Springer Science & Business Media.

Himanshu Choudhary, Aditya Kumar Pathak, Rajiv Ratan Saha, and Ponnurangam Kumaraguru. 2018. Neural machine translation for English-Tamil. In *Proceedings of the Third Conference on Machine Translation: Shared Task Papers*, pages 770–775, Belgium, Brussels. Association for Computational Linguistics.

Hideki Isozaki, Tsutomu Hirao, Kevin Duh, Katsuhito Sudoh, and Hajime Tsukada. 2010. Automatic evaluation of translation quality for distant language pairs. In *Proceedings of the 2010 Conference on Empirical Methods in Natural Language Processing*, pages 944–952, Cambridge, MA. Association for Computational Linguistics.

M. Kasthuri and S. Britto Ramesh Kumar. 2013. Rule based machine translation system from english to tamil. In *Proceedings of the 2013 International Conference on Information Technology and Applications*, ITA '13, pages 158–163, Washington, DC, USA. IEEE Computer Society.

Toshiaki Nakazawa, Chenchen Ding, Raj Dabre, Hideya Mino, Isao Goto, Win Pa Pa, Nobushige Doi, Yusuke Oda, Anoop Kunchukuttan, Shantipriya Parida, Ondej Bojar, and Sadao Kurohashi. 2019. Overview of the 6th workshop on Asian translation. In *Proceedings of the 6th Workshop on Asian Translation*, Hong Kong. Association for Computational Linguistics.

Kishore Papineni, Salim Roukos, Todd Ward, and Wei-Jing Zhu. 2002. Bleu: a method for automatic evaluation of machine translation. In *Proceedings of the 40th annual meeting on association for computational linguistics*, pages 311–318. Association for Computational Linguistics.

C Poornima, V Dhanalakshmi, KM Anand, and KP Soman. 2011. Rule based sentence simplification for english to tamil machine translation system. *International Journal of Computer Applications*, 25(8):38–42.

Loganathan Ramasamy, Ondřej Bojar, and Zdeněk Žabokrtský. 2012a. Morphological processing for english-tamil statistical machine translation. In *Proceedings of the Workshop on Machine Translation and Parsing in Indian Languages (MTPIL-2012)*, pages 113–122.

Loganathan Ramasamy, Ondřej Bojar, and Zdeněk Žabokrtskỳ. 2012b. Morphological processing for english-tamil statistical machine translation. In *Proceedings of the Workshop on Machine Translation and Parsing in Indian Languages*, pages 113–122.

Pramod Salunkhe, Aniket D Kadam, Shashank Joshi, Shuhas Patil, Devendrasingh Thakore, and Shrikant Jadhav. 2016. Hybrid machine translation for english to marathi: A research evaluation in machine translation:(hybrid translator). In *2016 International Conference on Electrical, Electronics, and Optimization Techniques (ICEEOT)*, pages 924–931. IEEE.

Rico Sennrich, Barry Haddow, and Alexandra Birch. 2015. Neural machine translation of rare words with subword units. *arXiv preprint arXiv:1508.07909*.

Kiril Simov, Petya Osenova, and Alexander Popov. 2016. Towards semantic-based hybrid machine translation between Bulgarian and English. In *Proceedings of the 2nd Workshop on Semantics-Driven Machine Translation (SedMT 2016)*, pages 22–26, San Diego, California. Association for Computational Linguistics.

Ilya Sutskever, Oriol Vinyals, and Quoc V Le. 2014. Sequence to sequence learning with neural networks. In *Advances in neural information processing systems*, pages 3104–3112.

Ashish Vaswani, Noam Shazeer, Niki Parmar, Jakob Uszkoreit, Llion Jones, Aidan N Gomez, Łukasz Kaiser, and Illia Polosukhin. 2017. Attention is all you need. In *Advances in neural information processing systems*, pages 5998–6008.

Fai Wong, Mingchui Dong, and Dongcheng Hu. 2006. Machine translation using constraint-based synchronous grammar. *Tsinghua Science and Technology*, 11(3):295–306.

Idiap NMT System for WAT 2019
Multi-Modal Translation Task

Shantipriya Parida
Idiap Research Institute,
Rue Marconi 19,
1920 Martigny,
Switzerland
`firstname.lastname@idiap.ch`

Petr Motlíček

Ondřej Bojar[*]
Charles University,
Faculty of Mathematics and Physics,
Institute of Formal and Applied Linguistics,
Malostranské náměstí 25, 118 00,
Prague, Czech Republic
`bojar@ufal.mff.cuni.cz`

Abstract

This paper describes the Idiap submission to WAT 2019 for the English-Hindi Multi-Modal Translation Task. We have used the state-of-the-art Transformer model and utilized the IITB English-Hindi parallel corpus as an additional data source. Among the different tracks of the multi-modal task, we have participated in the "Text-Only" track for the evaluation and challenge test sets. Our submission tops in its track among the competitors in terms of both automatic and manual evaluation. Based on automatic scores, our text-only submission also outperforms systems that consider visual information in the "multi-modal translation" task.

1 Introduction

In recent years, significant research has been done to address problems that require joint modelling of language and vision (Specia et al., 2016). The popular applications involving Natural Language Processing (NLP) and Computer Vision (CV) include image description generation (Bernardi et al., 2016), video captioning (Li et al., 2019), or visual question answering (Antol et al., 2015).

In the past few decades, multi-modality has received critical attention in translation studies, although the benefit of visual modality in machine translation is still in debate (Caglayan et al., 2019). The main motivation in multi-modal research in machine translation is the intuition that information from other modalities could help to find the correct sense of ambiguous words in the source sentence, which could potentially lead to more accurate translations (Lala and Specia, 2018).

---

[*] Corresponding author

		Tokens	
Set	Sentences	English	Hindi
HVG Train	28932	143178	136722
IITB Train	1.4 M	20.6 M	22.1 M
D-Test	998	4922	4695
E-Test	1595	7852	7535
C-Test	1400	8185	8665

Table 1: Statistics of our data: the number of sentences and tokens.

Despite the lack of multi-modal datasets, there is a visible interest in using image features even for machine translation for low-resource language. For instance, Chowdhury et al. (2018) train a multi-modal neural MT system for Hindi→English using synthetic parallel data only.

In this system description paper, we explain how we used additional resources in the text-only track of WAT 2019 Multi-Modal Translation Task. Section 2 describes the datasets used in our experiment. Section 3 presents the model and experimental setups used in our approach. Section 4 provides the official evaluation results of WAT 2019 followed by the conclusion in Section 6.

2 Dataset

The official training set was provided by the task organizers: Hindi Visual Genome (HVG for short, Parida et al., 2019a,b). The training part consists of 29k English and Hindi short captions of rectangular areas in photos of various scenes and it is complemented by three test sets: development (D-Test), evaluation (E-Test) and challenge test set (C-Test). We did not make any use of the images. Our WAT submissions were for E-Test (denoted "EV" in WAT official tables) and C-Test (denoted "CH" in WAT tables).

Proceedings of the 6th Workshop on Asian Translation, pages 175–180
Hong Kong, China, November 4, 2019. ©2019 Association for Computational Linguistics

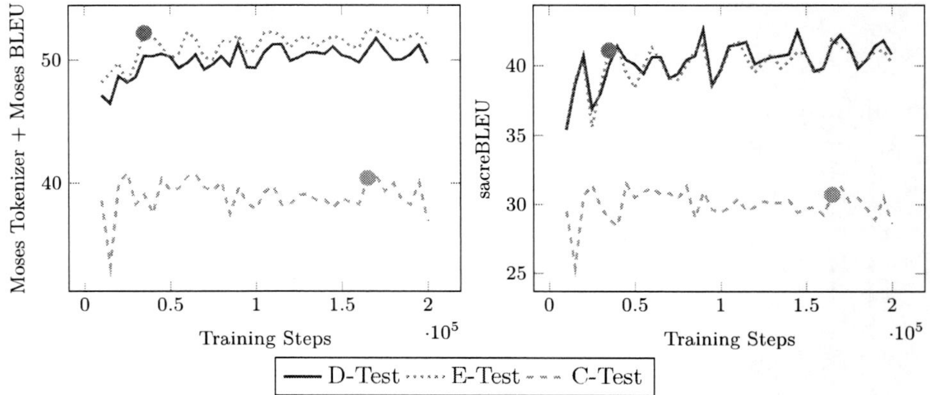

Figure 1: Learning curves in terms of BLEU score. The left plot is based on Moses tokenizer and BLEU score as implemented in Moses scorer. The right plot is sacreBLEU. The big round dots indicate which training iteration was used when producing our final submissions to WAT manual and automatic evaluation for E-Test and C-Test.

Additionally, we used the IITB Corpus (Kunchukuttan et al., 2017) which is supposedly the largest publicly available English-Hindi parallel corpus. This corpus contains 1.49 million parallel segments and it was found very effective for English-Hindi translation (Parida and Bojar, 2018).

The statistics of the datasets are shown in Table 1.

3 Experiments

We focussed only on the text translation task.

We used the Transformer model (Vaswani et al., 2018) as implemented in OpenNMT-py (Klein et al., 2017).[1]

3.1 Tokenization and Vocabulary

Subword units were constructed using the word pieces algorithm (Johnson et al., 2017). Tokenization is handled automatically as part of the pre-processing pipeline of word pieces.

We generated the vocabulary of 32k subword types jointly for both the source and target languages. The vocabulary is shared between the encoder and decoder.

3.2 Training

To train the model, we used a single GPU and followed the standard "Noam" learning rate

decay,[2] see Vaswani et al. (2017) or Popel and Bojar (2018) for more details. Our starting learning rate was 0.2 and we used 8000 warm up steps.

We ran only one training run.

We concatenated HVG and IITB training data and shuffled it at the level of sentences.

We let the model train for up to 200K steps, interrupted a few times due to GPU queueing limitations of our cluster. Following the recommendation of Popel and Bojar (2018), we present the full learning curves on D-Test, E-Test and C-Test in Figure 1.

We observed a huge difference between BLEU (Papineni et al., 2002) scores as implemented in the Moses toolkit (Koehn et al., 2007) and the newer implementation in sacreBLEU (Post, 2018). The discrepancy is very likely caused by different tokenization but the best choice in terms of linguistic plausibility still has to be made. In Figure 1, we show both implementations and see that the Moses implementation gives scores higher by 10 (!) points absolute. More importantly, it is a little less peaked, which we see as evidence for better robustness and thus hopefully the linguistic adequacy.

All of the test sets (D-, E- and C-Test) are independent of the training data and the training itself is not affected by them in any way.

---

[1] http://opennmt.net/OpenNMT-py/quickstart.html

[2] https://nvidia.github.io/OpenSeq2Seq/html/api-docs/optimizers.html

System and WAT Task Label	WAT BLEU	Our sacreBLEU	Our Moses BLEU	WAT Human
Our MMEV**TEXT**en-hi	**41.32**	41.1	52.18	**72.84**
Best competitor in MMEVMMen-hi	40.55	–	–	69.17
Our MMCH**TEXT**en-hi	**30.94**	30.7	40.40	**59.81**
Best competitor in MMCHMMen-hi	20.37	–	–	54.50

Table 2: WAT 2019 official automatic and manual evaluation results for English→Hindi (HINDEN) tasks on the E-Test (EV, upper part) and C-Test (CH, lower part), complemented with our automatic scores. Our scores are from the "TEXT", i.e. text-only, track while the "Best competitor" lines are from the "MM" (multi-modal) track. On each test set, the automatic scores are comparable, because the set of reference translations is identical for the two tracks. The manual scores are comparable to a lower extent because the text-only and multi-modal tracks were manually evaluated in two separate batches.

In other words, they all can be seen as interchangeable, only the choice which particular iteration to run must be done on one of them and evaluated on a different one.

At the submission deadline for E-Test, our training has only started, so we submitted the latest result available, namely E-Test translated with the model at 35K training steps. When submitting the translations of C-Test for the WAT official evaluation, we already knew the full training run and selected the step 165K where E-Test reached its maximum score. In other words, the choice of the model for the C-Test was based on E-Test serving as a validation set.

4 Official Results

We report the official automatic as well as manual evaluation results of our models for the evaluation and challenge test dataset here in Table 2. All the scores are available on the WAT 2019 website[3] and in the WAT overview paper (Nakazawa et al., 2019).

According to both automatic and manual scores, our submissions were the best in the text-only task (MM**TEXT), see the tables in Nakazawa et al. (2019).

Since the text-only and multi-modal tracks differ only in the fact whether the image is available and the underlying set of sentences is identical, we can also compare our result with the scores of systems participating in the multi-modal track (MM**MM). We show only the best system of the multi-modal track. Both on the E-Test and C-Test, our (text-only) candidates scored better in BLEU that the best competitor in the multi-modal track (41.32 vs. 40.55 on E-Test and 30.94 vs. 20.37

[3] http://lotus.kuee.kyoto-u.ac.jp/WAT/ evaluation/

on C-Test). Manual judgments also indicate that our translations are better than those of the best multi-modal system, but here the comparison has to be taken with a grain of salt. The root of the trouble is that the manual evaluation for the text-only and multi-modal tracks ran separately. While the underlying method (Direct Assessment, DA, Graham et al., 2013) in principle scores sentences in absolute terms, it has been observed by Bojar et al. (2017) that DA scores from independent runs are not reliably comparable. We indicate this by the additional horizontal lines in Table 2.

Figure 2 illustrates of our translation output.

5 Discussion

We did not explore the space of possible configurations much, we just ran training and observed the development of the learning curve. Our final results are nevertheless good, indicating that reasonably clean data and baseline settings of the Transformer architecture deliver good translations.

The specifics of the task have to be taken into account. The "sentences" in Hindi Visual Genome are quite short, only 4.7 Hindi and 4.9 English tokens per sentence. This is substantially less than the IITB corpus where the average number of tokens is 15.8 (Hindi) and 14.7 (English). With IITB mixed in the training data, the model gets a significant advantage, not only because of the better coverage of words and phrases but also due to the length. As observed by Kocmi and Bojar (2017) and Popel and Bojar (2018), NMT models struggle to produce outputs longer than the training data was. Our situation is the reverse, so our model "operates within its comfortable zone".

	English Input:	gold religious **cross** on top of golden ball
	Translated Output:	सोने की गेंद के शीर्ष पर स्वर्ण धार्मिक क्रॉसैं .
	Gloss:	Gold religious cross on top of golden ball
	English Input:	a blue wall beside tennis **court**
	Translated Output:	टेनिस कोर्ट के पास एक नीली दीवार हैं ।
	Gloss:	Blue wall near the tennis court
	English Input:	the tennis **court** is made up of sand and dirt
	Translated Output:	टेनिस कोर्ट रेत और गंदगी से बनी है।
	Gloss:	Tennis court is made of sand and dirt
	English Input:	A crack on the **court**
	Translated Output:	अदालत पर एक crack
	Gloss:	A crack on the judicial court

Figure 2: Sample Hindi output as generated for the challenge test set. The ambiguous source word is bolded in the English input, errors are underlined in the MT output and the gloss. The associated source images are given for the reference purpose only to judge our NMT system translation quality, we have not used any image features in our experiment.

Comparing the scores of D- and E-Test on the one hand and C-Test on the other hand, we see that D- and E-Test are much easier for the system. This can be attributed to the identical distributional properties of D-Test and E-Test as the model observed for HVG in the training data. According to Parida et al. (2019a), C-Test also comes from the Visual Genome but the sampling is different, each sentence illustrating one of 19 particularly ambiguous words (*focus* words in the following).

As shown in Figure 2, our system has generally no trouble in figuring out the correct sense of the focus words, thanks to the surrounding words in the context. The BLEU scores on C-Test are nevertheless much lower than on E-Test or D-Test. We attribute this primarily to the slight mismatch between HVG training data and C-Test. As can be confirmed in Table 1, the average sentence length in C-Test is 6.2 (Hindi) and 5.8 (English) tokens, i.e. 0.9–1.5 longer than the training data. Indeed, the model produces shorter outputs than expected and BLEU brevity penalty affects C-Test more (BP=0.907) than E-Test (BP=0.974).

By a quick visual inspection of the outputs, we notice that some rare words were not translated at all, for example, "dugout", "skiing", or "celtic". Most of the non-translated words are not the focus words of the challenge test set but simply random words in the sentences. The focus words that were not translated include: "springs", "cross" and some instance of the word "stand". We did not have the human capacity to review the translations of all the focus words but our general impression is that they were mostly correct. One example, the mistranslation of the (tennis) court is given at the bottom of Figure 2.

Finally, we would like to return to the issue of BLEU implementation pointed out in Section 3.2. The main message to take from this observation is that many common tools are not really polished and well tested for use on less-researched languages and languages not using Latin script. No conclusions can be thus drawn by comparing *numbers* reported across papers. A solid comparison can be only made with the evaluation tool fixed, as is the practice of WAT shared task.

6 Conclusion and Future Plans

In this system description paper, we presented our English→Hindi NMT system. We have highlighted the benefits of using additional text-only training data. Our system performed best among the competitors for the submitted track ("text-only") and also performs better than systems that did consider the image in the "multi-modal" track according to automatic evaluation. We conclude that for the general performance, more parallel data are more important than the visual features available in the image. A targeted manual evaluation would be however necessary to see if the translation of the particularly ambiguous words is better when MT systems consider the image.

As the next step, we plan to utilize image features and carry out a comparison study with the current setup. Also, we plan to experiment with the image captioning variant of the task.

Acknowledgments

At Idiap, the work was supported by an innovation project (under an InnoSuisse grant) oriented to improve the automatic speech recognition and natural language understanding technologies for German. Title: "SM2: Extracting Semantic Meaning from Spoken Material" funding application no. 29814.1 IP-ICT. And also supported by the EU H2020 project "Real-time network, text, and speaker analytics for combating organized crime" (ROXANNE), grant agreement: 833635.

At Charles University, the work was supported by the grants 19-26934X (NEUREM3) of the Czech Science Foundation and "Progress" Q18+Q48 of Charles University, and using language resources distributed by the LINDAT/CLARIN project of the Ministry of Education, Youth and Sports of the Czech Republic (projects LM2015071 and OP VVV VI CZ.02.1.01/0.0/0.0/16013/0001781).

References

Stanislaw Antol, Aishwarya Agrawal, Jiasen Lu, Margaret Mitchell, Dhruv Batra, C Lawrence Zitnick, and Devi Parikh. 2015. Vqa: Visual question answering. In *Proceedings of the IEEE international conference on computer vision*, pages 2425–2433.

Raffaella Bernardi, Ruket Cakici, Desmond Elliott, Aykut Erdem, Erkut Erdem, Nazli Ikizler-Cinbis, Frank Keller, Adrian Muscat, and Barbara Plank. 2016. Automatic description generation from images: A survey of models, datasets, and evaluation measures. *Journal of Artificial Intelligence Research*, 55:409–442.

Ondřej Bojar, Jindřich Helcl, Tom Kocmi, Jindřich Libovický, and Tomáš Musil. 2017. Results of the WMT17 Neural MT Training Task. In *Proceedings of the Second Conference on Machine Translation*, Copenhagen, Denmark. Association for Computational Linguistics.

Ozan Caglayan, Pranava Madhyastha, Lucia Specia, and Loïc Barrault. 2019. Probing the Need for Visual Context in Multimodal Machine Translation. *arXiv preprint arXiv:1903.08678*.

Koel Dutta Chowdhury, Mohammed Hasanuzzaman, and Qun Liu. 2018. Multimodal neural machine translation for low-resource language pairs using synthetic data. In *Proceedings of the Workshop on Deep Learning Approaches for Low-Resource NLP*, pages 33–42.

Yvette Graham, Timothy Baldwin, Alistair Moffat, and Justin Zobel. 2013. Continuous Measurement Scales in Human Evaluation of Machine Translation. In *Proceedings of the 7th Linguistic Annotation Workshop and Interoperability with Discourse*, pages 33–41, Sofia, Bulgaria. Association for Computational Linguistics.

Melvin Johnson, Mike Schuster, Quoc V. Le, Maxim Krikun, Yonghui Wu, Zhifeng Chen, Nikhil Thorat, Fernanda Viégas, Martin Wattenberg, Greg Corrado, Macduff Hughes, and Jeffrey Dean. 2017. Google's multilingual neural machine translation system: Enabling zero-shot translation. *Transactions of the Association for Computational Linguistics*, 5:339–351.

Guillaume Klein, Yoon Kim, Yuntian Deng, Jean Senellart, and Alexander M. Rush. 2017. OpenNMT: Open-source toolkit for neural machine translation. In *Proc. ACL*.

Tom Kocmi and Ondřej Bojar. 2017. Curriculum Learning and Minibatch Bucketing in Neural Machine Translation. In *Proceedings of Recent Advances in NLP (RANLP 2017)*.

Philipp Koehn, Hieu Hoang, Alexandra Birch, Chris Callison-Burch, Marcello Federico, Nicola Bertoldi, Brooke Cowan, Wade Shen, Christine Moran, Richard Zens, Chris Dyer, Ondřej Bojar, Alexandra Constantin, and Evan Herbst. 2007. Moses: Open Source Toolkit for Statistical Machine Translation. In *ACL 2007, Proceedings of the 45th Annual Meeting of the Association for*

Computational Linguistics Companion Volume Proceedings of the Demo and Poster Sessions, pages 177–180, Prague, Czech Republic. Association for Computational Linguistics.

Anoop Kunchukuttan, Pratik Mehta, and Pushpak Bhattacharyya. 2017. The IIT Bombay English-Hindi Parallel Corpus. *arXiv preprint arXiv:1710.02855*.

Chiraag Lala and Lucia Specia. 2018. Multimodal lexical translation. In *Proceedings of the Eleventh International Conference on Language Resources and Evaluation (LREC-2018)*.

Sheng Li, Zhiqiang Tao, Kang Li, and Yun Fu. 2019. Visual to text: Survey of image and video captioning. *IEEE Transactions on Emerging Topics in Computational Intelligence*.

Toshiaki Nakazawa, Chenchen Ding, Raj Dabre, Hideya Mino, Isao Goto, Win Pa Pa, Nobushige Doi, Yusuke Oda, Anoop Kunchukuttan, Shantipriya Parida, Ondřej Bojar, and Sadao Kurohashi. 2019. Overview of the 6th workshop on Asian translation. In *Proceedings of the 6th Workshop on Asian Translation*, Hong Kong. Association for Computational Linguistics.

Kishore Papineni, Salim Roukos, Todd Ward, and Wei-Jing Zhu. 2002. BLEU: a Method for Automatic Evaluation of Machine Translation. In *ACL 2002, Proceedings of the 40th Annual Meeting of the Association for Computational Linguistics*, pages 311–318, Philadelphia, Pennsylvania.

Shantipriya Parida and Ondřej Bojar. 2018. Translating short segments with nmt: A case study in english-to-hindi. In *21st Annual Conference of the European Association for Machine Translation*, page 229.

Shantipriya Parida, Ondřej Bojar, and Satya Ranjan Dash. 2019a. Hindi Visual Genome: A Dataset for Multimodal English-to-Hindi Machine Translation. *Computación y Sistemas*. In print. Presented at CICLing 2019, La Rochelle, France.

Shantipriya Parida, Ondřej Bojar, and Satya Ranjan Dash. 2019b. Hindi Visual Genome: A Dataset for Multimodal English-to-Hindi Machine Translation. *arXiv preprint arXiv:1907.08948*.

Martin Popel and Ondřej Bojar. 2018. Training tips for the transformer model. *The Prague Bulletin of Mathematical Linguistics*, 110(1):43–70.

Matt Post. 2018. A call for clarity in reporting BLEU scores. In *Proceedings of the Third Conference on Machine Translation: Research Papers*, pages 186–191, Belgium, Brussels. Association for Computational Linguistics.

Lucia Specia, Stella Frank, Khalil Sima'an, and Desmond Elliott. 2016. A shared task on multimodal machine translation and crosslingual image description. In *Proceedings of the First Conference on Machine Translation: Volume 2, Shared Task Papers*, pages 543–553.

Ashish Vaswani, Samy Bengio, Eugene Brevdo, Francois Chollet, Aidan Gomez, Stephan Gouws, Llion Jones, Łukasz Kaiser, Nal Kalchbrenner, Niki Parmar, Ryan Sepassi, Noam Shazeer, and Jakob Uszkoreit. 2018. Tensor2tensor for neural machine translation. In *Proceedings of the 13th Conference of the Association for Machine Translation in the Americas (Volume 1: Research Papers)*, pages 193–199. Association for Machine Translation in the Americas.

Ashish Vaswani, Noam Shazeer, Niki Parmar, Jakob Uszkoreit, Llion Jones, Aidan N Gomez, Łukasz Kaiser, and Illia Polosukhin. 2017. Attention is all you need. In *Advances in Neural Information Processing Systems*, pages 5998–6008.

WAT2019: English-Hindi Translation on Hindi Visual Genome Dataset

L. Sanayai Meetei
NIT Silchar
loisanayai@gmail.com

Thoudam Doren Singh
NIT Silchar
thoudam.doren@gmail.com

Sivaji Bandyopadhyay
NIT Silchar
sivaji.cse.ju@gmail.com

Abstract

A multimodal translation is a task of translating a source language to a target language with the help of a parallel text corpus paired with images that represent the contextual details of the text. In this paper, we carried out an extensive comparison to evaluate the benefits of using a multimodal approach on translating text in English to a low resource language, Hindi as a part of WAT2019 (Nakazawa et al., 2019) shared task. We carried out the translation of English to Hindi in three separate tasks with both the evaluation and challenge dataset. First, by using only the parallel text corpora, then through an image caption generation approach and, finally with the multimodal approach. Our experiment shows a significant improvement in the translation with the multimodal approach than the other approach.

1 Introduction

Hindi is the lingua franca in the Hindi belt of India, written in the Devanagari script, an abugida. It consists of 11 vowels and 33 consonants. Both Hindi and English belong to the same language family, Indo-European, but follows different word order. Hindi follows the Subject Object Verb (SOV) order while English follows the Subject Verb Object (SVO) order.

In addition to communication, learning a language covers a lot more things. It spreads culture, traditions, and conventions. A machine translation(MT) is the process of automatically generating a target human language from a source human language. With big companies such as Google offering decent translation to most of the high resource languages, interlingual communication becomes easy. The application of machine translation, can also be applied in our daily healthcare services (Wołk and Marasek, 2015; Yellowlees et al., 2015), government services, disaster management, etc. The methodology of machine translation system where the traditional statistical machine translation (SMT) (Koehn et al., 2007) is replaced by the neural machine translation (NMT) system, a MT system based on artificial neural network proposed by (Kalchbrenner and Blunsom, 2013), results to a better translation. Using deep learning and representation learning, NMT translate a source text to a target text. In the encoder-decoder model of NMT (Cho et al., 2014), the encoder encodes the input text into a fixed length of input vector and the decoder generates a sequence of words as the output text from the input vector. The system is reported to learn the linguistic regularities of both at the phrase level and word level. With the advancement in Computer Vision, the work on generating caption of an image is becoming popular. In an image caption generation model, a deep neural network based model is used to extract the features from the image, the features are then translated to a natural text using a language model.

Recently, research work on incorporating the features extracted from the image along with the parallel text corpora in a multimodal machine translation(MMT) is carried out in many shared translation task. The impact of combining the visual context in the MMT system has shown an increase in the robustness of machine translation (Caglayan et al., 2019). As a part of the shared task WAT2019, the main objective of our task is carry out the translation of English to Hindi. The remaining of this paper is structured as follows: Sec-

Proceedings of the 6th Workshop on Asian Translation, pages 181–188
Hong Kong, China, November 4, 2019. ©2019 Association for Computational Linguistics

tion 2 describe the related works, Section 3 illustrate the system architecture used in our model. Section 4 and Section 5 discuss the experimental setup and the result analysis respectively. Finally, concluding with our findings and the future scope of the work in Section 6.

2   Literature Review

With the introduction of neural machine translation, many approaches of the NMT model is carried out to improve the performance. Initially, because of the use of a fixed-length input vector, the encoder-decoder model of NMT suffers during the translation of long text. By introducing an attention mechanism (Bahdanau et al., 2014), the source text is no longer encoded into a fixed-length vector. Rather, the decoder attends to different parts of the source text at each step of the output generation. In their experiment (Bahdanau et al., 2014) of English to French translation task, the attention mechanism is observed to improve the translation performance of long input sentences.

The NMT translation of English to Hindi is carried out by (Mahata et al., 2019; Singh et al., 2017). Mahata et al. (2019) evaluate the performance of NMT model over the SMT system as a part of MTIL2017[1] shared task. The author reported that NMT performs better in short sentences while SMT outperforms NMT in translating longer sentences.

Sennrich et al. (2015) introduced an effective approach of preprocessing for NMT task where the text is segmented into subword units. The NMT model supports open-vocabulary translation where sequences of subword units encoded from the rare and unknown words are used. The proposed approach is reported to perform better than the back-off to a dictionary look-up (Luong et al., 2014) in resolving the out of vocabulary translation problem.

An automatic image caption generation system is a system that generates a piece of text that describes an input image. Kiros et al. (2014) introduced a multimodal neural network based image caption generation model. The model makes use of word representations and image features learned from deep neural networks. In the work by Vinyals et al. (2015), the authors proposed a neural and probabilistic framework for image caption generation system consisting of a vision Convolution Neural Network (CNN) followed by a language generating Recurrent Neural Network(RNN) trained to increase the likelihood of the generated caption text.

Calixto et al. (2017) reported a research work on various multimodal neural machine translation (MNMT) models by incorporating global features extracted from the image into attention based NMT. The author also evaluated the impact of adding synthetic multi-modal, multilingual data generated using phrase-based statistical machine translation(PBSMT) trained on the dataset from Multi30k (Elliott et al., 2016). The model where the image is used to initialize the encoder hidden state is observed to perform better than the other models in their experiment. The research work of MNMT for Hindi is very recent. Koel et al. (2018) report a MNMT work on English to Hindi translation by building a synthetic dataset generated using a phrase based machine translation system on a Flickr30k (Plummer et al., 2017) dataset.

3   System Architecture

In our model, the dataset from the Hindi Visual Genome[2] are used for three separate tasks: 1) Translation of English-Hindi using only the text dataset, 2) Generate the captions from the image, 3) Multimodal translation of English-Hindi using the image and the parallel text corpus. Figure 1 shows a brief representation of our working model. Following of this section illustrates the details of the dataset, the various methods used in our implementation for the three tasks.

3.1   Dataset

Hindi Visual Genome, HVG: The dataset used in our work is from the HVG (Parida et al., 2019) as a part of WAT2019 Multi-Modal Translation Task[3] . The dataset consists of a total of 31525 randomly selected images from Visual Genome (Krishna et al.,

---

[1]https://nlp.amrita.edu/mtil_cen/

[2]https://ufal.mff.cuni.cz/
hindi-visual-genome/
[3]https://ufal.mff.cuni.cz/
hindi-visual-genome/wat-2019-multimodal-task

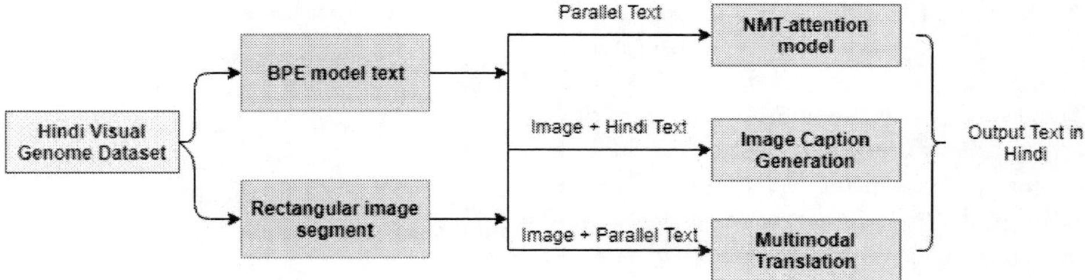

Figure 1: System Architecture

Dataset distribution	Items
Training set	28932
Development set	998
Evaluation set	1595
Challenge set	1400

Table 1: Hindi Visual Genome dataset details.

2017) and a parallel image caption corpus in English-Hindi for selected image segments. The details of the HVG corpus is shown in Table 1. Each item in Table 1 comprises of a source text in English, its translation in Hindi, the image and a rectangular region in the image. The text dataset represent the caption of the rectangular image segment.

3.2 Byte Pair Encoding (BPE)

BPE, a data compression technique proposed by Gage (1994) iteratively replaces the common pairs of bytes in a sequence with a single, unused byte. To handle an open vocabulary problem, we followed the word segmentation algorithm described at (Sennrich et al., 2015) where characters or character sequences are merged instead of common pairs of bytes. For example, the word "booked" is split into "book" and "ed", while "booking" is split into "book" and "ing". The resulting tokens or character sequences allows the model to generalize to new words. The method also reduces the overall vocabulary.

3.3 Neural Machine Translation

The neural machine translation uses RNN encoders and decoders where an encoder maps the input text to an input vector then a decoder decodes the vector into the output text. Following the attention mechanism of (Bahdanau et al., 2014), a bidirectional RNN in the encoder and, an alignment model paired with a LSTM in the decoder model is used.

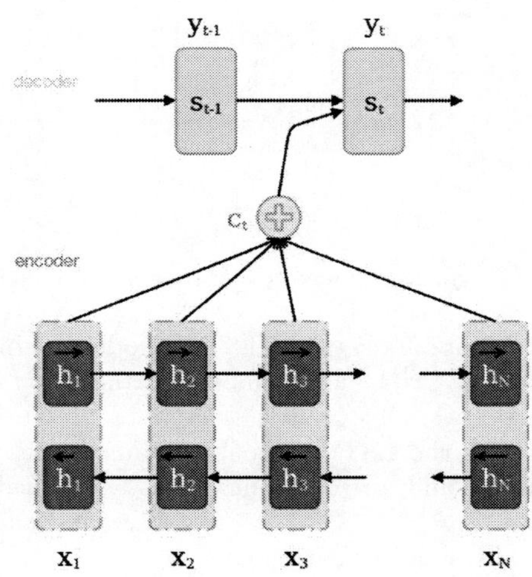

Figure 2: Neural Machine Translation model with attention mechanism

Figure 2 illustrate the attention model trying to generate the t-th target word y_t from a source sentence $(x_1, x_2, .., x_N)$ where the forward RNN encoder generates a forward annotation vectors sequence $(\vec{h_1}, \vec{h_2},...,\vec{h_N})$ and the backward RNN encoder generates a backward annotation vectors sequence $(\overleftarrow{h_1}, \overleftarrow{h_2},...,\overleftarrow{h_N})$. The concatenation of the two vectors gives the annotation vector at the time step i, as $h_i = [\vec{h_i};\overleftarrow{h_i}]$. The attention mechanism learns where to place attention on the input sequence as each word of the output sequence is decoded.

3.4 Image Caption Generation

With the hypothesis of CNN drawn from human visual handling framework, CNN provides a set of hierarchical filtering on image.

CNN in the end is able to extract latent features that represents a semantic meaning to the image. The combination of CNN with RNN makes use of the spatial and temporal features. A neural network based caption generator for an image using CNN model followed by RNN with BEAM Search(BS) for generating the language (Vinyals et al., 2015) is used in our system.

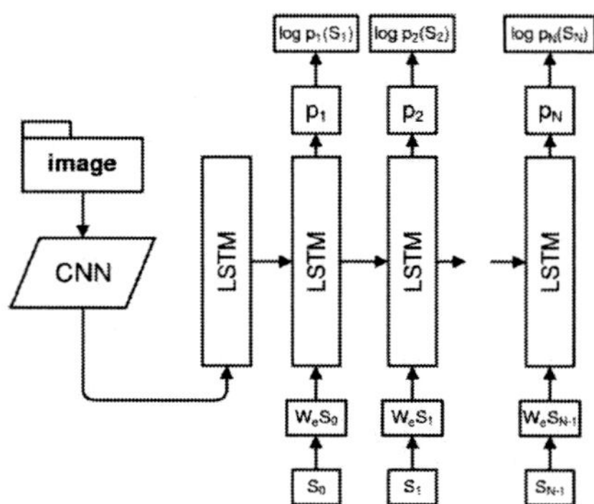

Figure 3: Image caption generation model

Figure 3 shows the LSTM model combined with a CNN image embedder and word embeddings. To predict each word of the sentence, the LSTM model is trained with the image and all preceding words as defined by $p(S_t|I, S_0, \ldots, S_{t-1})$. For an input image I and a caption description, $S = (S_0, \ldots, S_N)$ of I, the unrolling procedure of LSTM (Vinyals et al., 2015) is shown in the following equation:

$$x_{-1} = \text{CNN}(I) \tag{1}$$
$$x_t = W_e S_t, \quad t \in \{0 \ldots N - 1\} \tag{2}$$
$$p_{t+1} = \text{LSTM}(x_t), \quad t \in \{0 \ldots N - 1\} \tag{3}$$

A one-hot vector S_t of dimension equal to the size of the dictionary represent each word. A special start word, S_0 and a special stop word, S_N is used to mark the start and end of the sentence. The image with vision CNN and words by word embedding W_e are mapped to the same space as shown in Equation 1 and Equation 2 respectively. At instance $t = -1$, the image I is fed only once to deliver LSTM the content of the image. To generate the image caption, the BS iteratively examine the k best sentences up to time t as candidates for generating sentences of size $t+1$, keeping only the best k resulting from them.

3.5 Multimodal Machine Translation

In MMT, the image paired with the parallel text corpus is used to train the system. Using the multimodal neural machine translation (MNMT) model (Calixto et al., 2017), global features are extracted using a deep CNN based models.

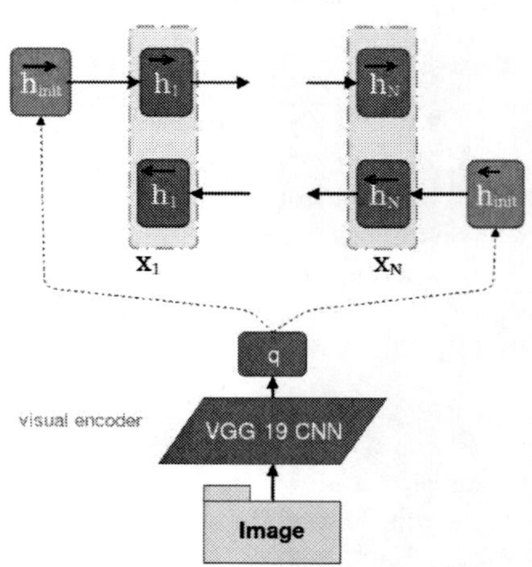

Figure 4: Multimodal translation model using image to initialize the hidden state of encoder

Using the global image feature vector ($q \in \mathbb{R}^{4096}$), a vector d is computed as follows:

$$d = W_I^2 \cdot (W_I^1 \cdot q + b_I^1) + b_I^2 \tag{4}$$

where W and b are image transformation matrices and bias vector respectively.

With bidirectional RNN at the encoder, the features are used to initialize the hidden states of the encoder. As shown in Figure 4, two new single-layer feed-forward networks are used to initialize the states of forward and backward RNN rather than initializing encoder hidden states with $\vec{0}$ (Bahdanau et al., 2014) as:

$$\vec{h}_{init} = \tanh(W_f d + b_f) \tag{5}$$

$$\overleftarrow{h}_{init} = \tanh(W_b d + b_b) \tag{6}$$

with W_f and W_b as the multi-modal projection matrices that project the image features d into the encoder forward and backward hidden states dimensionality, respectively, and b_f and b_b as bias vectors.

4 Experimental Setup

The translation of English to Hindi on the HVG dataset is evaluated in three separate tasks:

- Using only the text dataset.

- Using only the image dataset.

- Using both the image and the text dataset.

To carry out the experiment, the dataset from the HVG is processed as described in the following Subsection 4.1.

4.1 Dataset Preparation

Text: The text dataset is processed into a BPE format as describe in Subsection 3.2. The encoding-decoding of the text dataset to and from subword units is carried out using the open-source tool[4].

Example:

Raw text: outdoor blue mailbox receptacle

After processing: outdoor blue ma@@ il@@ box re@@ ce@@ p@@ ta@@ cle

Image: The image and description (English-Hindi pair) in HVG dataset are structured in such a format that, the caption describes only a selected rectangular portion of the image. With the image coordinates (X, Y. Width, Height) provided in the HVG dataset, the rectangular image segment from the original image is cropped as a part of processing. A sample is shown below in Figure 5.

(a)   (b)

Figure 5: (a) A sample image
(b) Image segment from (a) with *English caption:* woman with sunglasses holding a cellphone, *Hindi caption:* सेलफोन पकड़ने वाली स्त्री

---

[4] `https://github.com/rsennrich/subword-nmt`

With the model described in Section 3, the experimental setup for each of the three tasks are explained in the Subsections below.

4.2 NMT Text only Translation

Using the processed text data from Subsection 4.1, the translation of English-Hindi is carried out on a neural machine translation open-source tool based on OpenNMT (Klein et al., 2017). We used the attention mechanism of (Bahdanau et al., 2014). Along with other parameters such as learning rate at 0.002, Adam optimizer (Kingma and Ba, 2014), a dropout rate of 0.1, we train the system for 25 epoch.

4.3 Image Caption Generation

Our second task is to generate the caption of an image in Hindi. For this task, we trained our system (Subsection 3.4) with the processed images from Subsection 4.1 paired with its Hindi captions. For extracting the features from the image a 16-layer VGG (VGG16) model (Simonyan and Zisserman, 2014), pre-trained on the ImageNet dataset, is used. A 4096-dimensional vector generated by the VGG16 for each image is then fed to RNN Model with BEAM search. With BEAM search parameter set to three (number of words to consider at a time), the system is trained for 20 epoch.

4.4 Multimodal Translation

In our final task of multimodal translation of English to Hindi, the processed text and image dataset from Subsection 4.1 are fed into our model (Subsection 3.5). A pre-trained model, VGG19-CNN, is employed to extract the global features from the image. The system is trained for 30 epoch with a learning rate set to 0.002, dropout rate of 0.3 and using Adam optimizer.

5 Results and analysis

As a part of the Hindi Visual Genome (WAT2019 Multi-Modal Translation Task) shared task, we submitted in all the three task: 1) Text-only translation, 2) Hindi-only image captioning and 3) Multi-modal translation (uses both the image and the text), for the two types dataset (Parida et al., 2019): the Evaluation Test Set and the Challenge Test

Set . The experiment for the three tasks is carried out separately on both the test dataset.

Evaluation metrics: The evaluation of the translation system is carried out using three different techniques: AFMF (Banchs et al., 2015), BLEU (Papineni et al., 2002) score and RIBES (Isozaki et al., 2010).

Task	BLEU	RIBES	AMFM
TOT	20.13	0.57	0.61
HIC	2.59	0.15	0.41
MMT	28.45	0.63	0.68

Table 2: Results obtained in Evaluation Test Set.

Task	BLEU	RIBES	AMFM
TOT	5.56	0.37	0.46
HIC	0.00	0.08	0.38
MMT	12.58	0.48	0.55

Table 3: Results obtained in Challenge Test Set.

Table 2 and Table 3 shows the scores obtained by our system on the Evaluation Test Set and Challenge Test Set respectively. In Table 2 and Table 3, TOT, HIC, and MMT represents the text-only translation sub task system, automatic image caption generation system of Hindi-only image captioning sub task and the multi-modal translation (using both the image and the text) sub task system respectively. Three sample inputs with the different forms of an ambiguous word "stand" from the challenge test set and their outputs are shown in Table 4, Table 5 and Table 6.

From the above observations, we see that the results of multimodal translation outperforms the other methods. However, the evaluation of image caption generation is reported to achieve poor score. Reason being the evaluation metric used rely on the surface-form similarity or simply match n-gram overlap between the output text and the reference text, which fails to evaluate the semantic information describe by the generated text. Also, an image can be interpreted with different captions to express the main theme contained in the image. Hence, the poor performance report even though the generated caption text for the input image is observe to show reasonable quality of adequacy and fluency on random human evaluation. We can conclude that, for the case of image caption generation, there is a need for a different type of evaluation metrics.

6 Conclusion and Future Work

In this paper, we reported the evaluation of English-Hindi translation with different approaches as a part of WAT2019 shared task. It is observed that the multimodal approach of incorporating the visual features paired with text data gives significant improvement in translation than the other approaches. We also conclude that the same evaluation metrics used for the machine translation is not applicable to the automatic caption generation system, as the latter approach provides a good adequacy and fluency to the output text. In the future, we would like to investigate the impact of adding features in the BPE model. Furthermore, evaluating the system on a larger size of the dataset might give us more insight into the feasibility of the system in the real world applications.

Acknowledgments

This work is supported by Scheme for Promotion of Academic and Research Collaboration (SPARC) Project Code: P995 of No: SPARC/2018-2019/119/SL(IN) under MHRD, Govt of India.

References

Dzmitry Bahdanau, Kyunghyun Cho, and Yoshua Bengio. 2014. Neural machine translation by jointly learning to align and translate. *arXiv preprint arXiv:1409.0473*.

Rafael E Banchs, Luis F D'Haro, and Haizhou Li. 2015. Adequacy–fluency metrics: Evaluating mt in the continuous space model framework. *IEEE/ACM Transactions on Audio, Speech, and Language Processing*, 23(3):472–482.

Ozan Caglayan, Pranava Madhyastha, Lucia Specia, and Loïc Barrault. 2019. Probing the need for visual context in multimodal machine translation. *arXiv preprint arXiv:1903.08678*.

Iacer Calixto, Qun Liu, and Nick Campbell. 2017. Incorporating global visual features into attention-based neural machine translation. *arXiv preprint arXiv:1701.06521*.

Input Image and Text	Reference and Output by different Model Types
 Woman standing on tennis court	**Reference:** टेनिस कोर्ट पर खड़ी महिला Transliteration: tenis kort par khadee mahila **TOT:** टेनिस कोर्ट पर मनुष्य Transliteration: tenis kort par manushy *Translation: A man on a tennis court* **HIC:** एक व्यक्ति टेनिस खेल रहा है Transliteration: ek vyakti tenis khel raha hai *Translation: A person playing tennis* **MMT:** टेनिस कोर्ट पर खड़ी महिला Transliteration: tenis kort par khadee mahila *Translation: A woman standing on a tennis court*

Table 4: Sample 1 input and output

Input Image and Text	Reference and Output by different Model Types
 man stand on skateboard	**Reference:** आदमी स्केटबोर्ड पर खड़ा है Transliteration: aadmee sketabord par khada hai **TOT:** स्केटबोर्ड पर मनुष्य Transliteration: sketabord par manushy *Translation: Man on skateboard* **HIC:** व्यक्ति एक स्केटबोर्ड पर Transliteration: vyakti ek sketabord par *Translation: A person on a skateboard* **MMT:** व्यक्ति स्केटबोर्ड पर खड़ा है Transliteration: vyakti sketabord par khada hai *Translation: A person standing on a skateboard*

Table 5: Sample 2 input and output

Input Image and Text	Reference and Output by different Model Types
 A big tv on a stand	**Reference:** एक स्टैंड पर एक बड़ा टीवी Transliteration: ek staind par ek bada teevee **TOT:** एक सेलफोन पर एक बड़ा सा वैन Transliteration: ek selaphon par ek bada sa vain *Translation: A big van on a cellphone* **HIC:** इमारत के किनारे पर एक दीवार Transliteration: imaarat ke kinaare par ek deevaar *Translation: A wall on the side of the building* **MMT:** एक स्टैंड पर एक बड़ा टीवी Transliteration: ek staind par ek bada teevee *Translation: A big tv on a stand*

Table 6: Sample 3 input and output

Kyunghyun Cho, Bart Van Merriënboer, Caglar Gulcehre, Dzmitry Bahdanau, Fethi Bougares, Holger Schwenk, and Yoshua Bengio. 2014. Learning phrase representations using rnn encoder-decoder for statistical machine translation. *arXiv preprint arXiv:1406.1078*.

Koel Dutta Chowdhury, Mohammed Hasanuzzaman, and Qun Liu. 2018. Multimodal neural machine translation for low-resource language pairs using synthetic data. In *Proceedings of the Workshop on Deep Learning Approaches for Low-Resource NLP*, pages 33–42.

Desmond Elliott, Stella Frank, Khalil Sima'an, and Lucia Specia. 2016. Multi30k: Multilingual english-german image descriptions. In *Proceedings of the 5th Workshop on Vision and Language*, pages 70–74. Association for Computational Linguistics.

Philip Gage. 1994. A new algorithm for data compression. *The C Users Journal*, 12(2):23–38.

Hideki Isozaki, Tsutomu Hirao, Kevin Duh, Katsuhito Sudoh, and Hajime Tsukada. 2010. Automatic evaluation of translation quality for distant language pairs. In *Proceedings of the 2010 Conference on Empirical Methods in Natural Language Processing*, pages 944–952. Association for Computational Linguistics.

N. Kalchbrenner and P. Blunsom. 2013. Recurrent continuous translation models. In *Proceedings of the 2013 Conference on Empirical Methods in Natural Language Processing*, pages 1700–1709.

Diederik P Kingma and Jimmy Ba. 2014. Adam: A method for stochastic optimization. *arXiv preprint arXiv:1412.6980*.

Ryan Kiros, Ruslan Salakhutdinov, and Rich Zemel. 2014. Multimodal neural language models. In *International Conference on Machine Learning*, pages 595–603.

Guillaume Klein, Yoon Kim, Yuntian Deng, Jean Senellart, and Alexander M Rush. 2017. Opennmt: Open-source toolkit for neural machine translation. *arXiv preprint arXiv:1701.02810*.

P. Koehn, H. Hoang, A. Birch, C. Callison-Burch, N. Federico, M.and Bertoldi, B. Cowan, W. Shen, R. Moran, C.and Zens, and C. Dyer. 2007. Moses: Open source toolkit for statistical machine translation. In *Proceedings of the 45th annual meeting of the association for computational linguistics companion volume proceedings of the demo and poster sessions*, pages 177–180.

Ranjay Krishna, Yuke Zhu, Oliver Groth, Justin Johnson, Kenji Hata, Joshua Kravitz, Stephanie Chen, Yannis Kalantidis, Li-Jia Li, David A Shamma, et al. 2017. Visual genome: Connecting language and vision using crowdsourced dense image annotations. *International Journal of Computer Vision*, 123(1):32–73.

Minh-Thang Luong, Ilya Sutskever, Quoc V Le, Oriol Vinyals, and Wojciech Zaremba. 2014. Addressing the rare word problem in neural machine translation. *arXiv preprint arXiv:1410.8206*.

Sainik Kumar Mahata, Dipankar Das, and Sivaji Bandyopadhyay. 2019. Mtil2017: Machine translation using recurrent neural network on statistical machine translation. *Journal of Intelligent Systems*, 28(3):447–453.

Toshiaki Nakazawa, Chenchen Ding, Raj Dabre, Hideya Mino, Isao Goto, Win Pa Pa, Nobushige Doi, Yusuke Oda, Anoop Kunchukuttan, Shantipriya Parida, Ondřej Bojar, and Sadao Kurohashi. 2019. Overview of the 6th workshop on Asian translation. In *Proceedings of the 6th Workshop on Asian Translation*, Hong Kong. Association for Computational Linguistics.

Kishore Papineni, Salim Roukos, Todd Ward, and Wei-Jing Zhu. 2002. Bleu: a method for automatic evaluation of machine translation. In *Proceedings of the 40th annual meeting on association for computational linguistics*, pages 311–318. Association for Computational Linguistics.

Shantipriya Parida, Ondřej Bojar, and Satya Ranjan Dash. 2019. Hindi visual genome: A dataset for multimodal english-to-hindi machine translation. *arXiv preprint arXiv:1907.08948*.

Bryan A. Plummer, Liwei Wang, Christopher M. Cervantes, Juan C. Caicedo, Julia Hockenmaier, and Svetlana Lazebnik. 2017. Flickr30k entities: Collecting region-to-phrase correspondences for richer image-to-sentence models. *IJCV*, 123(1):74–93.

Rico Sennrich, Barry Haddow, and Alexandra Birch. 2015. Neural machine translation of rare words with subword units. *arXiv preprint arXiv:1508.07909*.

Karen Simonyan and Andrew Zisserman. 2014. Very deep convolutional networks for large-scale image recognition. *arXiv preprint arXiv:1409.1556*.

Sandhya Singh, Ritesh Panjwani, Anoop Kunchukuttan, and Pushpak Bhattacharyya. 2017. Comparing recurrent and convolutional architectures for english-hindi neural machine translation. In *Proceedings of the 4th Workshop on Asian Translation (WAT2017)*, pages 167–170.

Oriol Vinyals, Alexander Toshev, Samy Bengio, and Dumitru Erhan. 2015. Show and tell: A neural image caption generator. In *Proceedings of the IEEE conference on computer vision and pattern recognition*, pages 3156–3164.

Krzysztof Wołk and Krzysztof Marasek. 2015. Neural-based machine translation for medical text domain. based on european medicines agency leaflet texts. *Procedia Computer Science*, 64:2–9.

Peter Yellowlees, Steven Richard Chan, and Michelle Burke Parish. 2015. The hybrid doctor–patient relationship in the age of technology–telepsychiatry consultations and the use of virtual space. *International Review of Psychiatry*, 27(6):476–489.

SYSTRAN @ WAT 2019: Russian↔Japanese News Commentary task

Jitao Xu[†], MinhQuang Pham[††], TuAnh Nguyen[†], Josep Crego[†], Jean Senellart[†]
[†]SYSTRAN / 5 rue Feydeau, 75002 Paris, France
`firstname.lastname@systrangroup.com`
[‡]LIMSI, CNRS, Université Paris-Saclay 91405 Orsay, France
`firstname.lastname@limsi.fr`

Abstract

This paper describes SYSTRAN's submissions to WAT 2019 Russian↔Japanese News Commentary task. A challenging translation task due to the extremely low resources available and the distance of the language pair. We have used the neural Transformer architecture learned over the provided resources and we carried out synthetic data generation experiments which aim at alleviating the data scarcity problem. Results indicate the suitability of the data augmentation experiments, enabling our systems to rank first according to automatic evaluations.

1 Introduction

This paper describes the SYSTRAN neural MT systems employed for the 6th Workshop on Asian Translation (WAT) (Nakazawa et al., 2019), an open evaluation campaign focusing on Asian languages. This is our first participation in the workshop and the first year the workshop includes the Russian↔Japanese News Commentary task, with the objective of studying machine translation under extremely low resource conditions and for distant language pairs.

The lack of sufficient data together with the distance and richness of the language pair constitute very challenging conditions. A rather common situation in the translation industry, that motivated us to explore techniques that can help in the construction from scratch of efficient NMT engines. We present systems built using only the data provided by the organisers for both translation directions (Russian↔Japanese) and using the Transformer network introduced by (Vaswani et al., 2017). We enhance the baseline systems with several experiments that aim at alleviating the data scarcity problem. More precisely we run experiments following the back-translation method proposed by (Sennrich et al., 2016b) in which target

monolingual corpora are translated back into the source language. Thus, creating synthetic parallel data. In addition, we present an updated version of back-translation where synthetic data is created with higher diversity by means of side constraints.

The remaining of this paper is structured as follows: We first describe statistics of the datasets provided in Section 2. Section 3 outlines our neural MT system. In Section 4 we detail the data augmentation methods employed to alleviate data scarcity. Experiments are reported in Section 5. We analyse results in Section 6 and conclude in Section 7.

2 Resources

Datasets used for the evaluation can be found listed in the shared task web site[1]. WAT organisers kindly provide a manually aligned, cleaned and filtered Japanese↔Russian, Japanese↔English and English↔Russian train, development and test corpora (JaRuNC)[2] as well as a news domain Russian↔English corpus (NC)[3]. In addition, use of the next out-of-domain data is encouraged:

- Japanese↔English Wikipedia articles related to Kyoto (KFTT)[4].

- Japanese↔English Subtitles (JESC)[5],

- Japanese↔English asian scientific paper abstracts (ASPEC)[6],

---

[1]`lotus.kuee.kyoto-u.ac.jp/WAT/WAT2019`
[2]`github.com/aizhanti/JaRuNC`
[3]`lotus.kuee.kyoto-u.ac.jp/WAT/News-Commentary/news-commentary-v14.en-ru.filtered.tar.gz`
[4]`www.phontron.com/kftt/`
[5]`datarepository.wolframcloud.com/resources/Japanese-English-Subtitle-Corpus`
[6]`lotus.kuee.kyoto-u.ac.jp/ASPEC/`

Proceedings of the 6th Workshop on Asian Translation, pages 189–194
Hong Kong, China, November 4, 2019. ©2019 Association for Computational Linguistics

- Russian↔English transcriptions of TED talks (TED)[7],

- Russian↔English pair of the United Nations Parallel Corpus (UN)[8],

- The Russian↔English Yandex corpus v1.3 (Yandex)[9]

Statistics of the training bitexts are shown by Table 1, summarising for each language the total number of sentences, running words, vocabulary size and average sentence length. Note that despite listed as an official resource we do not use the ASPEC corpus as we never received the download link of the ASPEC corpus from the corpus owners. Statistics are computed after performing a light tokenisation by means of the OpenNMT tokeniser[10] (aggressive mode) which basically splits-off punctation. No additional parallel resources are used in our experiments.

Bitext		sent.	words	vocab.	L_{mean}
JaRuNC	ja	47.1K	1.3M	48.3K	26.9
	en		1.0M	51.2K	22.1
KFTT	ja	440K	10.9M	118K	24.9
	en		12.0M	173K	27.2
JESC	ja	2.8M	23.2M	155K	8.3
	en		25.6M	133K	9.2
ASPEC	ja	-	-	-	-
	en		-	-	-
JaRuNC	ru	82.1K	1.7M	140K	20.1
	en		1.9M	67.0K	23.0
NC	ru	279K	7.1M	204K	25.5
	en		7.6M	67.5K	27.2
TED	ru	185K	3.3M	165K	17.7
	en		3.9M	58.5K	21.0
Yandex	ru	1.0M	22.9M	704K	23.0
	en		25.2M	322K	25.2
UN	ru	11.7M	309M	870K	26.5
	en		340M	408K	29.2
JaRuNC	ru	12.4K	235K	42.0K	19.0
	ja		341K	21.9K	27.6

Table 1: *Statistics of training bitexts. Note that K stands for thousands and M for millions.*

Table 2 illustrates statistics of the development and test sets extracted from the corresponding JaRuNC corpora. We now include the number of out-of-vocabulary words. As it can be

seen, Japanese↔Russian parallel resources are extremely scarce with only 12,4K sentence pairs.

Side		sent.	words	vocab.	L_{mean}	OOV
Development (JaRuNC)						
ja		589	21.5K	3.5K	36.4	288
en			16.4K	3.7K	27.9	273
ru		313	7.6K	3.2K	24.3	278
en			8.3K	2.3K	26.4	83
ru		486	11.2K	4.4K	23.1	1297
ja			16.0K	2.9K	33.0	470
Test (JaRuNC)						
ja		600	22.5K	3.5K	37.5	302
en			16.9K	3.7K	28.2	316
ru		600	15.6K	5.6K	25.9	661
en			16.9K	3.7K	28.2	223
ru		600	15.6K	5.6K	25.9	1873
ja			22.5K	3.5K	37.5	661

Table 2: *Statistics of development and test sets.*

3 Neural MT System

We use the state-of-the-art Transformer model (Vaswani et al., 2017) implemented in `OpenNMT-tf`[11] toolkit (Klein et al., 2017). A neural network following the encoder-decoder architecture, where:

- Each word x_j in the input sentence x_1^J is encoded in a continuous space. Fixed positional embeddings are also added to the word vectors to represent a word embedding $\bar{x}_j$.

- The encoder is a self-attentive module that maps an input sequence of words $\bar{x}_1^J$ into a sequence of continuous representations h_1^J.

$$h_1^J = H_{enc}(\bar{x}_1^J; \theta_{enc})$$

where θ_{enc} are encoder parameters.

- The decoder is also a self-attentive module that at each time step outputs a single hidden state s_i, conditioned on the sequence of previously seen embedded target words $\bar{y}_{<i}$ and the encoder outputs h_1^J.

$$s_i = H_{dec}(h_1^J, \bar{y}_{<i}; \theta_{dec})$$

where θ_{dec} are decoder parameters.

---

[7] `wit3.fbk.eu`
[8] `cms.unov.org/UNCorpus/`
[9] `translate.yandex.ru/corpus?lang=en`
[10] `pypi.org/project/pyonmttok/`

[11] `github.com/OpenNMT/OpenNMT-tf`

- The hidden state s_i is projected to the output vocabulary and normalised with a $softmax$ operation resulting in a probability distribution over target words.

$$p(y_i|y_{<i}, x_1^J) = softmax(W \cdot s_i + b)$$

4   Data Augmentation

4.1   Back-translation

We follow the *back-translation* method proposed by (Sennrich et al., 2016b) in which target monolingual corpora are translated back into the source language. This synthetic parallel data is then used in combination with the actual parallel data to further train the model. This approach yields state-of-the-art results even when large parallel data are available, currently common practice in academia and industry scenarios (Poncelas et al., 2018).

4.2   Side Constraints

We propose a method to generate synthetic parallel data that uses a set of side constraints. Side constraints are used to guide the NMT model to produce distinct word translation alternatives based on their frequency in the training corpora. Furthermore, we employ a set of grammatical constraints (tense, voice and person) which introduce syntactic/semantic variations in translations. Thus, our method aims at enhancing translation diversity, a major drawback highlighted in back-translated data (Edunov et al., 2018). Similar to our work, side constraints have already been used on neural models in a number of different scenarios. To the best of our knowledge, side constraints were first employed to control politeness in a NMT by (Sennrich et al., 2016a). Domain-adapted translations using a unique network enhanced with side constraints is presented in (Kobus et al., 2017).

We consider 4 constraints regarding POS classes: *noun*, *verb*, *adjective* and *adverb*. For each constraint we build 3 clusters containing the set of words with H (high), M (medium) and L (low) frequency as computed over the training data. This is, the set of nouns occurring with highest frequency are arranged in the NH class, verbs with lower frequencies in VL, *etc.* We set the frequency thresholds to satisfy that the three clusters of a POS class have approximately the same number of occurrences in the training corpus.

Training source sentences are then tagged with the values seen on the corresponding target sentences of each POS class. Note that when a target sentence contains different values of a POS class, i.e.: two *nouns* one with high (H) frequency and another with low (L) frequency, or when no word is found belonging to one class we then use the value N (None). For instance, given the Russian sentence: Президент приезжает завтра (*the president arrives tomorrow*) we use as side constraints: VH, NH, AN, RH, since приезжает is a verb, президент is a noun and завтра is an adverb of high frequency, while adjectives do not appear in the sentence. Thus, the Japanese-Russian parallel sentence with corresponding side constraints illustrated in Table 3 is used in training to feed the model.

VH NH AN RH 明日大統領が到着します
⤳ Президент приезжает завтра

Table 3: French-German sentence pair with frequency constraints.

Note that when creating synthetic corpora, side constraint values are randomly generated to allow larger diversity of the generated language.

5   Experiments

5.1   Data Preprocessing

Before learning the translation network, data corresponding to each language is preprocessed following a similar workflow: word tokenisation + subword tokenisation. Tokenisation for English and Russian is performed using the OpenNMT tokeniser (aggressive mode). Japanese tokenisation is carried out by the MeCab[12] tokeniser. For subword tokenisation we trained a 30K byte-pair encoding (Sennrich et al., 2016c) (BPE) of each language, using separately English, Russian and Japanese training data.

5.2   Baseline Transformer

In order to alleviate the data scarcity problem, we introduce English as a third language in our baseline system to built a multi-lingual translation system following the work in (Firat et al., 2016). We concatenate both directions of all available Japanese-Russian, Japanese-English and Russian-English corpora to train our `base` model. We in-

---

[12]`github.com/taku910/mecab`

clude an additional token to the beginning of each source sentence to indicate the related target language (i.e. *@ru@* for Russian). In inference, the corresponding token (*@ru@* or *@ja@*) is used to request Russian or Japanese translation. Similarly, we consider an additional token to indicate whether the training sentence pair is in-domain or out-of-domain (i.e. *@in@* for in-domain data). All JaRuNC corpora and NC English-Russian corpus are considered in-domain data, the rest are deemed out-of-domain. In inference, translations are performed appending the *@in@* token.

Since BPE vocabularies were separately built for each language with 30K tokens, we then use a vocabulary of size 90K tokens for both source and target sides. Thus, covering all English, Russian and Japanese training data.

We train our model using the standard Transformer base model. We use Lazy Adam optimiser with the same learning rate decay schedule as (Vaswani et al., 2017). Learning rate is updated every 8 steps. We build our baseline model using a batch size of 3,072 over 400k steps on one GPU. The final models result of averaging the last 10 saved checkpoints in training.

Fine-tuning

We build a second network after fine-tuning the previous baseline network. For fine-tuning we use all in-domain data. More precisely Japanese-Russian (JaRuNC), Japanese-English (JaRuNC) and Russian-English (JaRuNC and NC) datasets in both translation directions (+FT (JaRuNC, NC)). Fine-tuning is performed during 80K additional steps for Japanese→Russian and 50K steps for Russian→Japanese.

Back-translation

We use the previously fine-tuned model to back-translate in-domain Russian and Japanese sentences of our datasets (aligned to English). This is, we back-translate the Japanese side of the Japanese-English (JaRuNC) corpus to extend the data available for the Russian→Japanese translation direction. Equivalently, we backtranslate the Russian side of the Russian-English (JaRuNC and NC) corpora to increase the amount of data available for the Japanese→Russian direction. Thus, building new synthetic Japanese*-Russian and Russian*-Japanese corpora. [13] Since our model is multi-lingual, we don't need additional networks

---

[13] We use * to denote synthetic data

to back-translate both Russian and Japanese sentences.

Given that we synthesised a larger number of Japanese*-Russian sentences than Russian*-Japanese we further synthesise additional data following another approach. We use English in-domain sentences (JaRuNC and NC) to produce Russian and Japanese translations. Thus, new Japanese*-Russian* synthetic bitexts become available. Translations are performed using two distinct uni-directional English→Russian and English→Japanese models. Following the same parameterisation used for the base model we train a new model considering all previous parallel data (+FT (JaRuNC, NC, BT, SYN)). Notice that following the same multi-stage strategy used in (Imankulova et al., 2019) our new model is built from +FT (JaRuNC, NC).

We also used our fine-tuned multi-lingual model to translate English sentences. However, the translation quality of the multi-lingual model is much poorer than uni-directional models. Thus, hurting the performance of the final model.

Side Constraints

As introduced in Section 4.2 we perform experiments synthesising using side constraints. Each Russian and Japanese source-side training sentence is extended with the side constraints previously described (corresponding to random frequency values of verbs, adjectives, nouns and adverbs) and are used as input sentences in order to generate the corresponding Japanese and Russian hypotheses. The synthesised parallel data is used together with the previous datasets to learn a new model (+FT (JaRuNC, NC, BT, SYN, SC)). Notice again that our new model is built from +FT (JaRuNC, NC).

6 Evaluation

All our results are computed following the BLEU (Papineni et al., 2002) score. Validation sets are used to select our best performing networks, while results shown in Table 5 are computed for the official test sets.

As it can be seen, all our experiments to alleviate data scarcity boosted translation performance. A light decrease in accuracy is observed when using SC data for Russian→Japanese translation. The improvement is remarkable for the Japanese→Russian task for which the BLEU score is doubled from 7 to more than 14 points.

System	Ru-Ja	Ja-Ru
base	9.76	6.95
+FT(JaRuNC,NC)	12.10	9.17
+FT(JaRuNC,NC,BT,SYN)	15.89	13.78
+FT(JaRuNC,NC,BT,SYN,SC)	15.39	14.36

Table 4: *BLEU score on JaRuNC testset.*

A final experiment is carried out considering our best performing setting so far. We repeat training work with a larger batch size of 6,144 during 250K iterations and using 3 GPUs.

batch size	Ru-Ja	Ja-Ru
3,072	15.89	**14.36**
6,144	**16.41**	-

Table 5: *BLEU score using a batch size = 6,144 with 3 GPUs.*

Given the tight schedule to submit our translations, we only run the experiment for the Russian→Japanese task. Bold figures indicate the BLEU scores of the best performing systems submitted for the evaluation.

7 Conclusions

We described SYSTRAN's submissions to WAT 2019 Russian↔Japanese News Commentary task. A challenging translation task due to the extremely low resources available and the distance of the language pair. Several data generation experiments were performed in order to alleviate data scarcity, one of the major difficulties of the translation task. Results showed the suitability of the experiments that boosted translation performance in both translation directions allowing our systems to rank first according to automatic evaluations.

Acknowledgements

We would like to thank the reviewers for their insightful comments.

References

Sergey Edunov, Myle Ott, Michael Auli, and David Grangier. 2018. Understanding back-translation at scale. In *Proceedings of the 2018 Conference on Empirical Methods in Natural Language Processing*, pages 489–500, Brussels, Belgium. Association for Computational Linguistics.

Orhan Firat, Kyunghyun Cho, and Yoshua Bengio. 2016. Multi-way, multilingual neural machine translation with a shared attention mechanism. In *Proceedings of the 2016 Conference of the North American Chapter of the Association for Computational Linguistics: Human Language Technologies*, pages 866–875, San Diego, California. Association for Computational Linguistics.

Aizhan Imankulova, Raj Dabre, Atsushi Fujita, and Kenji Imamura. 2019. Exploiting out-of-domain parallel data through multilingual transfer learning for low-resource neural machine translation. In *Proceedings of Machine Translation Summit XVII Volume 1: Research Track*, pages 128–139, Dublin, Ireland. European Association for Machine Translation.

Guillaume Klein, Yoon Kim, Yuntian Deng, Jean Senellart, and Alexander Rush. 2017. OpenNMT: Open-source toolkit for neural machine translation. In *Proceedings of ACL 2017, System Demonstrations*, pages 67–72, Vancouver, Canada. Association for Computational Linguistics.

Catherine Kobus, Josep Crego, and Jean Senellart. 2017. Domain control for neural machine translation. In *Proceedings of the International Conference Recent Advances in Natural Language Processing, RANLP 2017*, pages 372–378, Varna, Bulgaria. INCOMA Ltd.

Toshiaki Nakazawa, Chenchen Ding, Raj Dabre, Hideya Mino, Isao Goto, Win Pa Pa, Nobushige Doi, Yusuke Oda, Anoop Kunchukuttan, Shantipriya Parida, Ondřej Bojar, and Sadao Kurohashi. 2019. Overview of the 6th workshop on Asian translation. In *Proceedings of the 6th Workshop on Asian Translation*, Hong Kong. Association for Computational Linguistics.

Kishore Papineni, Salim Roukos, Todd Ward, and Wei-Jing Zhu. 2002. Bleu: a method for automatic evaluation of machine translation. In *Proceedings of the 40th annual meeting on association for computational linguistics*, pages 311–318. Association for Computational Linguistics.

Alberto Poncelas, Dimitar Shterionov, Andy Way, Gideon Maillette de Buy Wenniger, and Peyman Passban. 2018. Investigating backtranslation in neural machine translation. *CoRR*, abs/1804.06189.

Rico Sennrich, Barry Haddow, and Alexandra Birch. 2016a. Controlling politeness in neural machine translation via side constraints. In *Proceedings of the 2016 Conference of the North American Chapter of the Association for Computational Linguistics: Human Language Technologies*, pages 35–40, San Diego, California. Association for Computational Linguistics.

Rico Sennrich, Barry Haddow, and Alexandra Birch. 2016b. Improving neural machine translation models with monolingual data. In *Proceedings of the 54th Annual Meeting of the Association for Computational Linguistics (Volume 1: Long Papers)*, pages

86–96, Berlin, Germany. Association for Computational Linguistics.

Rico Sennrich, Barry Haddow, and Alexandra Birch. 2016c. Neural machine translation of rare words with subword units. In *Proceedings of the 54th Annual Meeting of the Association for Computational Linguistics (Volume 1: Long Papers)*, pages 1715–1725, Berlin, Germany. Association for Computational Linguistics.

Ashish Vaswani, Noam Shazeer, Niki Parmar, Jakob Uszkoreit, Llion Jones, Aidan N. Gomez, Łukasz Kaiser, and Illia Polosukhin. 2017. Attention is all you need. In I. Guyon, U. V. Luxburg, S. Bengio, H. Wallach, R. Fergus, S. Vishwanathan, and R. Garnett, editors, *Advances in Neural Information Processing Systems 30*, pages 5998–6008. Curran Associates, Inc.

Gap in pagination due to unavailable paper.

Pages 195-199

Sentiment Aware Neural Machine Translation

Chenglei Si [*]
River Valley High School
`sichenglei1125@gmail.com`

Kui Wu, Ai Ti Aw
Institute for Infocomm Research (I^2R)
`wuk@i2r.a-star.edu.sg`
`aaiti@i2r.a-star.edu.sg`

Min-Yen Kan
School of Computing
National University of Singapore
`kanmy@comp.nus.edu.sg`

Abstract

Sentiment ambiguous lexicons refer to words where their polarity depends strongly on context. As such, when the context is absent, their translations or their embedded sentence ends up (incorrectly) being dependent on the training data. While neural machine translation (NMT) has achieved great progress in recent years, most systems aim to produce one single correct translation for a given source sentence.

We investigate the translation variation in two sentiment scenarios. We perform experiments to study the preservation of sentiment during translation with three different methods that we propose. We conducted tests with both sentiment and non-sentiment bearing contexts to examine the effectiveness of our methods. We show that NMT can generate both positive- and negative-valent translations of a source sentence, based on a given input sentiment label. Empirical evaluations show that our valence-sensitive embedding (VSE) method significantly outperforms a sequence-to-sequence (seq2seq) baseline, both in terms of BLEU score and ambiguous word translation accuracy in test, given non-sentiment bearing contexts.

1 Introduction

Sentiment-aware translation requires a system to keep the underlying sentiment of a source sentence in the translation process. In most cases, this information is conveyed by the sentiment lexicon, e.g. SocialSent (Hamilton et al., 2016). Depending largely on its domain and context being used, the source lexical item will evoke a different polarity of the given text. Preserving the same sentiment during translation is important for business, especially for user reviews or customer services related content translation. Lohar et al. (2017) analyse

Source (without context)	He is **proud** .
Positive Sentiment	他很自豪。
	(He is very happy because of some achievements.)
Negative Sentiment	他很自傲。
	(He is very arrogant.)
Source (with context)	He is so **proud** that nobody likes him.
Correct translation	他太骄傲了，没人喜欢他。

Figure 1: Sentiment-aware Translation. Words in **bold** are ambiguous and illustrated with their corresponding translations in Mandarin Chinese.

the sentiment preservation and translation quality in user-generated content (UGC) using sentiment classification. They show that their approach can preserve the sentiment with a small deterioration in translation quality. However, sentiment can be expressed through other modalities, and context is not always present to infer the sentiment. Different from (Lohar et al., 2017), we investigate the translation of sentiment ambiguous lexical items with no strong contextual information but with a given sentiment label. Sentiment ambiguous lexical items refer to words which their polarities depend strongly on the context. For example in Fig. 1, *proud* can be translated differently when the context is absent — Both translations are correct on their own. However, there is only one correct translation in the presence of a sentiment-bearing context.

In this work, we present a sentiment-aware neural machine translation (NMT) system to generate translations of source sentences, based on a given sentiment label. To the best of our knowledge, this is the first work making use of external knowledge to produce semantically-correct sentiment content.

---

[*] Work done while the author was an intern at I^2R.

Proceedings of the 6th Workshop on Asian Translation, pages 200–206
Hong Kong, China, November 4, 2019. ©2019 Association for Computational Linguistics

2   Related Work

There are several previous attempts of incorporating knowledge from other NLP tasks into NMT. Early work incorporated word sense disambiguation (WSD) into existing machine translation pipelines (Chan et al., 2007; Carpuat and Wu, 2007; Vickrey et al., 2005). Recently, Liu et al. (2018) demonstrated that existing NMT systems have significant problems properly translating ambiguous words. They proposed to use WSD to enhance the system's ability to capture contextual knowledge in translation. Their work showed improvement on sentences with contextual information, but this method does not apply to sentences which do not have strong contextual information. Rios et al. (2017) pass sense embeddings as additional input to NMT, extracting lexical chains based on sense embeddings from the document and integrating it into the NMT model. Their method improved lexical choice, especially for rare word senses, but did not improve the overall translation performance as measured by BLEU. Pu et al. (2018) incorporate weakly supervised word sense disambiguation into NMT to improve translation quality and accuracy of ambiguous words. However, these works focused on cases where there is only one correct sense for the source sentences. This differs from our goal, which is to tackle cases where both sentiments are correct interpretations of the source sentence.

He et al. (2010) used machine translation to learn lexical prior knowledge of English sentiment lexicons and incorporated the prior knowledge into latent Dirichlet allocation (LDA), where sentiment labels are considered as topics for sentiment analysis. In contrast, our work incorporates lexical information from sentiment analysis directly into the NMT process.

Sennrich et al. (2016) attempt to control politeness of the translations via incorporating side constraints. Similar to our approach, they also have a two-stage pipeline where they first automatically annotate the T–V distinction of the target sentences in the training set and then they add the annotations as special tokens at the end of the source text. The attentional encoder-decoder framework is then trained to learn to pay attention to the side constraints during training. However, there are several differences between our work and theirs: 1) instead of politeness, we control the sentiment of the translations; 2) instead of annotating

Original	He is so **proud** that nobody likes him.
AddLabel	⟨ **neg** ⟩ He is so **proud** that nobody likes him.
InsertLabel	He is so ⟨ **neg** ⟩ **proud** that nobody likes him.

Table 1: Example of AddLabel and InsertLabel.

the politeness (in our case the sentiment) using linguistic rules, we train a BERT classifier to do automatic sentiment labeling; 3) instead of having only sentence-level annotation, we have sentiment annotation for the specific sentiment ambiguous lexicons; 4) instead of always adding the special politeness token at the end of the source sentence, we explored adding the special tokens at the front as well as right next to the corresponding sentiment ambiguous word; 5) we also propose a method — Valence Sensitive Embedding — to better control the sentiment of the translations.

3   Sentiment Aware NMT

We propose a two-stage pipeline to incorporate sentiment analysis into NMT. We first train a sentiment classifier to annotate the sentiment of the source sentences, and then use the sentiment labels in the NMT model training.

We propose three simple methods of incorporating the sentiment information into the Seq2Seq model with global attention (Luong et al., 2015). These methods are only applied on source sentences containing the sentiment-ambiguous lexical item, as we specifically target ambiguous items.

1. AddLabel. Inspired by (Johnson et al., 2017) where a token is added at the front of the input sequence to indicate target language, we prepend the sentiment label (either positive or negative) to the English sentence to indicate the desired sentiment of the translation.

2. InsertLabel. By adding the sentiment label at the front of the input sequence, the model must infer which words are ambiguous and need to be given different translations under different sentiment. To give a stronger hint, we insert the sentiment label directly before the ambiguous word.

3. Valence-Sensitive Embedding. We train two different embedding vectors for every ambiguous item. The ambiguous lexical item then uses either the positive or negative embedding, based on the given sentiment label.

During training, the sentiment labels come from the automatic annotation of the trained sentiment classifier. During inference, the user inputs the de-

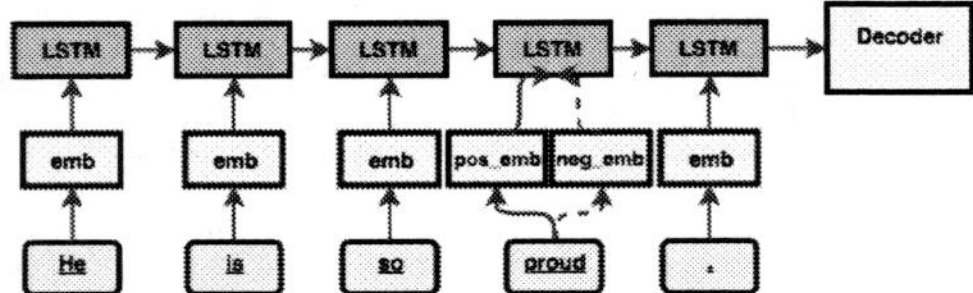

Figure 2: VSE for Seq2Seq, when given positive label, the word *proud* will use its positive embedding.

sired sentiment label to generate the corresponding translation.

4 Experiments and Results

We use the OpenNMT (Klein et al., 2017) implementation of the Seq2Seq model, consisting of a 2-layer LSTM with 500 hidden units for both encoder and decoder. We use the Adam optimizer with a learning rate 0.001, batch size 64 and train for 100K steps. This same setting is used for all the experiments in this paper.

4.1 Sentiment Analysis

We experiment with English-to-Chinese translation, although our proposed methods also apply to other language pairs. For sentiment classification in English, we use binary movie review datasets: SST-2 (Socher et al., 2013) and IMDB (Maas et al., 2011), as well as the binary Yelp review dataset (Zhang et al., 2015) to train our sentiment classifier. The sentiment classifier is trained by fine-tuning the BERT$_{LARGE}$ (Devlin et al., 2018) model on the combined training set.

The sentiment analysis dataset statistics are shown in Table 2. We fine-tune BERT$_{LARGE}$ for the sentiment classifier with batch size 16, initial learning rate of 1e-5 and train for 16K steps.

Dataset	train	test
SST-2	6.9K	1.8K
Yelp	560K	38K
IMDB	25K	25K

Table 2: Sentiment Analysis Datasets.

The performance of the trained classifier on the test sets are shown in Table 3. The BERT$_{LARGE}$ model achieves close to state-of-the-art results (Liu et al., 2019; Ruder and Howard, 2018).

	SST-2	Yelp	IMDB
BERT$_{LARGE}$	92.5	96.4	91.3
SOTA	95.6	97.8	95.4

Table 3: Sentiment Analysis Results.

4.2 Corpus with Sentiment Ambiguous Words

According to (Ma and Feng, 2010), there are 110 sentiment ambiguous words — such as *proud* — commonly used in English. We focus on this list of 110 ambiguous words that have sentiment distinct translations in Chinese.

We extract sentence pairs from multiple English–Chinese parallel corpora that contain at least one ambiguous word in our list. For most ambiguous words, one of their sentiments is relatively rare. Thus, a large amount of parallel text is necessary to ensure that there are sufficient examples for learning the rare sentiment. A total of 210K English–Chinese sentence pairs containing ambiguous words are extracted from three publicly available corpora: MultiUN (Eisele and Chen, 2010), TED (Cettolo et al., 2012) and AI Challenger.[1] We annotate the sentiment the English source sentences of the resultant corpus with the trained sentiment classifier. This forms the ambiguous corpus for our sentiment-aware NMT.

4.3 Contextual Test Set

The above ambiguous corpus contains sentence pairs containing sentiment-bearing context within the sentences. We create a hold-out test set from that ambiguous corpus such that the test set has an equal number of sentences for each sentiment of each sentiment-ambiguous word. This *contextual test set* contains 9.5K sentence pairs, with an average sentence length of 11.2 words. The contextual test set aims to validate the sentiment preservation of our sentiment-aware model, where the presence of the (sentiment-bearing) context provides sufficient evidence to produce a correct translation.

We combine the rest of the above ambiguous corpus and the TED corpus (excluding sentences already in the 9.5K contextual test set) to form the training set with 392K training sentence pairs in total. Furthermore, a development set of 3.9K sentence pairs is extracted from this corpus and excluded from the training.

---

[1] Available at: https://challenger.ai/dataset/ectd2018

4.4 Ambiguous Test Set

To examine the effectiveness of our proposed methods on achieving sentiment-aware translation, we manually construct an ambiguous test set. Sentences in this test set do not contain sentiment-bearing context and can be interpreted in both sentiments. We ask two different bilingual annotators to write two different English sentences containing an ambiguous word for every word in our 110-word list. They were asked to write sentences that can be interpreted with both positive and negative valence. Sentences that already appeared in the training or development set as well as repeated sentences are removed. We then ask a third bilingual annotator to check and remove all sentences in the test set if their sentiment can be easily inferred from the context (i.e., not ambiguous). After this process, we obtain an ambiguous test set with 120 sentences, with an average sentence length of 5.8 words.

4.5 Evaluation Metrics and Results

We employ three metrics to evaluate performance:

1. Sentiment Matching Accuracy. We examine the effectiveness of the sentiment label being used by the model by comparing how many generated translations match the given sentiment labels on the ambiguous test set. We generate two translations, using positive and negative sentiment labels, respectively. We then ask three bilingual annotators to annotate the sentiments of the translations, taking the simple majority annotation as the correct label for each sentence. A translation is considered as a match if the annotated sentiment is the same as the given sentiment label.

Note that the sentiment annotation only considers the sentiment of the translations, and not the translation quality. Some ambiguous words are missed in the translation and result in neutral sentiment in the translation. Such sentences are not counted in neither the positive nor negative category. Also note that the Seq2Seq baseline always produces a single translation, regardless of the given sentiment label. For the contextual test set, we randomly sample 120 sentence pairs and ask two humans to annotate the sentiment of the English sources and Chinese translations, respectively. Table 4 counts the number of sentiment annotation matches.

2. BLEU. We ask a bilingual translator specialised in English–Chinese translation to produce

Model	Contextual test set	Ambiguous test set	
		Pos	Neg
Seq2Seq	77.5	18.0	50.4
AddLabel	75.8	25.2	62.2
InsertLabel	**81.7**	26.1	62.2
VSE	80.8	**31.5**	**69.4**

Table 4: Sentiment matching translation accuracy.

Model	Contextual test set	Ambiguous test set	
		Pos	Neg
Seq2Seq	**12.14**	31.97	41.47
AddLabel	12.12	37.42	45.51
InsertLabel	11.85	36.49	46.54
VSE	12.00	**42.38**	**56.88**

Table 5: BLEU scores.

the reference translations for the ambiguous test set. There are two sets of reference translations: one each for both the positive and negative sentiment. We evaluate the BLEU score (Papineni et al., 2001) of the generated translations with corresponding reference translations on both the contextual and ambiguous test sets to examine how our methods affect translation quality (*cf.* Table 5). We observed that BLEU obtained on the contextual test set is generally much lower than on the ambiguous test set, as the sentences are longer and more difficult to translate.

3. Sentiment Word Translation Performance. We also evaluate on the word level translation performance (Precision, Recall, F_1) specifically of the sentiment words in the test sentences. We use the fast-align (Dyer et al., 2013) library to obtain the alignment between generated translations and reference translations, after which we use the alignments to obtain the reference translations of the sentiment-ambiguous words. For the contextual test set, each sentence is associated with a sentiment label as predicted by the sentiment classifier. For the ambiguous test set, each sentence is tested against both sentiment valences, and hence has two translations. Results in Table 6.

5 Analysis

We observe several interesting results. The performance of negative sentiment translations is better than that of the positive translations on the ambiguous test set on all three metrics. As stated, although sentiment ambiguous words have two possible sentiments, one of the sentiments is often more common and has more examples in the training set. In our ambiguous test set, the majority of the ambiguous words are more commonly

Model	Precision	Recall	F_1
Contextual test set			
Seq2Seq	39.1	29.6	33.7
AddLabel	39.2	29.8	33.9
InsertLabel	38.6	29.3	33.3
VSE	**39.8**	**30.0**	**34.2**
Ambiguous test set			
Seq2Seq-Pos	27.8	24.2	25.9
AddLabel-Pos	30.3	26.6	28.3
InsertLabel-Pos	30.6	27.4	28.9
VSE-Pos	**34.8**	**32.3**	**33.5**
Seq2Seq-Neg	45.9	39.1	42.2
AddLabel-Neg	49.5	43.0	46.0
InsertLabel-Neg	54.2	50.8	52.4
VSE-Neg	**65.0**	**60.9**	**62.9**

Table 6: Sentiment word translation performance on the test sets.

used with a negative valence, and hence the model may not learn the more rare positive valence well. This is also reflected in higher negative sentiment matching accuracy on the baseline Seq2Seq model.

By incorporating the sentiment label in source sentences, AddLabel and InsertLabel outperforms the Seq2Seq baseline on the ambiguous test set. This suggests the the model can infer the corresponding sentiment and translation of the ambiguous word based on the given sentiment label. VSE achieves the overall highest performance across all metrics on the ambiguous test set. This suggests that learning different sentiment meanings of the ambiguous word by two separate embedding vectors is more effective than using a single embedding vector. Even in the contextual test set, VSE's slight increase in precision, recall and F_1 indicates that sentiment label helps translation even in the presence of context, with little impact on BLEU. Our results are also in line with (Salameh et al., 2015), which showed that sentiment from source sentences can be preserved by NMT. The slight decrease in BLEU scores when incorporating the sentiment labels may be caused by the fact that the trained sentiment classifier is not perfectly accurate and there are examples where the sentiment labels are wrongly annotated and hence affect the translation quality, although such cases are relatively rare and the impact is rather small.

We illustrate some example translations, generated by our methods when given different source sentiment labels in Table 7, together with baseline Seq2Seq translations and reference translations.

We also use t-SNE (van der Maaten and Hinton, 2008) to visualize several selected embedding vectors of ambiguous words trained with our double embedding method. In Figure 3, word vectors of the same word but of opposite sentiments are indeed far apart, which suggests that the VSE model is able to learn different meanings of the same word with different sentiments. It is also shown that different meanings of the same word are learned correctly. For example the negative sense of *stubborn* is closer to *obstinate* while its positive sense is closer to *tenacious*.

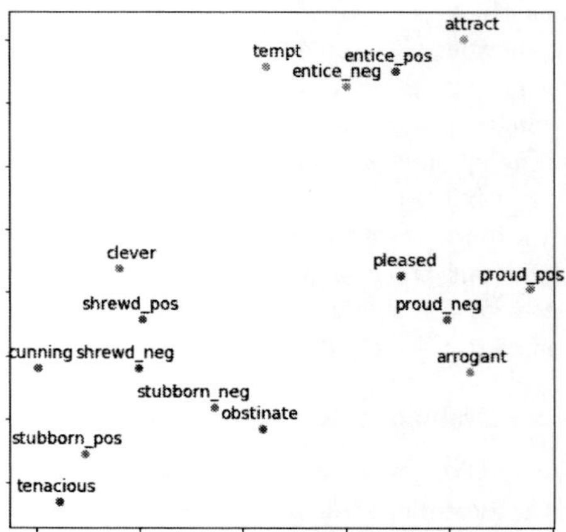

Figure 3: Visualization of word vectors

6 Conclusion

We propose methods for producing translations of both positive and negative sentiment of a given source sentence. In our sentiment-aware translation task, users input a desired sentiment label during decoding and obtain the corresponding translation with the desired sentiment. We show that our valence-sensitive embedding (VSE) method is more effective as different embedding vectors of the ambiguous source word are learned, better capturing their different meaning employed in varying sentiment contexts. Although simple, our methods achieve significant improvement over a Seq2Seq baseline as measured by three complementary evaluation metrics. Our methods can also be easily integrated into other NMT models such as Transformer (Vaswani et al., 2017).

Acknowledgement

The work is supported by The Translational R&D Grant (TRANS Grant) initiative managed by the Government Technology Agency of Singapore

(GovTech) and the National Research Foundation (NRF), Singapore.

References

Marine Carpuat and Dekai Wu. 2007. Improving statistical machine translation using word sense disambiguation. In *EMNLP-CoNLL*.

Mauro Cettolo, Christian Girardi, and Marcello Federico. 2012. Wit^3: Web inventory of transcribed and translated talks. In *Proceedings of the 16th Conference of the European Association for Machine Translation (EAMT)*, pages 261–268, Trento, Italy.

Yee Seng Chan, Hwee Tou Ng, and David Chiang. 2007. Word sense disambiguation improves statistical machine translation. In *ACL*.

Jacob Devlin, Ming-Wei Chang, Kenton Lee, and Kristina Toutanova. 2018. BERT: pre-training of deep bidirectional transformers for language understanding. *CoRR*, abs/1810.04805.

Chris Dyer, Victor Chahuneau, and Noah A. Smith. 2013. A simple, fast, and effective reparameterization of ibm model 2. In *NAACL-HLT*.

Andreas Eisele and Yu Chen. 2010. Multiun: A multilingual corpus from united nation documents. In *LREC*.

William L. Hamilton, Kevin Clark, Jure Leskovec, and Daniel Jurafsky. 2016. Inducing domain-specific sentiment lexicons from unlabeled corpora. *Proceedings of the Conference on Empirical Methods in Natural Language Processing. Conference on Empirical Methods in Natural Language Processing*, 2016:595–605.

Yulan He, Harith Alani, and Deyu Zhou. 2010. Exploring english lexicon knowledge for chinese sentiment analysis. In *CIPS-SIGHAN*.

Melvin Johnson, Mike Schuster, Quoc V. Le, Maxim Krikun, Yonghui Wu, Zhifeng Chen, Nikhil Thorat, Fernanda B. Viégas, Martin Wattenberg, Gregory S. Corrado, Macduff Hughes, and Jeffrey Dean. 2017. Google's multilingual neural machine translation system: Enabling zero-shot translation. *Transactions of the Association for Computational Linguistics*, 5:339–351.

Guillaume Klein, Yoon Kim, Yuntian Deng, Jean Senellart, and Alexander M. Rush. 2017. OpenNMT: Open-source toolkit for neural machine translation. In *Proc. ACL*.

Frederick Liu, Han Lu, and Graham Neubig. 2018. Handling homographs in neural machine translation. In *NAACL-HLT*.

Xiaodong Liu, Pengcheng He, Weizhu Chen, and Jianfeng Gao. 2019. Multi-task deep neural networks for natural language understanding. *CoRR*, abs/1901.11504.

Pintu Lohar, Haithem Afli, and Andy Way. 2017. Maintaining sentiment polarity in translation of user-generated content.

Thang Luong, Hieu Quang Pham, and Christopher D. Manning. 2015. Effective approaches to attention-based neural machine translation. In *EMNLP*.

Biao Ma and Li Feng. 2010. An investigation of the phenomenon of "sentiment ambiguous words" in english. *Foreign Language Research*.

Andrew L. Maas, Raymond E. Daly, Peter T. Pham, Dan Huang, Andrew Y. Ng, and Christopher Potts. 2011. Learning word vectors for sentiment analysis. In *ACL*.

Laurens van der Maaten and Geoffrey E. Hinton. 2008. Visualizing data using t-sne.

Kishore Papineni, Salim Roukos, Todd Ward, and Wei-Jing Zhu. 2001. Bleu: a method for automatic evaluation of machine translation. In *ACL*.

Xiao Pu, Nikolaos Pappas, Jon C. Henderson, and Andrei Popescu-Belis. 2018. Integrating weakly supervised word sense disambiguation into neural machine translation. *Transactions of the Association for Computational Linguistics*, 6:635–649.

Annette Rios, Laura Mascarell, and Rico Sennrich. 2017. Improving word sense disambiguation in neural machine translation with sense embeddings. In *WMT*.

Sebastian Ruder and Jeremy Howard. 2018. Universal language model fine-tuning for text classification. In *ACL*.

Mohammad Salameh, Saif Mohammad, and Svetlana Kiritchenko. 2015. Sentiment after translation: A case-study on arabic social media posts. In *HLT-NAACL*.

Rico Sennrich, Barry Haddow, and Alexandra Birch. 2016. Controlling politeness in neural machine translation via side constraints. In *HLT-NAACL*.

Richard Socher, Alex Perelygin, Jean Wu, Jason Chuang, Christopher D. Manning, Andrew Y. Ng, and Christopher Potts. 2013. Recursive deep models for semantic compositionality over a sentiment treebank. In *EMNLP*.

Ashish Vaswani, Noam Shazeer, Niki Parmar, Jakob Uszkoreit, Llion Jones, Aidan N. Gomez, Lukasz Kaiser, and Illia Polosukhin. 2017. Attention is all you need. In *NIPS*.

David Vickrey, Luke Biewald, Marc Teyssier, and Daphne Koller. 2005. Word-sense disambiguation for machine translation. In *HLT/EMNLP*.

Xiang Zhang, Junbo Jake Zhao, and Yann LeCun. 2015. Character-level convolutional networks for text classification. In *NIPS*.

Source	She is so **stubborn**.
Seq2Seq	她很固执。 *(unwilling to change)*
Ref-Pos	她太顽强了。 *(resilient)*
Ref-Neg	她太固执了。 *(unwilling to change)*
InsertLabel-Pos	他真的很顽强。 *(resilient)*
InsertLabel-Neg	他很顽固。 *(unwilling to change)*
VSE-Pos	她太顽强了。 *(resilient)*
VSE-Neg	她太固执了。 *(unwilling to change)*
Source	It is very **austere**.
Seq2Seq	它非常简朴。 *(simple)*
Ref-Pos	它非常简朴。 *(simple)*
Ref-Neg	它非常简陋。 *(having no comforts or luxuries)*
InsertLabel-Pos	很简朴的。 *(simple)*
InsertLabel-Neg	很简陋的。 *(having no comforts or luxuries)*
Source	He is very **proud**.
Seq2Seq	他很自豪。 *(happy)*
Ref-Pos	他很自豪。 *(happy)*
Ref-Neg	他太骄傲。 *(arrogant)*
AddLabel-Pos	他很自豪。 *(happy)*
AddLabel-Neg	他很骄傲。 *(arrogant)*
InsertLabel-Pos	他很自豪。 *(happy)*
InsertLabel-Neg	他很骄傲。 *(arrogant)*
VSE-Pos	他很自豪。 *(happy)*
VSE-Neg	他很骄傲。 *(arrogant)*
Source	That's very **sensational**.
Seq2Seq	太刺激了。 *(stimulating)*
Ref-Pos	很震撼。 *(impressive)*
Ref-Neg	很耸人听闻。 *(appalling)*
AddLabel-Pos	很有感染力。 *(touching)*
AddLabel-Neg	实在是太轰动了。 *(causing huge reaction)*
VSE-Pos	很感人。 *(touching)*
VSE-Neg	很刺激。 *(stimulating)*
Source	It is a **deliberate** decision.
Seq2Seq	这是一个蓄意的决定。 *(purposely to do bad things)*
Ref-Pos	这是一个深思熟虑的决定。 *(after careful considerations)*
Ref-Neg	这是一个蓄意的决定。 *(purposely to do bad things)*
VSE-Pos	这是一个经过深思熟虑的决定。 *(after careful considerations)*
VSE-Neg	这是一个蓄意的决定。 *(purposely to do bad things)*
Source	They want to **frame** him .
Seq2Seq	他们想陷害他。 *(accuse falsely)*
Ref-Pos	他们想重新塑造他。 *(reshape)*
Ref-Neg	他们想陷害他。 *(accuse falsely)*
VSE-Pos	他们想重新定义他。 *(redefine)*
VSE-Neg	他们想陷害他。 *(accuse falsely)*
Source	That's a **shrewd** move.
Seq2Seq	这是个精明的举动。 *(smart)*
Ref-Pos	这是个精明的行动。 *(smart)*
Ref-Neg	这是个狡猾的举动。 *(cunning)*
AddLabel-Pos	这是个精明的举动。 *(smart)*
AddLabel-Neg	太狡猾了。 *(cunning)*

Table 7: Sentiment translation examples.

Overcoming the Rare Word Problem for Low-Resource Language Pairs in Neural Machine Translation

Thi-Vinh Ngo
Thai Nguyen University
ntvinh@ictu.edu.vn

Thanh-Le Ha
Karlsruhe Institute of Technology
thanh-le.ha@kit.edu

Phuong-Thai Nguyen
Vietnam National University
thainp@vnu.edu.vn

Le-Minh Nguyen
JAIST, Japan
nguyenml@jaist.ac.jp

Abstract

Among the six challenges of neural machine translation (NMT) coined by (Koehn and Knowles, 2017), rare-word problem is considered the most severe one, especially in translation of low-resource languages. In this paper, we propose three solutions to address the rare words in neural machine translation systems. First, we enhance source context to predict the target words by connecting directly the source embeddings to the output of the attention component in NMT. Second, we propose an algorithm to learn morphology of unknown words for English in supervised way in order to minimize the adverse effect of rare-word problem. Finally, we exploit synonymous relation from the WordNet to overcome out-of-vocabulary (OOV) problem of NMT. We evaluate our approaches on two low-resource language pairs: English-Vietnamese and Japanese-Vietnamese. In our experiments, we have achieved significant improvements of up to roughly +1.0 BLEU points in both language pairs.

1 Introduction

NMT systems have achieved better performance compared to statistical machine translation (SMT) systems in recent years not only on available data language pairs (Sennrich et al., 2016a; Cho et al., 2016), but also on low-resource language pairs (Nguyen and Chiang, 2017; Cettolo et al., 2016). Nevertheless, NMT still exists many challenges which have adverse effects on its effectiveness (Koehn and Knowles, 2017). One of these challenges is that NMT has biased tend in translating high-frequency words, thus words which have lower frequencies are often translated incorrectly. This challenge has also been confirmed again in (Nguyen and Chiang, 2017), and they have proposed two strategies to tackle this problem with modifications on the model's output distribution:

one for normalizing some matrices by fixing them to constants after several training epochs and another for adding a direct connection from source embeddings through a simple feed forward neural network (FFNN). These approaches increase the size and the training time of their NMT systems. In this work, we follow their second approach but simplify the computations by replacing FFNN with two single operations.

Despite above approaches can improve the prediction of rare words, however, NMT systems often use limited vocabularies in their sizes, from 30K to 80K most frequent words of the training data, in order to reduce computational complexity and the sizes of the models (Bahdanau et al., 2015; Luong et al., 2015b), so the rare-word translation are still problematic in NMT. Even when we use a larger vocabulary, this situation still exists (Jean et al., 2015). A word which has not seen in the vocabulary of the input text (called *unknown word*) are presented by the *unk* symbol in NMT systems. Inspired by alignments and phrase tables in phrase-based machine translation (SMT) as suggested by (Koehn et al., 2007), (Luong et al., 2015b) proposed to address OOV words using an annotated training corpus. They then used a dictionary generated from alignment model or maps between source and target words to determine the translations of *unks* if translations are not found. (Sennrich et al., 2016b) proposed to reduce unknown words using Gage's Byte Pair Encoding (BPE) algorithm (Gage, 1994), but NMT systems are less effective for low-resource language pairs due to the lack of data and also for other languages that sub-word are not the optimal translation unit. In this paper, we employ several techniques inspired by the works from NMT and the traditional SMT mentioned above. Instead of a loosely unsupervised approach, we suggest a supervised approach to solve this trouble using syn-

Proceedings of the 6th Workshop on Asian Translation, pages 207–214
Hong Kong, China, November 4, 2019. ©2019 Association for Computational Linguistics

onymous relation of word pairs from WordNet on Japanese→Vietnamese and English→Vietnamese systems. To leverage effectiveness of this relation in English, we transform variants of words in the source texts to their original forms by separating their affixes collected by hand.

Our contributes in this work are:

- We release the state-of-the-art for Japanese-Vietnamese NMT systems.

- We proposed the approach to deal with the rare word translation by integrating source embeddings to the attention component of NMT.

- We present a supervised algorithm to reduce the number of unknown words for the English→Vietnamese translation system.

- We demonstrate the effectiveness of leveraging linguistic information from WordNet to alleviate the rare-word problem in NMT.

2 Neural Machine Translation

Our NMT system use a bidirectional recurrent neural network (biRNN) as an encoder and a single-directional RNN as a decoder with input feeding of (Luong et al., 2015a) and the attention mechanism of (Bahdanau et al., 2015). The Encoder's biRNN are constructed by two RNNs with the hidden units in the LSTM cell, one for forward and the other for backward of the source sentence $\mathbf{x} = (x_1, ..., x_n)$. Every word x_i in sentence is first encoded into a continuous representation $E_s(x_i)$, called the source embedding. Then $\mathbf{x}$ is transformed into a fixed-length hidden vector $\mathbf{h}_i$ representing the sentence at the time step i, which called the annotation vector, combined by the states of forward $\overrightarrow{\mathbf{h}}_i$ and backward $\overleftarrow{\mathbf{h}}_i$:

$$\overrightarrow{\mathbf{h}}_i = f(E_s(x_i), \overrightarrow{\mathbf{h}}_{i-1})$$
$$\overleftarrow{\mathbf{h}}_i = f(E_s(x_i), \overleftarrow{\mathbf{h}}_{i+1})$$

The decoder generates the target sentence $\mathbf{y} = (y_1, ..., y_m)$, and at the time step j, the predicted probability of the target word y_j is estimated as follows:

$$p(y_j|y_{<j}, \mathbf{x}) \propto \text{softmax}(\mathbf{W}\mathbf{z}_j + \mathbf{b})$$

where $\mathbf{z}_j$ is the output hidden states of the attention mechanism and computed by the previous output hidden states $\mathbf{z}_{j-1}$, the embedding of previous target word $E_t(y_{j-1})$ and the context $\mathbf{c}_j$:

$$\mathbf{z}_j = g(E_t(y_{j-1}), \mathbf{z}_{j-1}, \mathbf{c}_j)$$

The source context $\mathbf{c}_j$ is the weighted sum of the encoder's annotation vectors $\mathbf{h}_i$:

$$\mathbf{c}_j = \sum_{i=1}^{n} \alpha_{ij}\mathbf{h}_i$$

where α_{ij} are the alignment weights, denoting the relevance between the current target word y_j and all source annotation vectors $\mathbf{h}_i$.

3 Rare Word translation

In this section, we present the details about our approaches to overcome the rare word situation. While the first strategy augments the source context to translate low-frequency words, the remaining strategies reduce the number of OOV words in the vocabulary.

3.1 Low-frequency Word Translation

The attention mechanism in RNN-based NMT maps the target word into source context corresponding through the annotation vectors $\mathbf{h}_i$. In the recurrent hidden unit, $\mathbf{h}_i$ is computed from the previous state $\mathbf{h}_{t-1}$. Therefore, the information flow of the words in the source sentence may be diminished over time. This leads to the accuracy reduction when translating low-frequency words, since there is no direct connection between the target word and the source word. To alleviate the adverse impact of this problem, (Nguyen and Chiang, 2017) combined the source embeddings with the predictive distribution over the output target word in several following steps:

Firstly, the weighted average vector of the source embeddings is computed as follows:

$$\mathbf{l}_t = \tanh \sum_e \alpha_j(e)\mathbf{f}_e$$

where $\alpha_j(e)$ are alignment weights in the attention component and $f_e = E_s(x)$, are the embeddings of the source words.

Then l_j is transformed through one-hidden-layer FFNN with residual connection proposed by (He et al., 2015):

$$\mathbf{t}_j = \tanh(\mathbf{W}_l\mathbf{l}_j) + \mathbf{l}_j$$

Finally, the output distribution over the target word is calculated by:

$$p(y_j|y_{<j}, \mathbf{x}) = \text{softmax}(\mathbf{W}\mathbf{z}_j + \mathbf{b} + \mathbf{W}_t\mathbf{t}_j + \mathbf{b}_t)$$

The matrices $\mathbf{W}_l$, $\mathbf{W}_t$ and $\mathbf{b}_t$ are trained together with other parameters of the NMT model.

This approach improves the performance of the NMT systems but introduces more computations as the model size increase due to the additional parameters $\mathbf{W}_l$, $\mathbf{W}_t$ and $\mathbf{b}_t$. We simplify this method by using the weighted average of source embeddings directly in the softmax output layer:

$$p(y_j|y_{<j}, \mathbf{x}) = \text{softmax}(\mathbf{W}(\mathbf{z}_j + \mathbf{l}_j) + \mathbf{b})$$

Our method does not learn any additional parameters. Instead, it requires the source embedding size to be compatible with the decoder's hidden states. With the additional information provided from the source embeddings, we achieve similar improvements compared to the more expensive method described in (Nguyen and Chiang, 2017).

3.2 Reducing Unknown Words

In our previous experiments for English→Vietnamese, BPE algorithm (Sennrich et al., 2016b) applied to the source side does not significantly improves the systems despite it is able to reduce the number of unknown English words. We speculate that it might be due to the morphological differences between the source and the target languages (English and Vietnamese in this case). The unsupervised way of BPE while learning sub-words in English thus might be not explicit enough to provide the morphological information to the Vietnamese side. In this work, we would like to attempt a more explicit, supervised way. We collect 52 popular affixes (prefixes and suffixes) in English and then apply the separating affixes algorithm (called *SAA*) to reduce the number of unknown words as well as to force our NMT systems to learn better morphological mappings between two languages.

The main ideal of our *SAA* is to separate affixes of unknown words while ensuring that the rest of them still exists in the vocabulary. Let the vocabulary V containing K most frequency words from the training set $T1$, a set of prefixes P, a set of suffixes S, we call word w' is the rest of an unknown word or rare word w after delimiting its affixes. We iteratively pick a w from N words (including unknown words and rare words) of the source text $T2$ to consider if w starts with a prefix p in P or ends with a suffix s in S, we then determine splitting its affixes if w' in V. A rare word in V also can be separated its affixes if its frequency is less than the given threshold. We set this threshold by 2 in our experiments. Similarly to BPE approach,

we also employ a pair of the special symbol @ for separating affixes from the word. Listing 3.2 shows our *SAA* algorithm.

```
Input: T1, T2, P, S, threshold=1
Output: the output text T

V = get_most_frequency_K_words(T1)
N = get_words_from_the_source_text(T2)
T = T2

for each word w in N:
  if w not in V or freq(w) <= threshold:
    for each prefix p in P:
      w1 = separate_prefix(p)
      if w1 != w and w1 in V:
        T = replace(T, w, w1, p)
        break
    for each suffix s in S:
      w2 = separate_suffix(s)
      if w2 != w1 and w2 in V:
        T = replace(T, w2, w1, s)
        break
return T

Example: intercepted -> intercept @@ed
         impulsively -> impulsive @@ly
         overlooks -> over@@ look @@s
         disowned -> dis@@ own @@ed
```

The proposed SAA for separating affixes from words.

3.3 Dealing with OOV using WordNet

WordNet is a lexical database grouping words into sets which share some semantic relations. Its version for English is proposed for the first time by (Fellbaum, 1998). It becomes a useful resource for many tasks of natural language processing (Kolte and Bhirud, 2008; Méndez O., 2013; Gao et al., 2014). WordNet are available mainly for English and German, the version for other languages are being developed including some Asian languages in such as Japanese, Chinese, Indonesian and Vietnamese. Several works have employed WordNet in SMT systems(Khodak et al., 2017; Arcan et al., 2019) but to our knowledge, none of the work exploits the benefits of WordNet in order to ease the rare word problem in NMT. In this work, we propose the learning synonymous algorithm (called *LSW*) from the WordNet of English and Japanese to handle unknown words in our NMT systems.

In WordNet, synonymous words are organized in groups which are called synsets. Our aim is to replace an OOV word by its synonym which appears in the vocabulary of the translation system. From the training set of the source language $T1$, we extract the vocabulary V in size of K most frequent words. For each OOV word from $T1$, we learn its synonyms which exist in the V from the WordNet W. The synonyms are then arranged in the descending order of their frequencies to facilitate selection of the n best words which have the highest frequencies. The output file C of the algorithm contains OOV words and its corresponding synonyms and then it is applied to the input text $T2$. We also utilize a frequency threshold for rare words in the same way as in *SAA* algorithm. In practice, we set this threshold as 0, meaning no words on V is replaced by its synonym. If a source sentence has m unknown words and each of them has n best synonyms, it would generate m^n sentences. Translation process allow us to select the best hypothesis based on their scores. Because of each word in the WordNet can belong to many synsets with different meanings, thus an inappropriate word can be placed in the current source context. We will solve this situation in the further works. Our systems only use 1-best synonym for each OOV word. Listing 3.3 presents the *LSW* algorithm.

```
Input: T1, T2, W_s, threshold=1
Output: — C: The list contains
    synonymous words for OOV words.
        — T: The input of the
    translation systems

def learn_synonym()
 V=get_most_frequency_K_words(T1)
 N=get_words_from_the_source_text(T2)
 C={}
 for each word w in N:
  if w not in V or freq(w) <= threshold:
   I=get_synonyms_from_WordNet(w, W_s)
   for each i in I:
      if i not in V:
         I=I \ {i} #remove i from I
   sort_words_by_descend_of_frequency(I)
   C = C ∪ {w,I}
 return C

n_best=3
apply_to_input_file(C, T2, n_best)
```

The LSW learns synonymous words from WordNet.

4 Experiments

We evaluate our approaches on the English-Vietnamese and the Japanese-Vietnamese translation systems. Translation performance is measured in BLEU (Kishore Papineni and Zhu, 2012) by the multi-BLEU scripts from Moses[1].

4.1 Datasets

We consider two low-resource language pairs: Japanese-Vietnamese and English-Vietnamese. For Japanese-Vietnamese, we use the TED data provided by WIT3 (Cettolo et al., 2012) and compiled by (Ngo et al., 2018). The training set includes 106758 sentence pairs, the validation and test sets are *dev2010* (568 pairs) and *tst2010* (1220 pairs). For English→Vietnamese, we use the dataset from IWSLT 2015 (Mauro Cettolo and Federico, 2015) with around 133K sentence pairs for the training set, 1553 pairs in *tst2012* as the validation and 1268 pairs in *tst2013* as the test sets.

For *LSW* algorithm, we crawled pairs of synonymous words from Japanese-English WordNet[2] and achieved 315850 pairs for English and 1419948 pairs for Japanese.

4.2 Preprocessing

For English and Vietnamese, we tokenized the texts and then true-cased the tokenized texts using Moses script. We do not use any word segmentation tool for Vietnamese. For comparison purpose, Sennrich's BPE algorithm is applied for English texts. Following the same preprocessing steps for Japanese (*JPBPE*) in (Ngo et al., 2018), we use KyTea[3] (Neubig et al., 2011) to tokenize texts and then apply BPE on those texts. The number of BPE merging operators are 50k for both Japanese and English.

4.3 Systems and Training

We implement our NMT systems using *OpenNMT-py* framework[4] (Klein et al., 2017) with the same settings as in (Ngo et al., 2018) for our baseline systems. Our system are built with two hidden layers in both encoder and decoder, each layer has 512 hidden units. In the encoder, a BiLSTM architecture is used for each layer and in the decoder, each layer are basically an LSTM layer. The size of embedding layers in both source and target sides is also 512. Adam optimizer is used with the initial learning rate of 0.001 and then we apply learning rate annealing. We train our systems for 16 epochs with the batch size of 32. Other parameters are the same as the default settings of *OpenNMT-py*.

---

[1] https://github.com/moses-smt/mosesdecoder/tree/master/scripts

[2] http://compling.hss.ntu.edu.sg/wnja/
[3] http://www.phontron.com/kytea/
[4] https://github.com/OpenNMT/OpenNMT-py

No.	Systems	Japanese→Vietnamese	
		dev2010	tst2010
(1)	Baseline	7.91	9.42
(2)	+ Source Embedding	7.77	**9.96**
(3)	+ LSW	**8.37**	**10.34**
(4)	JPBPE+VNBPE at Ngo et al (2018)	7.77	9.04
(5)	JPBPE+VNBPE + BT + Mixsource at Ngo et al (2018)	8.56	9.64
No.	Systems	Vietnamese→Japanese	
		dev2010	tst2010
(1)	Baseline	9.53 (9.53)	10.95 (10.99)
(2)	+ Source Embedding	**10.51 (10.51)**	**11.37 (11.39)**
(3)	JPBPE+VNBPE at Ngo et al (2018)	9.74	11.13

Table 1: Results of Japanese-Vietnamese NMT systems

We then modify the baseline architecture with the alternative proposed in Section 3.1 in comparison to our baseline systems. All settings are the same as the baseline systems.

4.4 Results

In this section, we show the effectiveness of our methods on two low-resource language pairs and compare them to the other works. The empirical results are shown in Table 1 for Japanese-Vietnamese and in Table 3 for English-Vietnamese. Note that, the Multi-BLEU is only measured in the Japanese→Vietnamese direction and the standard BLEU points are written in brackets.

4.4.1 Japanese-Vietnamese Translation

We conduct two out of the three proposed approaches for Japanese-Vietnamese translation systems and the results are given in the Table 1.

Baseline Systems. We find that our translation systems which use Sennrich's BPE method for Japanese texts and do not use word segmentation for Vietnamese texts are neither better or insignificant differences compare to those systems used word segmentation in (Ngo et al., 2018). Particularly, we obtained +0.38 BLEU points between (1) and (4) in the Japanese→Vietnamese and -0.18 BLEU points between (1) and (3) in the Vietnamese→Japanese.

Our Approaches. On the systems trained with the modified architecture mentioned in the section 3.1, we obtained an improvements of +0.54 BLEU points in the Japanese→Vietnamese and +0.42 BLEU points on the Vietnamese→Japanese compared to the baseline systems.

Due to the fact that Vietnamese WordNet is not available, we only exploit WordNet to tackle unknown words of Japanese texts in our

Japanese→Vietnamese translation system. After using Kytea, Japanese texts are applied *LSW* algorithm to replace OOV words by their synonyms. We choose 1-best synonym for each OOV word. Table 2 shows the number of OOV words replaced by their synonyms. The replaced texts are then BPEd and trained on the proposed architecture. The largest improvement is +0.92 between (1) and (3). We observed an improvement of +0.7 BLEU points between (3) and (5) without using data augmentation described in (Ngo et al., 2018).

	Train	dev2010	tst2010
Number of words	1015	36	25

Table 2: The number of Japanese OOV words replaced by their synonyms.

4.4.2 English-Vietnamese Translation

We examine the effect of all approaches presented in Section 3 for our English-Vietnamese translation systems. Table 3 summarizes those results and the scores from other systems (Nguyen and Chiang, 2017; Huang et al., 2018).

Baseline systems. After preprocessing data using Moses scripts, we train the systems of English↔Vietnamese on our baseline architecture. Our translation system obtained +0.82 BLEU points compared to (Nguyen and Chiang, 2017) in the English→Vietnamese and this is lower than the system of (Huang et al., 2018) with neural phrase-based translation architecture.

Our approaches. The datasets from the baseline systems are trained on our modified NMT architecture. The improvements can be found as +0.55 BLEU points between (1) and (2) in the English→Vietnamese and +0.45 BLEU points (in *tst2012*) between (1) and (2) in the Vietnamese→English.

No.	Systems	English→Vietnamese	
		tst2012	tst2013
(1)	Baseline	26.91 (24.39)	29.86 (27.52)
(2)	+ Source Embedding	**27.41 (24.92)**	**30.41 (28.05)**
(3)	+ Sennrich's BPE	**26.96 (24.46)**	**30.10 (27.84)**
(4)	+ SAA	**27.16 (24.67)**	**30.60 (28.34)**
(5)	+ LSW	**27.46 (24.99)**	**30.85 (28.54)**
(6)	Nguyen and Chiang (2017)	-	26.7
(7)	Huang et al (2018)	-	28.07
No.	Systems	Vietnamese→English	
		tst2012	tst2013
(1)	Baseline	27.97 (28.52)	30.07 (29.89)
(2)	+ Source Embedding	**28.42 (29.04)**	**30.12 (29.93)**

Table 3: Results of English-Vietnamese NMT systems

For comparison purpose, English texts are split into sub-words using Sennrich's BPE methods. We observe that, the achieved BLEU points are lower Therefore, we then apply the *SAA* algorithm on the English texts from (2) in the English→Vietnamese. The number of applied words are listed in Table 4. The improvement in BLEU are +0.74 between (4) and (1).

	Train	tst2012	tst2013
Number of words	5342	84	93

Table 4: The number of rare words in which their affixes are detached from the English texts in the SAA algorithm.

Similarly to the Japanese→Vietnamese system, we apply *LSW* algorithm on the English texts from (4) while selecting 1-best synonym for each OOV word. The number of replaced words on English texts are indicated in the Table 5. Again, we obtained a bigger gain of +0.99 (+1.02) BLEU points in English→Vietnamese direction. Compared to the most recent work (Huang et al., 2018), our system reports an improvement of +0.47 standard BLEU points on the same dataset.

	Train	tst2012	tst2013
Number of words	1889	37	41

Table 5: The number of English OOV words are replaced by their synonyms.

We investigate some examples of translations generated by the English→Vietnamese systems with our proposed methods in the Table 6. The bold texts in red color present correct or approximate translations while the italic texts in gray color denote incorrect translations. The first example, we consider two words: *presentation* and the unknown word *applauded*. The word *presentation* is predicted correctly as *"bài thuyết trình"* in most cases when we combined source context through embeddings. The unknown word *applauded* which has not seen in the vocabulary is ignored in the first two cases (baseline and source embedding) but it is roughly translated as *"hoan nghênh"* in the *SAA* because it is separated into *applaud* and *ed*. In the second example, we observe the translations of the unknown word *tryout*, they are mistaken in the first three cases but in the *LSW*, it is predicted with a closer meaning as "bài kiểm tra" due to the replacement by its synonymous word as *test*.

5   Related Works

Addressing unknown words was mentioned early in the Statistical Machine Translation (SMT) systems. Some typical studies as: (Habash, 2008) proposed four techniques to overcome this situation by extend the morphology and spelling of words or using a bilingual dictionary or transliterating for names. These approaches are difficult when manipulate to different domains. (Trieu, 2016) trained word embedding models to learn word similarity from monolingual data and an unknown word are then replaced by a its similar word. (Madhyastha and España Bonet, 2017) used a linear model to learn maps between source and target spaces base on a small initial bilingual dictionary to find the translations of source words. However, in NMT, there are not so many works tackling this problem. (Jean et al., 2015) use a very large vocabulary to solve unknown words. (Luong et al., 2015b) generate a dictionary from alignment data based on annotated corpus to decide the hypotheses of unknown words. (Nguyen and Chiang, 2017) have introduced the solutions for dealing

Source	which presentation have you applauded the most this morning ?
Reference	bài thuyết trình nào bạn vỗ tay nhiều nhất trong sáng nay ?
Baseline	điều này có thể diễn ra trong buổi sáng hôm nay ?
+Source Embedding	bài thuyết trình nào có thể tạo ra buổi sáng hôm nay ?
+SAA	bài thuyết trình này có hoan nghênh buổi sáng hôm nay không ?
+LSW	điều gì đã diễn ra với bạn buổi sáng hôm nay ?
Source	I started this as a tryout in Esperance , in Western Australia .
Reference	tôi đã bắt đầu như một sự thử nghiệm tại Esperance , tây Úc .
Baseline	tôi bắt đầu như thế này như là một người đàn ông , ở phương Tây Úc .
+Source Embedding	tôi đã bắt đầu điều này như là một người đàn ap ở ven biển ở Tây Úc .
+SAA	tôi đã bắt đầu như thế này với tư cách là một người đàn ông trong lĩnh vực này , ở Tây Úc .
+LSW	tôi bắt đầu thí nghiệm này như một bài kiểm tra ở Quảng trường , ở Tây Úc .

Table 6: Examples of outputs from the English→Vietnamese translation systems with the proposed methods.

with the rare word problem, however, their models require more parameters, thus, decreasing the overall efficiency.

In another direction, (Sennrich et al., 2016b) exploited the BPE algorithm to reduce number of unknown words in NMT and achieved significant efficiency on many language pairs. The second approach presented in this works follows this direction when instead of using an unsupervised method to split rare words and unknown words into sub-words that are able to translate, we use a supervised method. Our third approach using WordNet can be seen as a smoothing way, when we use the translations of the synonymous words to approximate the translation of an OOV word. Another work followed this direction is worth to mention is (Niehues et al., 2016), when they use the morphological and semantic information as the factors of the words to help translating rare words.

6 Conclusion

In this study, we have proposed three difference strategies to handle rare words in NMT, in which the combination of methods brings significant improvements to the NMT systems on two low-resource language pairs. In future works, we will consider selecting some appropriate synonymous words for the source sentence from n-best synonymous words to further improve the performance of the NMT systems and leverage more unsupervised methods based on monolingual data to address rare word problem.

7 Acknowledgments

This work is supported by the project "Building a machine translation system to support translation of documents between Vietnamese and Japanese to help managers and businesses in Hanoi approach to Japanese market", No. TC.02-2016-03.

References

Mihael Arcan, John P. McCrae, and Paul Buitelaar. 2019. Polylingual wordnet. *CoRR*, abs/1903.01411.

Dzmitry Bahdanau, Kyunghyun Cho, and Yoshua Bengio. 2015. Neural machine translation by jointly learning to align and translate. *Proceedings of International Conference on Learning Representations*.

M Cettolo, J Niehues, S Stüker, L Bentivogli, R Cattoni, and M Federico. 2016. The IWSLT 2016 Evaluation Campaign. In *Proceedings of the 13th International Workshop on Spoken Language Translation (IWSLT 2016)*, Seattle, WA, USA.

Mauro Cettolo, Christian Girardi, and Marcello Federico. 2012. Wit³: Web inventory of transcribed and translated talks. In *Proceedings of the 16th Conference of the European Association for Machine Translation (EAMT)*, pages 261–268, Trento, Italy.

Eunah Cho, Jan Niehues, Thanh-Le Ha, Matthias Sperber, Mohammed Mediani, and Alex Waibel. 2016. Adaptation and combination of nmt systems: The kit translation systems for iwslt 2016. In *Proceedings of the ninth International Workshop on Spoken Language Translation (IWSLT), Seattle, WA*.

Christiane Fellbaum. 1998. Wordnet: An electronic lexical database. In *Bradford Books*.

Philip Gage. 1994. A new algorithm for data compression. In *C Users J., 12(2):23–38, February*.

Ningning Gao, Wanli Zuo, Yaokang Dai, and Wei Lv. 2014. Word sense disambiguation using wordnet semantic knowledge. *Advances in Intelligent Systems and Computing*, 278:147–156.

Nizar Habash. 2008. Four techniques for online handling of out-of-vocabulary words in arabic english statistical machine translation. In *Proceedings of the 46th Annual Meeting of the Association for Computational Linguistics*, pages 57–60.

Kaiming He, Xiangyu Zhang, Shaoqing Ren, and Jian Sun. 2015. Deep residual learning for image recognition. *2016 IEEE Conference on Computer Vision and Pattern Recognition (CVPR)*, pages 770–778.

Po-Sen Huang, Chong Wang, Sitao Huang, Dengyong Zhou, and Li Deng. 2018. Towards neural phrase-based machine translation. In *International Conference on Learning Representations*.

Sebastien Jean, Kyunghyun Cho, Roland Memisevic, and Yoshua Bengio. 2015. On using very large target vocabulary for neural machine translation. In *Proceedings of the 53rd Annual Meeting of the Association for Computational Linguistics and the 7th International Joint Conference on Natural Language Processing*, pages 1–10. Association for Computational Linguistics.

Mikhail Khodak, Andrej Risteski, Christiane Fellbaum, and Sanjeev Arora. 2017. Extending and improving wordnet via unsupervised word embeddings. *CoRR*, abs/1705.00217.

Todd Ward Kishore Papineni, Salim Roukos and Wei-Jing Zhu. 2012. Bleu: a method for automatic evaluation of machine translation. In *Proceedings of the 40th Annual Meeting of the Association for Computational Linguistics (ACL)*, pages 311–318.

Guillaume Klein, Yoon Kim, Yuntian Deng, Jean Senellart, and Alexander M. Rush. 2017. Opennmt: Open-source toolkit for neural machine translation. In *Proceedings of the 55th Annual Meeting of the Association for Computational Linguistics-System Demonstrations*, pages 67–72, Vancouver, Canada, July 30 - August 4, 2017. Association for Computational Linguistics.

Philipp Koehn, Hieu Hoang, Alexandra Birch, Chris Callison-Burch, Marcello Federico, Nicola Bertoldi, Brooke Cowan, Wade Shen, Christine Moran, Richard Zens, Chris Dyer, Ondřej Bojar, Alexandra Constantin, and Evan Herbst. 2007. Moses: Open source toolkit for statistical machine translation. In *Proceedings of the 45th Annual Meeting of the Association for Computational Linguistics Companion Volume Proceedings of the Demo and Poster Sessions*, pages 177–180, Prague, Czech Republic. Association for Computational Linguistics.

Philipp Koehn and Rebecca Knowles. 2017. Six challenges for neural machine translation. *Proceedings of the First Workshop on Neural Machine Translation*, abs/1706.03872:28–39.

S. G. Kolte and S. G. Bhirud. 2008. Word sense disambiguation using wordnet domains. In *2008 First International Conference on Emerging Trends in Engineering and Technology*, pages 1187–1191.

Minh-Thang Luong, Hieu Pham, and Christopher D. Manning. 2015a. Effective approaches to attention-based neural machine translation. In *Proceedings of the 2015 Conference on Empirical Methods in Natural Language Processing*, pages 1412–1421.

Thang Luong, Ilya Sutskever, Quoc V. Le, Oriol Vinyals, and Wojciech Zaremba. 2015b. Addressing the rare word problem in neural machine translation. *Proceedings of the 53rd Annual Meeting of the Association for Computational Linguistics and the 7th International Joint Conference on Natural Language Processing*, abs/1410.8206:11–19.

P.S. Madhyastha and C. España Bonet. 2017. Learning bilingual projections of embeddings for vocabulary expansion in machine translation. In *Proceedings of the 2nd Workshop on Representation Learning for NLP. pp.139-145. Association for Computational Linguistics, Vancouver, Canada (Aug 2017)*.

Sebastian Stüker Luisa Bentivogli Roldano Cattoni Mauro Cettolo, Jan Niehues and Marcello Federico. 2015. The iwslt 2015 evaluation campaign. In *International Conference on Spoken Language*.

Moreno-Armendáriz M.A. Méndez O., Calvo H. 2013. A reverse dictionary based on semantic analysis using wordnet. In *Advances in Artificial Intelligence and Its Applications, MICAI 2013. Lecture Notes in Computer Science, vol 8265. Springer, Berlin, Heidelberg*.

Graham Neubig, Yosuke Nakata, and Shinsuke Mori. 2011. Pointwise prediction for robust, adaptable japanese morphological analysis. In *Proceedings of the 49th Annual Meeting of the Association for Computational Linguistics: Human Language Technologies: Short Papers - Volume 2*, HLT '11, pages 529–533, Stroudsburg, PA, USA. Association for Computational Linguistics.

Thi-Vinh Ngo, Thanh-Le Ha, Phuong-Thai Nguyen, and Le-Minh Nguyen. 2018. Combining advanced methods in japanese-vietnamese neural machine translation. *2018 10th International Conference on Knowledge and Systems Engineering (KSE)*, pages 318–322.

Toan Q. Nguyen and David Chiang. 2017. Improving lexical choice in neural machine translation. *Proceedings of NAACL-HLT 2018*, pages 334–343.

Jan Niehues, Thanh-Le Ha, Eunah Cho, and Alex Waibel. 2016. Using factored word representation in neural network language models. In *Proceedings of the First Conference on Machine Translation: Volume 1, Research Papers*, pages 74–82.

Rico Sennrich, Barry Haddow, and Alexandra Birch. 2016a. Edinburgh Neural Machine Translation Systems for WMT'16. *arXiv preprint arXiv:1606.02891*.

Rico Sennrich, Barry Haddow, and Alexandra Birch. 2016b. Neural Machine Translation of Rare Words with Subword Units. In *Association for Computational Linguistics (ACL 2016)*.

Nguyen L. M. Nguyen P. T. Trieu, H. L. 2016. Dealing with out-of-vocabulary problem in sentence alignment using word similarity. In *Proceedings of the 30th Pacific Asia Conference on Language, Information and Computation: Oral Papers (pp. 259-266)*.

Neural Arabic Text Diacritization: State of the Art Results and a Novel Approach for Machine Translation

Ali Fadel, Ibraheem Tuffaha, Bara' Al-Jawarneh, and Mahmoud Al-Ayyoub

Jordan University of Science and Technology, Irbid, Jordan
{aliosm1997, bro.t.1996, baraaaljawarneh, malayyoub}@gmail.com

Abstract

In this work, we present several deep learning models for the automatic diacritization of Arabic text. Our models are built using two main approaches, viz. Feed-Forward Neural Network (FFNN) and Recurrent Neural Network (RNN), with several enhancements such as 100-hot encoding, embeddings, Conditional Random Field (CRF) and Block-Normalized Gradient (BNG). The models are tested on the only freely available benchmark dataset and the results show that our models are either better or on par with other models, which require language-dependent post-processing steps, unlike ours. Moreover, we show that diacritics in Arabic can be used to enhance the models of NLP tasks such as Machine Translation (MT) by proposing the *Translation over Diacritization* (ToD) approach.

1 Introduction

In Arabic and many other languages, diacritics are added to the characters of a word (as short vowels) in order to convey certain information about the meaning of the word as a whole and its place within the sentence. Arabic Text Diacritization (ATD) is an important problem with various applications such as text to speech (TTS). At the same time, this problem is a very challenging one even to native speakers of Arabic due to the many subtle issues in determining the correct diacritic for each character from the list shown in Figure 2 and the lack of practice for many native speakers. Thus, the need to build automatic Arabic text diacritizers is high (Zitouni and Sarikaya, 2009).

The meaning of a sentence is greatly influenced by the diacritization which is determined by the context of the sentence as shown in the following example:

كلم أحمد ...

Buckwalter Transliteration: klm >Hmd ...
Incomplete sentence without diacritization.

كَلَّمَ أَحْمَدٌ صَدِيقَهُ

Buckwalter Transliteration: kal~ama
>aHomadN Sadiyqahu
Translation: Ahmad talked to his friend.

كَلَمَ أَحْمَدٌ عَدُوَّهُ

Buckwalter Transliteration: kalama
>aHomadN Eaduw~ahu
Translation: Ahmad wounded his enemy.

The letters كلم "klm" manifests into two different words when given two different diacritizations. As shown in this example, كَلَّمَ "kal~ama" in the first sentence is the verb 'talked' in English, while كَلَمَ "kalama" in the second sentence is the verb 'wounded' in English.

To formulate the problem in a formal manner: Given a sequence of characters representing an Arabic sentence S, find the correct diacritic class (from Figure 2) for each Arabic character S_i in S.

Despite the problem's importance, it received limited attention. One of the reasons for this is the scarcity of freely available resources for this problem. To address this issue, the Tashkeela Corpus[1] (Zerrouki and Balla, 2017) has been released to the community. Unfortunately, there are many problems with the use of this corpus for benchmarking purposes. A very recent study (Fadel et al., 2019) discussed in details these issues and provided a cleaned version of the dataset with pre-defined split into training, testing and validation sets. In this work, we use this dataset and provide yet another extension of it with a larger training set and a new testing set to circumvent the issue that some of the existing systems have already be-

---

[1] https://sourceforge.net/projects/tashkeela

Proceedings of the 6th Workshop on Asian Translation, pages 215–225
Hong Kong, China, November 4, 2019. ©2019 Association for Computational Linguistics

en trained on the entire Tashkeela Corpus.

According to (Fadel et al., 2019), existing approaches to ATD are split into two groups: traditional rule-based approaches and machine learning based approaches. The former was the main approach by many researchers such as (Zitouni and Sarikaya, 2009; Pasha et al., 2014; Darwish et al., 2017) while the latter has started to receive attention only recently (Belinkov and Glass, 2015; Abandah et al., 2015; Barqawi and Zerrouki, 2017; Mubarak et al., 2019). Based on the extensive experiments of (Fadel et al., 2019), deep learning approaches (aka neural approaches) are superior to non-neural approaches especially when large training data is available. In this work, we present several neural ATD models and compare their performance with the state of the art (SOTA) approaches to show that our models are either on par with the SOTA approaches or even better. Finally, we present a novel way to utilize diactritization in order to enhance the accuracy of Machine Translation (MT) models in what we call *Translation over Diacritization* (ToD) approach.

The rest of the paper is organized as follows. The following section discusses the dataset proposed by (Fadel et al., 2019). Sections 3 and 4 discuss our two main approaches: Feed-Forward Neural Network (FFNN) and Recurrent Neural Network (RNN), respectively. Section 5 briefly discusses the related work and presents a comparison with the SOTA approaches while Section 6 describes our novel approach to integrate diacritization into translation tasks. The paper is concluding in Section 7 with final remarks and future directions of this work.

2   Dataset

The dataset of (Fadel et al., 2019) (which is an adaptation of the Tashkeela Corpus) consists of about 2.3M words spread over 55K lines. Basic statistics about this dataset size, content and diacritics usage are given in Table 1. Among the resources provided with this dataset are new definitions of the Diacritic Error Rate (DER), which is "the percentage of misclassified Arabic characters regardless of whether the character has 0, 1 or 2 diacritics", and the Word Error Rate (WER), which is "the percentage of Arabic words which have at least one misclassified Arabic character".[2] The redefinition of these measures is to exclu-

---

[2]DER/WER are computed with diacritization_stat.py

Table 1: Statistics about the size, content and diacritics usage of (Fadel et al., 2019)'s Dataset

	Train	Valid	Test
Words Count	2,103K	102K	107K
Lines Count	50K	2.5K	2.5K
Avg Chars/Word	3.97	3.97	3.97
Avg Words/Line	42.06	40.97	42.89
0 Diacritics (%)	17.78	17.75	17.80
1 Diacritic (%)	77.17	77.19	77.22
2 Diacritics (%)	5.03	5.05	4.97
Error Diacritics (%)	0	0	0

de counting irrelevant characters such as numbers and punctuations, which were included in (Zitouni and Sarikaya, 2009)'s original definitions of DER and WER. It is worth mentioning that DER/WER are computed in four different ways in the literature depending on whether the last character of each word (referred to as case ending) is counted or not and whether the characters with no diacritization are counter or not.

3   The Feed-Forward Neural Network (FFNN) Approach

This is our first approach and we present three models based on it. In this approach, we consider diacritizing each character as an independent problem. To do so, the model takes a 100-dimensional vector as an input representing features for a single character in the sentence. The first 50 elements in the vector represent the 50 non-diacritic characters before the current character and the last 50 elements represent the 50 non-diacritic characters after it including the current character.

For example, the sentence 'ذَهَبَ عَلِي', the vector related to the character 'ب' is as shown in Figure 1. As the figure shows, there are two characters before the character 'ب' and four after it (including the whitespace). The special token '<PAD>' is used as a filler when there are no characters to feed. Note that the dataset contains 73 unique characters (without the diacritics) which are mapped to unique integer values from 0 to 74 after sorting them based on their unicode representations including the special padding and unknown ('<UNK>') tokens.

Each example belongs to one of the 15 classes under consideration, which are shown in Figure 2. The model outputs probabilities for each

$\mathcal{X}$ = [<PAD>, ..., <PAD>, ذ, ه, ب, ' ', ع, ل, ي, <PAD>, ..., <PAD>]

Figure 1: Vector representation of a FFNN example.

Class Name	Class Shape	Class Name	Class Shape
No Diacritization	ب	Shadda	بّ
Fatha	بَ	Shadda + Fatha	بَّ
Damma	بُ	Shadda + Damma	بُّ
Kasra	بِ	Shadda + Kasra	بِّ
Fathatan	بً	Shadda + Fathatan	بًّ
Dammatan	بٌ	Shadda + Dammatan	بٌّ
Kasratan	بٍ	Shadda + Kasratan	بٍّ
Sukun	بْ		

Figure 2: The 15 classes under consideration.

class. Using a Softmax output unit, the class with maximum probability is considered as the correct output. The number of training, validation and testing examples from converting the dataset into examples as described earlier are 9,017K, 488K and 488K respectively.

Basic Model. The basic model consists of 17 hidden layers of different sizes. The activation function used in all layers is Rectified Linear Unit (ReLU) and the number of trainable parameters is about 1.5M. For more details see Appendix A. The model is trained for 300 epochs on an Nvidia Ge-Force GTX 970M GPU for about 16 hours using AdaGrad optimization algorithm (Duchi et al., 2011) with 0.01 learning rate, 512 batch size, and categorical cross-entropy loss function.

100-Hot Model. In this model, each integer from the 100-integer inputs is converted into its 1-hot representation as a 75-dimensional vector. Then, the 100 vectors are concatenated forming a 7,500-dimensional vector. Based on empirical exploration, the model is structured to have five hidden layers with dropout. It has close to 2M trainable parameters. For more details see Appendix A. The model is trained for 50 epochs on an Nvidia GeForce GTX 970M GPU for about 3 hours using Adam optimization algorithm (Kingma and Ba, 2014) with 0.001 learning rate, 0.9 beta1, 0.999 beta2, 512 batch size, and categorical cross-entropy loss function.

Embeddings Model. In this model, the 100-hot layer is replaced with an embeddings layer to learn feature vectors for each character through the training process. Empirically determined, the model has five hidden layers with only 728K trainable parameters. For more details see Appendix A. The model is trained with the same configurations as the 100-hot model and the training time is about 2.5 hours only.

Results and Analysis. Although the idea of diacritizing each character independently is counter-intuitive, the results of the FFNN models on the test set (shown in Table 2) are very promising with the embeddings model having an obvious advantage over the basic and 100-hot models and performing much better than the best rule-based diacritization system Mishkal[3] among the systems reviewed by (Fadel et al., 2019) (Mishakl DER: 13.78% vs FFNN Embeddings model DER: 4.06%). However, these models are still imperfect. More detailed error analysis of these models is available in Appendix A.

4 The Recurrent Neural Network (RNN) Approach

Since RNN models usually need huge data to train on and learn high-level linguistic abstractions, we prepare an external training dataset following the guidelines of (Fadel et al., 2019). The extra training dataset is extracted from the Classical Arabic (CA) part of the Tashkeela Corpus and the Holy Quran (HQ). We exclude the lines that already exist in the previously mentioned dataset. Note that, with the extra training dataset the number of unique characters goes up to 87 (without the diacritics). Table 3 shows the statistics for the extra training dataset.

The lines in the dataset are split using the following 14 punctuations ('.', ',', '،', ':', '؛', '؟' , '(', ')', '[', ']', '{', '}', '«' and '»'). After that, the lines with length more than 500 characters (without counting diacritics) are split into lines of length no more than 500. This step is necessary for the training phase to limit memory usage within a single batch. Note that the splitting procedure is omitted within the prediction phase, e.g., when calculating DER/WER on the validation and test sets. Moreover, four special tokens ('<SOS>', '<EOS>', '<UNK>' and '<PAD>') are used to prepare the input data before feeding it to the model. '<SOS>' and '<EOS>' are added to the start and the end of the sequences, respectively. '<UNK>' is used to represent unknown characters not seen in the training dataset. Finally, '<PAD>' is appended to pad the sequences within the same batch.

---

[3]https://tahadz.com/mishkal

Table 2: DER/WER comparison of the different FFNN models on the test set

DER/WER	w/ case ending	w/o case ending	w/ case ending	w/o case ending
	Including 'no diacritic'		Excluding 'no diacritic'	
Basic model	9.33% / 25.93%	6.58% / 13.89%	10.85% / 25.39%	7.51% / 13.53%
100-Hot model	6.57% / 20.21%	4.83% / 11.14%	7.75% / 19.83%	5.62% / 10.93%
Embeddings model	**5.52% / 17.12%**	**4.06% / 9.38%**	**6.44% / 16.63%**	**4.67% / 9.10%**

Table 3: Extra training dataset statistics

	Extra Train
Words Count	22.4M
Lines Count	533K
Avg Chars/Word	3.97
Avg Words/Line	42.1
0 Diacritics (%)	17.79
1 Diacritic (%)	77.16
2 Diacritics (%)	5.03
Error Diacritics (%)	0

Four equivalent special tokens are used as an output in the target sequences.

Basic Model. Several model architectures are trained without the extra training dataset. After some exploration, the best model architecture is chosen to experiment with different techniques as described in details throughout this section.

The exploration is done to tune different hyperparameters and find the structure that gives the best DER, which, in most cases, leads to better WER. Because the neural network size have a great impact on performance, we primarily experiment with the number of Bidirectional CuDNN Long Short-Term Memory (BiCuDNNLSTM) (Appleyard et al., 2016) layers and their hidden units. By using either one, two or three layers, the error significantly decreases going from one layer to two layers. However, it shows slight improvement (if any) when going from two layers to three layers while increasing the training time. So, we decide to use two BiCuDNNLSTMs in further experiments as well as 256 hidden units per layer as using less units will increase the error rate while using more units does not significantly improve it. Then, we experiment with the size and depth of the fully connected feed-forward network. The results show that the depth is not as important as the size of each layer. The best results are produced with the model using two layers with 512 hidden units each. All experiments are done using Adam optimization algorithm, because different optimizers like Stochastic Gradient Descent, Adagrad and Adadelta do not converge to the optimal minimal fast enough and RMSprop, Nadam and Adamax give the same or slightly worse results. The number of character features to learn in the embedding layer that gives the best results is 25, where more features leads to little improvement and more overfitting, and less features makes the training harder for the network. This is probably due to the input vocabulary being limited to 87 different characters. We also experiment with training the models for more than 50 epochs, but the return is very little or it makes the learning unstable and eventually causes exploding gradients leaving the network with useless predictions, unable to learn anymore. The best model is structured as shown in Figure 3.

The training is done twice: with and without the extra training dataset, in order to explore the impact of the dataset size on the training phase for the diacritization problem. This has led to reduced overfitting. A weights averaging technique over the last few epochs is applied to partially overcome the overfitting issue and obtain a better generalization.

Models in all following experiments are trained on Google Colab[4] (Carneiro et al., 2018) environment for 50 epochs using an Nvidia Tesla T4 GPU, Adam optimization algorithm with 0.001 learning rate, 0.9 beta1, 0.999 beta2, 10^{-7} epsilon, 256 batch size, and categorical cross-entropy loss function.

Conditional Random Field (CRF) Model. A CRF classifier is used in this model instead of the Softmax layer to predict the network output. CRF is usually more powerful than Softmax in terms of sequence dependencies in the output layer which exist in the diacritization problem. It is worth mentioning that CRF is considered to be "a best practice" in sequence labeling problems. However, in this particular problem, the results show that CRF

[4] http://colab.research.google.com

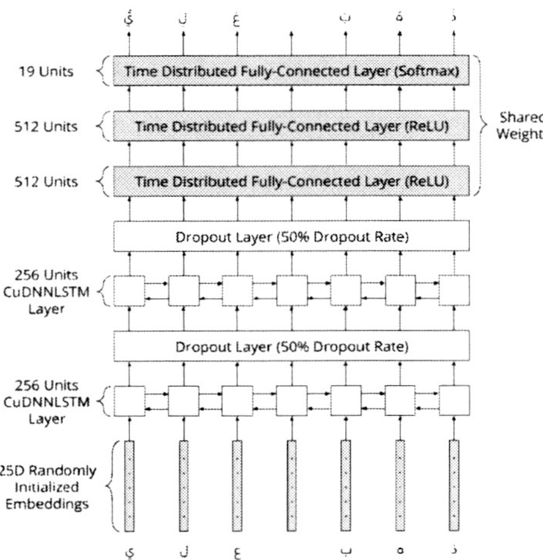

Figure 3: RNN basic model structure.

performs worse than Softmax in most cases except for WER results when training without the extra dataset which indicates that, even with worse DER results, CRF is able to make more consistent predictions within the same word.

Block-Normalized Gradient (BNG) Model. In this model, (Yu et al., 2017)'s BNG method is applied to normalize gradients within each batch. This can help accelerate the training process. According to (Yu et al., 2017), this method performs better in RNN when using optimizers with adaptive step sizes, such as Adam. It can also lead to solutions with better generalization. This coincides with our results.

Discussion and Analysis. The results of the RNN models on the test set (shown in Table 4) are much better than the FFNN models by about 67%. To show the effect of the weights averaging technique, Table 5 reports the DER/WER statistics related to the BNG model after averaging its weights over the last 1, 5, 10, and 20 epochs. Studying the confusion matrices for all the models suggests that the Shadda class and the composite classes (i.e., Shadda + another diacritic) are harder to learn for the network compared to other classes. However, with the extra training dataset, the network is able to find significantly better results compared to the results without the extra training dataset, especially for the Shadda class.

The comparison method for calculating DER/WER without case ending skips comparing the diacritization on the end of each word. This

skip improves the best DER to 1.34% (vs 1.69%) and best WER to 2.91% (vs 5.09%) which is a 26% improvement in DER and 43% improvement in WER. This is because the diacritic of the last character of the word usually depends on the part of speech tag making it harder to diacritize. However, we note that the actual last character of the word may come before the end of the word if the word has some suffix added to it.

Arabic sentence	هذا هو كتابه	قرأ كتابه	مكتوب في كتابه
English translation	This is his book	He read his book	It's written in his book
Part of speech tag	subject	object	genitive

Figure 4: Case ending different diacritization with different part of speech tag.

Consider the example shown in Figure 4. The word 'كتابه' means 'his book' where the last character 'ـه' is the suffix representing the pronoun 'his', and the letter before it may take three different diacritics depending on its part of speech tagging. More detailed error analysis of these models available in Appendix B.

Furthermore, an Encoder-Decoder structure (seq2seq) was built using BiCuDNNLSTMs to encode a sequence of characters and generate a sequence of diacritics, but the model was not able to successfully learn the alignment between inputted characters and outputted diacritics. Other attempts tried encoding the sentences as sequences of words and generate a sequences of diacritics also terribly failed to learn.

The BNG model performs the best compared to other models described above. So, it is used for comparison with other systems in the following section.

5 Comparison with Existing Systems

As mentioned earlier, the efforts on building automatic ATD is limited. A recent study (Fadel et al., 2019) surveyed existing approaches and tools for ATD. After discussing the limitations in closed-source tools, they divided existing approaches to ATD into two groups: traditional rule-based approaches (Zitouni and Sarikaya, 2009; Pasha et al., 2014; Shahrour et al., 2015; Alnefaie and Azmi, 2017; Bebah et al., 2014; Azmi and Almajed, 2015; Chennoufi and Mazroui, 2017; Darwish et al., 2017; Fashwan and Alansary, 2017; Alqahtani et al., 2019) and machine learning based approaches (Belinkov and Glass, 2015; Abandah

Table 4: DER/WER comparison of the different RNN models on the test set

DER/WER	w/ case ending	w/o case ending	w/ case ending	w/o case ending
	Including 'no diacritic'		Excluding 'no diacritic'	
Without Extra Train Dataset				
Basic model	2.68% / 7.91%	2.19% / 4.79%	3.09% / 7.61%	2.51% / 4.66%
CRF model	2.67% / 7.73%	2.19% / 4.69%	3.08% / 7.46%	2.52% / 4.60%
BNG model	**2.60% / 7.69%**	**2.11% / 4.57%**	**3.00% / 7.39%**	**2.42% / 4.44%**
With Extra Train Dataset				
Basic model	1.72% / 5.16%	1.37% / 2.98%	1.99% / 4.96%	1.59% / 2.92%
CRF model	1.84% / 5.42%	1.47% / 3.17%	2.13% / 5.22%	1.69% / 3.09%
BNG model	**1.69% / 5.09%**	**1.34% / 2.91%**	**1.95% / 4.89%**	**1.54% / 2.83%**

Table 5: DER/WER comparison showing the effect of the weights averaging technique on BNG model

DER/WER	Averaged Epochs	w/ case ending	w/o case ending	w/ case ending	w/o case ending
		Including 'no diacritic'		Excluding 'no diacritic'	
Without	1	2.73% / 8.08%	2.21% / 4.80%	3.16% / 7.79%	2.54% / 4.68%
extra	5	2.64% / 7.80%	2.14% / 4.64%	3.04% / 7.49%	2.46% / 4.52%
train	10	**2.60% / 7.69%**	**2.11% / 4.57%**	**3.00%/ 7.39%**	**2.42% / 4.44%**
dataset	20	2.61% / 7.73%	**2.11% / 4.56%**	3.01% / 7.42%	**2.42% / 7.42%**
With	1	1.97% / 5.85%	1.61% / 3.55%	2.20% / 5.61%	1.82% / 3.45%
extra	5	1.73% / 5.20%	1.38% / 3.02%	1.98% / 4.98%	1.58% / 2.92%
train	10	1.70% / 5.13%	1.35% / 2.94%	1.96% / 4.92%	1.55% / 2.85%
dataset	20	**1.69% / 5.09%**	**1.34% / 2.91%**	**1.95% / 4.89%**	**1.54% / 2.83%**

et al., 2015, 2017; Barqawi and Zerrouki, 2017; Moumen et al., 2018; Mubarak et al., 2019). The extensive experiments of (Fadel et al., 2019) showed that neural ATD models are superior to their competitors especially when large training data is available. Thus, we limit our attention in this work to such models.

According to (Fadel et al., 2019), the Shakkala system (Barqawi and Zerrouki, 2017) performs the best compared to other existing systems using the test set and the evaluation metrics proposed in (Fadel et al., 2019). Considering our best model's results mentioned previously, it is clear that our model outperforms Shakkala on the testing set after splitting the lines to be at most 315 characters long (Shakkala system limit), which causes a slight drop in our best model's results. However, since Shakkala was also trained on Tashkeela Corpus, we develop an auxiliary test set extracted from three books from Al-Shamela Library[5] ,'تاج العروس من جواهر القاموس' 'الفتاوى الكبرى لابن تيمية' and 'فتح الباري شرح صحيح البخاري' using the

[5]http://shamela.ws

same extraction and cleaning method proposed by (Fadel et al., 2019) while keeping only lines with more than 80% "diacritics to Arabic characters" rate. The extracted lines are each split into lines of lengths no more than 315 characters (without counting diacritics) which is the input limit of the Shakkala system. This produces a test set consisting of 443K words. Table 6 shows the results comparison with Shakkala.

A comparison with the pre-trained model of (Belinkov and Glass, 2015) is also done using the test set and the evaluation metrics of (Fadel et al., 2019) while splitting the lines into lines of lengths no more than 125 characters (without counting diacritics) since any input with length more than that causes an error in their system. The results show that (Belinkov and Glass, 2015)'s model performs poorly. However, we note that (Belinkov and Glass, 2015)'s system was trained and tested on the Arabic TreeBank (ATB) dataset which consists of text in Modern Standard Arabic (MSA). So, to make a fair comparison with (Belinkov and Glass, 2015)'s system, an auxiliary dataset is built from the MSA part of the Tashkeela Corpus using the same extraction and cleaning method proposed

Table 6: Comparing the BNG model with (Barqawi and Zerrouki, 2017) in terms of DER/WER on the test set

DER/WER	w/ case ending	w/o case ending	w/ case ending	w/o case ending
	Including 'no diacritic'		Excluding 'no diacritic'	
(Fadel et al., 2019) Testing Dataset Results				
Our best model	**1.78% / 5.38%**	**1.39% / 3.04%**	**2.05% / 5.17%**	**1.60% / 2.96%**
Barqawi, 2017	3.73% / 11.19%	2.88% / 6.53%	4.36% / 10.89%	3.33% / 6.37%
Auxiliary Testing Dataset Results				
Our best model	**5.98% / 15.72%**	5.21% / 11.07%	**5.54% / 13.21%**	**4.85% / 9.02%**
Barqawi, 2017	6.41% / 17.52%	**5.12% / 10.91%**	6.82% / 15.92%	5.32% / 9.65%

Table 7: Comparing the BNG model with (Belinkov and Glass, 2015) in terms of DER/WER on the test set

DER/WER	w/ case ending	w/o case ending	w/ case ending	w/o case ending
	Including 'no diacritic'		Excluding 'no diacritic'	
Classical Arabic Testing Dataset Results				
Our best model	**1.99% / 6.10%**	**1.48% / 3.25%**	**2.30% / 5.88%**	**1.70% / 3.17%**
Belinkov, 2015	31.26% / 75.29%	29.66% / 59.46%	35.78% / 74.37%	33.67% / 57.66%
Modern Standard Arabic Testing Dataset Results				
Our best model	**8.05% / 23.56%**	**6.85% / 16.12%**	**8.29% / 21.10%**	**7.16% / 14.41%**
Belinkov, 2015	31.77% / 75.02%	29.21% / 59.40%	37.13% / 73.93%	33.82% / 58.03%

by (Fadel et al., 2019) keeping only lines with more than 80% "diacritics to Arabic characters" rate. This test set consists of 111K words. The results are reported in Table 7. In addition to the poor results of (Belinkov and Glass, 2015)'s system, its output has a large number of special characters inserted randomly. These characters are removed manually to make the evaluation of the system possible.

Finally, we compare our model with (Abandah et al., 2015)'s model which, to our best knowledge, is the most recent deep-learning work announcing the best results so far. To do so, we employ a similar comparison method to (Chennoufi and Mazroui, 2017)'s by using the 10 books from the Tashkeela Corpus and the HQ that were excluded from (Abandah et al., 2015)'s test set. The sentences used for testing our best model are all sentences that are not included in the training dataset of (Fadel et al., 2019) or extra training dataset on which our model is trained. To make the comparison fair, we use the same evaluation metric as (Abandah et al., 2015), which is (Zitouni and Sarikaya, 2009)'s. Moreover, the characters with no diacritics in the original text are skipped similarly to (Abandah et al., 2015). The results are shown in Table 8. It is worth mentioning that the results of (Abandah et al., 2015) include post-processing techniques, which improved DER by 23.8% as reported in (Abandah et al., 2015). It can be easily shown that, without this step, our model's results are actually superior.

All codes related to the diacritization work are publicly available on GitHub,[6] and are also implemented into a web application[7] for testing purposes.

6 Translation over Diacritization (ToD)

Word's diacritics can carry various types of information about the word itself, like its part of speech tag, the semantic meaning and the pronunciation. Intuitively, providing such extra features in NLP tasks has the potential to improve the results of any system. In this section, we show how we benefit from the integration of diacritics into Arabic-English (Ar-En) Neural Machine Translation (NMT) creating what we call Translation over Diacritization (ToD).

Dataset Extraction and Preparation. Due to the lack of free standardized benchmark datasets for Ar-En MT, we create a mid-size dataset using the following corpora: GlobalVoices v2017q3, MultiUN v1, News-Commentary v11, Tatoeba v2, TED2013 v1.1, Ubuntu v14.10, Wikipedia v1.0 (Tiedemann, 2012) downloaded from

Table 8: Comparing the BNG model with (Abandah et al., 2015) in terms of DER/WER on the test set

| | DER | | WER | |
	w/ case ending	w/o case ending	w/ case ending	w/o case ending
Our best model	2.18%	1.76%	**4.44%**	**2.66%**
Abandah, 2015	**2.09%**	**1.28%**	5.82%	3.54%

Table 9: Vocab size for all sequences types before and after BPE step

| Language | Vocab Size | |
	Before BPE	After BPE
English	113K	31K
Original Arabic	224K	32K
Diacritized Arabic	402K	186K
Diacritics Forms	41K	15K

the OPUS[8] project. The dataset contains 1M Ar-En sentence pairs split into 990K pairs for training and 10K pairs for testing. The extracted 1M pairs follow these conventions: (i) The maximum length for each sentence in the pair is 50 tokens, (ii) Arabic sentences contain Arabic letters only, (iii) English sentences contain English letters only, and (iv) the sentences do not contain any URLs.

The Arabic sentences in the training and testing datasets are diacritized using the best BNG model. After that, Byte Pair Encoding (BPE)[9] (Sennrich et al., 2015) is applied separately on both English and original (undiacritized) Arabic sequences to segment the words into subwords. This step overcomes the Out Of Vocabulary (OOV) problem and reduces the vocabulary size. Then, diacritics are added to Arabic subwords to create the diacritized version. Table 9 shows the number of tokens before and after BPE step for English, Original Arabic and Diacritized Arabic as well as the Diacritics forms when removing the Arabic characters.

Model Structure The model used in the experiments is a basic Encoder-Decoder sequence to sequence (seq2seq) model that consists of a BiCuD-NNLSTM layer for encoding and a CuDNNLSTM layer for decoding with 512 units each (256 per direction for the encoder) while applying additive attention (Bahdanau et al., 2014) on the outputs of the encoder. As for the embeddings layer, a single randomly initialized embeddings layer with vector size 64 is used to represent the subwords

[8]http://opus.nlpl.eu
[9]https://github.com/rsennrich/subword-nmt

when training without diacritics. Another layer with the same configuration is used to represent subwords' diacritics, which is concatenated with the subwords embeddings when training with diacritics. The model structure shown in Figure 5.

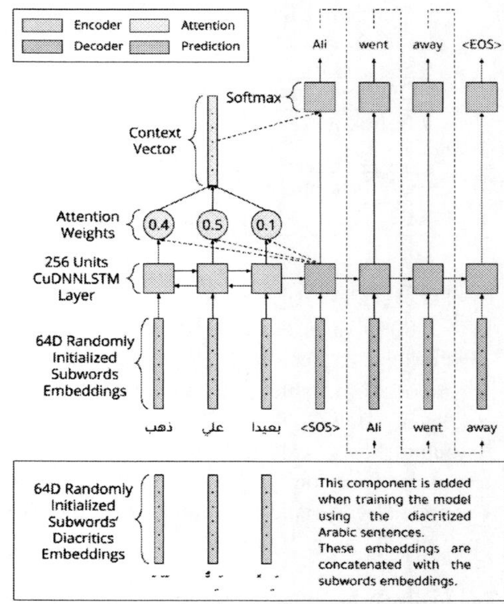

Figure 5: ToD model structure.

Results and Discussion To explore the effect of the Arabic diacritization on the NMT task, we experiment with training both with and without diacritics. The models are trained for 50 epochs using an Nvidia Titan Xp GPU, Adam optimization algorithm with 0.001 learning rate, 0.9 beta1, 0.999 beta2, 10^{-7} epsilon and 256 batch size.

The structure for training the model with diacritics may vary. We experiment with two variations where the first one uses the diacritized version of the sequences, while the other one uses the original sequences and the diacritics sequences in parallel. When merging diacritics with their sequences, we get more variations of each word depending on its different forms of diacritization, therefore expanding the vocabulary size. On the other hand, when separating diacritics from their sequences, the vocab size stays the same, and diacritics are added separately as extra input.

The results in Table 10 show that training the model with diacritization compared to without diacritization improves marginally by 0.31 BLEU score[10] when using the 'with diacritics (merged)' data and improves even more when using the 'with diacritics (separated)' data by 1.33 BLEU score. Moreover, the training time and model size increases by about 20.6% and 41.4%, respectively, for using the 'with diacritics (merged)' data, while they only increase by about 3.4% and 4.5%, respectively, for using the 'with diacritics (separated)' data. By observing Figure 6, which reports the BLEU score on all three models every 5 epochs, it is clear that, although the 'with diacritics (merged)' model converges better at the start of the training, it starts diverging after 15 epochs, which might be due to the huge vocab size and the training data size.

By analysing Figure 6, we find that BLUE score converges faster when training with diacritics (merged) compared to the other two approaches. However, it starts diverging later on due to vocabulary sparsity. As for with diacritics (separated), the BLUE score has higher convergence compared to without diacritics while also maintaining stability compared to with diacritics (merged). This is because separating diacritics solves the vocabulary sparsity issue while also providing the information needed to disambiguate homonym words.

We note that, concurrently to our work, another work on utilizing diacritization for MT has recently appeared. (Alqahtani et al., 2019) used diacritics with text in three downstream tasks, namely Semantic Text Similarity (STS), NMT and Part of Speech (POS) tagging, to boost the performance of their systems. They applied different techniques to disambiguate homonym words through diacritization. They achieved 27.1 and 27.3 BLUE scores without and with diacritics, respectively, using their best disambiguation technique. This is a very small improvement of 0.74% compared to our noticeable improvement of 4.03%. Moreover, our approach is simpler and it does not require to drop any diacritical information.

All codes related to the ToD work are publicly available on GitHub[11].

---

[10]BLEU scores are computed with multi-bleu.perl

[11]`https://github.com/AliOsm/translation-over-diacritization`

Table 10: Translation over Diacritization (ToD) results on the test set

Model	Training Time	Model Size	Best BLEU Score
Without	**29 Hours**	**285MB**	33.01
Merged	35 Hours	403MB	33.32
Separated	30 Hours	298MB	**34.34**

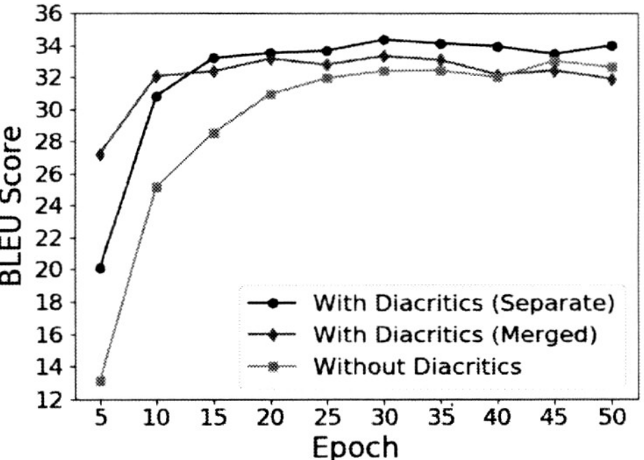

Figure 6: Testing dataset BLEU score while training.

7 Conclusion

In this work, we explored the ATD problem. Our models, which follow two main approaches: FF-NN and RNN, proved to be very effective as they performed on par with or better than SOTA approaches. In the future, we plan on investigating the sequence to sequence models such as RNN Seq2seq, Conv Seq2seq and Transformer. In another contribution of this work, we showed that diacritics can be integrated into other systems to attain enhanced versions in NLP tasks. We used MT as a case study and showed how our idea of ToD improved the results of the SOTA NMT system.

Acknowledgments

We gratefully acknowledge the support of the Deanship of Research at the Jordan University of Science and Technology for supporting this work via Grant #20180193 in addition to NVIDIA Corporation for the donation of the Titan Xp GPU that was used for this research.

References

Gheith Abandah, Alaa Arabiyat, et al. 2017. Investigating hybrid approaches for arabic text diacritization with recurrent neural networks. In *2017 IEEE Jordan Conference on Applied Electrical Engineering and Computing Technologies (AEECT)*, pages 1–6. IEEE.

Gheith A Abandah, Alex Graves, Balkees Al-Shagoor, Alaa Arabiyat, Fuad Jamour, and Majid Al-Taee. 2015. Automatic diacritization of arabic text using recurrent neural networks. *International Journal on Document Analysis and Recognition (IJDAR)*, 18(2):183–197.

Rehab Alnefaie and Aqil M Azmi. 2017. Automatic minimal diacritization of arabic texts. *Procedia Computer Science*, 117:169–174.

Sawsan Alqahtani, Hanan Aldarmaki, and Mona Diab. 2019. Homograph disambiguation through selective diacritic restoration. In *Proceedings of the Fourth Arabic Natural Language Processing Workshop*, pages 49–59.

Jeremy Appleyard, Tomas Kocisky, and Phil Blunsom. 2016. Optimizing performance of recurrent neural networks on gpus. *arXiv preprint arXiv:1604.01946*.

Aqil M Azmi and Reham S Almajed. 2015. A survey of automatic arabic diacritization techniques. *Natural Language Engineering*, 21(3):477–495.

Dzmitry Bahdanau, Kyunghyun Cho, and Yoshua Bengio. 2014. Neural machine translation by jointly learning to align and translate. *arXiv preprint arXiv:1409.0473*.

Ahmad Barqawi and Taha Zerrouki. 2017. Shakkala, arabic text vocalization.

Mohamed Bebah, Chennoufi Amine, Mazroui Azzeddine, and Lakhouaja Abdelhak. 2014. Hybrid approaches for automatic vowelization of arabic texts. *arXiv preprint arXiv:1410.2646*.

Yonatan Belinkov and James Glass. 2015. Arabic diacritization with recurrent neural networks. In *Proceedings of the 2015 Conference on Empirical Methods in Natural Language Processing*, pages 2281–2285.

Tiago Carneiro, Raul Victor Medeiros Da Nóbrega, Thiago Nepomuceno, Gui-Bin Bian, Victor Hugo C De Albuquerque, and Pedro Pedrosa Reboucas Filho. 2018. Performance analysis of google colaboratory as a tool for accelerating deep learning applications. *IEEE Access*, 6:61677–61685.

Amine Chennoufi and Azzeddine Mazroui. 2017. Morphological, syntactic and diacritics rules for automatic diacritization of arabic sentences. *Journal of King Saud University-Computer and Information Sciences*, 29(2):156–163.

Kareem Darwish, Hamdy Mubarak, and Ahmed Abdelali. 2017. Arabic diacritization: Stats, rules, and hacks. In *Proceedings of the Third Arabic Natural Language Processing Workshop*, pages 9–17.

John Duchi, Elad Hazan, and Yoram Singer. 2011. Adaptive subgradient methods for online learning and stochastic optimization. *Journal of Machine Learning Research*, 12(Jul):2121–2159.

Ali Fadel, Ibraheem Tuffaha, Bara' Al-Jawarneh, and Mahmoud Al-Ayyoub. 2019. Arabic text diacritization using deep neural networks. In *ICCAIS*.

Amany Fashwan and Sameh Alansary. 2017. Shakkil: an automatic diacritization system for modern standard arabic texts. In *Proceedings of the Third Arabic Natural Language Processing Workshop*, pages 84–93.

Diederik P Kingma and Jimmy Ba. 2014. Adam: A method for stochastic optimization. *arXiv preprint arXiv:1412.6980*.

Laurens van der Maaten and Geoffrey Hinton. 2008. Visualizing data using t-sne. *Journal of machine learning research*, 9(Nov):2579–2605.

Rajae Moumen, Raddouane Chiheb, Rdouan Faizi, and Abdellatif El Afia. 2018. Evaluation of gated recurrent unit in arabic diacritization. *International Journal of Advanced Computer Science and Applications (IJACSA)*, 9(11).

Hamdy Mubarak, Ahmed Abdelali, Hassan Sajjad, Younes Samih, and Kareem Darwish. 2019. Highly effective arabic diacritization using sequence to sequence modeling. In *Proceedings of the 2019 Conference of the North American Chapter of the Association for Computational Linguistics: Human Language Technologies, Volume 1 (Long and Short Papers)*, pages 2390–2395.

Arfath Pasha, Mohamed Al-Badrashiny, Mona T Diab, Ahmed El Kholy, Ramy Eskander, Nizar Habash, Manoj Pooleery, Owen Rambow, and Ryan Roth. 2014. Madamira: A fast, comprehensive tool for morphological analysis and disambiguation of arabic. In *LREC*, volume 14, pages 1094–1101.

Rico Sennrich, Barry Haddow, and Alexandra Birch. 2015. Neural machine translation of rare words with subword units. *arXiv preprint arXiv:1508.07909*.

Anas Shahrour, Salam Khalifa, and Nizar Habash. 2015. Improving arabic diacritization through syntactic analysis. In *Proceedings of the 2015 Conference on Empirical Methods in Natural Language Processing*, pages 1309–1315.

Jörg Tiedemann. 2012. Parallel data, tools and interfaces in opus. In *Lrec*, volume 2012, pages 2214–2218.

Adams Wei Yu, Lei Huang, Qihang Lin, Ruslan Salakhutdinov, and Jaime Carbonell. 2017. Block-normalized gradient method: An empirical study for training deep neural network. *arXiv preprint arXiv:1707.04822*.

Taha Zerrouki and Amar Balla. 2017. Tashkeela: Novel corpus of arabic vocalized texts, data for auto-diacritization systems. *Data in brief*, 11:147.

Imed Zitouni and Ruhi Sarikaya. 2009. Arabic diacritic restoration approach based on maximum entropy models. *Computer Speech & Language*, 23(3):257–276.

Author Index